Innovating Democracy

Innovating Democracy

Democratic Theory and Practice
After the Deliberative Turn

Robert E. Goodin

OXFORD
UNIVERSITY PRESS

OXFORD
UNIVERSITY PRESS

Great Clarendon Street, Oxford OX2 6DP

Oxford University Press is a department of the University of Oxford.
It furthers the University's objective of excellence in research, scholarship,
and education by publishing worldwide in

Oxford New York

Auckland Cape Town Dar es Salaam Hong Kong Karachi
Kuala Lumpur Madrid Melbourne Mexico City Nairobi
New Delhi Shanghai Taipei Toronto

With offices in

Argentina Austria Brazil Chile Czech Republic France Greece
Guatemala Hungary Italy Japan Poland Portugal Singapore
South Korea Switzerland Thailand Turkey Ukraine Vietnam

Oxford is a registered trade mark of Oxford University Press
in the UK and in certain other countries

Published in the United States
by Oxford University Press Inc., New York

British Library Cataloguing in Publication Data
Data available

Library of Congress Cataloging in Publication Data
Data available

Typeset by SPI Publisher Services, Pondicherry, India
Printed in the UK on acid-free paper by
the MPG Books Group

ISBN 978-0-19-954794-4

To the memory of Iris Marion Young

Contents

Preface

Familiar problems look different, and new problems emerge, after the deliberative turn in democratic theory. These essays represent attempts at coming to terms with that latest turn. Recasting democratic theory in light of the deliberative turn is very much a work in progress for the community of democratic theorists at large. The essays collected in this book represent instalments on that larger project, not a remotely final grand synthesis.

These essays were written over the first decade of the twenty-first century. During that time I was working with John Dryzek and Avi Tucker on a project on 'The Theory & Practice of Deliberative Democracy' (DP0342795) and on another with Geoff Brennan, Nic Southwood, and Lina Eriksson on 'Norms, Reasons and Values' (DP DP0663060), both with funding from the Australian Research Council, which is gratefully acknowledged. Around then, ANU's Research School of Social Sciences was quite possibly the best place in the world to work on these topics: Dave Estlund, Christian List, and Gerry Mackie were long-term visitors; John Ferejohn, Claus Offe, and Anne Phillips recurring Adjunct Professors; and Simon Niemeyer, John Parkinson, and Carolyn Hendriks PhD students. I am grateful to them all for their stimulation, advice, and encouragement.

The essays collected in this book were originally presented at an array of conferences and seminars at ANU, Chinese Academy of Social Sciences, European University Institute, Harvard University, Norwegian University of Science and Technology at Trondheim, University of Amsterdam, University of British Columbia, University of Canterbury at Christchurch, University of Edinburgh, University of Paris V, and University of Turku. Helpful comments, then and later, have been received from an embarrassingly long list of colleagues, in addition to those already mentioned: Bruce Ackerman, Tjitske Akkerman, Gustaf Arrhenius, André Bächtiger, Lars Bergström, John Braithwaite, Geoff Brennan,

Dave Brown, Peter Cane, Louise Clery, Keith Dowding, Jim Fishkin, Marc Fleurbaey, Mark Francis, Nancy Fraser, Christoph Freghe, Archon Fung, Andreas Føllesdal, Diane Gibson, Carol Gould, Joanna Goven, John Grin, Peter A. Hall, Peter Dobkin Hall, Iain Hampsher-Monk, Kasper Møller Hansen, Carol Harlow, Bob Haveman, Karl Hinrichs, Heidi Hurd, Magnus Jiborn, Bora Kandra, Dick Katz, Andrew Knops, Frances Kunreuther, Niki Lacey, Eerik Lagerspetz, Claudia Landwehr, Julian Le Grand, Christian List, Carolyn Lukensmeyer, Mark Lyons, Doug MacLean, Jenny Mansbridge, Jerry Mashaw, Marcel Maussen, Peter McCarthy, Daniel McDermott, Martha Minow, Michele Micheletti, Mark Moore, Michael Moore, Richard Mulgan, Hannu Nurmi, Laurie Paul, Thomas Pogge, Martin Rein, Mike Ridge, Susan Rose-Ackerman, Shawn Rosenberg, Nancy Rosenblum, Chuck Sabel, Andy Sabl, Mike Saward, Colin Scott, Maija Setälä, Vivienne Shue, Graham Smith, David Soskice, Rob Sparrow, Judith Squires, Jürg Steiner, Cass Sunstein, Lawrence Susskind, Torbjörn Tännsjö, Folke Tersman, Doug Torgerson, Laura Valentini, Robert van der Veen, Mark Warren, Albert Weale, Steve Weatherford, Donald Wittman, Iris Marion Young, and Laura Zurita. I am grateful to them all, and to four excellent anonymous referees for OUP, for invaluable comments on this book as a whole.

Most of these chapters have been previously published, sometimes in substantially different form. I am grateful to my publishers and co-authors for permission to reprint here from the following:

Robert E. Goodin and John S. Dryzek, 'Deliberative Impacts: The Macropolitical Uptake of Mini-publics'. *Politics & Society*, 34(#2) (June 2006), 219–44, © Sage Publications.

Robert E. Goodin and Simon J. Niemeyer, 'When Does Deliberation Begin? Internal Reflection versus Public Discussion in Deliberative Democracy'. *Political Studies*, 51(#4) (Dec. 2003), 627–49, © Blackwell Publishers.

'Talking Politics: Perils and Promise'. *European Journal for Political Research*, 45(#2) (March 2006), 235–61, © Blackwell Publishers.

'Enfranchising All Affected Interests, and Its Alternatives'. *Philosophy & Public Affairs*, 35(#1) (Jan. 2007), 40–68, © Blackwell Publishers.

'Democratic Accountability: The Distinctiveness of the Third Sector'. *Archives Européenes de Sociologie*, 44(#3) (2003), 359–96, © Cambridge University Press.

'Sequencing Deliberative Moments'. *Acta Politica*, 40 (July 2005), 182–96, © Palgrave Macmillan.

Robert E. Goodin and Michael Saward, 'Dog Whistles and Democratic Mandates'. *Political Quarterly*, 76(#4) (Oct.–Dec. 2005), 471–6, © Blackwell Publishers.

'Representing Diversity'. *British Journal of Political Science*, 34(#3) (July 2004), 453–68, © Cambridge University Press.

Like my last book's, this book's cover art was selected with the help of Lea Ypi; I thank her for that, for valuable comments on the book as a whole, and for much else.

List of Figures and Tables

Figures

Tables

1

Introduction

The sort of democracy that triumphed with the fall of the Berlin Wall is democracy of a distinctly minimalist sort. People vote to determine their rulers; votes are counted, winners declared; those elected rule for a time, facing the electorate once again at the end of that time.

There is much that might go wrong even with that minimalist set of democratic procedures. Who gets to vote is a big question: if people are unjustifiably excluded from voting, that compromises the quality of even the most minimalist sort of democracy. Who actually turns out to vote is another big issue: if too few of those qualified actually vote, the strength of the winner's mandate is democratically compromised. The counting of votes is a fraught issue, not only in places where whole ballot boxes end up in the river but also in places where 'hanging chad' can decide an election. How long those elected can rule, and who decides when they must face the electorate again, is of considerable consequence from a democratic point of view. In all those familiar ways, even the most minimalist sort of democracy is far from unproblematic.

Beyond all that, however, minimalist democracy is widely seen to be problematic precisely because it is so minimalist. All it asks of citizens is to cast a ballot from time to time: in most places, if and only if they feel like it. Minimalist democracy does not ask that citizens inform themselves before they vote. It does not ask them to pay attention to public debates on the issues of the day. It does not ask them to get together with others to discuss the issues. It does not ask them to justify their voting decision to anyone else. Still less does it ask people to take a position publicly to get actively involved in campaigning to persuade others that they should vote the same way.

From the point of view of minimalist democracy, it is of course essential that people be *permitted* to do all those things. But by minimalist

1

standards, democracy does not *require* people to do any of those things. Indeed, the institutional architecture of minimalist democracy is predicated precisely on the assumption that most people will not do most of those things most of the time. The task of institutional design for a minimalist democracy is generally seen as being to make democracy robust against those failings.

A wide range of critics have long insisted that that is simply not good enough, from a democratic point of view. Democracy should be designed in such a way as to encourage people to come together to discuss common problems and agree to solutions. Democracy should be designed in such a way as to enable citizens to see things from each other's point of view, understanding others' interests and arguments as well as one's own. Democracy should be designed in such a way as to encourage citizens to engage actively with one another in the joint management of their collective affairs, and in that way to develop their own capacities and perspectives.

Those are familiar themes from a long list of democratic theorists, running from Rousseau and Mill through Macpherson and Pateman down to Barber and Mansbridge.[1] That bundle of concerns has travelled under different banners in different generations: 'developmental' or 'participatory' or 'strong' democracy. There are very real differences at the level of detail among all those specific theories, of course, but their basic animus is pretty much the same.

In most recent years, democratic theory has taken a 'deliberative' turn.[2] Again, there are genuinely important differences of detail between deliberative democracy and those other forms. But once again, the basic animus is pretty much the same. Deliberative democrats tell us, most fundamentally, that we should shun merely adding up votes in favour of talking together.

What especially distinguishes the deliberative democracy movement is its concern with finding ways of putting the theory into practice. A host of micro-deliberative innovations—Citizens' Juries, Consensus Conferences, Deliberative Polls[3]—show us what deliberative democracy might look like in miniature. The 'deliberative quality' of parliamentary assemblies

---

[1] Rousseau (1762), Mill (1859), Macpherson (1973, 1977), Pateman (1970), Barber (1984), and Mansbridge (1980).

[2] The phrase is Bohman's (1998). Seminal texts include: Manin (1987), Cohen (1989, 1996, 1998), Dryzek (1990, 2000), Bohman (1996, 1998), Benhabib (1996), Chambers (1996), Gutmann and Thompson (1996, 2004), Habermas (1996), and Rawls (1997/1999). See more generally the papers collected in Bohman and Rehg (1997) and Elster (1998a).

[3] All are described in Chapter 2.

has been assayed, and ways of improving it recommended.[4] Ways of connecting micro-deliberations to macro-political decision-making have been trialled. Of course, all democratic theorists would like to see their theories put into practice. But deliberative democrats have been far more assiduous in joining up their theory with practice than most.

1.1. Incorporating Deliberation

The first question for any democratic theory is who is included. The history of expansion of the franchise traces the unfolding of that issue in a vote-counting context. The same issue obviously arises within deliberative democracy. Who gets a say? Who is entitled to speak?

This is a strangely under-explored issue within democratic theory, in both its vote-counting and its voice-hearing modes.[5] There are of course all sorts of arbitrary and ad hoc ways of answering the question, in practice. But if we are seeking a genuinely principled way of answering the question, we are I think driven in a radically expansionist direction. In principle, virtually everyone in the world ought to be entitled to a say in virtually any decision of virtually any polity anywhere in the world, as I argue in Chapter 7.

Of course, it is going to be awfully hard to implement that ideal in practice, even thinking of democracy purely in terms of voting. It is going to be all the harder to implement when thinking of democracy in terms of talking. If everyone in the world has to listen to everyone else for even a nanosecond before making a collective decision, each decision would take longer than a normal human lifespan.[6]

Deliberative democracy is a model growing out of small-scale face-to-face interactions. To apply it to any larger scale—even modest-sized towns, much less the world at large—requires some different institutional structure.[7] Deliberative democrats need to find ways of linking the virtues of small-scale deliberation with decision-making for larger-scale societies.

One way would be to build a micro-deliberation into the heart of the formal decision processes of the larger society, in any of the various ways

---

[4] Steiner et al. (2004) and Steenbergen et al. (2002).

[5] Although there were worries early on that the 'mannerly' requirements of deliberation might unduly exclude certain sorts of people (Young 1996/1997a, 2000: ch. 2; Sanders 1997), relaxing those requirements was the obvious solution (Dryzek 2000: ch. 3).

[6] Dahl (1970: 67–8) and Goodin (2003b: ch. 9) cf. Dryzek (2001).

[7] Indeed, the organizational structure of legislatures themselves is a response to the need to limit demands on time spent talking in plenary session (Cox 2006).

3

canvassed in Chapter 2. Porto Alegre Participatory Budgeting does that, having local meetings discuss broad budgetary issues and elect representatives to carry those concerns forward in higher-level deliberations.[8] British Columbia did that when using a micro-deliberative Citizens' Assembly to frame a recommendation to be put to a referendum concerning a new electoral system.[9]

Other times, micro-deliberations relate to formal decision-making machinery in more diffuse ways. Often they serve as something more akin to 'market-testing': will this idea sell, or not? The 'Listening to the City' America*Speaks* micro-deliberation persuaded New York City planners that the initial proposal for rebuilding on the World Trade Centre site would not.

Market-testing might sound like a derisive description. But in truth it is an important contribution, not just from the crassly careerist perspective of politicians seeking election but also from the perspective of the loftiest democratic theory. Good decisions, democratic or otherwise, require that we 'scope the range of the possible'—what the possible problems and options are, what the possible positions and solutions might be.

Sensitizing us in those ways to the perspectives and interests, experiences and concerns of others is one of the main things that talking together helps us do, as I show in Chapters 4 and 5. Even when talk does not 'settle' things, it clarifies them. By talking together, we understand more. We see why people take the positions they do, and sometimes that gives us more reason to embrace that position ourselves. We probably will have to settle things by voting rather than merely talking—and we should probably want to do so, given that conversations can be arbitrarily path dependent (Chapter 6). Nevertheless, talking together does make an important contribution, in getting all the relevant alternatives and considerations onto the table.

Even just the anticipation of having to defend our position to others can help push us to internalize their perspectives and reflect systematically on such information as we have, thus leading us to make better decisions from a democratic point of view. Indeed, on the evidence of Chapter 3, that might be one of the principal mechanisms at work in all micro-deliberations.

If so, that is a very good thing. The reason is simply one of scale, again. In any moderately diverse society, there is no realistic chance of capturing the full range of diversity within any modest-sized deliberative body. That

---

[8] Baiocchi (2001) and Fung and Wright (2003*a*).   [9] Warren and Pearce (2008*a*).

is true not just of the novel mini-publics described in Chapter 2. It is equally, and more importantly, true of legislative assemblies themselves, as I show in Chapter 12. Although called 'representative assemblies', they can never hope fully to 'mirror' a diverse society, having representatives of all of the full range of cross-cutting dimensions of diversity physically present in the chamber itself. The most we can hope is that our representative assemblies will be sufficiently diverse to 'represent the sheer fact of diversity'. Even so, awareness of that fact might hopefully lead to a situation in which such representatives are present to project themselves imaginatively into the positions of a range of people missing from the assembly, and to realize that they are legislating for a society that is more complex and diverse than the microcosm sitting in the chamber itself.

/ Sensitivity to difference ?

1.2. Enriching Democracy

Although micro-deliberative innovations have been the focal point for much recent excitement within democratic theory and practice, simply bolting those onto existing democratic institutions is not an adequate response to the challenge of democratizing the contemporary world. Instead, aspects of the deliberative ideal must be adapted for and incorporated in the core elements of democratic institutions as they already exist. Furthermore, elements of the deliberative ideal can help us see new modes of democratic governance, outside those old familiar institutional structures.

In going back to rethink democratic theory as a whole, the first question posed in Part II is how the demos is constituted. Who is included, and who is excluded? Who gets a say, and who does not, in what the demos democratically decides to do? That threshold question is addressed in Chapter 7.

In practice, the demos has historically been territorially defined. From a principled point of view, that was only ever a rough approximation to anything that is remotely morally defensible. Sharing a territory in itself hardly matters, from a principled point of view. Still, back in the day that most interactions people had were within the boundaries of their country's own territory, territoriality might not have been a bad approximation to what really mattered, which is whose interests are affected by your own actions and choices and whose actions and choices affect your interests. Even before the latest round of globalization, and still more after, it has simply ceased to be the case that the effects of our actions and choices stop at the territorial boundaries of our own countries. Democratically, we really ought to reconstitute our demos to reflect that fact: ideally including within it everyone whose interests are affected by our actions and choices, or at the very least adapting democratic practice within our unjustifiably restricted demos to reflect its democratic shortcomings in that respect.

One way of addressing the challenge of more global democratic accountability, in the absence of a single world government, is to think in broader terms of accountability. We know well what democratic accountability means within the context of a state. We think too little about what accountability of a broadly democratic sort might mean outside the state—in the market sector, for one obvious example. But we also think way too little about what distinctive mechanisms of accountability, again of a broadly democratic sort, might be available within civil society. Chapter 8 suggests that 'network accountability' is the distinctively discursive mode of democratic accountability operating within that realm. That is a mode of accountability that can bind non-governmental actors across political boundaries. It is a distinctly deliberative mode of 'discursive accountability', relying more on naming-and-shaming than on threats-and-sanctions. But it is no less effective for that.

Within the state, democratic decision-making of the ordinary sort involves a sequence of contributions by a large array of actors. In trying to make that sequence more deliberative overall, we ought to be sensitive to the different role that those actors play at each stage of those democratic deliberations—and we ought to have different deliberative expectations of each of them. Democratic decision-making is a matter of 'distributed deliberation', as Chapter 9 dubs it; and we need to be thinking in terms of 'sequencing deliberative moments' within that larger, differentiated system of democratic decision-making.

Political parties are central players in that larger system of 'distributed deliberation' within real-existing democracies—and rightly so, Chapter 10 argues. It is through them that the deliberations of the electorate at large are coordinated, so voters end up talking about the same thing and coming to a shared understanding of what should be inferred from a vote one way rather than another. In a small-scale group, this happens automatically when people start talking together.[10] Among mass electorates, we need some focal points—most typically provided by political parties—in order to achieve such shared understandings of the meaning of a vote.

[10] List et al. (2007).

And it is democratically essential to achieve that, if the people are to 'give laws to themselves'.

If everyone has a different understanding of what it is they are supporting, then the fact that everyone seems to support the 'same' thing will be democratically meaningless. They do not support the same thing at all, only seemingly the same thing under lots of different descriptions. Any law they enact would have no ratio, any government they elect would have no real democratic mandate. That is the fundamental perversity of 'dog whistle politics', whereby political parties send coded messages that will be heard one way by their core supporters and another way altogether by others (Chapter 11). Political parties engaging in that sort of behaviour are fundamentally undermining democratic deliberation—and ironically enough doing so in ways that fundamentally undermine their own democratic reason for being.

The story about 'dog whistle politics' brings us back to where we began this chapter, the shortcomings of minimalist accounts of democracy. At the heart of that model is the mechanical aggregation of people's votes. What the story about 'dog whistle politics' emphasizes is the need to attend to the propositional content of people's votes when aggregating them. When adding up 'votes for going to war', you have to make sure that all the votes you add together really are for 'going to war'. If in some voting machines Column 1 represented 'going to war' and in some Column 1 represented 'going to water' (and there is no way of retrospectively recovering which is which machine-by-machine, to rectify the error), then simply summing the number of votes for Column 1 yields a meaningless result. Thus, even in the most minimalist democracy, you can never merely aggregate people's votes: you must attend to their reasons as well.

1.3. Reasoning Democracy

We are in a period of high innovation, both within democratic theory and within democratic practice. The 'deliberative turn' has provided much of the impetus for both. In many ways, the innovations occasioned by it have gone beyond classically deliberative themes and mechanisms. We nonetheless have the 'deliberative turn' very largely to thank for the reinvigoration of democracy in all its new and increasingly unbounded forms.

Inevitably, however, deliberative democracy can only supplement rather than supplant the institutional apparatus of representative democracy as we know it. Representative assemblies will not disappear, political parties will not disappear, international fora will not disappear, policy networks will not disappear. Deliberative democrats need to figure out how to fit their peculiar contribution to existing institutions of representative democracy, just as practitioners of democratic politics have to figure out how to incorporate deliberative insights. Chapter 13 attempts to begin the task of rethinking the roles of existing democratic institutions in new deliberative terms, at the same time as recasting those deliberative ideals in terms of the sticky institutional realities of existing democracies.

Part I

Micro-Deliberation

2

Making use of mini-publics

with John S. Dryzek

When democratic theory took its 'deliberative turn', one of the most immediate worries lay in how large groups of individuals could genuinely deliberate together. With too many people, genuine deliberation is just not possible: there is just not enough time.

Various solutions have been suggested. Some theorists place their hopes in conventional institutions of government such as legislatures or courts, some in civil society, others in e-networks or mass-mediated deliberation, yet others in empathetic imaginings.[1]

Still other deliberative democrats place their hopes in 'mini-publics'. These are designed to be groups small enough to be genuinely deliberative and representative enough to be genuinely democratic—although they rarely meet standards of statistical representativeness, and they are never representative in the electoral sense. Such mini-publics include Deliberative Polls, Consensus Conferences, Citizens' Juries, Planning Cells, and many others (briefly described in Section 2.1).

Importantly, different though all these designs are from one another, what they all share is their reliance on small-group deliberations in mini-publics composed of ordinary citizens. That is what distinguishes them from a raft of other recent democratic innovations.[2] The suggestion is that deliberation in these mini-publics is representative of—and hence can substitute for—deliberation among mass publics that simply cannot deliberate together in the same ways.[3]

---

[1] See, variously: Bessette (1994), Rawls (1997/1999), Habermas (1996), Dryzek (2000, 2001), Norris (2001), Page (1996), and Goodin (2003*b*).

[2] Gastil and Levine (2005) and Smith (2005).

[3] It is that 'substitution' that led me elsewhere to call this 'ersatz' (Goodin 2003: 174–6).

Here is an early and influential image of a mini-public from Robert Dahl, the pre-eminent democratic theorist of the past generation:

Suppose an advanced democratic country were to create a 'minipopulus' consisting of perhaps a thousand citizens randomly selected out of the entire demos. Its task would be to deliberate, for a year perhaps, on an issue and then to announce its choices. The members of a minipopulus could 'meet' by telecommunications. One minipopulus could decide on the agenda of issues, while another might concern itself with a major issue. Thus one minipopulus could exist for each major issue on the agenda.... It could be attended—again by telecommunications—by an advisory committee of scholars and specialists and by an administrative staff. It could hold hearings, commission research, and engage in debate and discussion.

'In these ways', Dahl writes, 'the democratic process could be adapted once again to a world that little resembles the world in which democratic ideas and practices first came to life.'[4]

Dahl envisages such a minipopulus 'not as a substitute for legislative bodies but as a complement'.[5] Some writers suggest democratic designs in which the deliberations of a mini-public chosen by lot would literally substitute for those of an elected representative assembly, but such authoritative assemblies have hardly been seen since Ancient Greece.[6] The sorts of mini-publics I shall be focusing on in this chapter are not normally like that. In these designs, the ordinary institutions of representative democracy remain sovereign, and micro-deliberative mechanisms merely provide inputs into them. These inputs are more formal in some cases, less formal in others, but rarely does the mini-public itself share sovereignty over the decision at hand. Thus arises the problem at the heart of the present chapter: how to link the micro to the macro.

By 'macro' I mean the larger political system and its need for authoritative collective decisions. When it comes to the macro-political impact, more than direct impact on the content of public policy will turn out to be at issue, as we shall see. Still, mini-publics of the sort here generally can have real political impact only by working on, and through, the broader public sphere, ordinary institutions of representative democracy, and administrative policymaking.[7] In this chapter, I attempt

---

[4] Dahl (1989: 342), cf. Dahl (1970: 149–53). Technology has come a long way since Dahl was writing, and organization of a minipopulus online would now be quite straightforward.

[5] Just as Budge (1996: ch. 7) envisages direct-democratic mechanisms complementing representative democracy.

[6] Burnheim (1985).

[7] On the basis of his survey, Ryfe (2005: 61) remarks, 'Interestingly, I have come across few examples... of policy officials [being] explicitly bound by the decisions of deliberative groups... in the United States.... Instead, most initiatives focus... either on education or

to map ways in which that might happen, providing apt illustrations of each. Democratic theory now accords central roles to deliberating citizens, but large questions remain unresolved concerning how citizen deliberation can be consequential in democratic practice. This chapter will begin answering such questions by cataloguing, tracing, and illustrating available paths of impact.

2.1. Mini-Publics: A Brief Survey

Recent years have seen a burgeoning of innovative democratic techniques. In a report for the UK POWER project, Graham Smith lists 57.[8] Some are proposals specifically for electoral reform. Others involve improved consultative procedures. Still others involve e-initiatives or expansions of familiar instruments of direct democracy, such as referenda.[9] Here I shall be concentrating more narrowly on mini-publics.

These are designs in which small groups of people deliberate together.[10] This chapter will be focusing on mini-publics with some claim to representativeness of the public at large. Representation is something of a conceptual thicket in political theory.[11] Mini-publics definitely cannot claim electoral representation. Nor do they necessarily claim statistical representativeness.[12] All 'some claim to representativeness' need mean is that the diversity of social characteristics and plurality of initial points of view in the larger society is substantially present in the deliberating mini-public. Social characteristics and viewpoints need not be present in the same proportions as in the larger population, nor need members of the mini-public be accountable to the larger population in the way elected representatives are.

In focusing on mini-publics with claims to representativeness, this chapter stresses forums involving non-partisan lay citizens. Thus, this chapter says little about familiar consultative mechanisms in which participants exclusively self-select or are selected on the basis of their partisanship—public inquiries, stakeholder dialogues, mediation,

---

consultation. Put another way, most initiatives imagine that the ultimate impact of deliberation is on public opinion and not the policy-making process'.

[8] Smith (2005).   [9] Lupia and Matsuaka (2004).

[10] Sometimes many such small groups meet simultaneously or sequentially, at the same venue or at separate ones.

[11] Saward (2003) and Mansbridge (2003b).

[12] Among the mini-public designs this chapter discusses, only one (the Deliberative Poll) asserts that claim.

regulatory negotiation, and so forth—except for purposes of comparison. Many of the macro-impact issues this chapter addresses will also arise in these kinds of partisan forums, though in principle impact should be more straightforward, given that key players in the macro system are often present in partisan deliberative forums.[13]

Because of that focus on mini-publics with some claim to representativeness, this chapter will say little about mini-public heading exercises that rely completely on self-selection.[14] Of course, there is an element of self-selection in all deliberative microcosms: citizens must agree to participate, and many decline.[15] In some designs, participants are selected from among those who have registered an interest in participating in this kind of forum via a website or phone line. Yet these designs remain very different from those that rely completely on self-selection, which are likely to attract only strong partisans.

These other sorts of mini-publics are important too, of course. One of them—perhaps the most widely discussed recent innovation in participatory-cum-deliberative decision-making, especially when it comes to direct impact on policymaking—is Participatory Budgeting in the Brazilian city of Porto Alegre. Begun there in 1989 and spreading to many other cities in Brazil and Latin America in subsequent years, Participatory Budgeting involves three tiers of decision-making: first, a set of popular Regional Assemblies, open to all; then Regional Budget Forums, whose members are elected by the Regional Assemblies; and finally, Municipal Budget Councils elected by Regional Assemblies.[16] Certainly Participatory Budgeting is a great success in participatory terms.[17] It is also a great success in terms of macro-political impact, with budget priorities and representatives to the Forums and Councils being determined by direct vote in the popular Regional Assemblies. But these mini-publics are different from the sort discussed in the rest of this chapter in that, there, the participants are either self-selected (in the case of the Regional Assemblies) or elected (by the Regional Assemblies, for the other two tiers).

[13] For a comparison that suggests this generalization does not always hold, see Hendriks, Dryzek, and Hunold (2007).

[14] Fung (2003a) says much more about those.

[15] For example, in the British Columbia Citizens' Assembly on Electoral Reform discussed below, some 26,500 people were invited to express interest in being included in the Assembly; 1,441 participants were invited to attend a selection meeting after indicating interest, of which 964 actually attended; and 158 participants were randomly selected from that number (Warren and Pearse 2008b).

[16] Baiocchi (2001).

[17] Some 8.4% of the adult population of Porto Alegre report having participated in Assemblies at some point over the previous five years (Baiocchi 2001; Fung 2003a).

Complete reliance on self-selection is also true of another much-discussed set of cases involving 'community policing' in Chicago.[18] Substantial amounts of control are devolved onto 'beat meetings', where small groups of police and citizens engage in 'deliberative problem-solving' on an ongoing basis. These are certainly instances of genuine empowerment of local communities; and when everything goes well (as it sometimes does not), they involve genuine micro-level deliberations across the lay and professional participants. But since 'beat meetings' were simply open meetings, participants were self-selected and hence not a microcosm of the ordinary public. The same is true of community consultations conducted in connection with Oregon health care reform.[19]

This chapter also does not discuss deliberation in courts, legislatures, and administrative agencies, though they figure centrally in some theories of deliberative democracy.[20] Formal institutions of government have constitutional power or statutory authority to determine outcomes. Their members have that authority by virtue of having been formally elected or appointed to certain offices of state. Of course, in a system of mixed government, there will be other branches or officials that may try to ignore or override their determinations, so the problem at the heart of the present chapter might thus arise in a different way there too. But formally empowered bodies generally have a different kind of claim for their determinations to be taken seriously than do the mini-publics upon which this chapter focuses. The latter have no constitutional claim to share in formal macro-political decision-making. At most, and very rarely, they have a politically (but not constitutionally) guaranteed place in policymaking on a particular issue. The more usual case is that mini-publics lack formal power or authority in the macro-political system. They might sometimes have been established by some public authority. They might report to

---

[18] Fung (2001, 2004). In the companion case Fung discusses—Chicago community schooling—lay members of the Local School Councils were actually elected.

[19] When the Oregon Basic Health Care Act foresaw 'difficult and controversial choices' being required concerning 'the categories of medical conditions and treatments that would be covered by public health insurance', it enjoined the Health Services Commission to make that determination 'based on values established in a community participatory process'. As part of that process, some 46 community meetings involving 1,003 residents throughout the state were held, to 'build consensus on the values to be used to guide health service allocation decisions'. Those meetings were, by all accounts, exemplary in their deliberative quality. But 'meetings were voluntary and little effort seems to have been expended to recruit from disadvantaged communities'; and in consequence participation was 'skewed...toward a narrow band of professionals and citizens of high socioeconomic status' (Fung 2003: 357). Many of the participants were actually health care professionals.

[20] Bessette (1994) and Uhr (1998).

it. But when they do, their reports are purely advisory and lack even any presumptive law-making power of their own. The problem of how the macro-political 'takes up' their micro-deliberative input thus arises in acute form.

Among the most interesting forms of mini-public are the following:[21]

- *Citizens' Juries*, initiated in the USA by Ned Crosby and the Jefferson Centre he founded in 1974, have been run sporadically there and more widely in other countries since. Citizens' Juries receive information, hear evidence, cross-examine witnesses, and then deliberate on the issue at hand. Typically, but not invariably, the Citizens' Jury has been commissioned by some public agency to whom its recommendations are addressed. Citizens' Juries were especially common in Blair's Britain.[22] In Canada in 2004, the government of Ontario appointed a Minister for Democratic Renewal to preside over the establishment of Citizens' Juries of 12–24 citizens, selected by stratified sampling to promote demographic representativeness and who deliberated over 2–4 days to provide advice on specific aspects of the province's budget.[23] *Planning Cells* in Germany operate broadly similarly, with a number of deliberating groups running in parallel in a longer, multistage process.[24]

- *Consensus Conferences*, initiated by the Danish Board of Technology in 1987, have been run there and across the world with some frequency since.[25] In the original Danish model, a small group of 15 lay citizens holds two weekend-long preparatory meetings to set the agenda for a four-day public forum; there, experts give testimony and are questioned, after which the lay panel retires to write a report presented at the end of the fourth day to a press conference, typically attracting attention from politicians and the media. In Denmark, that public forum is then followed by a set of local debates, also organized by the Board of Technology. A 2003 enactment of the US Congress specifies Consensus Conferences as one way in which the responsible agency can discharge its obligation of 'ensuring that ethical, legal,

---

[21] A more complete catalogue can be found in Gastil and Levine (2005).

[22] For details, see: www.jefferson-center.org/; Coote and Lenaghan (1997), Crosby and Nethercut (2005) and Lenaghan, New, and Mitchell (1996).

[23] Galloway (2004).

[24] For details, see: www.planungszelle.de/; Dienel (2005) and Hendriks (2005a).

[25] For details, see: Joss and Durand (1995), Hendriks (2005a) and Sclove (2005).

environmental and other appropriate social concerns... are considered during the development of nanotechnology'.[26]

- *Deliberative Polls*, initiated by James S. Fishkin and his Centre for Deliberative Polling in 1988, have now been run in several countries around the world.[27] Deliberative Polls gather a random sample of between 250 and 500 citizens. They hear evidence from experts, break up into smaller groups (around 15 people each) to frame questions to put to the experts, and then reassemble in plenary session to pose these questions to panels of experts. Before-and-after surveys of participants are taken to measure both information acquisition and opinion change over the course of the event. Large and expensive enterprises, Deliberative Polls are typically run in collaboration with media outlets, which publicize the results. In their book *Deliberation Day*, Ackerman and Fishkin propose that this model be expanded into a nationwide Deliberative Poll before national elections, involving simultaneous events across the country in which literally all citizens would be invited to participate.[28]

- America*Speaks*, founded by Carolyn Lukensmeyer in 1997, organizes a series of '*21st Century Town Meetings*'.[29] These are one-day events involving between 500 and 5,000 people deliberating on some specific issue. Participant selection procedures vary, but efforts are made to ensure reasonably representative samples of citizens. They operate through moderated small-group discussions at demographically mixed tables of 10–12 people. Feedback from these tables is immediately pooled via networked computers and sifted by the organizers to form the basis for subsequent discussions. Large video screens present data, themes, and information in real time over the course of the deliberations. As themes emerge and votes are taken, recommendations gel. Key stakeholders produce background materials and, together with public authorities, typically attend the event. The most famous America*Speaks* Town Meetings were a pair called 'Listening to

---

[26] US Congress (2003). In the version of the bill that originally passed the House of Representatives, Consensus Conferences alone were specified, but that was amended in the Senate to specify instead 'mechanisms such as citizens' panels, consensus conferences, and educational events, as appropriate'.

[27] For details, see: cdd.stanford.edu/polls/docs/summary/; Fishkin (1991, 1997) and Fishkin and Farrar (2005).

[28] Ackerman and Fishkin (2004).

[29] For details, see: www.americaspeaks.org/services/town_meetings/index.htm (accessed 10 July 2005) and Lukensmeyer, Goldman, and Brigham (2005).

the City: Rebuilding Lower Manhattan' after the 9/11 destruction—more of which is described below.

- *National Issues Forums*, an initiative of the Kettering Foundation, annually convenes a US-wide network of over 3,000 locally sponsored public forums of varying sizes and selection procedures to discuss selected issues.[30] The Foundation collates feedback into reports that it then circulates to elected officials. Drawing on the National Issues Forums, a Deliberative Poll called the National Issues Conference was convened in the run-up to the 1996 US presidential elections; the event was broadcast on PBS, anchored by Jim Lehrer, and had an estimated 10 million viewers.[31] In the small town of Kuna, Idaho, public officials regularly convene Study Circles on this model to deliberate and advise on issues that are likely to prove controversial.[32]

- '*GM Nation?*' was a 'public debate' organized by (but at arm's-length from) the UK government as part of a national consultation on genetically modified food in June 2003.[33] The main debate of some 675 'open community meetings' involved individuals who were purely self-selected; that component of the debate is not therefore the sort of mini-public upon which this chapter focuses. There was, however, another component of 'GM Nation?' that did involve deliberative groups of the sort of interest here. To provide more structured analysis of community response to the issues and to serve as a cross-check for results from the open meetings, organizers also convened 10 'Narrow

[30] For details, see: www.nifi.org/forums/about.aspx (accessed 10 July 2005) and Melville, Willingham, and Dedrick (2005).

[31] Fishkin (1995: 177–203). Another 2003 National Issues Forums Deliberative Poll, also in collaboration with McNeil-Lehrer Productions, focused on 'America in the World' (Fishkin, Luskin, and Brady 2003).

[32] In Fung's description (2006: 677–8):

citizens are invited to learn about the issue in more detail and deliberate with one another and with officials about the merits and costs of various options over the course of several days. Following the national study circles model, participants in these events are given briefing materials and organized into small, facilitated discussion groups. In these groups and in large group discussions composed of the whole, members develop opinions about the issues and options at stake and prepare questions and recommendations for policy makers. These popular deliberations sometimes validate decision makers' views and galvanize community members in favor of certain policy positions. Sometimes, however, the deliberations reveal objections and latent preferences that cause representatives and other officials to modify their proposals. Citizens often come to understand and appreciate the reasons that favor various proposals and positions in their deliberations with officials. Between one and several hundred residents typically participate in these study circles. Over the past five years, Kuna has convened study circles on issues ranging from multimillion-dollar school bonds to student drug testing, local tax policy, and town planning.

[33] For details, see: www.gmnation.org.uk/ (accessed 10 July 2005).

but Deep' groups. Each of these groups held two day-long meetings a fortnight apart providing their views on issues that arose in the open meetings.

2.2. Possible Pathways to Influence

How might mini-publics affect political decision-making? Possible modes of influence are many and varied. So too are the possible ways in which the macro-political system might 'abuse' mini-publics, using them in ways that undermine the democratic or deliberative quality of the larger political process. The aim of this chapter is to catalogue the various ways mini-publics might possibly affect the macro-political system, for better or for worse, providing instances of each. A detailed catalogue is useful in countering those who are sceptical of the impact of such innovations, and in illuminating the subtle as well as the obvious ways they can make a difference.

2.2.1. Actually Making Policy

The limiting case of actually 'making policy' occurs when a forum is formally empowered as part of a decision-making process. Cases are still rare, though they might become increasingly common.[34]

Perhaps the most surprising success story along these lines is the 2005 Chinese Deliberative Poll in Zeguo. Participants were asked how the township should allocate funds across some thirty proposed public infrastructure projects, and the government committed in advance to implementing recommendations of the Deliberative Poll. The results of their deliberation surprised the leadership, but their recommendations were indeed faithfully implemented.[35]

Another famous recent case of mini-publics forming part of the formal political process is the Citizens' Assembly on Electoral Reform in British

[34] The 2003 statute discussed in n. 22 above that includes Consensus Conferences as part of US policymaking on nanotechnology is a clear signal of movement in that direction, though there is no guarantee of formal incorporation.

[35] Fishkin et al. (2006). Ironically, deliberative mini-publics are probably a preferred form of democratization in the People's Republic of China precisely because they do not constitute a challenge to one-party rule, on which more will be said in Section 10.2.1. While the Deliberative Poll may have democratized, after a fashion, that particular set of budgetary choices, it is hard to see how even a large series of Deliberative Polls can democratize the body of law as a whole.

Columbia.[36] That Assembly, composed of 160 randomly selected citizens, was established by a unanimous enactment of the provincial legislature and charged with the task of recommending an electoral system for the province. If it recommended changed arrangements, the provincial government committed itself to putting that proposal to the electorate at large in a referendum at the next year's elections.

After an initial set of weekend meetings to inform members concerning alternative electoral systems, the Assembly held 50 public hearings (attended by 3,000 citizens and receiving 1,600 written submissions) and then spent 6 weekends deliberating. In December 2004, it recommended a version of single-transferable vote that was put to referendum the next May.

The Citizens' Assembly was constituted as a formal part of the political system. It was legislatively charged with making a recommendation that would automatically go onto the ballot as a referendum proposal. That was an ironclad commitment from the provincial government from the start. In that central respect, the macro-political uptake of this mini-public's recommendation was hardwired.

Of course, it was then an open question whether or not the Citizens' Assembly's recommendations would be approved in that referendum. Ultimately it was not.[37] Still, having a guarantee that its recommendations will be considered, even if they are ultimately rejected, is importantly different from having no guarantee that they will be considered at all, which is the case with purely advisory recommendations of mini-publics of the sort discussed next.

2.2.2. Taken Up in the Policy Process

The much more frequent case occurs when a mini-public provides recommendations to ordinary macro-political processes, with no formal guarantee that the recommendations will be taken any further (much less adopted and implemented) in the macro-political process. Sometimes organizers of a forum will seek assurance in advance from government officials that the forum will be taken up in the political decision-making

---

[36] See: www.citizensassembly.bc.ca/public (accessed 13 July 2005). For background see Gibson (2002) and Warren and Pearse (2008a), and the interim report of the Assembly (British Columbia Citizens' Assembly on Electoral Reform 2004).

[37] To pass the proposal had to win 60% of the valid votes in 60% of the electoral districts; the Assembly's proposals passed the second test but failed the first, winning only 57.69% of total votes. See www.elections.bc.ca/elections/ge2005/fnalrefresults.htm (accessed 13 July 2005).

process; this is a standard feature of the America*Speaks* procedure and a not-uncommon feature of Citizens' Juries. In Denmark, there is an expectation (although no formal legal requirement) for Parliament and political parties to respond explicitly to the recommendations of Consensus Conferences organized by the Danish Board of Technology. For an example of ways in which Danish Consensus Conferences have directly influenced legislation, note that the 'conferences that were held in the late 1980s influenced the Danish Parliament to pass legislation limiting the use of genetic screening in hiring and insurance decisions, to exclude genetically modified animals from the government's initial biotechnology research and development program, and to prohibit food irradiation for everything except dry spices'.[38] Of course it cannot be proven that the Consensus Conference was the decisive influence; sceptics might say this is what government policy would have been anyway.

In at least one peculiar case, a policymaker allegedly guaranteed in advance that he would *not* respond to the recommendations of a citizen's forum. A citizen's jury on container deposit legislation financed by the government of New South Wales was seen as a potential source of threat by the beverage industry, which reportedly secured a commitment in advance from Premier Bob Carr that no legislation would be introduced, whatever the jury recommended.[39]

Mini-publics involve (at most) 'only a few hundred [citizens] who are given a chance to learn, think and deliberate'. Yet they can make claims to represent informed public opinion on an issue. Indeed, the designers of Deliberative Polls claim that participants 'are a scientifically chosen random sample and their views therefore represent what the ... people would think if they became similarly more knowledgeable about ... policy....'.[40] They thus 'represent what the public would think about the issue if it were motivated to become more informed and to consider competing arguments'.[41]

That fact might give mini-publics the power to influence public policymaking in various ways. One might be that policymakers take the opinion of people informed in the course of these events as authoritative, in preference to 'raw' public opinion. 'The judgment of a minipopulous', Dahl says,

---

[38] Sclove (2005).   [39] Hendriks (2005*b*: ch. 4).
[40] Fishkin, Luskin, and Brady (2003: 19).
[41] Fishkin (2003: 128); see similarly Fishkin (1995: 163, 173).

would 'represent' the judgment of the demos. Its verdict would be the verdict of the demos itself, if the demos were able to take advantage of the best available knowledge to decide what policies were most likely to achieve the ends it sought. The judgments of the minipopulus would thus derive their authority from the legitimacy of democracy.[42]

Of course, it is an open question whether decision-makers will prefer this kind of public opinion to raw and uninformed public opinion (or lack of opinion) that the mass of ordinary voters will still exhibit. Electoral considerations might dictate a preference for the latter.

Positive influence is, however, possible. As a way of discharging their statutory public-consultation requirements, eight electric utilities in different parts of Texas commissioned Deliberative Polls between 1996 and 1998, asking customers how they preferred that future electricity requirements to be met. The results showed a sharp increase in participants' support for investments in energy conservation measures, and also strong willingness to pay more for energy if it came from renewable sources.

The results of these Deliberative Polls affected public policy in two ways, one very direct and the other only slightly less so. First, 'as a result of the deliberative polls, the utility companies began to integrate consumer values about energy choices into their [Integrated Resource Plan] filings [to the state Public Utility Commission] . . . ; and decisions that followed tended to include renewable energy investments, paid for by all consumers. Several of the companies also received regulatory approval to start renewable energy marketing ("green pricing") programs on a pilot basis'.[43]

Second, 'in 1999, the Texas Legislature enacted Senate Bill 7, which'— among other things—'established a renewable energy development standard that requires all for-profit retail sellers of electricity to obtain approximately 3% of their electricity supplies from renewable energy sources by 2009. . . . The legislation also set new conservation goals . . . '. Cautious commentators say,

While it would be disingenuous to suggest that the results of the deliberative polling process alone were responsible for the regulatory and legislative changes that followed, the polls did, for the first time, provide for public consultation in a systematic and scientific manner . . . The contribution of the deliberative polls was to provide a measurement of what is important to those affected by energy statutes and regulation—the public. . . . The deliberative polling results validated what advocates of renewable energy, energy efficiency and low-income assistance

---

[42] Dahl (1989: 342).   [43] Lehr et al. (2003: 9).

had argued for some time but could not necessarily prove: that customers support these public benefits expenditures and are willing to pay for them.[44]

A less cautious conclusion is suggested by their report's subtitle: 'How Deliberative Polling helped build 1,000 MW of new renewable energy projects in Texas?'.

Certainly their organizer is bullish in attributing these policy changes to the effects of his Deliberative Polls. Fishkin proudly proclaims that

based on the results of the Deliberative Polls, [the Texas Utility Commissioners] implemented plans that yielded the largest investments in renewable energy in the history of the state. Later the legislature, when it de-regulated the utility industry, used the results of the Deliberative Poll to justify including a substantial renewable energy portfolio in the legislation.[45]

2.2.3. Informing Public Debates

In a Pew Charitable Trust survey of organizations sponsoring citizen dialogues of one sort or another, no less than 45 per cent reported that 'one of their major goals was simply to provide information'.[46] Information would flow both to those involved directly in policy debates and (ideally) to larger publics. One way to influence broader publics is via media coverage of deliberative events.[47] Advocates of mini-publics characteristically argue that the media should give more publicity to their results. 'Why so little coverage?' they ask. 'Shouldn't informed public opinion count for more than uninformed public opinion?'[48] The answer to this second question may not be straightforward, as has just been noted.

Such media coverage might influence people's behaviour in various ways. It might lead them to become more interested in the topic and acquire more and better information about it.[49] Media coverage of mini-publics might also alter people's policy preferences directly, if they became persuaded that they ought to shift their own preferences in line with those of their more informed but otherwise identical counterparts.[50]

---

[44] Lehr et al. (2003: 9).   [45] Fishkin (2003: 132).

[46] Quoted in Fung (2003a: 349).   [47] Fishkin (2003: 131).

[48] Fishkin, Luskin, and Brady (2003: 19).

[49] 'By giving substantial coverage to [mini-publics], the media could stimulate a broader debate about what information and knowledge people need to make informed pronouncements about ... policy', say Fishkin, Luskin, and Brady (2003: 19).

[50] A Deliberative Poll, as Fishkin (1995: 163) puts it, 'has a recommending force: these are the conclusions citizens would come to, were they better informed on the issues and had the opportunity and motivation to examine those issues seriously. ... If such a poll were broadcast before an election or a referendum, it could dramatically affect the outcome'.

According to Fishkin, 'In the Deliberative Poll before the 1999 Australian referendum', for example, 'we can clearly see from other polls that the broadcasts and newspaper articles had a significant effect'[51]—albeit one that had dissipated by the time voting took place.

Another Australian case of a mini-public informing public debate is that of a Consensus Conference on genetically modified foods that took place in 1999.[52] Prior to the conference, public debate on this issue was minimal. The conference helped raise the profile of the issue, receiving substantial media coverage, and it was cited in subsequent legislative debates. Monsanto, the main commercial sponsor of genetic technology, was forced to change its communications strategy. The company dispatched a representative to the Consensus Conference who treated it as a public relations occasion, patronizing the citizen participants as being in need of a bit of instruction and reassurance about the safety of the technology.[53] This representative was so chastened by the citizen's panel's hostile reaction that, when it came to delivery of the report, he had retreated from his reserved seat on the floor of the chamber to the obscurity of the balcony. For the first time Monsanto realized it could lose the public relations battle, and needed to take public scepticism more seriously. Along with Monsanto, the Commonwealth Scientific and Industrial Research Organization (a pro-GM government body) became aware of the need to engage the public in dialogue, rather than simply educate and inform. The Consensus Conference recommended caution in proceeding with the technology, but did not recommend a ban or moratorium.

That was also the case with Danish procedures of technology assessment more generally. There, even Danish Council of Industry representatives agree that

corporations have benefited from their nation's participatory approach to technology assessment because 'product developers have worked in a more critical environment, thus being able to forecast some of the negative reactions and improve their products in the early phase'. For example, Novo Nordisk, a large Danish biotechnology company, reevaluated its research and development strategies after a 1992 panel deplored the design of animals suited to the rigors of existing agricultural systems but endorsed the use of genetic engineering to help treat incurable diseases. The firm now wants to concentrate on work more likely to win popular approval, such as animal-based production of drugs for severe human illnesses.[54]

---

[51] Fishkin (2003: 131).   [52] Hendriks (2005*b*: ch. 5).
[53] Hendriks (2005*b*: 117–18).   [54] Sclove (2005).

2.2.4. *Shaping Policy by Market-Testing*

The phrase 'market-testing' points to an analogy with commerce, and there are indeed instances of commercial ventures benefiting in just this way from politically commissioned mini-publics. The cases of Texas utility companies, Monsanto and Novo Nordisk discussed above are cases in point. But politicians need to 'market-test' their proposals too.

The key question, to which mini-publics can provide a clear answer, is: 'Can we sell this to the public, however hard we try, however much we increase public awareness, information, etc.?' Much of the consultative apparatus traditionally used by governments—public inquiries and Green Papers in the UK, remiss procedures in Scandinavia,[55] Congressional hearings in the USA—have long had that as their aim, however dubious the marketing language might seem from the viewpoint of some democratic ideals. Marketing experts have long used 'focus groups' to market-test products, and political consultants have been using the same techniques for years to market-test political pitches.

Mini-publics of the sorts described above can serve the same function for the macro-political system more generally. Sometimes sponsors get a clear and surprising 'yes' to the question 'Can we sell this to people?' as with the Deliberative Polls on renewable energy in Texas in the example discussed above. Sometimes they get a clear 'no'.

A case of the latter sort comes from World Trade Centre site planning. The pair of America*Speaks* 21st Century Town Meetings, 'Listening to the city', had a clear—if, in the first instance, primarily negative—impact on plans for rebuilding lower Manhattan after the 9/11 attacks.[56]

One major concern of the owner of the site, the Port Authority, was to replace rapidly all the commercial space that had been lost on the site in order to restore the $120 million annual revenue stream it had lost. But the Lower Manhattan Development Corporation—the agency responsible for approving the plans—'wanted to learn as much as they could about the public's evaluation of the elements that made up those concept plans—and they got that information'. This willingness may have had more to do with a desire to avoid political trouble than a genuine

[55] Goodin (2003*b*: ch. 8).
[56] For details on the event, see: www.listeningtothecity.org/ (accessed 13 July 2005) and Civic Alliance to Rebuild Downtown New York (2002). For a brief gloss, see Fung (2006: 678–9).

wish to learn from informed public opinion. However, the upshot of the 'Listening to the City' exercise was a 'unanimous' and 'resounding rejection' of these Port Authority priorities.[57]

As summarized by the official report of the proceedings,

people voiced strong objections to elements of all six proposals, particularly the dense office and commercial development they called for. Participants said that although the concept plans seemed to meet the Port Authority's desire to replace the offices, retail space and hotel rooms destroyed on September 11, they did not provide an appropriate setting for a memorial, nor did they reflect the economic realities facing the city and the metropolitan area.

A consensus was quickly reached that all the proposals were fundamentally inadequate.[58]

This political uptake of the message was as prompt as the message was clear, as the official report describes it:

The messages generated by this committed, energized assembly—one of the largest gatherings of its kind—reached decision-makers quickly and unmistakably.... 'Listening to the City' had a direct and swift impact on the fate of these concept plans. Just weeks after the six plans were introduced as a starting point for discussing, the program they were based upon was set aside, largely because of the sharp criticism at 'Listening to the City' and other public feedback.... Shortly after 'Listening to the City', LMDC and the Port Authority pledged that a new program will be developed.

It is a perfectly fair comment to say that 'other than skewering the six plans and calling for a reduction in the amount of commercial space, the meeting hadn't produced many concrete recommendations for how to design the site'.[59] The impact of this mini-public was thus of a largely negative sort, at least in the first instance. Still, vetoing all six initial proposals and forcing a rethink of the fundamental planning concepts upon which they all rested is a clear accomplishment of the market-testing sort. This may not have been the intention of the planning authorities, who in subsequent years were able to shift policy back to more standard commercial concerns. And while the organizers of 'Listening to the City' stress its impact, there were parallel debates in the broader public sphere whose tone was equally critical of the plans, so it is hard to determine just how decisive this particular mini-public was.

[57] Carolyn Lukensmeyer, President of America*Speaks*, quoted in Susan Rosegrant (2003: 20).
[58] Civic Alliance (2002: 11).   [59] Rosegrant (2003: 20).

Another example of market-testing is the 'GM Nation?' exercise in the UK.[60] The exercise did not achieve the endorsement of GM foods sought by the pro-GM forces in the British Government that launched it. Neither did the process enjoy high esteem among the public at large: 'many actions and statements by government around the time of the debate' tended 'to undermine the credibility of the debate process'; and there was in consequence 'widespread cynicism among both participants and the wider public about the likely impact of the debate on government policy'.[61]

Nonetheless, there were clear messages emerging from both the 'open community meetings' and the more genuinely deliberative 'Narrow but Deep' components. 'Key messages' as summarized in the Executive Summary of the official report of the exercise were as follows:

1. People are generally uneasy about GM.
2. The more people engage in GM issues, the harder their attitudes and more intense their concerns.
3. There is little support for early commercialization.
4. There is widespread mistrust of government and multinational companies.
5. There is a broad desire to know more and for further research to be done.[62]

In a nutshell, 'the key message was caution'.[63]

In important respects, the UK Government in its official response stubbornly refused to accept that message:

We take public concern very seriously, and we recognize the need to address the people's legitimate anxieties about GM crops. But having weighed up all the evidence, we have concluded that we should continue to assess each GM crop on an individual case-by-case basis. . . . We have looked at [people's] concerns carefully, and we have concluded that for the most part the regulatory regime which is now

---

[60] A similar story can be told about the Nuclear Waste Management Organization's public consultation in Canada in 2002 (Johnson 2007).

[61] Horlick-Jones et al. (2004).   [62] Heller (2004: 6–7).

[63] As the report summarizes the 'key message' in continuous prose: 'Most people wanted to delay the commercialisation of the GM crops to allow for more debate and research, and case-by-case testing of individual crops, followed by strict policing. People wanted proof that GM crops would be safe for human health and the environment and many wanted additional proof that GM crops would produce some benefit for the consumer' (Heller 2004: 42, para. 192).

in place is capable of addressing them, but that on some issues further action is required.[64]

Thus, despite the Government's insistence that all was well, the 'GM Nation?' debate—and especially its more genuinely deliberative 'Narrow but Deep' component, by which Government explicitly set most store[65]— succeeded in extracting some 'further action' from Government. These specific measures came in the areas of 'providing choice for consumers and farmers', 'mandatory labelling for consumers', and steps to ensure the 'coexistence' of GM and non-GM crops.[66] Beyond these specific measures, the Government committed itself, first and foremost, to 'protect human health and the environment through robust regulation of GM crops on a case-by-case basis, consistent with the precautionary principle'.[67]

In a way that changes nothing. The case-by-case regulatory structure remains the same; the precautionary principle has long been official policy, both in the UK and the EU. Protecting human health and the environment are policy objectives of long standing. Every regulatory regime purports to be 'robust'. But the UK government wanted to change matters in a pro-GM direction, and in this it did not succeed.

Even—or perhaps especially—where the upshot of the market-testing is a frustrating 'no', politicians are clearly better off knowing it to be a lost cause before staking too much of their reputations and political capital on it. And it is not just good for politicians, in a narrowly careerist sense: it is good for the macro-political system—in terms of its functionality, its legitimacy, and its democratic responsiveness—not to try to force wildly unacceptable proposals down citizens' throats.

2.2.5. Legitimating Policy

Mini-publics can help legitimate public policies in whose process of production they play a part, however symbolic that part may be. Recall Dahl's words, quoted earlier: 'The judgments of a minipopulus would "represent" the judgment of the demos . . . [and] would thus derive their authority

[64] UK Department for Environment, Food & Rural Affairs (UK DEFRA 2004: 12, 13, paras. 4.3, 4.9).
[65] UK Department for Environment, Food & Rural Affairs (UK DEFRA 2004: 11, paras. 3.2–3.5).
[66] UK Department for Environment, Food & Rural Affairs (UK DEFRA 2004: 13, para. 4.9).
[67] UK Department for Environment, Food & Rural Affairs (UK DEFRA 2004: 3, para. 1).

from the legitimacy of democracy'.[68] As such they would lend legitimacy to particular policy recommendations.

That was certainly the aim of the Chinese Deliberative Poll discussed in Section 2.2.1. In the words of the Zeguo Town Party Secretary, 'Although I gave up some final decision-making power, we gain more power back because the process has increased the legitimacy for the choice of priority projects and created public transparency in the public policy decision-making process. Public policy is therefore more easily implemented'.[69]

In the UK, similarly, Citizens' Juries had been heavily promoted in the UK by the Institute for Public Policy Research, an independent think-tank co-founded by Patricia Hewitt who went on to become a Labour MP and then Secretary of State for Health. Citizens' Juries have been widely used in the UK to resolve a raft of knotty local issues. One example concerns plans to reconfigure hospital services in Hewitt's own Leicester constituency. The city of Leicester had three main hospitals: Leicester Royal Infirmary; Leicester General; and Glenfield. The Leicestershire Health Authority grew concerned that

'planned care' services for chronic disease and rehabilitation were suffering because acute care was taking up too many resources. Following four years of consultation and planning with hospital-based specialists and other medical interests, they proposed concentrating accident and emergency services at the Leicester Royal Infirmary and General, moving some other acute services from Glenfield, and devoting Glenfield to planned care services.[70]

When the Health Authority announced that plan in late 1999, however, 'a storm of protest erupted' centring mainly around the fact that it would involve relocating 'a heart unit and breast care services [that] had just been set up at Glenfield largely thanks to major public appeals for donations rather than direct government spending'. A petition opposing the plan collected 150,000 signatures, the media were mobilized, and MPs and local councillors got involved.

At the suggestion of Patricia Hewitt, a Citizens' Jury was established to help the Health Authority find a way out of the conundrum. It met for four days in March 2000, hearing witnesses and deliberating. In its recommendations, the Citizens' Jury endorsed the Health Authority's desire for one of the city's hospitals to specialize in 'planned care'; but 'to the

---

[68] Dahl (1989: 342). On deliberative legitimation, see further: Manin (1987), Knight and Johnson (1994) and Parkinson (2003, 2006).
[69] Jiang Zhaohua, quoted in Fishkin et al. (2006: 24).   [70] Parkinson (2004b: 384).

delight of the protestors', it recommended that that site be the General, not Glenfield. The Health Authority accepted that recommendation and set about implementing it.[71]

As one of the leading health administrators involved in the process is quoted as having said:

You could look at it [the Citizens' Jury] as being a way out for us in a particular messy situation.... We almost got to the point where there was an impasse.... It [the Citizens' Jury] was the single biggest factor that freed up the next steps in the review process.... If we hadn't done that Jury, we would not have got through.[72]

Thus beyond its clear impact on policy (the sort of 'take-up' effect discussed in Section 2.2.2), the citizens' jury played a key role in legitimating policy in the eyes of divided and sceptical publics.

Mini-publics can lack the sort of legitimacy possessed by representatives who have been elected, or even appointed to 'act on behalf' of the public. Even statistically representative samples as claimed in deliberative polling hold no 'commissions' from the public at large. They have not been 'authorized' by them to speak on their behalf.[73] The sheer numbers participating in an event may, however, increase legitimating force. This is why America*Speaks* typically seeks very large numbers, much larger than required by statistical significance (even if the sample were statistically representative, which it is not), or to make sure all points of view are present. 'Thousands' has a legitimating impact greater than 'hundreds'. (One America*Speaks* pamphlet is actually entitled 'Millions of Voices'.)

The decisions of bodies with formal legal authority might be more widely respected across the rest of the macro-political system the more conspicuously they involve the deliberative engagement of a wide, representative group of ordinary citizens. Even though they eventually failed by a narrow margin in the subsequent referendum, the recommendations of the Citizens' Assembly on Electoral Reform enjoyed more credence than they otherwise would have done precisely for their having emerged from protracted deliberations among a representative sample of citizens of British Columbia.[74]

Mini-publics will not necessarily promote legitimacy in the eyes of sceptical publics, who may suppose the real aim is to 'sell' a policy, rather than genuinely to listen to public views on the matter (this is

---

[71] Parkinson (2004*a*: 374).   [72] Quoted in Parkinson (2004*b*: 386).
[73] Parkinson (2004*a*) and Brown (2006).   [74] Ferejohn (2008).

different from the market-testing described earlier). Scepticism here can draw on long experience with public inquiries whose conclusion is pre-ordained, or whose impacts are minimal if they depart from their script. Publics can be doubtful that macro-political actors will take any notice of what mini-publics conclude, particularly if they come to the 'wrong' conclusions. The minimally responsive official Government response to the 'GM Nation?' exercise in the UK is just the last in a long list of such experiences.

Finally, mini-publics designed to legitimize certain policies can some-times end up legitimizing activist disobedience. For oppositional groups that feel an obligation to give the system 'one last chance', a mini-public might well look like that 'last best chance'. Suppose that the recommen-dations of that mini-public vindicate the position of these oppositional groups, but that the macro-political system fails to respond appropriately to the clear recommendations of the public in its more informed and reflective form. Or it might become clear that the forum was being used by governmental actors to buy time, in the hope public attention to the issue would wane. Oppositional groups might reasonably conclude that more activist responses are then warranted.[75]

2.2.6. Confidence-Building/Constituency-Building

Participatory processes may promote 'empowerment' in the psychological or sociological rather than the strictly legal–political sense.[76] Even if the consultative procedures are purely advisory, the mobilization of people to participate in them often has two further effects, both of which are of indirect political consequence. One is to give people participating in the consultation a psychological boost in confidence—and often on good grounds, insofar as they acquired additional information, insights, and skills in the course of engaging in the process.[77] A second effect is sociological: insofar as large groups of people were mobilized to par-ticipate in the consultative process, groups thus mobilized will be in a better position to bring political pressure to bear on the macro-political system in other (e.g. electoral) ways as well. Note that most members of the British Columbia Citizens' Assembly participated actively in public

---

[75] Fung 2005.
[76] Fung (2003a: 349–50, 352), Fung and Wright (2003a: 30), Levine, Fung, and Gastil (2005: 278).
[77] Luskin, Fishkin, and Jowell (2002).

debate leading up to the referendum after their formal role had ceased, and they were no longer being paid.[78]

How much difference mini-publics make in these indirect ways to the operation of the macro-political system depends largely upon just how 'micro' they are, that is, on just how few or many citizens are involved in them, though media coverage may help compensate for small numbers. A Citizens' Jury or Consensus Conference involves only 12–20 citizens. In other cases, however, moderately large numbers of people are involved in the mini-public. America*Speaks* Town Meetings involve up to 5,000 people, for example. That is a small fraction of the total population of New York City, yet mobilizing that many people on a highly sensitive issue like rebuilding on the World Trade Center site can make a real difference to the way the macro-political system processes that issue. In another example, consider the community meetings to advise on the implementation of the Oregon Basic Health Care Act: 1,003 people is a small proportion of total citizens of Oregon, but their having met in 46 committee meetings across the state arguably helped to constitute a powerful constituency in support of that scheme.[79]

For a simple, telling example, consider the case of the Reconnecting Communities and Schools project in South Carolina in 1998–2000. The process was to convene

a series of public meetings...under the auspices of a steering committee comprised of citizens selected by the school district as broadly representative of the community...to discuss their aspirations for the community, what keeps people apart and what brings them together in the community, and what role the schools should play in the community. After completion of the public meetings, the steering committee would select 50 citizens reflecting the demographics of the community in terms of ethnicity, age, social class, residence and parental status to come together in a 'community conversation' to forge an 'agreement' that would outline what they hope different segments of the local area would do to reconnect schools with the community.[80]

Such Reconnecting experiments had a great many very useful schooling-specific outcomes in all three communities in which they were conducted. But the one in Horry County had empowering effects of a dramatic sort. By way of background, 'as part of its economic development strategy, South Carolina allows local governments to grant tax exemptions to

---

[78] Warren and Pearse (2008*b*).

[79] Fung (2003: 358) and Jacobs, Marmor, and Oberlander (1999: 161–80).

[80] Weatherford and McDonnell (2007: 187).

particular kinds of business park developments'. When Horry County authorities proposed granting such an exemption for a large development that would result in substantial lost revenue for the local schools, which are of course funded from the tax revenues from which the developers were being exempted, the school district filed a suit against the city and county.

This lawsuit is unprecedented, and represents an assertion that school districts should have an equal standing in local development decisions from which they have traditionally been sidelined. School district officials were clear in saying that they could not have filed this lawsuit without Reconnecting:

- [A member of the school board said], 'A few years ago the school district would have had no choice but to take what . . . the county planning commission gave them, but Reconnecting has shown the Superintendent and the board what the community wants us to do, and it has given the community a reason to support the district's decision to stand up and fight'.

- [A school district official reports,] 'it would be hard for anyone to argue that the same thing would have happened without Reconnecting. When I had to go out and make our case to the people, they were listening with "new ears", and they could see that it just didn't make sense to go on diverting tax money from education to subsidize developers at the same time that the community wants to make itself a center of growth for high tech R&D'.[81]

2.2.7. Popular Oversight

Participatory, consultative mechanisms also sometimes serve as a means of public oversight forcing official accountability.[82]

All mini-publics serve this function to some extent, insofar as they take testimony (albeit typically on a voluntary basis) from representatives of public agencies and from their critics. They might serve this function more successfully had they the power (de jure or de facto) to require public officials to appear before them to testify. To serve this function most successfully would require ongoing or recurring mini-publics, rather than one-off micro-deliberations.[83]

A model might be the 'community policing' arrangements in Chicago. These do not qualify as mini-publics in our terms, purely because 'beat meetings' are 'open' to all comers, such that self-selection effects are greater. Still, levels of participation have been high: some '12 per cent of

---

[81] Weatherford and McDonnell (2007: 201).
[82] Fung (2003: 349–50) and Fung and Wright (2003: 29–30).   [83] Fung (2003a: 360).

adults in Chicago report that they have attended at least one community-policing meeting'; and, 'reversing the ordinary participation bias, residents from poor and less well-educated neighborhoods turn out at much higher rates than those from wealthy ones...because they have high stakes—increasing their own physical security—in the issue at hand'.[84] Whether or not 'beat meetings' themselves qualify as our sort of mini-publics, they provide an example of how other sorts of deliberations could be organized and empowered to provide greater popular oversight of public authorities.

As described by Fung:

Deliberation in community policing beat meetings is structured according to a...problem-solving process. Police and residents begin by using a 'brainstorming' process to generate a comprehensive list of crime and safety problems in their neighborhood. They then agree to focus on two or three listed items as priority issues, then pool information and perspectives to develop analyses of these problems. From these analyses, they construct strategies and a division of labor to implement these strategies. The success of the strategies is assessed in subsequent meetings. Groups typically try to develop additional strategies to address stubborn problems or take on new problems after resolving old ones. This short feedback loop between planning, implementation, and assessment increases both the practical capabilities and the problem-solving success of residents and police officers in each beat.[85]

In addition to this sort of creative, collaborative problem-solving, 'beat meetings' also serve to monitor police performance directly. 'The poor quality of police performance and their shirking is a frequent topic of beat meeting discussions. This deliberative design thus increases the accountability of street-level police officers'.[86]

'Beat meetings' provide a model of mini-public oversight of street-level activities of public authorities. The US statute specifying the use of Consensus Conferences, Citizens' Juries, and the like to provide public input into nanotechnology research and development policy provides an example at the 'policy' end of the spectrum.[87]

2.2.8. Resisting Co-option

A standard complaint with government consultative mechanisms is that they 'co-opt' opponents of proposed policies. By 'bringing them into

[84] Fung (2003a: 359).   [85] Fung (2001: 81).   [86] Fung (2003a: 360).
[87] US Congress (2003).

34

the process', co-optive arrangements can deprive these groups of any legitimacy for continuing opposition to the policies, once they have been approved by processes in which the groups have participated. 'They have had their say, and they lost fair and square' is what would-be co-opters hope that people will be thinking.[88]

This could be more of an issue with consultative processes involving large organized groups than it is with deliberative processes involving small(ish) numbers of ordinary citizens. Critics complain of pressure towards consensus in deliberative designs oriented towards generating a list of agreed 'recommendations'.[89] But that pressure is felt by, at most, the small(ish) number of individuals involved. Even if they are somehow co-opted in the process, the vast majority of citizens have not been directly touched by that process, and no organized group of policy advocates or opponents has been defanged—though they still might fear this.[90]

Beyond all that, the discursive component of mini-publics makes their proceedings particularly hard to predict or control, and hence unsuited to cooption. A case in point is the Clayoquot Sound Scientific Panel, a discursive design a bit different from the kind under discussion here, because it involved stakeholders as deliberators.

When the British Columbia government was under pressure to take measures to prevent clear-cutting of ancient forests on Clayoquot Sound, it appointed 'a "scientific panel" of experts to determine world class forestry guidelines....'. Initially, 'this move...was greeted by considerable skepticism by many who viewed the formation of the scientific panel as a typical technocratic effort to quell dissent while maintaining established patterns of power....Things, however, did not turn out as expected'. Torgerson explains:

The scientific panel consisted not only of scientists and conventional experts, but also of several representatives of the First Nations, who exerted a significant impact on the panel....As it developed, the scientific panel thus incorporated diverse perspectives, including that of traditional ecological knowledge....The success of the panel members in bridging often divergent orientations was a result of serious work to develop common understandings, particularly including efforts by First Nations representatives to educate other members of the panel about their outlook. It is notable, however, that the other members turned out to be receptive....[91]

---

[88] Selznick (1949) and Saward (1992).

[89] Avoiding this is the unique virtue of the Deliberative Poll, which merely reports shifts in opinion on the same questions among the group after the event; that advantage comes at the cost that the citizen participants cannot craft solutions or proposals, only choose from the questionnaire options set in advance.

[90] Hendriks (2005b).   [91] Torgerson (2003: 129–31).

The recommendations that have come out of the Scientific Panel reflect this broadened understanding. 'No one now claims that the scientific panel was a technocratic cover-up. The criticism instead is that the recommendations of the panel, although accepted by the provincial government, have not been fully implemented'. Thanks to the deliberative component in the process, the Scientific Panel turned out to be anything but an exercise in co-optive politics.

2.3. Conclusion

Highlighting as this chapter has done modes of successful impact goes against the grain of a long tradition in policy studies that delights in exposing failure. Of course it is not hard to identify limits and failures when it comes to mini-publics; this is hardly surprising given their novelty and the challenge they often present to political power constituted in more conventional terms. Sometimes the mini-publics' deliberations pass almost unnoticed, getting little attention from the press, the public, or the politicians. In one case, presenters at a Deliberative Poll on UK health policy could not even recall the event at all a couple of years later.[92] Even when the events get a fair amount of publicity at the time, they are often soon enough swamped by other stories. The French Conférence de Citoyens sur les Organismes Génétiquement Modifiés was held in June 1998, when media attention was fixed on the soccer World Cup competition which France was hosting and went on to win. Similarly the October 1999 Deliberative Poll was held a week before the referendum on whether Australia should become a republic. The Poll showed a massive shift in favour of a republic; it had excellent media coverage (it was sponsored and reported heavily by a major national newspaper; it was broadcast live on the Australian Broadcasting Corporation television network and featured in the popular 'Sixty Minutes' program); opinion polls early the next week showed significant movement in favour of the republic, with the heavily reported results of the Deliberative Poll being the only plausible cause.[93] But by week's end, when voting actually took place, that effect had worn off and the referendum lost decisively.

Yet stories of failure, however entertaining (and occasionally instructive), ought not be enough to satisfy those interested in building a more deliberative democracy. There are good reasons in normative

[92] Parkinson (2006).   [93] Fishkin (2003: 131).

democratic theory to accord ordinary citizens a more central place in political processes, and mini-publics provide one such way that overcomes the problem of size that has so plagued participatory theories more generally.[94] As has been seen, there are cases in practice where this has been done to good effect. Innovative mini-publics genuinely have, from time to time, had major impacts on macro-politics. The kinds of effects are varied. The most readily conceptualized—direct influence on the content of policy—is just one such effect. Occasionally it can be observed, in terms of determining the referendum question on electoral reform in British Columbia, influencing Danish policy on irradiated food, or emboldening Texas utilities to invest more heavily in renewable energy even if at slightly higher prices to consumers. However, in complex political processes, one should not be surprised when it proves hard to trace the direct impact of any particular input, be it a discursive design, a piece of policy analysis, the pressure exerted by a lobby group, the campaign of a social movement, or the content of a party manifesto. Sometimes the impact on policy was of a negative sort, a matter of deliberative market testing leading to veto of a proposal—slowing the introduction of GM crops in Britain and forcing Lower Manhattan urban planners back to the drawing board. Other times the impact was in terms of legitimation—providing a way out of a tricky situation that enabled the Leicestershire Health Authority to dedicate one of its three hospitals to 'planned care' without alienating key stakeholders.

This chapter has mapped and illustrated some democratic possibilities. What it has not done is to generate and test systematic explanations concerning why sometimes impact is achieved, and why sometimes it is not. What is most needed is not so much more research on this question as more mini-publics—both in order to populate the social scientists' sample and, more importantly, in order to improve democratic practice.

---

[94] Carson and Martin (1999).

3

When does deliberation begin?

with Simon J. Niemeyer

The 'deliberative turn' in contemporary political philosophy constituted two turns at once. First, as has already been said, it represented a turn within democratic theory away from 'aggregative' or 'vote-centric' models of democracy. Deliberative democracy gives pride of place to the discussing of reasons, rather than the sheer tallying of votes.[1]

Second, and perhaps less remarked upon, the 'deliberative turn' represented a turn within political philosophy more generally away from internal reflections and towards models giving pride of place to actual interpersonal engagement.[2] Political theorists used to ask themselves, hypothetically, what they would agree behind a Rawlsian 'veil of ignorance'.[3] Rawls invites us to imagine that as a discussion involving everyone affected by the decision. But, significantly, that discussion is supposed to occur purely in each person's *own* imagination. It is an exercise to 'be undertaken by the solitary thinker'.[4]

'This is deliberation of a sort', Dryzek retorts, 'but only in terms of the weighing of arguments in the mind, not testing them in real political interaction... [It] downplays the *social* or interactive aspect of deliberation.'[5] For contemporary deliberative democrats, actual

---

[1] Miller (1992) and Dryzek (2000: chs. 1–2).   [2] Ackerman (1989).

[3] Rawls (1971). The counterfactualization involved has much in common, of course, with 'ideal observer' theory (Firth 1952), with 'ideal preference utilitarianism' (Brandt 1979), and, indeed, with Habermas' (1984) 'ideal speech situation'—although Habermas of course was always anxious to promote actual discourse approximating that ideal and always reluctant to draw substantive political inferences directly from speculations about what would follow from that (White 1980; Habermas 1995).

[4] Dryzek (2000: 15).

[5] Dryzek (2000: 15); see similarly: Manin (1987: 348) and Gutmann and Thompson (1996: 37–8). Steenbergen et al. (2002) are of course right to enter the converse objection that, in 'talk-centric' models of democracy, talk as such is not necessarily very deliberative.

discourse—'recurrent communicative interaction'[6]—is absolutely essential to democratic legitimation. Hard though it may be to actualize the 'ideal deliberative procedure' in any real-world 'discursive designs', that is very much the goal.[7]

What deliberative democrats prioritize is 'talking as a decision procedure'.[8] They cherish the 'forum', and the forum is more than just a noticeboard.[9] It intrinsically involves discussion and disputation, not simply the exchange of information (important though information-pooling undeniably is to the deliberative process: I say more of this in Chapters 4–5). Deliberative democracy requires that citizens actually, not just hypothetically,

exchange views and debate their supporting reasons concerning public political questions. They suppose that their political opinions may be revised by discussion with other citizens; and therefore these opinions are not simply a fixed outcome of their existing private or nonpolitical interests. It is at this point that public reason is crucial. . . . [10]

It insists upon political institutions that

guarantee participation in all deliberative and decisional processes . . . in a way that provides each person with equal chances to exercise the communicative freedom to take a position on criticizable validity claims.[11]

Both Habermas and the later Rawls, and a raft of deliberative democrats with them, regard it as democratically crucial for citizens to engage in actual rather than merely hypothetical discourse in an array of public fora.

Surely it is axiomatic that democratic legitimation can come only through public processes. Hypothetical imagined discourse—imagining what you would say if you were in their shoes, and letting the conversation play out in your own head (what I call 'deliberation within'[12])— can never substitute for the external democratic validation that comes

---

[6] Dryzek (1990: 43).   [7] Cohen (1989) and Dryzek (1990: chs. 2, 4–5).

[8] Schauer (1999). Cohen (1998: 193) insists that 'deliberative democracy cannot be distinguished simply by its emphasis on discussion' because 'on any view of democracy, . . . discussion is important, if only because of its essential role in pooling private information, against a background of asymmetry in its distribution'. Surely, deliberative democracy attaches relatively greater weight and priority to discussion than do other models of democracy, however.

[9] Elster (1986).   [10] Rawls (1997/1999: 138–9).

[11] Habermas (1996: 127) and, more generally, §§3.3 and 7.1.2. Notice, however, that Habermas (1996: 107) still formulates his key 'discourse principle' in hypothetical terms: 'Just those action norms are valid to which all possibly affected persons *could* agree as participants in rational discourses' (emphasis added).

[12] Goodin (2000c).

from more overtly political processes. It can only be a supplement, never a substitute.[13] It leaves plenty of work still to be done by discussion—along with voting, bargaining, petitioning, suing, and all the other inter-personal acts of democratic politics.

Nevertheless, important parts of that process are the imaginative and empathetic projections at the heart of 'deliberation within'—calling to mind others and asking oneself 'what would they say?'[14] Indeed, on the evidence to be presented below, that might even be a more important part of the process than is the dialogic and discursive element that is so cherished by contemporary deliberative democrats.

3.1. The Nature of 'Deliberation'

Deliberation, Aristotle and Hobbes tell us, begins when we 'turn our minds' to something: individually, in the case of choosing some personal course of action; collectively, in the case of choosing some joint course of action.[15]

What it means to 'turn our mind' to something collectively is conven-tionally understood (just as deliberative democrats would have it) most centrally to involve discussing it among ourselves. Thus, juries officially begin to 'deliberate' only once they reach the jury room and discuss the case together after all the evidence has been heard. So the judge admonishes them, at the beginning of the trial.[16]

Likewise, deliberative assemblies formally begin to deliberate only after the chairperson has called the meeting to order and put a question to

---

[13] Albeit an important supplement in all sorts of ways, not least in helping to overcome the 'size' constraints of mass democracy (Goodin 2000b: ch. 9).

[14] Goodin (2000c, 2003b).

[15] Aristotle (1984a: book vi, 1984c: book 1, chs. 3–4) and Hobbes (1651: ch. 6).

[16] 'Model Jury Instructions' have the judge instructing the jury in the following terms: '*First*, you are not to discuss this case with anyone, including your fellow jurors, mem-bers of your family, people involved in the trial, or anyone else, nor are you allowed to permit others to discuss the case with you. If anyone approaches you and tries to talk to you about the case, please let me know about it immediately; *Second*, do not read any news stories or articles or listen to any radio or television reports about the case or about anyone who has anything to do with it; *Third*, do not do any research, such as consulting dictionaries, searching the Internet or using other reference materials, and do not make any investigation about the case on your own; . . . *Fifth*, do not make up your mind about what the verdict should be until after you have gone to the jury room to decide the case and you and your fellow jurors have discussed the evidence. Keep an open mind until then' (US Court of Appeals, Ninth Circuit, Office of the Circuit Exec-utive 2002: §1.9; 'Model Instructions' are identical for civil and criminal cases, on these points).

members for debate. So *Robert's Rules of Order* says.[17] So judges suppose, in what they count as the judicially cognizable 'legislative history' of the assembly's deliberations: legislative intent is judicially inferred from reports of discussions of formal groups formally assembled, not the private intentions of the bill's sponsors and supporters as recorded in their diaries or notes or off-the-record comments.[18]

In all those ways, we are led to suppose (with contemporary deliberative democrats) that deliberation—in the sorts of collective settings that characterize political life, anyway—consists principally in interpersonal communications, paradigmatically conversational, dialogic, or discursive in form.

This chapter queries that proposition. Its thesis is that much (maybe most) of the work of deliberation occurs well before the formal proceedings—before the organized 'talking together' ever begins.

'Deliberation', the *Oxford English Dictionary* tells, consists essentially in 'the *consideration* and *discussion* of the reasons for and against a measure by a number of councillors.'[19] In that definition, 'consideration' should, I suggest, enjoy pride of place.

Even among deliberative democrats, discussion is not (usually) seen as an end in itself. It is supposed instead to be a means to a more considered, reasoned decision. The whole point of deliberation, political or otherwise, is usually to make our decision processes more 'reflective': to help us *choose* a course of action, after due consideration, rather than merely *picking* some course of action after hardly a moment's thought, with scant regard to evidence or argument.[20]

Certainly 'consideration' necessarily comes temporally prior to 'discussion'. An internal process of weighing of reasons necessarily precedes any participation in a public discursive interchange. That, after all, is how you decide what position to take in the ensuing public discussion. Ideals of deliberative democracy may require that we go into public discussions with an 'open mind', in the sense of a willingness to change our opinions in light of subsequent evidence and argument. But if everyone came to the process with a completely open mind, to the extent that no one was prepared to take any position to start with, the deliberations would have nowhere to begin.

---

[17] An extraordinary majority is required to suppress a question without debate, which *Robert's Rules of Order* (Robert 1876/1951: §28, p. 109) treats as a 'fundamental principle' of a 'deliberative assembly'.

[18] McKinney and Sweet (2002).   [19] Second definition; emphasis added.

[20] Manin (1987: 351–4) and Ullmann-Margalit and Morgenbesser (1977).

Internal-reflective processes are also involved in responding to the arguments and evidence presented by others in discussion. Much of the work in understanding what others are saying, whether in a formal meeting or an everyday conversation, inevitably occurs inside your own head. You 'get' their jokes, catch their allusions, complete their 'conversational implicatures', fill in suppressed premises of their argument-sketches, and so on.[21]

Empathetic extensions of that sort are crucial in enabling us to make sense of one another over the course of discussions, democratic or otherwise. So too, I would argue, do they loom large in the run-up to those discussions. And so too might they do likewise, I would suggest, even in the absence of any formal discussions. Imagining yourself in the place of another, for purposes of trying to understand what the other is saying, is broadly of a cloth with imagining yourself in the place of another, for purposes of trying to understand what the other is or might be feeling or desiring. The motivations might be different, but the process is broadly the same.[22]

As a modest step towards establishing those larger arguments, this chapter examines how deliberations actually proceeded in a citizens' jury on an Australian environmental issue. There, just as my model of 'democratic deliberation within' hypothesizes, deliberation of the more internal-reflective sort did indeed precede—and did indeed do more to change people's attitudes than—formal group deliberations of the more discursive sort.

3.2. The Case Study: A Citizens' Jury Assesses the Bloomfield Track

The findings here reported grow out of a 'citizens' jury' convened on the Cairns campus of James Cook University in January 2000.[23] Its task was to discuss policy options for the Bloomfield Track, a controversial unimproved road running through the Daintree rainforest,

---

[21] Grice (1975) and Mansbridge (1999a).

[22] Goodin (2003b: ch. 9). In explaining how 'discourse ethics' gets the sort of 'intersubjectivity' that it requires, Habermas (1995: 117) similarly says that it 'rests on . . . a joint process of "ideal role taking"' in which 'everyone is required to take the perspective of everyone else, and thus project herself into the understandings of self and world of all others'. cf. Young (1997b).

[23] The design of this exercise deviated marginally from that of Ned Crosby, who has copyrighted the term: 'scare quotes' ought to therefore be understood as implicit in all subsequent uses of the term in this chapter.

in the Wet Tropics World Heritage area on the far northeast coast of Australia.

3.2.1. *The Issue*

The Bloomfield Track is a public road, accessible only by four-wheel-drive vehicle, running between the Cape Tribulation and the Bloomfield River. The Track itself is ~30 km in length, forming part of a longer 181 km route between Cairns and Cooktown in the far north of Queensland.

Constructed amid controversy in the mid-1980s, the Track's stated purpose was to provide access for locals in the isolated areas north of the Bloomfield River as an alternative to the longer (190 km) inland route already in existence.

Relative trip times for both routes vary according to the conditions and the driver.[24] In good weather, the Bloomfield Track shortens travel time between remote northern towns and larger population centres to the south; it is also enjoyed by tourists seeking a 'wilderness experience'.

Being part of the Wet Tropics, however, periods of heavy rainfall are common. Flooded creeks can render the Track impassable, and muddy conditions mean that steep grades turn treacherous, particularly for heavy vehicles. These factors undermine the Track's utility as a means of access. Furthermore, the resulting erosion impacts on the region's ecology.

Sensitivities surrounding the Bloomfield Track are heightened by the fact that, forming as it does part of a larger World Heritage-listed Wet Tropics, the Daintree region is recognized as embracing ecological values of international importance. The area through which the Track passes contains the last significant example of continuous mountain-to-coastal rainforest in Australia.[25] It also comprises the only example where such rainforest abuts inshore coral reefs, promoted by the tourist board as 'where the rainforest meets the reef'.

Proponents of the Track have consistently appealed to the need for access of the Bloomfield community. Its detractors have steadfastly emphasized its direct impact on rainforest and the symbolically important abutting reef.

Those stated arguments both for and against the Bloomfield Track have often concealed deeper political motivations. Its construction in

---

[24] Work is currently underway to upgrade the inland route to a two-lane bitumen road, however, and that will reduce travel time on the inland route considerably; this forms an important part of our story, below.

[25] Webb (1984).

the mid-1980s was the result of a complex interplay of tensions within and between different levels of government (local, state, and federal) and a desire to play off parochial concerns in the region against broader appeals to environmental values.[26] State and local powerbrokers cynically overrode 'due process' requirements, smoothing the way for its construction. Protesters attempted to impede its construction through a series of desperate tactics that backfired, playing into the hands of proponents of the Track keen to exploit anti-environmental sentiments in the local community for their own ends.

Such was the intensity of the campaign that the claims and counter-claims of various protagonists remain salient years later. The same stylized antimony—'community access' versus 'erosion and the reefs'—continues to dominate public discourse in the region to this day, despite the many subtle and interconnected considerations associated with the future of the Track.

3.2.2. The Jury

The Far North Queensland Citizens' Jury met to consider policy options for the Bloomfield Track as part of publicly funded academic research into the use of deliberative processes to inform public policymaking. Although its aim was to work towards agreed recommendations, this Jury had no formal connection to any official policy process, as citizens' juries often do.[27]

A jury of twelve citizens was selected on a random stratified basis from among 300 respondents to 2,000 letters sent out to randomly selected addresses in the Far North Queensland region. All those selected were residents of the region, most of relatively long standing (two-thirds of jurors had lived in the area over a decade). The jury was demographically mixed: there were seven women, five men; five were aged 40 or under, seven aged over 40; two had ten years of schooling, five had twelve, and three had tertiary education (another two were secondary school-leavers who then had returned for tertiary training). Jurors were similarly mixed in their occupations. One (Koda[28]) was a qualified marine biologist working as an environmental consultant; another (Janine) was an indigenous woman born in the Daintree and employed as a community worker in the area.

---

[26] Niemeyer (2002).   [27] Smith and Wales (2000).
[28] A number of jurors chose pseudonyms to preserve their anonymity.

The Far North Queensland Citizens' Jury met over four days in January 2000. The first day was devoted to a site visit and background briefings.[29] The second and third days were spent hearing and questioning technical witnesses and community representatives. The fourth day was given over to formal discussions among jurors themselves.

3.2.3. The Evidence

Technical witnesses testified on issues to do with engineering, planning, the environment, and impact of the Bloomfield Track on the reef and tourism. Community views were represented by the Mayors of the two local Councils (Douglas and Cook) through which the Track travelled, and the local councillor for the Bloomfield region, whose residents would be most intimately affected by any decision on the Track.

Without attempting to summarize all that was said over the course of those two days of testimony and questioning by members of the jury, I would highlight two points as particularly salient to the arguments of rest of this chapter.

The first concerns the issue of damage to the inshore coral reef from runoff from the Track. A representative from the Great Barrier Reef Marine Park Authority testified that, while there was clear evidence of erosion around the Track and of extra silt in nearby streams in consequence, there was currently no evidence that that runoff was causing any damage to the coral reef abutting the shore.

The second concerns the importance of the Track in providing access to the people living north of the Daintree River to larger towns further south. One witness presented evidence on planning issues that high-lighted alternatives to the Bloomfield Track for assess to the region. He particularly pointed to the upgrade presently underway on the existing inland highway. Once complete, it will be a two-lane bitumen road, passable in all weather; and despite being 160 km longer, it will provide access for most vehicles at many times of the year that is as fast or faster than the Bloomfield Track.

3.2.4. The Verdict

Jurors were polled as to their preferences over five policy options for the Bloomfield Track at the very beginning and the very end of the exercise,

---

[29] The intention was to travel all the way to the Bloomfield region, but delays along the way (including the rescue of tourists stranded in the middle of a river crossing) forced the group to turn back earlier than that.

when they first arrived and when they were about to leave. The options they were asked to rank-order were the following:

- Bituminize, upgrading the Track to two-wheel drive, all-weather standard;
- Upgrade the Track to a dirt road suitable for two-wheel-drive vehicles;
- Stabilize the Track, fixing specific trouble spots (such as steep grades) but leaving it as a four-wheel-drive track;
- Status quo, maintaining the Track in its present condition as a four-wheel-drive roadway; and
- Close the Track and rehabilitate the area.

Jurors' preferences over those policy options shifted dramatically from the beginning to the end of the jury process. Initially, the jury displayed a weak preference for 'stabilizing the Track' (the first choice of four jurors and the second of another three) or 'maintaining the status quo' (the first choice of three jurors and the second choice of another five). At the outset, closing the Track was the least-preferred option (indeed, it was literally the last preference of over half—fully seven—of the twelve jurors).

By the end, a strong (but still not unanimous) preference had emerged for closing the Bloomfield Track. That was the clear first choice of fully seven of the twelve jurors, and the first or second choice of all but two of them.

Looking across jurors' rankings as a whole confirms those impressions gleaned from inspection of 'top preferences' alone. A 'Borda count' (assigning five points to a juror's top-ranked option, four points to that juror's next-to-top option, and so on) shows that the 'closure' option shifted from being the lowest-ranked option at the beginning of the process to being the highest-ranked option at the end of the process.[30]

3.3. When and Why Did Attitudes Shift?

Thus, people's policy preferences changed over the course of the jury process. But when and why did that occur?[31]

---

[30] These results are also confirmed by the findings made by the jury as a group, which were communicated as a Jurors' Report (Niemeyer and Blamey 2003).

[31] For a much fuller discussion of changes of preferences in relation to attitudes, and the broader mechanisms driving the change, see the larger work upon which this chapter is based (Niemeyer 2002).

3.3.1. *Shifting Positions*

To surmise the processes underlying changes in policy preferences, jurors' attitudes were surveyed at three points in the process.[32] Jurors were given a questionnaire consisting of 42 propositions related to these issues, and they were asked to indicate whether they agreed or disagreed with each proposition, on a scale of −4 to +4.[33]

This same questionnaire was administered to jurors on three separate occasions. The first was at the beginning of day 1, when the group first assembled and before anything else occurred. The second was at the end of day 3, after testimony from all the witnesses had been heard but before the discussions that constitute the formal 'jury deliberation' had begun. The third was at the end of those formal deliberations, as jurors were about to leave on day 4.

I shall refer to everything that happened between the first questionnaire and the second questionnaire—the site visit, background briefings, presentations by and interrogation of witnesses—as the 'information phase' of the jury process. I shall refer to everything that happened between the second questionnaire and the third questionnaire—the formal group deliberations of the jury as a jury, aimed at moving towards recommendations—as the 'discussion phase' of the jury.

Of course, much of the work of the first phase was done discursively. Witnesses talked, they were interrogated, and so on. Such questioning and challenging is crucial to the learning process. Furthermore, even in the first phase of the jury, there was much talking among jurors themselves, both informally (over lunch and tea) and formally (in deciding what questions to ask of witnesses). And of course, much of the work that was done in the first phase lay not so much in literally 'conveying propositional content' as in establishing the preconditions for genuine deliberation: attentiveness, openness, willingness to change one's position as appropriate, and so on.[34] So when referring to the first phase

---

[32] Policy preferences were surveyed at only two points in the process: at the very beginning and at the very end. No survey of policy preferences themselves was taken in the middle of the jury process for fear that, on the simple ranking over only five policy options, jurors might attempt to be consistent with their ranking in the previous survey (Dillehay et al. 1966). The attitudinal questionnaire, in contrast, asked jurors to respond to 42 propositions fully, each on a 9-point scale. There seemed much less risk of jurors striving for consistency over successive rankings on that much more complex task.

[33] Texts of those propositions, together with mean scores at each stage in the process, can be found in Niemeyer (2002).

[34] Grice (1975) and Midgaard (1980).

Table 3.1. Changes in attitudes, by phase

Juror	Mean absolute change in ranking across all 42 propositions during the	
	Information phase	Discussion phase
Adventure	2.45	1.45
Aswad	2.45	1.43
Boat	2.26	1.45
Janine	2.52	1.17
Julie	1.64	2.00
Keith	2.79	1.43
Koda	1.29	0.45
Matilda	1.50	0.64
Pearl	2.50	1.62
Rastus	2.05	1.17
Snoopy	2.31	1.40
Tamara	1.69	1.24
Mean (standard deviation)	2.12 (0.48)	1.29 (0.41)

as the 'information phase', that term should be construed very broadly. Still, it seems proper to dub it as the 'information phase' of the jury, since that—rather than discussion and deliberation—remains the formal, official task of the citizens' jury during that phase of the proceedings. Such discursive interactions as occur in the interstices of those proceedings are informal and incidental, and in that sense broadly of a cloth with the informal interactions that occur in the interstices of various other aspects of everyday life organized around other ends.

When referring to the second phase as the 'discussion phase', that should be construed correspondingly narrowly. By 'discussion' there, I mean what deliberative democrats mean by 'deliberation': collectively organized conversations among a group of coequals aiming at reaching (or moving towards) some joint view on some issues of common concern.[35]

Analysing changing responses to the repeated questionnaires enables us to pinpoint 'when' and 'why' the attitudes of citizens' jurors (and hence their preferences[36]) changed. Table 3.1 presents the basic results, first juror-by-juror and then overall. The first column reports change between the first stage and the second stage of the jury process—between the time when the jury first assembled and the end of the 'information phase'. The

[35] Cohen (1989).

[36] Analysis of the results show that responses to these propositions map well onto policy preference: the changes to each concur with one another (Niemeyer 2002).

second column shows change between the second stage and the third stage of the process—during the 'discussion phase', when jurors formally deliberated among themselves.

The scores reported in Table 3.1 for each juror represent the mean of the absolute change, on the nine-point scale, of that juror's assessments, averaging across all 42 propositions. The final row represents the mean change per phase, averaging across all the jurors.

It is clear from Table 3.1 that the bigger change, by a wide margin, occurred in the minds of jurors *before* the jury's formal discussions began.[37] Jurors' ranking of each proposition shifted, on average, 2.12 places on the nine-point scale over the course of the first 'information phase' of the proceedings. During the second phase of the proceedings, during which jurors discussed these issues formally among themselves, their rankings shifted, on average, only 1.29 places on that nine-point scale.[38] Formal tests of statistical significance confirm the fact that the first shift is, indeed, significantly greater than the second ($t = 4.57$, $p < .001$).[39]

To say that the 'information phase' produced the much greater change in juror attitudes is not, of course, to say that the 'discussion phase' made no difference. Even just measured in terms of attitude-shifts, jurors changed, on average, 1.29 places on a nine-point scale over that second phase; and by some absolute standard that might be considered a non-negligible change.[40] And of course discussion might 'firm up' opinion, and embolden people to act upon it, even if it does not actually change their opinions.

Thus, to say that the 'information phase' of the citizens' jury was much more important in producing the observed shifts in jurors' policy preferences is not to say that the 'discussion phase' was of utterly

[37] Furthermore, that is not because jurors came to adopt a 'citizen's' rather than 'consumer's' perspective only over the course of the first days of the citizens' jury: other responses analysed in depth in Niemeyer (2002) shows that they had already shifted to 'citizen-mode' upon arrival on the very first day of the jury.

[38] It might be thought that discussion has latent effects on attitudes that would not be picked up over the course of a single day's discussion. Such informal evidence as we have on this point suggests it did not, in this case. Jurors reconvened informally for a 'debriefing' on the results of the research six months after the citizens' jury concluded. Although the attitude questionnaire was not re-administered at that point, jurors were asked whether they had changed their positions subsequently on the Track. Only one juror had done so—and that not because of what was said in the jury, but rather because he had taken the opportunity to drive the length of the Track after the jury finished.

[39] Other tests suited to non-parametric data confirm that conclusion.

[40] It is less than the smallest possible random shift, on the calculations reported in footnote 26. But depending on just where the shifts come and on just how finely balanced things were beforehand, shifts of that magnitude might nonetheless be big enough to 'make all the difference', politically.

no consequence. It is instead merely to say that it was of much less consequence than the 'information phase'—contrary to the expectations of discursive democrats who would have us privilege conversation over cogitation as politically the most important mode of deliberation.

3.3.2. Subjective Perceptions

The finding in Table 3.1 of great changes in jurors' attitudes during the first 'information phase' of the jury, followed by only modest changes during the second 'discussion phase' of the jury, tallies with the subjective perceptions of jurors themselves. In a post-jury 'exit survey' completed just as they were leaving, jurors were asked: 'If your preferred option changed since the beginning of the Citizens' Jury, what do you think helped to change your mind?' Jurors were asked to rank four possible factors:

- *Learning more*: 'The fact that I learnt a great deal about the Bloomfield Track and its implications.'
- *Listening to witnesses*: 'Listening to the views of the speakers who came to present as witnesses.'
- *Shift in perspective*: 'The fact that I had to look at the issue from the perspective of what is best for the community rather than what I personally would like to see happen.'
- *Group discussion*: 'The fact that I had to discuss the issues with other members of the jury and justify my reasons to others.'

Juror replies are shown in Table 3.2.

According a high priority to the last column ('group discussion') would be to say that the 'discussion phase' mattered more in changing their opinion. According a high priority to either of the first two columns would tend to suggest that the 'information phase' mattered more. The correspondence is not perfect.[41] But as a broad interpretation of juror responses, that seems warranted.

Among the eight jurors who perceived that their preferences over policy options had changed, it thus seems relatively clear that the 'information'

---

[41] It is logically possible that respondents would have picked the first column to represent the 'more inclusive' option, supposing the 'learning' to which it refers embraces everything they learned over the course of the whole process (from witnesses, background briefings, site visits, *and* group discussions). Similarly, it is conceivable that the last column might not capture all the influence of discussion; literalists might not rank that column high if what they thought important about group discussion was, for example, listening to others rather than having to defend one's own position.

Table 3.2. Perceived sources of change

Juror	Sources of change (Rank[a])			
	Learning more	Listening to witnesses	Shift in perspective	Group discussion
Adventure	1	3	2	4
Boat	1	2	3	4
Janine	2	1	3	4
Koda	3	1	4	2
Matilda	2	3	1	4
Pearl	3	2	1	4
Rastus	1	3	4	2
Snoopy	1	4	2	3
Mean rank	1.75	2.38	2.5	3.38
Borda rank	1	2	3	4

[a]Where 1 is the highest possible ranking and 4 the lowest.

rather than the 'discussion' aspects of the jury were more responsible for the changes. No one thought that 'group discussion' was the most important factor in changing their opinion; three-quarters of them thought it was the least important factor. 'Learning more' about the Bloomfield Track and 'listening to witnesses' were the most important factors in changing fully three-quarters of jurors' minds.

3.3.3. *Potential Implications for Deliberative Democracy*

Recall the central thesis of this chapter: Internal-reflective processes of 'democratic deliberation within' are relatively more central to the process of democratic deliberation, and external-collective processes of formal discursive interactions less central, than commonly supposed.

On its face, the evidence presented in this chapter would seem to count as telling support for that thesis. Jurors' attitudes really do seem to have changed much more substantially *before* formal discussion actually began, and much less substantially *during* formal discussions.

Of course it is perfectly possible for deliberation to have a major effect even if it changes no attitudes (by strengthening people's confidence in their prior attitudes, e.g., or by emboldening them to act upon them[42]). Still, in the case under study policy preferences and attitudes *did* change; and explaining that change is essential to the analysis of the deliberative processes involved in the case at hand.

[42] That may be linked to the role of formal public discussion in legitimating outcomes (Manin 1987; Cohen 1989). It may just be linked to the familiar phenomenon of 'groupthink' (Sunstein 2000, 2002).

51

It is also perfectly true, as I have already acknowledged, that even during the initial 'information phase' of the jury a fair bit of informal discussion occurred among jurors (over tea and meals, on the site visit, etc.) and between jurors and the witnesses (whom they questioned, as well as listened to). The fact that this discussion in the first phase of the jury was informal rather than formal might, for some deliberative democrats, make it a model of deliberation in the 'public sphere' of 'civil society' (more of which is given in Chapters 8 and 13) rather than within the formal processes of political deliberation, which might be better modelled by the jury's second 'discussion phase'.[43]

Still, it is worth recalling that these jurors were mostly very long-term residents of the area, and that the Bloomfield Track had long been a contentious issue within the public sphere of which they were already part. Something in the initial phase of the jury made a difference to them, which informal discussions in the public sphere had previously not. That, too, requires explanation.

3.4. Are the Results Epiphenomenal?

Before trumpeting too boldly any conclusions about the relative importance of internal-reflective 'democratic deliberation within' versus 'external-collective' deliberations among these jurors, I must first consider the possibility that these results might be purely epiphenomenal in various possible ways.

3.4.1. *Order of the Phases*

One reason might have to do with the order in which the phases of the jury were sequenced. Maybe whichever phase comes first always has most effect, regardless of which phase it is.

One way to test that hypothesis would be to alter the sequence of the phases. That is to say, have a formal group discussion before any formal presentation of information (followed then by yet another discussion phase after the information has been heard). If the speculation here in view were correct, the first discussion phase should have more effect than either of the two subsequent phases.

Resource constraints did not permit experimentation with multiple variations in research design. Hence, I cannot say for sure what would

---

[43] Habermas (1996: ch. 8), Chambers (1996), and Dryzek (2000: ch. 4).

have happened had the order of phases been altered in deliberations on the Bloomfield Track. But evidence from elsewhere suggests that it probably would not have made much difference.

The alternative sequence—'discussion/information/discussion'—is precisely what is employed in Deliberative Polls.[44] Under that experimental design, just as under this one, 'information effects' turn out to be substantial and 'small group' discussion effects to be small.[45] Deliberative Polls and citizens' juries are of course very different discursive designs, so it is impossible to infer with complete confidence from one to the other. Still, such evidence as we have from elsewhere suggests that different research designs would not have greatly changed the findings reported in this chapter.

3.4.2. Duration of the Phases

Another reason for thinking these results might be epiphenomenal has to do with the differing duration of the two phases of the jury process. Remember that the first phase of the jury process lasted three days whereas the second lasted only one. Statistically, it might seem to be only expected that more change would occur, purely at random, over the longer (first) phase than the shorter (second) phase.

Certainly if events occur purely at random and at a fixed rate, we would expect thrice as many such *events* over a period that lasts thrice as long. We would, for example, expect to see thrice as many atoms decay from U-238 to U-235 over a three-day period as over a one-day period. The *amount* of U-235 increases cumulatively over time, however, only because the change is not random but rather unidirectional. Thrice as much U-235 is created in thrice as long a period, purely because none of it ever changes back into U-238. Random changes, in contrast, proceed in all directions. Random changes can be (and often are) mutually cancelling, in consequence, as things change and change back over time. That makes purely random changes non-cumulative over time.

In a purely random process (involving a large enough number of events for the law of large numbers to apply), the extent of change in a distribution—here, of jurors' beginning and ending positions—would be statistically expected to be literally identical, regardless of the duration of the period over which the changes (and changes back) occurred. How

---

[44] Fishkin (1995: 171–2).   [45] Luskin, Fishkin, and Jowell (2002: 474–8).

big, on average, a random change would be statistically expected to be depends purely on the initial distribution, and not at all on the duration of the process.[46]

3.4.3. *Continuous Unidirectional Change?*

Purely random change, then, would not have produced the pattern of results found in Table 3.1. But suppose jurors—like radioactive isotopes— always moved in one particular direction continuously over time. Then the changes would indeed be cumulative over time, just as is the amount of U-235 formed from the decay of U-238. If that hypothesis were true, the fact that jurors changed more during the first period than the second could indeed be because it lasted longer than the second.[47]

Changes in jurors' attitudes were not continuous and unidirectional across both phases of the jury process, however. Instead, jurors shifted their attitudes towards *different* propositions during the two different phases of the jury process.

That is clear from Figure 3.1. There, the *x*-axis represents the change in the mean score of each proposition, on the −4 to +4 scale, during the first ('information') phase, from the first time the questionnaire was administered to the second. The *y*-axis represents the change in the mean score of each proposition during the second ('discussion') phase, from the second time the questionnaire was administered to the third.

Suppose the process were one of continuous unidirectional change over time, and hence the only reason for more change over the first phase than the second is that the first lasted three times as long. On that hypothesis, we should expect to see a strong positive correlation between those two patterns of change, with the slope of regression line being proportional to the duration of each period. On this deflationary hypothesis, the same

---

[46] If everyone were initially congregated at one or the other (or at both) ends of a 9-point scale on all items, everyone would have most 'room' to move. There, a completely random redistribution would be statistically expected to lead to a mean change of 4.00 places. Were everyone initially congregated at the midpoint on all items, they would have least 'room' to move; and there, a completely random redistribution would be statistically expected to lead to a mean change of 2.22 places. Were everyone initially distributed randomly (and hence equally) over all 9 positions on all items, a completely random redistribution would be statistically expected to lead to a mean change of 2.96 places.

[47] The sheer *fact* that more change occurred in the first phase would be explained, but *how much* more would remain unexplained. Although the 'information phase' lasted three times as long, it yielded less than twice as much change in average juror positions (2.12 as compared to 1.29). But there is no need to explore that, given the evidence below that the change was not continuous and unidirectional in any event.

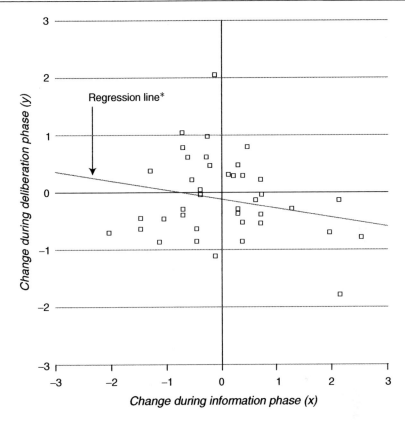

Figure 3.1. Change to average statement score

Note: *$y = 0.12 - 0.16x, r^2 = 0.051$.

items that changed most in the first phase should also be expected to have changed most in the second phase; that is why the correlation should be expected to be positive. And on this deflationary hypothesis the rate of such change is expected to be constant; that is why the amount of change should be proportional to the duration of each period, and we should therefore expect a third as much change over the second period, which lasted a third as long.

Were this deflationary hypothesis completely correct, we should thus expect to see a perfect fit to a regression line of $y = 0.33x$. What we actually see in Figure 3.1, instead, is quite the contrary. Instead of the strong positive correlation predicted by the deflationary hypothesis, Figure 3.1 shows instead virtually no correlation ($r^2 = .05$) and an essentially flat regression line ($b = -0.16$).

Whatever was going on here, it clearly was not a process of continuous unidirectional change across both phases of the jury. The items on which juror opinion changed most in the first phase were not the same as those on which they changed most in the second phase. Hence, the observation of more change in juror attitudes during the first 'information phase' than the second 'discussion phase' is not purely an artefact of their differing duration.

3.4.4. Discussion as a Corrective?

Finally, by just reporting aggregates ('the mean absolute change in each juror's ranking across all 42 propositions'), Table 3.1 might obscure important patterns in how much and in what direction jurors' views changed on *particular* propositions in different phases of the jury process. Formal group discussions during the second phase of the jury might, for example, serve as a 'corrective', helping jurors overcome the overreactions they might have had to the information they had been presented during the first phase of the jury.

If that were the case, we would expect to see the opposite pattern expected on the reasoning of Section 3.4.3: items on which there had been large negative shifts in the first phase of the jury should experience large positive shifts in the second phase, and vice versa. That is to say, we should on this hypothesis expect a perfect fit of the data in Figure 1 to the top-left to bottom-right diagonal, $y = -x$.

Figure 3.1 shows only a little weak evidence of some such 'clawing back' during the 'discussion phase' of the jury. While it is true that the slope of the regression line in Figure 1 is indeed negative, as this hypothesis predicts, it is only very weakly negative ($b = -0.16$, rather than $b = -1.0$ that this hypothesis predicts). Furthermore, the fit even to that regression line is itself very weak ($r^2 = .05$).

3.5. What Really Happened in this Citizens' Jury?

Let us now look more closely at the particular propositions on which the average change in juror attitudes was large. Upon examination, clear differences emerge in the topics preoccupying jurors in the first and the second phases of the process.

There were two main changes in jury attitudes during the first 'information phase' of the jury. Initially, jurors had been concerned about the impact of the Bloomfield Track on the coral reefs nearby. By the midpoint of the jury process, those worries had been largely allayed.[48] And initially jurors thought the Track was important not only for tourism but also as an access road for people living in remote northern towns. By the midpoint of the jury process, that concern had also been dissipated.[49]

During the 'discussion phase' of the jury, a similarly large change occurred in attitudes towards only one proposition. That proposition was: 'I will be made worse off by any decision about the Bloomfield Track.' Initially jurors worried that that might be true, and their wariness had not dissipated by the midpoint of the jury (if anything, it had increased somewhat). Over the course of the 'discussion phase', however, jurors became more comfortable that that was not true.

What is missed in that analysis of attitudes that changed is, of course, any account of attitudes that were constant across time. Among this group of jurors, there was a strong and unchanging commitment of jurors to preserving the integrity of the Daintree rainforest through which the Bloomfield Track runs.

The proposition on which jurors' views were strongest was, 'We don't need to worry too much about environmental damage in the Daintree region because future generations will be better able to deal with these problems than we are.' Among all 42 propositions to which jurors were asked to respond, that proposition achieved the highest mean score (strongly negative) on both the first questionnaire and the last questionnaire.

The effect of the 'information phase' of the jury was to deflate the overblown rhetoric, about reef damage on one side and about the need for road access on the other. That highly symbolic way of framing the

[48] The largest changes during the 'information phase' of the jury came with respect to three propositions: 'Erosion from the Bloomfield Track is permanently damaging the coral reefs that fringe the beaches below' dropped 2.08 places in the 9-point scale; 'Erosion from the Bloomfield Track does not cause siltation or damage to the fringing inshore reefs between Cape Tribulation and Cooktown' rose 2.50 places; and 'The coral reefs along the foreshore below the Bloomfield Track are not badly affected by the road' rose 2.08 places.

[49] 'The most important use of the Bloomfield Track is for tourism' rose 2.08 places in the 9-point scale over the 'information phase', between the first questionnaire and the middle questionnaire. In the final questionnaire, jurors once again reacted negatively to this proposition, just as they had in the first questionnaire. But from the context, we can infer that they were reading the question differently at these different points in the process. In initially denying that the most important use for the Track is tourism, jurors were expressing concern for the needs of residents to the north; by the midpoint of the jury, those concerns with access for residents to the north had dissipated, given the upgrade underway to the inland route. On the last occasion, in rejecting the proposition that 'the most important use of the Bloomfield Track is for tourism', jurors were saying that they *especially* did not want the track used just for tourism.

question had long dominated public discussions of the Track, thus providing ready attitudinal crutches upon which people could rely whenever asked about the issue.[50]

The effect of the testimony from the technical witnesses was to break that symbolic frame. Advised by experts that there was no clear cause for concern on either of those scores, jurors settled back to let their views on the Track be determined by their strong underlying attitudes towards the importance of protecting the rainforest itself. The damage that the Track was causing to the World Heritage rainforest might be more modest in scale than eco-alarmists claimed it was causing to the reef. But that more modest damage was more clearly demonstrable. Once jurors allowed themselves to focus on it, their policy preferences became much clearer and more nearly univocal.[51]

3.6. Are the Findings Generalizable?

3.6.1. *From This Citizens' Jury to Others?*

What happened in this particular case, as in any particular case, was in some respects peculiar unto itself. The problem of the Bloomfield Track had been well known and much discussed in the local community for a long time. Exaggerated claims and counter-claims had become entrenched, and unreflective public opinion polarized around them.

In this circumstance, the effect of the first 'information phase' of deliberative processes was to brush away those highly polarized attitudes, dispel the myths and symbolic posturing on both sides that had come to dominate the debate, and liberate people to act upon their attitudes towards the protection of rainforest itself.

The key point, from the perspective of 'democratic deliberation within', is that that happened in the earlier stages of deliberation—before the formal discussions ('deliberations', in the discursive sense) of the jury process ever began. The simple process of jurors seeing the site for themselves, focusing their minds on the issues, and listening to what experts

---

[50] Sears (1993).

[51] The three jurors who ranked Closure as their second rather than their first choice did so explicitly (according to group discussions and post-jury probing) because they thought more evidence was needed on precisely this point. All three made it clear that, if that evidence were forthcoming, Closure would indeed become their first-choice policy option as well.

had to say did all the work in changing jurors' attitudes. Talking among themselves, as a jury, did virtually none of it.

The same might happen in cases very different from this one, however. Suppose that instead of highly polarized symbolic attitudes, what we have at the outset is mass ignorance or mass apathy or non-attitudes. There again, people's engaging with the issue—focusing on it, acquiring information about it, thinking hard about it—would be something that is likely to occur earlier rather than later in the deliberative process. And more to the present point, it is something that is most likely to occur within individuals themselves or in informal interactions, well in advance of any formal, organized group discussion.

There is much in the large literature on attitudes and the mechanisms by which they change to support that speculation.[52] Consider, for example, the literature on 'central' versus 'peripheral' routes to the formation of attitudes.

Before deliberation, individuals may not have given the issue much thought or bothered to engage in an extensive process of reflection.[53] In such cases, positions may be arrived at via peripheral routes, taking cognitive shortcuts or arriving at 'top of the head' conclusions, or even simply following the lead of others believed hold similar attitudes or values.[54] These shorthand approaches involve the use of available cues such as 'expertness' or 'attractiveness'[55]—not deliberation in the internal-reflective sense I have described. Where peripheral shortcuts are employed, there may be inconsistencies in logic and the formation of positions, based on partial information or incomplete information processing.

'Central' routes to the development of attitudes, by contrast, involve the application of more deliberate effort to the matter at hand, in a way that is more akin to the internal-reflective deliberative ideal. Importantly for the thesis of this chapter, there is nothing intrinsic to the 'central' route that requires group deliberation. Research in this area stresses instead the importance simply of 'sufficient impetus' for engaging in deliberation, such as when an individual is stimulated by personal involvement in the issue.[56]

---

[52] For overviews and applications, see: Zaller (1992), Sniderman (1993), and Kinder and Herzog (1993).

[53] In such cases, we might apply the term 'cognitive miser' for someone who engages in minimal reflection of issue at hand (Taylor 1981).

[54] Lupia (1994).   [55] Petty and Cacioppo (1986).

[56] Petty and Cacioppo (1986), Johnson (1989), and Sears (1993: 144).

The same is true of 'online' versus 'memory-based' processes of attitude change.[57] The suggestion here is that we lead our ordinary lives
largely on autopilot, doing routine things in routine ways without
much thought or reflection. When we come across something 'new',
we update our routines—our 'running' beliefs and procedures, attitudes,
and evaluations—accordingly. But having updated, we then drop the
impetus for the update into deep-stored 'memory'. A consequence of this
procedure is that, when asked in the ordinary course of events 'what we
believe' or 'what attitude we take' towards something, we easily retrieve
what we think but we cannot so easily retrieve the reasons why. That more
fully reasoned assessment—the sort of thing I have been calling internal-
reflective deliberation—requires us to call up *reasons* from stored memory
rather than just consulting our running online 'summary judgements'.

Crucially for the present discussion, once again, what prompts that
shift from online to more deeply reflective deliberation is not necessarily
interpersonal discussion. The impetus for fixing one's attention on a topic,
and retrieving reasons from stored memory, might come from any of a
number of sources: group discussion is only one. And again, even in the
context of a group discussion, this shift from 'online' to 'memory-based'
processing is likely to occur earlier rather than later in the process, often
before the formal discussion ever begins.

All this is simply to say that, on a great many models and in a great
many different sorts of settings, it seems likely that elements of the pre-
discursive process are likely to prove crucial to the shaping and reshaping
of people's attitudes in a citizens' jury-style process. The initial processes
of focusing attention on a topic, providing information about it, and
inviting people to think hard about it are likely to provide a strong
impetus to internal-reflective deliberation, altering not just the information people have about the issue but also the way people process that
information and hence (perhaps) what they think about the issue.

What happens once people have shifted into this more internal-
reflective mode is, obviously, then an open question. Maybe people would
then come to an easy consensus, as they did in their attitudes towards
the Daintree rainforest.[58] Or maybe people would come to divergent
conclusions; and they then may (or may not) be open to argument and
counterargument, with talk actually changing minds.

---

[57] Chaiken, Wood, and Eagley (1996: 709), Druckman and Lupia (2000), and Lupia (2002,
2003).

[58] Sunstein's (2000, 2002) evidence about 'group polarization' within mock juries suggests
this might be a common pattern.

The claim of this chapter is not that group discussion will always matter as little as it did in this citizens' jury.[59] The claim is instead merely that the earliest steps in the jury process—the sheer focusing of attention on the issue at hand and acquiring more information about it, and the internal-reflective deliberation that that prompts—will invariably matter more than deliberative democrats of a more discursive stripe would have us believe. However much or little difference formal group discussions might have, on any given occasion, the pre-discursive phases of the jury process will invariably have a considerable impact on changing the way citizens' jurors approach an issue.

3.6.2. From Citizens' Juries to Ordinary Mass Politics?

In a citizens' jury sort of setting, then, it seems that informal, pre-group deliberation—'deliberation within'—will inevitably do much of the work that deliberative democrats ordinarily want to attribute to the more formal discursive processes. What are the preconditions for that happening? To what extent, in that sense, can findings about citizens' jury be extended to other larger or less well-ordered deliberative settings?

Even in citizens' juries, deliberation will work only if people are attentive, open, and willing to change their minds as appropriate. So too in mass politics. In citizens' juries the need to participate (or the anticipation of participating) in formally organized group discussions might be the 'prompt' that evokes those attributes. But there might be many other possible 'prompts' that can be found in less formally structured mass political settings.

Here are a few ways citizens' juries (and all cognate micro-deliberative mini-publics[60]) might be different from mass politics, and in which lessons drawn from that experience might not therefore carry over to ordinary politics:

- A citizens' jury concentrates people's minds on a single issue. Ordinary politics involve many issues at once.

- A citizens' jury is often supplied a background briefing that has been agreed by all stakeholders.[61] In ordinary mass politics, there

---

[59] It may matter much more where there is a less sharp distinction between factual questions and values than in this case, or where value disagreements loom larger than they did here. Those are precisely the sorts of disputes that many deliberative democrats (e.g. Ackerman 1989; Gutmann and Thompson 1996) have most in mind, of course.

[60] Luskin, Fishkin, and Jowell (2002: 459) say much the same about Deliberative Polls.

[61] Smith and Wales (2000: 58).

is rarely any equivalent common ground against which debates are conducted.

- A citizens' jury separates the process of acquiring information from that of discussing the issues. In ordinary mass politics, those processes are invariably intertwined.

- A citizens' jury is provided with a set of experts. They can be questioned, debated, or discounted. But there is a strictly limited set of 'competing experts' on the same subject. In ordinary mass politics, claims and sources of expertise often seem virtually limitless, allowing for much greater 'selective perception'.

- Participating in something called a 'citizens' jury' evokes certain very particular norms: norms concerning the 'impartiality' appropriate to jurors; norms concerning the 'common good' orientation appropriate to people in their capacity as citizens.[62] There is a very different ethos at work in ordinary mass politics, which are typically driven by flagrantly partisan appeals to sectional interest (or utter disinterest and voter apathy).[63]

- In a citizens' jury, you think and listen in anticipation of the 'discussion phase', knowing that you soon will have to defend your views in a discursive setting where they will be probed intensively.[64] In ordinary mass political settings, there is no such incentive for paying attention.

It is perfectly true that citizens' juries are 'special' in all those ways. But if being special in all those ways makes for a better—more 'reflective', more 'deliberative'—political process, then those are design features that we ought try to mimic as best as we can in ordinary mass politics as well.

There are various ways that that might be done. Briefing books might be prepared by sponsors of American presidential debates (the League of Women Voters, and such like) in consultation with the stakeholders

---

[62] Again, however, Table 3.2 shows that jurors themselves thought that this was the next least important influence on them.

[63] Mill (1861: ch. 10) argued for public rather than secret voting on the grounds that that would make voters think of the ballot as a 'public trust' rather than as a 'private right', and force them to defend their votes in terms of the common good rather than letting it be dictated by narrow self-interest.

[64] Table 3.2 shows that jurors themselves did not feel this as much of an influence, although of course it might have acted upon them subliminally. Other experiments show 'that individuals who are told that they will have to discuss their judgments publicly are more likely to possess more information more objectively' (Ryfe 2005: 57; see further Tetlock 1983a, 1983b, 1985).

involved. Agreed panels of experts might be questioned on prime-time television. Issues might be sequenced for debate and resolution, to avoid too much competition for people's time and attention. Variations on the Ackerman-Fishkin proposal for a 'Deliberation Day' before every election might be generalized, with a day every few months being given over to small meetings in local schools to discuss public issues.[65]

All that is rather visionary, perhaps. And (although it is clearly beyond the scope of this discussion to explore them in depth) there are doubtless many other more-or-less visionary ways of introducing into real-world politics analogues of the elements that induce citizen jurors to practice 'democratic deliberation within', even before the jury discussion gets underway. Here, I must content myself with identifying those features that need to be replicated in real-world politics in order to achieve that goal—and with the 'possibility theorem' that is established by the fact that (as sketched immediately above) there is at least one possible way of doing that for each of those key features.

3.7. Deliberation Before Discourse

The aim of this chapter has been to point out the virtues—and centrality—of the sort of deliberation that goes on inside people's heads privately, and among citizens informally, well before formal public deliberations ever get underway. People engage in those sorts of private and informal deliberations all the time. That they do is crucial to the functioning of politics, writ large or small.

Empathy requires no harangues. It may not even be compatible with them. One of the most important things of which the Far North Queensland Citizens' Jury has reminded us is the possibility of internal empathetic reflections shaping citizens' attitudes even towards the politically mute, such as a World Heritage rainforest. In that spirit, let us leave the last word to one of the jurors, Matilda, who when asked 'what changed your mind?' replied simply, 'Being in the rainforest itself, especially when the driver turned off the engine.'

[65] Ackerman and Fishkin (2002).

4

Talking politics: perils and promise

Previous chapters have shown how deliberation works, and how it might fit into macro-political processes. I now want to stand back and assess whether and why deliberation—understood as 'talking politics'—might or might not be a good thing, politically.

I start with the observation that, in its 'deliberative turn', democratic theory has lost sight of something that was once common wisdom among all practitioners of politics. 'The core idea' of deliberative democracy, Gutmann and Thompson say, 'is simple: when citizens . . . disagree morally, they should continue to reason together to reach mutually acceptable decisions.'[1]

But canny politicians of all sorts have long known that, politically, some things are better left unsaid. Even at age fourteen, George Washington recognized 'avoid taking firm positions on contentious issues' as a maxim worth noting in his copybook of *Rules of Civility and Decent Behaviour in Company and Conversation.*[2]

Nor is it simply a matter of what topics may appropriately be raised at the dinner table. There have always been certain things (their particulars varying across time and place) that are deemed better left undiscussed, even in the most political (and, indeed, democratic) of fora.[3] A limiting case might be Lebanon's refusal to take a census of its population since 1932, for fear of exacerbating intercommunal tensions. But across a range of less dramatic cases, political actors often appreciate the benefits of

---

[1] Gutmann and Thompson (1996: 1). Similarly, in Cohen's words (1998: 186), deliberative democracy is 'free public reasoning among equals who are governed by the decisions'.

[2] Washington (1746/1988: prop. 69).

[3] In certain places, of course, the conventional wisdom was that nothing or virtually nothing should be subject to general political discussion: but my focus here is on democratic polities.

leaving much unsaid. Contemporary commentators on the theory and practice of negotiation, for example, remark: 'By tying our tongues about a sensitive question, we can secure forms of cooperation and fellowship otherwise beyond reach'; and, 'When anger and misperception are high, some thoughts are best left unsaid'.[4]

Of course, the impolitic is sometimes the essence of politics. Awkward issues must sometimes be confronted and resolved, one way or another, politically. However much we might politically wish to 'leave things undecided', we cannot practice avoidance forever.[5] Sometimes awkward topics might *have* to be broached. That has always been known, too. Still, the once-common wisdom held that, on many topics and in many circumstances, it would be better to avoid broaching tender topics insofar as possible.

Deliberative democratic theory, in contrast, tends to emphasize the ubiquitous importance of talk. It must be talk of a certain sort, to be sure. In an 'ideal speech situation' it would be mutually respectful, eschewing bullying, domination, or recourse to any power beyond the 'forceless force of the better argument'.[6] In a non-ideal world with power inequalities overlaying social differences, talk (and other modes of communication) of a more rambunctious and less disciplined form might be more appropriate.[7] And in any case, the time for deliberation must at some point end and a decision (however provisionally) be settled upon.[8] Be that as it may, the deep-background assumption that is shared by discourse ethics and deliberative democracy is that 'talk' (in suitably extended sense) is always good, whatever the topic.

Insofar as that proposition is queried in contemporary literature, it is queried by realist sceptics anxious to assert almost exactly the opposite. They say that political talk is always (or anyway can always be) bad: it is (or anyway always can be) purely strategic and manipulative; it can always lead to domination by special interests and to worse decisions overall for the vast majority.[9] Furthermore, that is true whatever the topic of the

---

[4] Holmes (1988: 19) and Fisher and Ury (1983: 37).

[5] Sunstein (1996a) and Bickel (1962: 133).

[6] Cohen (1989) and Habermas (1984, 1987, 1996).

[7] Sanders (1997), Young (2000: ch. 2), Dryzek (2000: ch. 3), and Gutmann and Thompson (1996: 2–3, 135–8).

[8] Gutmann and Thompson (2002: 169–72) and Shapiro (2002).

[9] For informal arguments to this effect, see Przeworski (1998), Stokes (1998), Shapiro (1999), cf. Mackie (1998). For similar arguments predating the 'deliberative turn' in democratic theory, see Edelman (1988) and Gamson (1992). For game-theoretic demonstrations, see Austen-Smith (1990), Austen-Smith and Banks (1996), Feddersen and Pesendorfer (1998),

talk. Just like deliberative democrats, and unlike the more discriminating once-common wisdom, realist sceptics treat all political discourse as pretty much on a par, making little effort to distinguish between different topics of political conversation.

This chapter begins by revisiting that once-common wisdom, attempting to catalogue topics sometimes deemed undiscussable in ordinary political discourse, even in genuinely democratic polities. Let me be clear from the start as to the point of the taxonomy. It amounts to nothing more than 'soft advice', of a broadly pragmatic sort, as regards what sorts of topics can and cannot usefully be discussed politically. I shall not be using this taxonomy to say what sorts of reasons can legitimately count as normatively permissible 'public reasons'.[10] Still less is this a taxonomy designed to regulate political speech, legislatively prohibiting certain propositions from being uttered publicly. My aim here is merely to map out circumstances in which talking is pragmatically pointless or politically inadvisable.

The main aim is for that taxonomy to serve as a springboard, enabling me to say something more general about when and why talking might actually help to resolve issues. Section 4.2 will sketch two distinct models. The first operates in terms of pooling information, in quest of the truth. The second operates in terms of probing premises, in search of the source of our differences.

Section 4.3 then brings those two models to bear back on questions of politically undiscussable issues. There are many things that it is pointless to talk about, from either perspective (although there might be good reasons in terms of both to talk some about what exactly the limits of those things might be). But having come to appreciate the premise-probing function that discussion can serve, many of the things we might otherwise deem too sensitive to discuss can be seen to be well worth discussing after all.

---

and Austen-Smith and Feddersen (2006). Note that the game-theoretic demonstrations show that strategic misrepresentation of one's true beliefs or preferences can sometimes lead to better outcomes from the point of view of the group as a whole.

[10] Rawls (1997/1999: 136–7) fleshes out his notion as follows: 'Citizens are reasonable when viewing one another as free and equal in a system of social cooperation over generations, they are prepared to offer one another fair terms of cooperation according to what they consider the most reasonable conception of political justice...The criterion of reciprocity requires that when those terms are proposed as the most reasonable terms of fair cooperation, those proposing them also think it at least reasonable for others to accept them, as free and equal citizens....' See similarly Cohen (1989) and Gutmann and Thompson (1996).

4.1. A Partial Taxonomy of the Politically Undiscussable

Although it was once common wisdom even in genuinely democratic polities that some issues ought to be deemed politically undiscussable, there was rarely much discussion of any general sort about what exactly caused some issues to fall into that category. Like the US Supreme Court's view of pornography, that once-common wisdom seemed simply to recognize instances of politically undiscussable issues when it saw them.

Here I attempt to impose a bit more order on the sorts of examples that constituted the once-common wisdom through such 'one-case-at-a-time' procedures. As a rough first cut, we can distinguish two broad classes of topics that the once-common wisdom deemed to be politically undiscussable. In the first class of cases, discussion is thought to be simply pointless, owing to something about the pragmatics of the discourse at hand. In the second, there is something politically inadvisable about discussing those issues. I shall offer multiple examples and subspecies of each. In so doing, I broadly follow Rawls, who proceeds analogously (albeit with rather different examples and categories) in sketching the domain of reasonable, irresolvable disagreement in politics.[11]

I draw examples from a deliberate range of political experience, in hopes of capturing as much of the phenomenon as possible. Those examples range across unmannerly words as well as impolitic topics, procedural sensitivities as well as substantive ones, and contentious means as well as divisive ends. They involve private fora as well as public ones, and a wide variety of subspecies of each. All those distinctions clearly matter: clearly, things that are 'undiscussable' or 'unspeakable' in one place can be, and often are, perfectly fit subjects for discussion by other people in other places at other times or in different ways. What concerns me here is not with finding things that are 'undiscussable' *tout court*, however. Instead, my concern is with the phenomenon of 'undiscussability' or 'unspeakability' itself—why and in what sense some things might be thought to fall into some such categories, at all.

4.1.1. *Pointless Discussions*

Some topics are simply 'not subject to rational discourse' because discussion of them is, for one reason or another, pragmatically pointless. Here are some ways in which that might be true.

---

[11] Rawls (1993: 54–8; 2001: 35–6).

DEBATING WHETHER TO CLOSE DEBATE

Consider, first, things that it makes no *sense* to discuss. A prime example of this is provided by rules of parliamentary procedure classifying motions to close debate as being themselves 'not debatable'.[12]

Reflect for a moment upon the problem to which motions to close debate are a solution. Those motions aim to bring the issue to a vote, if members are ready to vote. To make such motions themselves debatable would be pragmatically counterproductive. It would simply serve to perpetuate a filibuster, preventing the question of whether debate should be closed from itself being brought to a vote. In that respect, allowing debate on motions to close debate would make no *pragmatic sense*.

In certain circumstances, it might not make any *logical* sense to debate motions to close debate. That occurs when the only reasons to be offered in favour of continuing debate are the fact that there remain first-order arguments for or against the proposition that have not yet been discussed. But of course *that* proposition cannot be further discussed, except by actually introducing into the discussion those hitherto neglected arguments into the debate over whether to end debate. Debates over the second-order question of whether to end debate would then collapse, logically, into debate over the first-order proposition on the table for debate.

Of course, there are plenty of other arguments for ending or continuing debate, other than that all possible arguments for and against the proposition have not yet been fully considered. We might argue to continue debate out of fairness: there are some people who have not yet had their say (even if we do not expect them to say anything materially different than what we have already heard). We might argue to end debate out of a sense of urgency: the barbarians are at the gates, or it is time for dinner. It would not be logically senseless to allow a debate of that sort on whether or not to close debate. But it usually seems sufficiently senseless (either logically or pragmatically) to allow discussion of motions to close debate that most parliamentary manuals simply prohibit it.

DELIBERATING OVER THE IMPOSSIBLE

According to one of the more famous maxims of modern moral philosophers, 'ought implies can'. There is no pragmatic point in telling people (or in people telling themselves) that they ought to do something, if there

---

[12] Robert (1876/1951: §§17, 24, 29, 30).

is no way in which they can do it. The point of morality is to be action-guiding, and there is no pragmatic point to moralizing when it cannot serve that role. Modern policy scientists say, similarly, that 'feasibility is part of desirability'.[13] There is no pragmatic point in policy advisors commending courses of action that are impossible for policy-makers to pursue.

A sensible rule for the conduct of deliberative assemblies might similarly hold that things that are impossible ought to be struck off the agenda. As Hobbes observed long ago, '[O]f things past, there is no deliberation; because manifestly impossible to be changed; nor of things known to be impossible... because men know... such deliberations vain'.[14] If no resolution of the assembly can change some state of affairs, there is no pragmatic point in the assembly's deliberating over what it should do about that state of affairs. It can make various symbolic gestures: it can express sympathy, or outrage, or hope. But it cannot make any material difference to the outcome.

Of course, what matters here is not so much the fact of impossibility as the *perception* of it. To continue the quotation from Hobbes: 'of things impossible, which we think possible, we may deliberate, not knowing it is in vain'. Conversely, thinking something impossible leads us to fail to deliberate on it—wrongly, of course, if our perceptions of impossibility are in error.

Rigging perceptions of impossibility in such a way as to keep things off the agenda is a classic trick of political manipulation. Bentham bemoaned how 'the plea of impossibility offers itself at every step, in justification of injustice in all its forms'.[15] And there is evident truth to that claim, as, for example, manipulation of intelligence information during international crises suggests.[16]

What is and is not possible is thus itself properly subject to dispute, and appropriate for debate. Undiscussability sets in only after we have satisfied ourselves that something really *is* impossible. At that point, though, there really is no pragmatic purpose to be served in discussing the matter further.[17]

---

[13] Wildavsky (1979: 216).   [14] Hobbes (1651: book 1, ch. 6).

[15] Bentham (1827: vol. 7, p. 285).

[16] The Iraq war is the latest case; the Cuban Missile Crisis was an earlier one (Goodin 1982: ch. 7).

[17] Even the Melian discourse was over feasible alternatives: 'fight and lose' versus 'surrender to Athens without a fight' (Thucydides 1972, book 5).

IRRESOLVABLE ISSUES

If we see the purpose of debate as being to 'resolve' an issue, one way or another, then there is no point in debating issues that are irresolvable. Irresolvability might come about in either of two ways.

Issues can be irresolvable, first, because no resolution of the assembly can resolve those issues. That is to say, they are beyond the power, competence, or control of the assembly. No human assembly can, by its enactment alone, reduce the distance from the earth to the moon. Likewise, no human assembly, by its enactments, can change the past (as opposed to how the past is taught in schools). There is pragmatically no point in any human assembly debating such matters, because there is nothing that their enactments can do, one way or the other, to change those things.

Issues can be irresolvable, second, because the assembly is unable to come to any resolution concerning them. That is to say, under whatever decision rules the assembly operates, there is no proposition that can command support of a decisive number of voters. Or, as a variation on that theme, no proposition commands the *stable* support of a decisive majority: any motion enacted one day gets repealed the next.[18] Then the issue is irresolvable, in the sense that the assembly cannot come to any *resolute* solution.

UNDECIDABLE ISSUES

Topics can be 'not worth discussing' in a further, related respect. This occurs with topics on which we disagree, but on which our disagreements cannot be resolved by discussion alone (or even in large part).

Imagine a group of physicists pondering Einstein's claims, circa 1910. They disagree as to the merits of his theories of relativity. Through discussion, they can clarify exactly what the content of the claims are; they can sort out misunderstandings; they can check the mathematics for internal consistency. Those are real contributions. Nonetheless, they stop far short of resolving the larger issue: 'But is it *true?*' Everyone agrees that the crucial test is whether, during the next solar eclipse, light can be shown to be bent by the sun's gravitational field. Everyone agrees that there is no point in discussing the matter further, until then: they will just have to wait for the results of that 'natural experiment'.

Sometimes social and political issues are rather like that. We disagree; and after a certain amount of discussion, we agree that no further

[18] Riker (1983); cf. Mackie (2003).

discussion is likely to resolve our disagreement. Just occasionally, we might also agree what further evidence (akin to that of the solar eclipse) might actually resolve our disagreement. More often in socio-political affairs, we simply 'agree to disagree' (or more precisely, to leave the question open) and we set up social institutions that work around that.[19]

One way we do that is by creating separate enclaves, within which each of us can operate according to our own beliefs, trying to avoid situations that would force adjudication across those enclaves. Writ large, this is the classic Westphalian order: the religion of each place is deemed to be the religion of its prince, which other princes are required to respect. Writ nationally, it is the 'non-establishment' clause of the First Amendment to the US Constitution ('Congress shall make no law respecting an establishment of religion, or prohibiting the free exercise thereof'). Writ small, it is the 'free speech' clause in that same Amendment, prohibiting the Congress from restricting the free speech of citizens, and allowing each citizen to think and say whatever s/he likes. All of those are responses to differences over matters of fact that cannot be decided through further discussion. Instead of attempting to decide which is right, we allow (as best we can) all to flourish, each in its own way and each in its own separate sphere.

More mundane policy discourse might sometimes have broadly the same structure. Take the case of the safe storage of radioactive wastes from nuclear power-generating plants. The problem is how to store lethal poisons for a period measured in terms of geologic time, which human science can model only extraordinarily imperfectly. If we had to guess where best to place such poisons, we would put them in the bottom of salt mines where the geology has (so far) been stable for a very long time. But we have no firm guarantee that they will remain stable, geologically, for an equally long time into the future.[20] There may be crucial experiments, like the solar eclipse in the case of Einstein's theory, which could resolve the essentially factual issue. But those 'natural experiments' may well lie too far in the future to do us any good in framing current policy.

RADICALLY DIVISIVE ISSUES

There is one remaining quasi-logical reason that a group might find an issue undiscussable. That is that the group cannot resolve that issue and, at the same time, remain together as a group. These issues are such that any resolution would cause the group to splinter. Groups cannot

---

[19] Sunstein (1996a, 1996b); cf. Aumann (1976).   [20] Goodin (1982: ch. 9).

resolve such issues, because in the process of resolving them the groups themselves cease to exist. The resolution effaces the resolver.[21]

One classic case in point is slavery in the early history of the American republic. The 1789 US Constitution explicitly forbad Congress from prohibiting (or hence sensibly discussing prohibiting) the importation of slaves until 1808.[22] Then, in 1836, the US House of Representatives adopted a 'gag rule' that remained in force for a further nine years precluding issues of slavery from being debated on the floor of the House.[23] The political calculus underlying that gag rule (substantially borne out by subsequent developments) was that whichever way the issue of slavery was resolved would be inimical to the survival of the USA as a single country, and of the US Congress as the authoritative deliberative assembly legislating for it.

The logical form of this problem—the resolution *literally* effacing the resolver—is a relatively rare phenomenon. Other cases are sometimes likened to it: abortion or euthanasia, for example.[24] While those are obviously hotly disputed issues, they are (probably) not divisive in the literal sense that slavery proved to be. Resolving those issues one way or another will undoubtedly be highly contentious. But it will (probably) not lead to the extinguishing of the deliberative, resolving agency, in anything like the same way that resolving the issue of slavery one way or another clearly credibly threatened to do throughout the first half of the nineteenth century in America.

Of course, the parenthetical 'probably' is of signal importance in those contexts. We can never be absolutely certain, *ex ante*, what contentious topics are so contentious that any resolution of them will literally split the polity apart. Constitutional ruptures are often the unintended consequences of a chain of events, substantially unpredictable in advance. So there is no sure way of telling ahead of time what topics might prove to be too divisive even to discuss, and cautious politicians might reasonably give such topics a very wide berth in consequence of these inherent uncertainties.

---

[21] This is the limiting case of Section 4.2.2's category of topics deemed politically undiscussable because 'impolitic'. The difference between 'dissolving the decision-making unit', as opposed merely to 'upsetting people' (perhaps very badly), seems sufficiently great to constitute a difference in kind. In practice, of course, it might often be hard to tell in advance which category in any given situation is going to be an instance of.

[22] Art. 1, sec. 9, para. 1.

[23] A resolution 'relating in any way ... to the subject of slavery or the abolition of slavery shall, without being either printed or referred, be laid on the table, and ... no further action whatever shall be had thereon' (quoted in Holmes 1988: 31).

[24] Luker (1984).

4.1.2. *Impolitic Discussions*

Sometimes issues are undiscussable, not because it is in any sense pragmatically pointless to discuss them but instead because it would be impolitic to discuss them. Doing so would be imprudent by reason of the reactions it would evoke from others.

VISCERAL RESPONSE

Some topics might be undiscussable because they are not amenable to rational discourse, and that is due not (as before) to some reason internal to topics themselves but rather (here) to the reactions of others.

Think of sensitivities of a more tactile sort: part of the body that is 'sensitive to the touch'. When you touch that spot (when you 'tread on tender toes'), you evoke an involuntary response. The person jerks, yelps, pulls away—quite uncontrollably.

Those are all physical responses to physical stimuli. But we sometimes think of verbal stimula evoking wholly involuntary responses of roughly the same sort. That is the theory underlying the doctrine of 'fighting words'. Those are words which, 'by their very utterance inflict injury or tend to incite an immediate breach of the peace.... [A]ppellations "damned racketeer" and "damned Fascist" are epithets likely to provoke the average person to retaliation, and thereby cause a breach of the peace'.[25] When someone calls you some deeply offensive name, your reason is blinded. 'In the heat of the moment' you respond (largely) involuntarily to overwhelming verbal provocation.

Many restrictions found in manuals of parliamentary procedure on 'unparliamentary language' are presumably rooted in a similar thought. Parliamentarians are prohibited from, to quote Jefferson's *Manual*, 'speaking reviling, nipping, or unmannerly words against a particular member' because the inevitable response in kind will lead to a hopeless deterioration in the quality of the debate.[26]

One reason for not raising whole issues that are 'sensitive' in similar ways might be that doing so evokes a visceral response, beyond the bounds of reason. In a racially deeply divided society, political discourse can easily spin out of rational control whenever politicians 'play the race card'—whenever they raise the issue of race—at all.[27] The visceral response evoked by the mere mention of topics that are 'sensitive' in this way makes such issues rationally undiscussable.

[25] Murphy (1942: 574).   [26] Jefferson (1801: §17, pp. 374–7).
[27] Kinder and Sanders (1996) and Mendelberg (2001).

How seriously we want to take this argument might depend on either (or both) how reasonable or on how incorrigible the associated visceral response really is. Often we are inclined to reply, 'Get a grip!' To many people or groups who would ask us to censor political debate to protect their sensitivities (and not incidentally to protect their interests in so doing) we might be inclined to say the same thing. It is just not reasonable that their (real or pretended) lack of self-control should be allowed to control our collective agenda like that.

But suppose that, however unreasonable, people's visceral responses in these respects really are incorrigible. They simply cannot 'get a grip', however hard they try. When these topics arise, they just inevitably fly off the handle, and become utterly incapable of rational discourse. That would be an unfortunate fact about those people, and about the political community containing them. Still, it may well be a fact that that community will have to work around, in superintending its collective affairs. Topics inevitably triggering such irrational responses have to be avoided.[28] Either that, or else the attendant irrationality coped with, when we decide that those topics cannot or should not be avoided.

TENDER TOPICS

Certain topics are sometimes deemed to be discursively 'off limits' on the grounds that merely raising the topic will be hurtful to someone or another.

The old playground chant has it that 'sticks and stones can break my bones but words can never hurt me'. But that is palpably false. Words can indeed 'do' things.[29] Among them are many harmful things: 'sentence', 'disbar', 'banish', 'defame', 'demean', and 'degrade'. The US Supreme Court draws a sharp distinction between 'speech' (which is always to be free) and 'action' (which can be restricted depending on its consequences). But that distinction is clearly untenable, as modern feminist jurisprudes have made abundantly clear.[30]

This thought provides another ground for restrictions on 'unparliamentary language' in manuals on parliamentary procedure. The reason you ought not call another fellow member of parliament a 'blighter' might not be so much that that will evoke an automatic, almost visceral response in

---

[28] Especially insofar as they can costlessly be avoided, i.e. insofar as 'such utterances are no essential part of any exposition of ideas, and are of such slight social value as a step to truth that any benefit that may be derived from them is clearly outweighed by the social interest in order and morality' (Murphy 1942: 574).
[29] Austin (1962). [30] Mackinnon (1993).

kind. The reason may simply be that such name-calling does some actual harm to someone, insofar as it offends the sensitivities of some members (in addition, of course, serving no useful parliamentary purpose).

Analogous reasoning might justify keeping whole items off the political agenda. Merely raising the topic can sometimes profoundly offend certain segments of the community. Spokesmen for the Muslim community in Australia, for example, purport to take offence at the mere discussion of banning the export of live sheep to the Middle East, where they are slaughtered in ways that animal liberationists deem cruel. The objection, notice, is precisely to the ban being *discussed*: to treat it as an open question, up for discussion, whether their deepest beliefs are to be respected or not.[31] Debates over whether the Holocaust really happened, or over what role coastal African tribes played in kidnapping blacks from the interior for the slave trade, are sometimes likewise subject to bans on grounds of the offence that the sheer discussion would cause to insular minorities within the community.

How seriously we should take claims that something should not be publicly discussed, merely on account of the offence that would be given to some sector of the community by its being discussed, obviously depends upon how 'reasonable' we think it is for them to feel offended.

The reasonableness of their taking offence is, note, a separate question from the Rawls-style question about the 'reasonableness' of their beliefs as such.[32] We might well think the metaphysics of Islam rationally groundless, yet still think that it would be perfectly reasonable for believers to take offence that we would even contemplate (much less impose) a ban on ritual practices that they believe to be morally obligatory.

Note, further, that we might sometimes regard the sheer fact that someone will take offence a sufficient ground for desisting from doing (or even discussing) something, even if we do not think them reasonable to take offence. It is enough that pornography offends women to justify its being banned; we do not need also to believe that they have good grounds for feeling offended (though most of us do); we would regard it as inappropriate for an opponent of such a ban to protest that the

---

[31] Imagine, for an even clearer case, someone proposing that we debate whether to rescind someone else's rights. Given the intimate connections between 'rights', 'status', and 'dignity' (Feinberg 1970), the sheer proposal that we debate that question would rightly be regarded as an affront to the people whose rights would be involved. Treating it as an open question, politically up for grabs, whether or not to treat them as dignified members of the community is itself to deny them that dignity, quite apart from how the vote subsequently turns out.

[32] Rawls (1993: ch. 2).

women have no grounds for feeling offended, that the offended parties are overreacting or misinterpreting the intentions of purveyors or consumers of pornography. Sometimes, at least, we are prepared to suppose that sensitivities are good grounds for taking certain topics off the agenda, no further questions asked.

SECRETS

'Sensitive', recall, is the lowest grade of confidentiality under the Official Secrets Act. Matters that are 'sensitive' in that sense are matters that are not open to general public discussion.

Official Secrets, and confidences more generally, refer to facts that can be shared—and hence topics that can be discussed fully—only among that subset of people privy to confidential information. Sometimes that precludes any general public discussion of those topics at all. But even where there can be some scope for general public discussion of such issues, that ought not be the decisive determinant of policy in areas where the public is necessarily not privy to the full facts. Or so it is standardly said, anyway.[33]

Official Secrets are only one particularly dramatic example of privacy constraints on public discussion, however. Here I shall focus instead upon privacy interests and secrets that it would deeply upset certain people to have made public. A particularly dramatic case arose in Australia when a group of Aboriginal women tried to block construction of the Hindmarsh Island bridge, claiming that the island involved was a site of ritual significance to women of their group but since the rituals concerned were 'secret women's business' they could not be disclosed in open court.[34]

Still less dramatic instances of privacy constraints on public discussion occur all the time. Editors find themselves in contempt of court if they put into the public domain matters that are *sub judice*, under consideration in court. Matters that are 'commercial in confidence' cannot be publicly discussed, even when the commercial contract is with a public agency: and many have commented on how contracting out public services has, in that way, effectively served to shield providers of public services from proper scrutiny and accountability to the public at large.[35]

[33] Gutmann and Thompson (1996: ch. 3). Arthur Schlessinger (1973: 361), however, declares that '99 percent of the information necessary for intelligent judgment is available to any careful reader of the *New York Times*, the *Washington Post* or the *Congressional Record*'.

[34] The veracity of those claims is disputed: the findings of a Royal Commission (Stevens 1996) that declared them to be 'fabricated' were overruled in an appeal to the Federal Court (Brisbane *Courier-Mail*, 21 August 2001).

[35] Australian Senate (2003) and Minow (2003: 38).

Whether privacy interests should trump the public interest in discussion of those issues is a balancing act to be performed on a case-by-case basis. The case of Official Secrets is marginally easier, structurally anyway, insofar as it puts public interest against public interest: the public's interest in knowing and discussing the matters against the public's interest that is being protected by preventing certain facts from becoming public and hence available to one's enemies. Other cases are trickier insofar as they pit the public interest (in revealing and discussing the facts) against private interests (in keeping the facts confidential). But in all cases it is a matter of balancing.

In that balancing, there is no reason to think that one side will *always* carry the greater weight. 'State secrets' and 'privacy interests' are often offered as if they were absolute trumps, excluding consideration of all other reasons.[36] Undoubtedly they are strong reasons that will usually trump most others. And when they do, whole rafts of topics might disappear from the list of legitimate topics for general public discussion. But we cannot simply let the matter be settled by the sheer fact of a claim being lodged by some interested parties (state officials in the one case; in the other, groups who want to keep their own business secret). The public's counterclaim of a 'right to know and discuss' always needs to be weighed in the balance, even if often it will be outweighed.[37] Institutionally it is courts that typically serve this function, and it is one they need to protect all the more assiduously in times of trouble.[38]

POLITICAL CONVENIENCE

It can sometimes simply be politically prudent to keep certain divisive issues off the agenda, purely out of low-level considerations of political convenience—keeping coalitions together, keeping influential persons sweet, and so on.[39]

In general, it is smart politics to agree what we can agree, and to ignore the rest (for the moment, anyway). By maintaining their focus on what unites them, parties to a coalition can achieve what is achievable. By ignoring what might divide them, they preserve the coalition as an effective force for doing what it can.

---

[36] Raz (1975) and Goodin (1982: ch. 11).

[37] Bovens (2002). Recall Jefferson's reaction to the secrecy of the Philadelphia Constitutional Convention: 'I am sorry that they began their deliberations by so abominable a precedent as that of tying up the tongues of their members. Nothing can justify this example but . . . ignorance of the value of public discussion' (quoted in Gutmann and Thompson 1996: 115).

[38] Waldron (2003).   [39] Holmes (1988: 19).

In Britain, for example, the Conservative Party has long been deeply divided over Europe. Some members fervently want to join the European Monetary Union; others want equally fervently to remain outside it. The question splits the party down the middle, threatening to destroy the party altogether as an effective political force. The best hope for the Tories is to keep the issue off the agenda altogether.

Of course, other things being equal, the fact that the issue would split the Tories is an irresistible reason for *other* parties to press the issue. But other things might not be equal. Those other parties might themselves also be at risk of splitting over the issue. Or they may fear that if the Tories split, the political forces thereby unleashed would be dangerous (to their own parties, or the country, or whatever). Or they may think, more simply, that any major reconfiguration of the political landscape entails risks and transition costs that are better avoided, from the point of view of all concerned. For those sorts of reasons, parties on all sides might conspire to keep off the agenda topics that would upset the existing coalition dynamics.

4.2. What Political Deliberation Can Accomplish

Partial though that catalogue inevitably is, it gives some sense of the kinds of reasons we might have for supposing that certain topics might be better left undiscussed, politically. Next I propose to explore the other side of the question: how, in general, *can* political deliberations contribute to the resolution of unsettled questions? Borrowing from Rawls, I explore in this section two models. Section 4.3 will bring these two discussions into joint focus, asking how political deliberations might contribute in each of those ways to come to terms even with issues that might initially seem politically undiscussable. In the case of sensitive issues, of course, 'coming to terms' might take various different forms. 'Coming to an agreed solution' is one, of course; but that may often be more than we can reasonably hope for. Simply 'desensitizing' an issue might be a good outcome—'resolving' the issue, after a fashion, without exactly 'solving' it. That, I shall conclude, is the larger contribution that political deliberation and discussion is likely to make, when dealing with sensitive issues in highly polarized settings.

4.2.1. Two Contributions: The Gospel According to Rawls

In his first, best book John Rawls points to two ways in which 'an ideally conducted discussion among many persons is more likely to arrive at the correct conclusion'.[40] Although he does not distinguish them as sharply as I will, I hope to show that they are indeed two distinct contributions.

Rawls starts from the assumption that participants are acting in good faith in sincere pursuit of the common good.[41] He thinks that agents motivated thusly are more likely to reach the right results by deliberating and deciding matters jointly, due (firstly) to a relatively mechanical aspect of information-pooling:

> If we ask how likely it is that the majority opinion will be correct, it is evident that the ideal procedure bears a certain analogy to the statistical problem of pooling the views of a group of experts to arrive at a best judgment. Here the experts are rational legislators able to take an objective perspective because they are impartial. The suggestion goes back to Condorcet that if the likelihood of a correct judgment on the part of the representative legislator is greater than that of an incorrect one, the probability that the majority vote is correct increases as the likelihood of correct decision by the representative legislator increases. Thus we might be tempted to suppose that if many rational persons were to try to simulate the conditions of the ideal procedure and conducted their reasoning and discussion accordingly, a large majority anyway would almost certainly be right.[42]

This is the 'epistemic' argument for democratic deliberation. In embracing it, Rawls sets himself in a clear lineage from Aristotle through Mill.[43] The former spoke of 'the wisdom of the multitude'; the latter pointed to the role of freedom of thought and speech in winnowing true opinion from false. And those sorts of propositions have entered into today's conventional wisdom about democratic theory and practice. Gutmann and Thompson, for example, invite us to

---

[40] Rawls (1971: 358)

[41] Here is how Rawls (1971: 357) describes that assumption: 'In the ideal procedure, the decision reached is not a compromise, a bargain struck between opposing parties trying to advance their ends. The legislative discussion must be conceived not as a contest between interests, but as an attempt to find the best policy as defined by the principles of justice. I suppose, then, as part of the theory of justice, that an impartial legislator's only desire is to make the correct decision in this regard, given the general facts known to him. He is to vote solely according to his judgment. The outcome of the vote gives an estimate of what is most in line with the conception of justice.'

[42] Rawls (1971: 357–8). See similarly: cf. Waldron (1989: 1322–3; 1999: 135), Estlund (1993: 93), and Gaus (1997: 150; 2003: 157–64).

[43] Aristotle (1984b: 1281a43–b9, p. 66) and Mill (1859: ch. 2).

think of the requirement of actual deliberation as analogous to a feature of scientific inquiry. Reciprocity is to justice in political ethics what replication is to truth in scientific ethics.... The process of deliberation has...epistemic value. Decisions are more likely to be morally justifiable if decision-makers are required to offer justifications for policies to other people, including those who are both well informed and representative of the citizens who will be most affected by the decisions.[44]

That epistemic argument is the first model Rawls offers for how deliberation might help us 'arrive at the correct conclusion', politically. But for reasons discussed below, Rawls himself does not want to rely too heavily upon that epistemic argument alone. He therefore goes on to offer a second argument that is (on my reading if not Rawls's own) separate and distinct from the first:

we normally assume that an ideally conducted discussion among many persons is more likely to arrive at the correct conclusion (by a vote if necessary) than the deliberations of any one of them by himself. Why should this be so? In everyday life the exchange of opinion with others checks our partiality and widens our perspective; we are made to see things from the standpoint of others and the limits of our vision are brought home to us... The benefits of discussion lie in the fact that even representative legislators are limited in knowledge and the ability to reason. No one of them knows everything the others know, or can make all the same inferences that they can draw in concert. Discussion is a way of combining information and enlarging the range of arguments.[45]

In his own exposition of it, Rawls seems to think of this being merely another, less mechanical form of 'information-pooling'. As analyzed below, however, this argument might actually be quite distinct, having more to do with 'premise-probing' than information-pooling.

4.2.2. Resolving Disagreements: Information-Pooling

Consider Rawls's two suggestions in turn. According to the first, deliberation in good faith can lead to 'correct' solutions through information-pooling of an almost mechanical sort. The mechanical process in question is most often thought of as a simple democratic aggregation of votes.

This result finds its most formal, robust expression in the Condorcet Jury Theorem. So long as each individual brings his or her own *independent* judgement to bear on the *same issue*, and individuals are on average

[44] Gutmann and Thompson (2002: 158).   [45] Rawls (1971: 358–9).

more likely to vote for the correct outcome than any incorrect one, then the Condorcet Jury Theorem shows that the plurality among a *large number of voters* is almost certain to be correct in its judgement.[46]

Condorcet's result is an incredibly powerful one. It shows that if voters are 51% likely to be right in a two-option choice, then the probability that the correct answer will be chosen by a majority among 10,001 voters is 97.8%. In a three-option choice, if voters are just a little more likely to choose correctly than randomly (if on average voters are 34% likely to be right), the probability that the correct answer will be chosen by a plurality among 10,001 voters is 81.4%.

There is no magic or mystery in these results. They are really nothing more than reflections of the law of large numbers. If people are on average 51% likely to be right, then among a very large group the chances are very high that the vote for the right answer is very close to 51% (and in any case well over 50%). If people are on average 34% likely to be right, then among a very large group the chances are very high that the vote for the right answer is very close to 34% (and in any case well over 33.333 . . . %).[47]

Although most commonly phrased in terms of voting, the Condorcet Jury Theorem can easily be rephrased in terms of 'judgement' more generally. That version would say: so long as each informant brings *independent* judgement to bear on the *same subject*, and individuals' judgements are on average *more likely to be correct* than in error, then the most common judgement among a *large number of individuals* is almost certain to be the correct judgement.

The Condorcet Jury Theorem is about group decisions. A parallel result can be derived from Bayesian models to show that under those same conditions the beliefs of individuals will track the truth increasingly closely. In a Bayesian model, an individual starts with (*a*) a 'prior' assessment of the probability of some proposition being true and (*b*) an assessment of the 'conditional probability' that some specific thing will happen if the proposition is true and (*c*) the 'conditional probability' that same thing will happen if the proposition is not true. Bayes's Formula then tells us how we should use those conditional probabilities

---

[46] Condorcet (1785). Among the seminal articles reintroducing that theorem into mainstream democratic theory are Barry (1964: 9), Grofman, Owen, and Feld (1983), Grofman and Feld (1988), and List and Goodin (2001).

[47] Goodin (2003*b*: ch. 5); the Bayesian analogue to this result is discussed in Goodin (2003*b*: ch. 6).

to update our prior probability assessment in light of the evidence as it comes in.[48]

Bayes's Rule is the cornerstone of standard prescriptive decision theory, in mathematics and statistics. Its natural home is in the science lab: there, the proposition in question is some 'scientific hypothesis'; and outcomes of experimental procedures are which we conditionalize our beliefs about the probability of its being true upon. To transfer this model to the political realm, we need merely think of each other person's vote as an additional piece of evidence, upon which basis we should update our own beliefs in line with Bayes's Rule.

Just as in the science laboratory, so too in the electorate: so long as the information (the result of any given experiment, in the lab; the views of any given voter, in the election) is more likely to be correct than not, then the more pieces of information you have arguing in one direction the more likely you should think that is to be true, after Bayesian updating. Exactly how quickly you become exactly how convinced depends upon the exact values of your prior and conditional probabilities. But broadly speaking, in the Bayesian model of individual belief-revision, just as in the Condorcet Jury Theorem model of group decision, the process is a rapidly increasing function of the number of more-reliable-than-not informants.[49]

These analytic results are broadly borne out by the results of a variety of real-world experiences. In one experiment, fifty-six students were asked to guess how many beans there were in a jar that actually contained 850 beans; averaging across the estimates of all the students, the 'group estimate' was closer than that of all but one of the students. In another experiment, contestants at a county fair were asked to guess the weight of an ox: the average guess across all the contestants was 1,197 lb; the actual weight was 1,198 lb. The most established 'prediction market', the Iowa Electronic Markets, predicts the outcome of US presidential elections better than most sample polls, predicting the 2004 outcome within a tenth of a percent.[50]

---

[48] Specifically, $p_{\phi|x} = [(p_{x|\phi})(p_\phi)]/[(p_{x|\phi})(p_\phi) + (p_{x|not-\phi})(p_{not-\phi})]$, where p_ϕ is the 'prior probability' which she originally assigned to the proposition ϕ; $p_{x|\phi}$ is the 'conditional probability' which she assigns to event x occurring given that ϕ is true (and $p_{x|not-\phi}$ the corresponding conditional probability that she assigns to event x occurring given that not-ϕ is true); and $p_{\phi|x}$ is the 'updated' (revised or 'posterior') probability which she assigns to ϕ being true, given that x has occurred.

[49] Young (1988) and Goodin (2003b: ch. 6); for calculations, see Goodin (2002: appendix).

[50] Sunstein (2006: 110). For an argument to use prediction markets to implement public policy, see Hanson (2003).

All that looks like good news for democracy-as-information-pooling.[51] All those models provide powerful grounds for thinking that collective judgements are likely to be much more reliable than individual ones. But these models also have strict limits of which we must be mindful, perhaps especially in applying them to sensitive issues. I shall highlight those limits by reference to the Condorcet Jury Theorem, but most of what I say in that connection generalizes to all other information-pooling models of democracy as well.

First, note that people have to be talking (or voting) about the 'same issue' as one another. Rawls, above, stipulates, for example, that everyone is voting in good faith on what they perceive to be in the public interest, rather than their own private interests. People voting on 'what is in my interest', when their interests differ, are voting on *different* questions— in which case the information-pooling arguments of the Condorcet Jury Theorem simply do not apply.[52]

With sensitive issues, that is sometimes precisely the problem. One reason an issue might be too sensitive to be resolved through democratic deliberation is precisely that some groups' interests are too deeply at stake to expect them to transcend their own positions and perspectives, and see the situation from a more Archimedean point of view that can be common to all. Slavery in Antebellum America might be one such example, racial politics in the post-Reconstruction South another.

Where that is the problem, there are no grounds for thinking that political deliberation will help resolve it. Certainly there is no reason for thinking that the Condorcet Jury Theorem guarantees that the political majority will be correct in its resolution of such issues.

Second, note that the Condorcet Jury Theorem crucially depends on an assumption about people's epistemic competence. Specifically, the average voter must be more likely to be right than wrong (or, more generally, to be more likely to favour the correct option more than any other). If that is not the case, then the mathematics of the theorem literally goes into reverse: if the average voter is more likely wrong than right, the majority

---

[51] Perhaps too good, in various respects. One is that, among a very large group of voters, even very narrow proportional majorities are almost certainly correct; in these terms a 75% majority is virtually no more persuasive than a 50.0001% majority. Another is that, among a very large group of voters, on the assumptions here specified, there seem to be no rational grounds for persisting opposition to that almost-certainly-correct majority (Goodin 2002; 2003b: ch. 7).

[52] Przeworski (1999: 28–9).

among a large group of voters is all the more certain to be wrong. That is why Rawls, along with many others, says it 'would be a mistake' to rely too heavily on this theorem alone.[53]

In certain ways, that reticence is excessive.[54] Still, there may be cases in which voters should indeed be expected to be 'worse than random' at picking the right outcomes. Psychologists tell us about a wide range of cognitive and perceptual errors to which humans generally are prone.[55] Of course, if each person were at risk merely of judging wrongly each in his or her own way, their errors would cancel each other out and the Condorcet Jury Theorem would still hold. But given that each person judges wrongly in ways that s/he shares with others, owing to certain constants of human psychology, such a 'common-mode failure' can indeed lead the majority into error.

In highly structured, highly divisive political systems of the sort where political sensitivities abound, voters receive the bulk of their information about broader public issues from much the same sources: one of a handful of television stations, newspapers, political parties, etc.[56] The combination of shared signals and shared psychologies threaten, at least in some important cases, to undermine that assumption. Thus, for example, a divided society with a yellow press regularly pushing people's 'hot buttons' is not one in which one can seriously expect democratic deliberations to lead the majority to reach 'correct' determinations. There, a key requirement of the Condorcet Jury Theorem would be missing.

---

[53] Rawls (1971: 357–8). See similarly: Waldron (1989: 1322–3; 1999: 135), Estlund (1993: 93), and Gaus (1997: 150).

[54] All that the Condorcet Jury Theorem requires is that voters be 'better than random' at picking the right outcome, and 'better than random' is a very low standard. People who know absolutely nothing about an issue would choose sides on it purely at random. Furthermore, the Condorcet Jury Theorem merely asks that voters on *average* are better than that (Grofman, Owen and Feld 1983)—which is compatible with lots of voters being worse than random.

[55] People's judgements are systematically distorted by how choices are 'framed' (they will react differently to a description framed in terms of losses rather than gains, even though the situation depicted by those two alternative descriptions is identical); they are systematically distorted by 'anchoring effects' (what is the status quo or 'default' option); they are systematically affected by the judgements of others around them (adjusting their own reports to fit those of others); and they are systematically striving to reduce 'cognitive dissonance' (to avoid believing two things at the same time that, while logically consistent, nonetheless have pragmatically opposing implications). See Kahneman, Slovic, and Tversky (1982), Kahneman and Tversky (2000), Kuran (1995), and Sunstein (2006: ch. 2).

[56] Again, that would not compromise in itself the mathematics underlying the Condorcet Jury Theorem, so long as each voter brought his or her own independent perspective (his or her own 'private' information) to bear when reacting to the shared mass stimulus. Insofar as that is true, Rawls (1971: 358) worries wrongly that discussion among legislators violates the independence that the Condorcet proof requires is based on a misunderstanding of what is actually required (Goodin 2003*b*: ch. 5).

Third, information-pooling models like the Condorcet Jury Theorem and Bayes's Rule say, in essence, that the more independent observers who tell you something is true, the more likely it is to be true. But that works only to the extent that they really are *independent* observers. Insofar as they are themselves all relying on the same source of evidence, the fact that they concur does not tell you much. Where people have no independent information above and beyond what they read in the one daily newspaper, the fact that thousands of them there agree is evidence only that that is what that one newspaper said.[57] But in terms of information-processing models like the Condorcet Jury Theorem, that constitutes just *one* report, not thousands, of what is true.

Similar problems arise with interdependent 'bloc' voting. Where one person votes some way, just because the leader of his or her bloc said to vote that way, the effective number of independent points of view for Condorcet Jury Theorem purposes is not the thousands of voters but the handful of bloc leaders. In deeply divided societies, where there are tightly organized blocs of voters who systematically vote whatever way the leaders of their blocs say, the presuppositions of information-processing models like the Condorcet Jury Theorem would once again fail. There, the ordinary political process of open debate and a free vote is virtually no much more likely to choose the 'correct' outcome.[58]

Fourth, and somewhat more informally, the Condorcet Jury Theorem presupposes a world in which everyone is prepared to believe that every other is roughly as likely to be correct in his or her judgement as one is oneself. Suppose instead we have a divided and highly polarized society, where people suppose that they and people like them ('having similar opinions to them') are more likely to be right than wrong, and that people unlike them ('having dissimilar opinions to them') are more likely to be wrong than right. Then each side would be perfectly warranted by the logic underlying the Condorcet Jury Theorem in believing that they are right—and in believing that all the more firmly, because others say that they are wrong. Where opinion is deeply polarized in this particular way, there is no epistemic point in discussing things with others: their views

---

[57] 'No' independent information is obviously an extreme case: most people bring *some* independent perspective to bear in reading what they have read. How much of an independent perspective is required to make the Condorcet Jury Theorem work is something that, to my knowledge, has not been explored formally. But informally it seems clear that there must be some trade-off between 'degrees of interdependence' and 'numbers of voters'; so in a very large electorate, there can be very substantial (but not total) interdependence among voters, and the Theorem will still hold good.

[58] Goodin (2006).

are immediately discredited by the sheer fact that they disagree with one's own.

Fifth, and perhaps most obviously, the Condorcet Jury Theorem is applicable only where 'truth' is at stake, where as a matter of pure fact one outcome is objectively the 'correct' outcome. Consider in contrast more evaluative tasks, where there is no objectively correct answer: whether boysenberry ice cream tastes good, for example. That is just a matter of taste, and the fact that most people's tastes differ from mine does not provide any sort of epistemic warrant for me supposing that the majority view of this matter must be the correct one.

Morality is not purely a matter of taste, of course. Even if it is purely a social convention, there is a right and wrong of the matter as to whether that *is* our convention—and people whose convention it is should all have some independent access to that fact. 'Moral realists' would go further, insisting that there are facts about morality that are as objective as any other facts about the world—and once again, those are facts to which each individual should presumably have some independent access.

Most evaluative tasks lie somewhere in between the polar cases of thinking boysenberry ice cream is good and thinking that torturing babies is wrong. Elements of objective fact (of various sorts) and of subjective value (of various degrees) are intermixed, in complex ways, in any evaluative exercise. And contentious matters requiring political resolution certainly usually involve both evaluative and more ordinarily epistemic issues. In those mixed fact-and-value disputes, more purely information-pooling of the sort envisaged by the Condorcet Jury Theorem certainly has something substantial to contribute to that more purely epistemic task, even if it cannot settle everything (not in exactly the same way, in any case) on the evaluative front.[59]

---

[59] Stronger claims are sometimes made. Gutmann and Thompson (2002: 158), for example, say that 'the epistemic allure of deliberation is especially great when the justification for a decision must combine factual and evaluative matters'. In 'most health care decisions', for example, 'while experts may be the best judges of scientific evidence, they have no special claim to finding the right answer about priorities when degrees of risk and trade-offs of costs and benefits are involved'. Even granting that experts have no claim to expertise on those latter matters, it is an open question whether the public do either: whether, in other words, risk preferences ought to be regarded as tastes which ought to be respected or as truths to be discovered. Only if they have some objective truth status would the contribution of public deliberation on them be properly described as 'epistemic'.

4.2.3. *Desensitizing Disagreements: Premise Probing*

The long and the short of those various considerations is this: Where there are deep social divisions, there may be no good reason to suppose that the deliberative process is likely to work via information-pooling to resolve matters.

Discussion and deliberation have a very different role to play in those circumstances. Rather than leading to conclusions that are compelling from an epistemic point of view, deliberation in these other sorts of cases can serve a 'premise-revealing' function. That in turn can help to demonstrate the reasonableness of different points of view, thus 'desensitizing' if not literally 'resolving' the issue.

In any piece of formal reasoning, premises are required before conclusions can be derived. The conclusions are justified by reference to the premises and rules of inference, but the premises themselves are just 'assumed to be true', without argument.[60] Of course, premises and conclusions typically nest in chains of reasoning. What serve as premises in one piece of reasoning will have been established by the conclusions of another piece of reasoning. But at some point, the chain has to stop. Some premises just have to be 'taken as true', without argument.

Working back up those chains of reasoning, the boldest hope would be to find some 'overlapping consensus' as regards those basic unargued-for premises. There, the hope is to find some such 'basic' premises upon which everyone can agree, however different may be the conclusions and first-order beliefs that they then go on to derive from them. Maybe the fundamental principle, which each of us elaborates in our own different way, is the utilitarian one of maximizing the surplus of pleasure over pain. Or maybe it is satisfying the will of some God or gods. Or maybe it is the golden rule. Or whatever.

It is of course a purely contingent matter whether or not we will be able to find some such basic premises that are shared as common ground among all parties to the conversation. That just depends on the nature of the beliefs afoot within the political community. Sometimes the trick might work. Often, presumably, it will not.

---

[60] It is equally true in formal logic as pure mathematics: 'the proper business of the pure mathematician is to derive theorems from postulated assumptions, and... it is not his concern as a mathematician to derive whether the axioms he assumes are actually true' (Nagel and Newman 1964: 11).

A more modest hope along similar lines would be to find an 'overlapping consensus' of a more pragmatic sort, wherein everyone converges (each for his different reasons) on the same conclusion.[61] Whether or not this can be done, too, is a contingent matter, depending again on the particular beliefs afoot within the community.

Discussion obviously has an important role to play in probing both those possibilities. In talking through our differences, we might well find that there are certain premises that we share; and we can then start looking more closely at where exactly our approaches begin to diverge. Or in talking around our differences, we might find that we can easily enough agree on what needs to be done, just so long as we keep our deep disagreements over 'first principles' out of the discussion.[62] If political deliberation succeeds in either task, it will have been a great success. This is Gutmann and Thompson's explicit ambition.[63]

Here, however, I want to focus on ways in which political discussion and debate might still succeed, without accomplishing anything nearly as grand as either of those goals. Even if political discussion and debate does not so much produce a 'consensus', even of these contingent 'overlapping consensus' sorts, it may nonetheless reveal the premises underlying the conclusions of the various parties to the discussion. And that can be a major contribution in its own right.

The thought is just this: in ordinary discourse, we generally proceed on the assumption that others are pretty much like us. Rather than belabouring the point, we typically offer the merest of gestures towards arguments, expecting others to catch the allusions.[64] We talk principally in terms of conclusions, offering in ordinary discussion only the briefest argument-sketch hinting at the reasoning leading us to those conclusions.

We do so precisely so as not to belabour the point, needlessly. As discussion and deliberation proceed, however, we discover we are not on exactly the same wavelength. It becomes clear, upon probing, that the other just does not 'get our point'. At various points each of us says to the other, 'But why on earth do you believe *that*?' By way of explanation, we proceed to elaborate in fuller detail our underlying reasoning.

In so doing, we proceed to excavate the underlying premises. We do so, either until we reach premises upon which we can both agree (thus

---

[61] Rawls (1993: Lec. 4). As Rawls (2001: 33) says in his *Restatement*: 'The fundamental concepts, principles and virtues of the political conception are theorems, as it were, of [i.e. derived from] their comprehensive views.'

[62] Sunstein (1996b: ch. 2; 1996a).

[63] Gutmann and Thompson (1996, 2004: 11–12, 79–90).   [64] Grice (1975, 1989).

achieving an 'overlapping consensus' of the sort described above) or else until we hit primitive assumptions for which we can offer no further underlying premises.

The former is of course the more satisfactory scenario. But even in that latter, less happy scenario, going through that discursive process together might help to reassure people, in a divided society, of the 'reasonableness' of those on the other side of the social division.[65] Indeed, it might do so in two respects.

First of all, simply by going through this process of displaying our reasoning, we reassure one another that our position is not arbitrary or groundless. Others might think your grounds are not *good* grounds; but once this process gets underway (and assuming it proceeds in moderately good faith) at least those others cannot seriously believe that you have *no grounds*. Displaying chains of reasoning to one another in these ways shows everyone that one another's beliefs are reasoned, even if they are not in the end persuaded that they are right.

There is a second way this process can sometimes help to desensitize disputes. Suppose that in the course of these discussions the excavation of premises gets all the way back to everyone's 'first principles'. Everyone is then reduced to saying, 'Well, that seems to be as far as I can go in explaining to you why I believe as I do: I cannot think of any deeper premise from which that premise can be derived; I just take that to be indubitably true'.[66] In that scenario, everyone will have to concede that they are in a symmetrical argumentative position to everyone with whom they are disagreeing.

Up to this point, recall, the others have shown themselves reasonable in the sense of being willing to give reasons—just as you have. But at this point both of you are stumped. Argumentatively, you have fought one another to a standstill. There is nothing to do at that point except to declare it a draw—or go to war. Of course, you can at this point simply give up the arguing game and resort to force. But having been drawn that deeply into the arguing game, you will presumably be reluctant to take up cudgels at that point. More likely you will declare it a draw, argumentatively, and either leave things undecided (if you can afford to) or simply put the matter to a vote (if a decision one way or the other is strictly required).[67]

---

[65] Which is how 'difference' becomes a 'resource for democratic communication' for Young (2000: ch. 3), and how the phenomenology of 'listening' works for Bickford (1996: ch. 5).

[66] cf. Norman (1998).

[67] On 'leaving things undecided', see Sunstein (1996a, 1996b).

'Reasonable disagreement' is a fact of life in complex societies. Rawls discusses the phenomenon by reference to 'comprehensive doctrines': religious worldviews and such like.[68] But similar phenomena arise in connection with disagreements over matters of a more mundane and less cosmic sort. Deliberating together with others who profoundly disagree with us over sensitive and contested issues might, through the premise-revealing dynamics I have sketched, lead to broadly that sort of result.[69]

4.3. The Politically Undiscussable Revisited

All this suggests that there might be considerable scope for public discussion and debate even of sensitive issues. Discussion and debate can make a considerable contribution towards helping us come to terms with those issues, even if not strictly resolve them.

Some topics (those discussed in Section 4.2.1) may remain pragmatically pointless to discuss. Of course, even where there are limits on what can usefully be debated, those limits *themselves* can often be profitably subjected to discussion and debate. While there is literally no point debating what to do about things that are impossible, it is well worth discussing whether or not something really is impossible. There may be no point in debating something that is beyond the power of the assembly to resolve; but it is well worth discussing whether or not this thing really is within the power of the assembly. Maybe we cannot openly debate whether some particular fact should be kept secret (openly debating it makes the fact public), but we can and should debate the general principles of public policy classifying some things secret. And even as regards issues that we clearly cannot resolve by discussion alone, discussion is important in clarifying the nature of our disagreements (to show us that the disagreements really are of that sort) and in helping us see what further facts might be needed actually to resolve the issue. In all these connections, there might

[68] Rawls (1993: 60) hopes that his citizens will come to see that 'it is not in general unreasonable to affirm any one of a number of reasonable comprehensive doctrines. We recognize that our own doctrine has (and can have) for people generally, no special claims on them beyond their own view of its merits. Others who affirm doctrines different from ours are, we grant, reasonable also, and certainly not unreasonable. Since there are many reasonable doctrines, the idea of the reasonable does not require us, or others, to believe any specific reasonable doctrine, though we may do so'.

[69] 'Mutual accommodation' in the face of 'deliberative disagreement', in Gutmann and Thompson's terms (1996: 73–94).

well be some pragmatic point to discussions, if not exactly 'of' anyway 'related to' items in this first category of topics that might be deemed politically undiscussable.

We might not literally 'put these things to a vote', in the mechanical way the Condorcet Jury Theorem envisages. But in all those cases the general 'weight of opinion' can and should ordinarily loom large in deciding of how to circumscribe the bounds of discussability in all those ways. The great exception to that rule comes in cases of deeply divided societies. There, there is no particular reason to think that the opinion of the majority faction is necessarily likely to be right. In those cases, the 'weight of opinion' cannot literally 'resolve' any issues. At most, discussion there might help desensitize issues in the second 'premise-probing' way I have sketched.

With respect to the second class of politically undiscussable topics— ones that merely seem 'impolitic' to discuss—discussion can help in that second way, if not the first. In a highly polarized setting, maybe discussion cannot hope literally to 'establish truths', as in other contexts it might via Condorcet Jury Theorem sorts of processes. Still, by helping us understand the suppressed premises involved in others' reasoning, public deliberation can help us see others as 'reasonable' (albeit, in our own view, still wrong); and seeing them as reasonable can help us live with our differences. Even if we cannot expect literally to 'resolve' issues like that through public discussion, there might nonetheless be a genuinely useful purpose to be served in pondering together why people might find some topics so tender as to be generally undiscussble.[70]

Once we have seen through that sort of a discussion *why* people would take offence or would react in some uncontrolled way to such discussion, we might have discussed the matter enough to satisfy all concerned. We will have come to see that they had their reasons for reacting in that way. Even if those are reasons that we do not share, the sheer fact that those others can be seen to have reasons that are on a par with our own can qualify those people in our eyes as 'reasonable'.

In short, people can be seen to be 'reasonable' without being 'right'. We can go far towards desensitizing contentious issues, without resolving

---

[70] Perhaps at first brush there may seem to be an air of paradox in 'discussing why something is undiscussable', akin in certain respects to that associated with 'debating whether to close debate'. But the paradox is more apparent than real. We can discuss *why* someone might take moral offence at being called certain names or at taking a vote on whether or not to outlaw their religious observances, without actually *calling* the person that name or actually *putting* the observances to a vote.

them, merely by showing ourselves each to be reasonable in our differing ways of approaching those issues. If political deliberation, in its premise-probing mode, can help to do that, it will have made a major contribution towards defusing issues that might otherwise poison public life. Talking politics can always hope to make that more modest sort of contribution towards desensitizing sensitive issues—ones we might initially have been tempted to deem 'undiscussable' altogether.

5

How talk informs

When democratic theory took its deliberative turn, what it deliberately turned away from was, as I have said, 'aggregative democracy'. Democracy as deliberative democrats understand it centrally involves people in giving one another reasons, not simply in adding up people's votes. That is the central claim of deliberative democracy.[1]

In principle, there are many mechanisms by which we might ascertain the reasons that other people have for judging things as they do. One way certainly would be for them to tell us face-to-face.[2] Another is for them to write a letter to the editor of our local newspaper, or give an interview to the local radio station.[3] Yet another is for them to put a bumper sticker on their car or spray-paint graffiti on the wall of our local supermarket.[4] Yet another is for us simply to imagine ourselves in their place, and try hard to think what we would say if we were in their shoes.[5]

Among all these ways of ascertaining other people's reasons, the first—face-to-face communication—has come to enjoy pride of place among deliberative democrats. They freely admit that all those other things happen too. Indeed, they freely admit that those other channels of communication can be essential to effective deliberation, at least in certain circumstances. In particular, they admit that those other communication channels have to supplement (and maybe even substitute for) face-to-face deliberation in large-scale mass democracy. All those concessions and qualifications notwithstanding, talking face-to-face clearly remains the paradigm case of deliberation for deliberative democrats.

---

[1] The terms are conventionally credited to Miller (1992) but the fundamental distinction arguably dates from Riker (1983).
[2] Laslett (1956).   [3] Page (1996).   [4] Young (2000).   [5] Goodin (2003b).

What deliberative democrats want, then, is for people to *talk face-to-face*.[6] *Why* they want them to do that is to tap the 'wisdom of the multitude' by *pooling information*.[7] One variation is Aristotle's: different people know different things; if they got together and pooled everything that any of them knew, then together they would know more things than any of them knew separately.[8] Another variation on that theme is Condorcet's: the larger the group of minimally competent observers, the more confident we can be in the group's collective judgement. Yet another form of information to be pooled concerns our premises.

Putting together the 'what' and the 'why', 'deliberative democracy' can be defined as 'information pooling by means of talk'. There is nothing incoherent about that aspiration. Talking together is certainly one way of pooling information. Notice, however, that that is only one among many ways of pooling information. All the other ways of communicating with one another mentioned earlier are also ways of conveying information. Hence the puzzle at the heart of this chapter: insofar as the reason 'why' we want deliberative democracy is just to pool information,[9] then what justifies so much emphasis on one particular means of pooling information (talking face-to-face), to the exclusion of other equally good ways of pooling information?

Notice that on the Condorcet Jury Theorem and analogous Bayesian models of information pooling of the sort discussed in Section 4.2.2 there would be no need whatsoever for people to talk together.[10] You need merely feed your information mechanically into the decision process. Indeed, the Condorcet Jury Theorem procedures are almost as mechanical as the model of aggregative democracy that deliberative democrats so malign. Whereas aggregative democracy simply counts qualified votes, the Condorcet procedure simply counts competent opinions; and the

---

[6] Fishkin's model (1995: 33) was inspired by Laslett (1956); see further Fishkin and Laslett (2003b: 1).

[7] Those like Cohen (1989: 22, 1996: 99–101) who emphasize the legitimation function of deliberation might prefer to phrase this in terms of giving one another 'reasons'. Here, 'information' should be understood in a suitably generic way that embraces information about others' beliefs and desires and principled commitments as well as information about more mundane facts about the natural world.

[8] 'Some appreciate one part, some another, all together appreciate all' (Aristotle 1984b: 1281a 43–69, p. 66).

[9] And that may not be the only reason, as the discussion of 'premise probing' in Section 4.2.3 has shown.

[10] It is sometimes thought that the Condorcet Jury Theorem's requirement that jurors act independently of one another actually precludes any communication between them; but all that really matters is that they each form their own independent judgment after they have talked.

option supported by the most competent opinions is deemed the winner. Bayesian decision-making, updating our judgements in light of feedback from others, does much the same.

I am not saying that those are the only or even necessarily the very best ways of pooling information. But clearly they are very respectable ways of pooling information, which do not necessarily involve any face-to-face talk. Furthermore, the Condorcet Jury Theorem is itself often invoked by deliberative democrats precisely to justify the 'why' of deliberative democracy: the Condorcet Jury Theorem, as I have said, provides a powerful demonstration of the value of pooling different people's information. Ironically, in the Condorcet Jury Theorem, that effect can be achieved perfectly well without the very thing that deliberative democrats say is what they want, which is talking face-to-face.

In this chapter, I attempt to bring the 'why' and the 'what' of deliberative democratic theory into closer alignment. I begin by pointing to various ways in which pooling information in the ordinary mechanical way might mislead us, in ways that talking together can help us avoid. Having thus identified some of the functions of talking in small-scale, face-to-face settings, I then turn to consider how we might institutionalize the functional equivalent of that for large-scale political decision-making where it is literally impossible for everyone to talk with one another face-to-face.

5.1. Pooling Information, Mechanically versus Discursively

When talking about 'pooling information in the ordinary mechanical way', I am not going to be evoking any particularly fancy or refined model. Basically, I will be talking simply in terms of a generic Bayesian procedure of updating our beliefs in light of information received from others, how much depending on the credence we attach to their reports. If someone whom you think to be a tolerably reliable reporter tells you that something is true, then you adjust upwards your own assessment of the probability that it is true. If someone else whom you trust tells you the same thing, you do so again. What could be more natural?

Mechanically pooling information like that is going to be distinguished from pooling information 'discursively'. In the mechanical process, you simply take some probability numbers and enter them into Bayes's Formula, and that formula yields your new 'updated' probability of the proposition being true. The discursive process differs in allowing you to probe not only what the other person's probability assessment is but also why she thinks that to be so.

What is particularly interesting in the context of our present discussion is that some of what you learn from talking to someone about why she thinks as she does constitutes information that would lead you either to increase or decrease our confidence in her as a reliable reporter. (In Bayesian terms, it would alter the conditional probability we assign to something being true if she says it is true.) Here are some examples.

5.1.1. *Should the Numbers Count?*

Ordinarily when mechanically pooling information, the more people who say something is true the more confident we should be that that proposition is indeed true. As Locke advises us in his chapter on probability in *An Essay Concerning Human Understanding*, 'As the number of testifiers increases, so it becomes more likely that that they testify is true'.[11]

This is sometimes derided as 'groupthink' or the 'common knowledge fallacy'.[12] And sometimes we might of course be overly influenced by the fact that everyone around us says something, denying the evidence of our own eyes that one line really is longer than another, and so on.[13]

Still, in good Bayesian terms, it generally makes a lot of sense to think that the more people who say something is true, the more likely it is to be true. But of course that only makes sense if you think that those people are tolerably reliable informants. If instead you think they are all liars, or heavily biased, then the sheer fact that there are a lot of them asserting the same proposition does not give you any (or anyway, nearly as much) reason to revise your own assessment. Still, such pathologies are reasonably rare in ordinary social life. Most people most of the time are moderately good informants about most sorts of things. Or anyway, we tend to assume they are, unless we have some particular reason for thinking otherwise.

When we get to talking to people about why they think as they do, however, it typically becomes clear that some people's opinions should count for lots more than others'. It might become clear that some people

---

[11] Locke (1975: book IV, ch. 15, § 5); quoted in Shapin (1994: 213).

[12] Janis (1982) and Sunstein (2006: 84).   [13] Asch (1956) and Bond and Smith (1996).

have specialized knowledge that others lack. Your interlocutor might have been trained as a civil engineer, which makes his assessment of the probability that a bridge will collapse in a high wind much more reliable than just the ordinary untrained person's.[14]

Or again, your interlocutor might have experiences that others do not. On the basis of their experiences, most white Americans doubted O. J. Simpson's claim that the police had framed him, because the experience of most white Americans of the police is that they simply do not do that sort of thing. But in the experience of black Americans, they definitely do. Learning that your interlocutor is black, and that blacks (like O. J. Simpson) have systematically different experiences with the police, would once again make you weigh your black interlocutor's assessment much more heavily than the average white person's.[15]

On the basis of talking with people, then, you might decide some people's information or experience is such that their opinions should weigh much more heavily than others'. Having decided that, you might well end up overturning the ordinary propensity within Condorcet-Bayes reasoning to 'go with the majority'. The opinion of a more reliable minority, if it is sufficiently more reliable, might weigh more heavily with you than the opinion of a less reliable majority.

That is of course precisely as it should be on good Bayesian logic, I hasten to add. The credence we place on any given informant's report is a crucial part of Bayesian calculations. My point here is merely that oftentimes it is by talking to people—by pooling information with them discursively, rather than just taking the probability assessments they give us and mechanically cranking through the Bayesian formula— that we discover that some informants are more credible than others. Having discovered that fact, we can (and should) adjust our Bayesian calculations accordingly. But had we proceeded to the Bayesian calculation straightaway, without talking with them about the reasons for their opinions, we might never have discovered that crucial fact— a fact crucial to proper implementation of the Bayesian aggregation itself.

[14] Locke (1975: book IV, ch. 15, §§1, 4) once again advises us to consider 'the skill of the witnesses' in assessing testimony.

[15] This case is represented in Locke by the parable of the Dutch ambassador testifying to the King of Siam that in his country water sometimes froze so hard that elephants (were there any in Holland) could walk on it; the ambassador has experience of living in both Holland and Siam, in a way the King does not, so the King should attach extra credence to the ambassador's report (Locke 1975: book IV, ch. 15, §5).

5.1.2. Adjusting for Known Biases

Here is another way in which it helps to pool information discursively rather than merely mechanically. Sometimes by talking to someone you can discover that he has a pile of prejudices or prior commitments that will inevitably bias his reports in one particular direction.

If you had no reason to suppose your informant was biased—if you had no reason to doubt that she was as reliable when reporting P as she is when reporting not-P—then when mechanically updating your own beliefs in light of her reports you would give either report from her equal weight. But once you have had a chance to talk with her and discover the extent and direction of her biases, you no longer would treat either sort of report from her the same.

Naturally, you would discount reports from her that go 'with the grain' of her known biases. You know she is not going to be too hard on her own favourite theories.[16] When scientists in the pay of the tobacco industry publish reports denying any link between smoking and cancer, one simply takes no notice.

But it would be wrong simply to ignore reports from biased observers altogether.[17] Occasionally (perhaps only very occasionally) the reports we receive from biased observers go against the grain of their known biases. In those cases, information from biased observers would be epistemically highly useful—and it would be all the more so because of their biases.

Suppose some scientist who has staked his professional career on the proposition that smoking does not cause cancer is suddenly seen to be reporting that, in fact, smoking does cause cancer. We can be pretty confident that that scientist has come to that conclusion grudgingly. We can be pretty confident that he has double-checked his facts many times. We can be pretty sure that he would not have made this report—so contrary to all he has published previously—unless he were really very confident that this report is correct. And knowing that he has subjected his reports that 'go against the grain' to special scrutiny of this sort, we ourselves can be all the more confident in the veracity of those reports.

In other words, evidence from biased observers can be one-way decisive. It will be of little epistemic use to us when (as is most often the case) it 'goes with the grain of the informant's known biases'. But it can be of

---

[16] A survey of 206 articles examining the nutritional effects of drinks found that industry-funded studies were up to eight times more likely to be positive towards the drinks than publicly funded studies (Lesser et al. 2007; reported in Curtis 2007).

[17] Which is Locke's advice, i.e. 'Believe people who have no reason to misrepresent how things are' (Locke 1975: book IV, ch. 15, §§4–5; quoted in Shapin 1994: 223).

considerable epistemic use to us when (as occasionally happens) it 'goes against the grain of the informant's known biases'.[18]

Again, this is something that ought clearly to be taken into account in any proper Bayesian updating procedure. When you discover that someone is biased in favour of proposition P, then the conditional probability you attach to the proposition that 'P is true, given that she says it is true' ought to fall; and conversely, the conditional probability that you attach to the proposition that 'not-P is true, given that she says it is true' ought to rise.

My point is not that Bayesians are oblivious to these considerations, nor do I deny that they have machinery to take them into account. My point is merely that if we were just pooling information in the more mechanistic ways, we might never discover that our informants were indeed biased in these ways. More discursive methods of information pooling can help alert us to that fact, which even mechanistic information-pooling Bayesians agree is a crucial fact.

5.1.3. Overcoming Caution

Here is another setting in which discursive rather than merely mechanical pooling of information might yield further important information that we would like to take into account.

Imagine you are a member of a jury, and the case you are hearing is a tort action in which a large corporation is being sued over a large oil spill that has caused considerable environmental damage. The plaintiff asks for damages of $2 million. That sounds like an awfully lot of money to you; then again, it was an awfully big oil spill, and a lot of sea life was destroyed by it. So, as you sit listening to the judge summing up the case, you privately conclude that $2 million is probably about the right damages. Having taken a course in statistics, you then remember that you should not only choose a 'point estimate'; you should also choose a 'confidence interval'. So you decide, again privately, that so far as you are concerned the right result is awarding the plaintiff $2 million, plus or minus a half million; you are 95% sure that the right result lies somewhere within that interval.

Here comes the interesting twist in the tale. Suppose you all retire to the jury room and the foreperson of the jury straightaway asks everyone to write down on a piece of paper two things: (*a*) whether or not they

[18] These arguments are elaborated more fully in Goodin (2007*a*).

think the defendant is guilty; and (*b*) if guilty, what damages ought to be awarded against the defendant.

You have no hesitation in writing, 'Guilty'. But over the amount of damages, you hesitate. Two million dollars is, after all, a lot of money, and you are naturally cautious in making judgements involving that much money. So when writing down your vote for damages, you do not report your point estimate ($2 million) but rather something towards the bottom end of your confidence interval ($1.75 million, say). That is the cautious thing to do, and you are a cautious person, at least when it comes to sums of money as massive as that.

There are two ways the jury decision-making might proceed at this point. The way real juries proceed is, of course, discursively: real jurors would talk through their reasons for the judgements they have just written down. But suppose that every member of the jury has written down exactly what you wrote down: '(*a*) guilty; (*b*) $1.75 million'. One can easily imagine a jury foreperson, anxious to get home, seizing upon the fact of that unanimity and announcing, 'Well, we all seem to be of one mind, so let's go back into court and announce that as our verdict'. That would, in effect, be to aggregate jurors' opinions mechanically rather than discursively.

What would that mechanical pooling of information of jurors miss out? Well, obviously, their reasoning that underlay the judgements that they have written down. The crucial bit of that reasoning, in the story I have just been telling, is the fact that each of the jurors—acting independently—might have been cautiously underreporting her 'true' ('point') estimate of how much damages ought to be awarded. You know you did. Maybe all the others did likewise.

Suppose, therefore, you put your hand up in response to the foreperson's proposal, and suggest that instead of simply polling the jury and reporting back the unanimity thus uncovered, you go around the jury table and ask everyone to state briefly the reasoning that led them to the conclusions they have just written on that piece of paper. Suppose that when you do that, you discover that everyone had indeed been reasoning exactly like you: everyone thought that the right amount of damages would be $2 million; but everyone was being cautious and reporting something towards the lower end of their confidence interval, and hence the unanimous (under)report of $1.75 million. Having heard that discussion, and perhaps recalling the Condorcet Jury Theorem, everyone on the jury would then be emboldened to revert to their original point estimate of $2 million. Their prudent caution when forming a private judgement is overcome by confirmation from many other independent and equally reliable jurors.[19]

This general sort of phenomenon is sometimes actually observed, both in psychological experiments and in actual juries. Some people—most famously, Cass Sunstein—deride it as 'group polarization' and deem it a pathological aspect of group deliberation, another manifestation of 'groupthink'.[20] But what if what drives 'group polarization' is the perfectly logical sequence of adjustments I have just been describing?[21] If that is what underlies it, then 'group polarization' looks more like 'correcting for caution that is no longer warranted'—which is surely something that we would rationally like to see happen.

So too would Bayesians, of course. Again, it is not as if they would have any objection in the least to these sorts of adjustments occurring; on the contrary, they would insist upon them. My point, once again, is merely that if we were simply mechanically aggregating judgements— counting how many jurors voted for damages of $1.75 million on the original tally sheets—we would never have uncovered the crucial piece of evidence that everyone agrees we should also take into account. It was only through discussion within the jury that everyone discovered that everyone else had originally returned an estimate that they themselves thought was 'on the low side' of what they really thought it should have been. Discursive information-pooling allowed that fact to emerge, in a way that mechanical information-pooling had not.

5.1.4. *Averting Unwelcome Cascades*

Another advantage of discursively rather than just mechanically pooling information is that that might help avert unwelcome cascades. By a 'cascade' I mean a sequence of moves in which each is an exaggerated version of the last; and by calling it an 'unwelcome cascade' I mean merely that everyone involved would have preferred where they started to where they ended up as a result of that process.

Here is the sort of thing I have in mind.[22] Suppose you live in a quiet neighbourhood, near but not too near the centre of Washington. Your

---

[19] I have sketched this scenario in Goodin (2007*b*).

[20] Sunstein (2002, 2006: 95). The evidence on the Group Polarization Effect is less unambiguous than Sunstein suggests, however; see e.g. Luskin, Fishkin, and Jowell (2002: 477 ff.).

[21] For what it is worth, there is social psychological evidence that people's confidence in their estimates increases after group discussion, particularly if they find others agree with them; see Baron et al. (1996).

[22] The example is adapted from Goodin and Jackson (2007).

neighbours are all busy people, and you only ever really have a chance to talk to them at the annual Christmas street party that you host. But you know they are all well-informed (indeed, some work for the CIA), sensible people. It has been a trying time in Washington: terrorists have crashed a plane into the Pentagon; there has been anthrax in the postal system; everyone is nervous. But you yourself do not think that there is all that much to fear from another terrorist attack.

Suddenly you see that your neighbour in the house on the corner has put duct tape around his windows. You had heard of others doing that as protection against a gas attack. You did not yourself think that remotely warranted, but maybe your neighbour knows something you do not. So on the basis of those inputs—the sheer observation of your neighbour's duct-tape windows, and what you infer about how likely he must think terrorist attacks are—you use Bayes's Formula to adjust your own assessment of the probability of a gas attack. It rises from 5% to 10%, in your updated view. Of course you are naturally risk-averse, particularly when it comes to really big threats like a gas attack. So that rise is enough to induce you to put duct tape on your windows, too. And then your neighbour down the street, seeing that two of you have duct tape in your windows, 'mechanically' updates her own probability assessments in light of those two new pieces of information; perhaps she started at 5% and now thinks gas attack is 15% likely. Accordingly, she hurries to tape her own windows. And so on up and down the street.

The effect of all that 'mechanical' Bayesian updating will have been a cascade, as first one and then the next of the neighbours cues on each other's behaviour and the judgements they infer underlay that behaviour. Come Christmas, the whole street's windows are all taped up. As a result of all the 'mechanical' Bayesian updating, everyone on the street thinks that gas attack is virtually imminent.

But it is Christmas, after all. So notwithstanding the terrorist threat you persist in your traditions and invite the whole street to your house for your annual party. For the first time all year you actually have a chance to chat with your neighbours. The imminent threat of gas attacks naturally looms large in those conversations. And once you all get to talking about it, you realize that nobody knows much more than you do about that threat; you were all just responding to what each other was doing, in putting up duct tape. You are all hugely relieved; you all enjoy a good laugh. But then you start wondering how this duct-tape business ever got started, and you trace it back to the fellow who lives on the corner. You wander over to where he is standing, and ask what special knowledge he had about the threat of gas attacks, that led him to tape up his own windows. 'Gas attacks?' he exclaims; 'Nothing to do with gas attacks! My wife had contracted pneumonia and we had to seal off any drafts!'

Now, if you had had a chance to talk to your neighbour on the corner, before drawing false inferences about what was leading him to tape up his windows, the cascade would never have occurred. And of course Bayesians would regret those false inferences as much as anyone else: if the evidence is being misinterpreted, the mechanisms of Bayes's Formula will be misled. So again, I am not telling Bayesians anything they do not already know.

My point is merely that it took 'discursive information-pooling'—the Christmas party—to bring out the fact that what we were all assuming was evidence of one thing (the probability of a gas attack) had nothing at all to do with that.

When updating our beliefs mechanically, using Bayes's Formula, we were doing so unaware of just how slender was an evidence base upon which we were relying. In updating her beliefs in light of the fact that both the person in the corner house and I have put duct tape on our windows, for example, our next neighbour was unwittingly just double-counting the evidence that the person living on the corner taped his windows: she simply did not realize, until talking to me at the Christmas party, that I did not know anything that the person living on the corner did not know.[23] And all of us were doing our updating, unaware that even the first-mover's beliefs were being fundamentally misinterpreted (nothing to do with gas attack, everything to do with his wife's pneumonia).

5.1.5. Promoting Welcome Cascades

Not all cascades are necessarily unwelcome ones, of course. Sometimes they result in us all being in a position that we prefer to the one we started out in. Let me close this catalogue with an example of that.

Consider the case of Chinese footbinding.[24] Arguably, at least at some point, nobody wanted to do that to their daughters. But everybody thought everybody else did; and your own daughter would not be able

[23] For a discussion of this sort of error, see Goodin and Jackson (2007). The judicious Hooker (1989: I, p. 13; quoted in Shapin 1994: 233) understood as much: 'Though ten persons be brought to give testimony in any cause, yet if the knowledge they have of the thing whereunto they come as witnesses appear to have grown from some one amongst them, and to have spread itself from hand to hand, they all are in force but as one testimony.'

[24] This example is loosely adapted from Mackie (1996). The more general point is pursued in a variety of applications by Kuran (1995).

to attract a marriage partner (in the right social class anyway) unless she looked like everyone else's daughter in that respect.

If we were restricted simply to mechanically aggregating external evidence, the conclusion would seem to be clear. From the fact that every girl (in this social class anyway) has her feet bound, it seems natural to infer that everybody (except me) wants to bind their daughters' feet.

Were we able to pool information discursively, however, it would become immediately apparent that the only reason I bind my daughter's feet is that I think you want to bind your daughter's, and vice versa—and so on for every other parent, and indeed for every marriage partner, in the community. Once a few of us stop the practice, and our daughters nonetheless find suitable partners, many others will immediately follow suit. We will see a cascade—this time, a welcome cascade—putting an end to that cruel practice.

Again, this is fundamentally just a matter of correcting false beliefs. And again, Bayesians are of course all in favour of correcting false beliefs. The point is just that mechanical means of pooling information, through manipulations of Bayes's Formula, would not necessarily have helped to correct those false beliefs. It took more discursive methods of information pooling to do that.

5.2. How Discursive Information-Pooling Helps

Those are some examples of how we might reach better decisions by pooling information discursively rather than merely mechanically. The list is not exhaustive; there may be whole broad categories that I have overlooked. Still, the examples on that list are sufficiently numerous and diverse as to convince me that this is not a quirky or isolated phenomenon.

What can we say about the general structure of the phenomenon? How exactly does discursive information-pooling improve our decisions across all these examples?

It does so, most fundamentally, by providing us with more information. Sometimes the extra information concerns the reliability of our informants. By talking to our informants, we discover that some of them have specialized information or distinctive experience that makes their reports more reliable; or we discover by talking to them that they are generally biased against precisely the sort of conclusion they have reached in this case, making their support for that conclusion all the more persuasive. Other times the extra information concerns the proper interpretation of the information that others are conveying to us. Once we get talking to our fellow jurors, we discover that each of them has cautiously underreported our true estimate of the appropriate damage award; once we get talking to our neighbours, we discover that none of us have any new information on the risk of terrorist attack and that we were all just misinterpreting the duct tape on our first neighbour's window; once we get talking to other parents, we realize that none of us really wants to bind our daughter's feet, and each of us was only doing it because we thought others expected it.

In short: pooling information discursively yields extra information, and that extra information proves crucial to reaching the right conclusions in examples I have been discussing. Furthermore, and most crucially for present purposes: that is information we would have missed had we just been pooling information mechanically, cranking through Bayes's Formula or taking a majority vote in a Condorcet-style jury. Once we have the extra information, we can of course feed that additional information into those more mechanical information-pooling procedures. But in the examples I have been describing, it took the discursive procedure to uncover that extra information in the first place.

Although talking face-to-face is how that extra information came to light in the particular examples I have been describing, however, that is not the only logically possible way in which that information might have come to light. In most of those cases, anyway, it is logically possible for the same information to have been uncovered without any face-to-face interaction at all. If we asked people to write down their estimate of the probability that the Sydney Harbour Bridge will collapse in a high wind, we could at the same time have asked them to write down their highest degree and what subject it was in. We could then have collated probability estimates according to whether people had higher qualifications in civil engineering or not, reporting the results back to all our informants and asking them to revise their own probability estimates in light of the distribution thus generated. You get the information about some people's expertise in that way, without any face-to-face conversations. Or again, the distinctive experiences of black Americans with the police could have been conveyed to people through a newspaper story about an academic study. The foreperson of the jury could have asked jurors to write down on the paper not a single number but rather their confidence interval. And so on.

In a few of the cases, however, it is harder to think how the crucial information might have emerged without people getting together and comparing notes. That is particularly the case in the last two instances of people misinterpreting others' actions. Sure, the man who lives in the corner house could have taped a note to his window explaining that his wife had pneumonia, and that is why he is taping around his windows. But it would quite possibly never occur to him to think that his neighbours were misinterpreting his actions as protection against terrorist attacks, or hence to put such a note in the window to dispel those misinterpretations.

The same is broadly true of all the other examples as well, once you begin to think about it. Sure, we could collect information on people's highest degree, or on their race, but it would not occur to us to do so unless we had some reason to believe that that information was going to be important. True, there might be academic studies aplenty to support the conclusion that it will be. But the way we get the idea that that extra information might be important in the very first place—before the studies have been done—is most typically by talking to people (in those cases, people with different knowledge bases or different patterns of experience with the police).

Thus, while there are (usually) ways other than talking face-to-face by which the extra information in question might be elicited and conveyed, talking face-to-face in a small-group setting is usually the best way to discover what extra information might need to be elicited and conveyed in those other ways.

5.3. Perfecting Information Pools for Mass Publics

This chapter has pointed to cases in which 'discursive information-pooling' is required to help identify *further* information that needs to be collected, somehow, from people before we precipitously pool in mechanical fashion (by voting, or such like) such information as we already have from them. Since that 'discursive information-pooling' usually needs to be done face-to-face, it is inevitably a small-scale enterprise. Talking simply takes too much time, among any remotely large group.

Of course, macro-political decision-making cannot be delegated to small groups of unelected deliberators. The decisions of small, unelected groups inevitably lack democratic legitimacy. But as Chapter 2 has shown, those micro-deliberative processes can be used as 'focus groups', to help us discover discursively what further information we need to collect and disseminate to democratic decision-makers before mechanically aggregating their views.

Political parties use small-scale 'focus groups' to 'market test' big ideas all the time, of course. There is generally a sense that there is something sleazy or illicit in that. Not least is the fact that politicians tend to use such focus groups, not to decide what to do, but rather to determine how best to 'sell' what they have already decided to do. Even those sleazy uses of micro-deliberative mechanisms might still serve democratic ends, however: recall from Section 2.2.4 the stories of how the New York Port Authority discovered that it simply could not 'sell' its original plan for rebuilding the World Trade Centre site to the New York public, and how the British government discovered that it simply could not sell genetically modified farming to the British public.

On the sort of analysis I have been developing, there are other good purposes served by small-scale deliberative groups talking face-to-face about what matters to people. In that way, such groups can help to identify what might be major lines of cleavage and what more information needs to be collected from the general public. The results of these micro-deliberations are not in and of themselves determinative of policy, of course. They merely constitute a way of discovering, by pooling information on the only scale that information can be pooled discursively, what other sorts of information we ought collect from people more broadly before pooling the views of the general public more mechanically.

That larger pooling of everyone's views, which must inevitably be done through those more mechanical voting processes in any large society, is what is democratically authoritative. But that democratically authoritative decision will be a far better one—more genuinely informed, in ways that matter to those making it themselves—if what is thus being aggregated is informed by smaller-scale discursive explorations of what sort of information might matter.

6

First talk, then vote

Certainly talk can be enormously informative in all the ways seen in previous chapters. Certainly talk can be an important aid in making good decisions.[1] But deliberative democrats say that they want to treat 'talk as a decision procedure'.[2] Should we *literally* adopt 'talk' as our decision procedure? Should we make decisions *purely* by talking together?

In any moderately large community, of course, deliberation must almost inevitably be supplemented by voting as the ultimate decision procedure. It is simply unrealistic to expect any moderately large group to come to complete consensus, however long they talk together. Critics of deliberative democracy press that point forcefully.[3] Deliberative democrats themselves usually concede that point without much fuss. Joshua Cohen, for example, acknowledges that 'even under ideal conditions there is no promise that consensual reasons will be forthcoming. If they are not, then deliberation concludes with voting, subject to some

---

[1] 'Can be', in deference to the fact that the evidence on whether or not group discussion improves the quality of decisions (Hastie 1986; Sunstein 2006: chs. 2–3). The evidence suggests, however, that groups learn faster than isolated individuals (Blinder and Morgan 2000; Kocher and Sutter 2005), and that there are increases in accuracy more often in groups that were heterogeneous rather than homogeneous in their initial opinions (Corfman and Kahn 2005).

[2] Schauer 1999. In Elster's (1998b: 1) words, 'The idea of deliberative democracy...is decision making by discussion among free and equal citizens.' I take it that deliberative democrats want 'talk' in order to reach a decision, and not merely as an end in itself or as a means to some other end (like 'building a sense of community' or 'teaching people to be good citizens who take other people's views into account'). At the very least, it would be self-defeating publicly to announce those other goals, in just the way that Elster (1986) shows it would be to publicly announce that the purpose of trial by jury is not to make good decisions on the case at hand but rather to train citizens for democracy.

[3] None more so than Przeworski (1998: 141): 'deliberative theorists...wish away the vulgar fact that under democracy deliberation ends in voting'. See similarly: Gould (1988: 18, 126–7) and Saward (1998: 64).

form of majority rule'.[4] Thus, deliberative democrats concede the pragmatic point, typically in a spirit of resigned acceptance.[5]

Here I shall offer a more principled reason for embracing the rule,
'first talk, then vote'. 'First talk', because talk can be a good 'discovery
procedure', as has already been shown. 'Then vote', because construed
as a decision procedure talk can be fatally flawed by 'path dependency',
rendering its outcomes indeterminate or arbitrary.[6]

Talking together can be a good way of getting all the options on the
table and exploring their strengths and weaknesses. It can be a good way
of sensitizing people to the perspectives of others. It can be a good way
of reminding people of just how diverse a community it is that will be
bound by the rules that they adopt. All that is an important input into
the decision process. But after having heard all that in the preceding
democratic conversation people ought to go away and vote, taking all
that into account.

6.1. What Kind of a Decision Procedure Is Talk?

When deliberative democrats talk of 'talk as a decision procedure', what
kind of decision procedure is it that they have in mind? What are its most
salient features, and what are its natural consequences?

[4] Cohen (1989: 23); see similarly Cohen and Sabel (1997: 320–1) and Manin (1987).
Habermas (1979: 90, 1982: 257–8) himself concedes that consensus might be an unattainable ideal, a point that other deliberative theorists make even more emphatically (e.g.
Bohman 1995; Dryzek 1990: 16–17). As Elster (1986: 115) says, 'One can discuss only for
so long, and then one has to make a decision, even if strong differences of opinion should
remain.... [E]ven assuming unlimited time for discussion, unanimous and rational agreement
might not necessarily ensue. Could there not be legitimate and unresolvable differences of
opinion over the nature of the common good? Could there not even be a plurality of ultimate
ends?'

[5] Dryzek (2000: 170), making a virtue of necessity, proclaims: 'In a pluralistic world,
consensus is unattainable, unnecessary and undesirable.' He thinks it is 'unnecessary'
because there can be 'incompletely theorized agreements' (Sunstein 1996a) 'in which participants agree on a course of action, but for different reasons'. While that certainly
relaxes the requirement of consensus, there is obviously no guarantee that even that
weaker form of consensus can always, or often, be found among large and heterogeneous
groups.

[6] A certain sort of deliberative democrat might shrug her shoulders and say: 'Any
outcome arrived at through due deliberation is as good as any other; the fact that a
deliberation in which the same people had spoken in a different order would have
yielded a different outcome in no way impugns the outcome actually reached.' But
I take it that most deliberative democrats are 'epistemic democrats' as well, valuing
deliberative procedures at least in part because they are more likely to yield 'correct' outcomes where there is some independent truth of the matter for decisions to
track.

6.1.1. *Talk as a Serial Process with Dynamic Updating*

Talk as a decision procedure has many peculiar features. Many of them can be very attractive, in ways already discussed. Standing back from all of these specific and attractive attributes, however, talk has one generic feature that makes it unattractive as a decision procedure.

To bring this feature into sharp focus, recall the central contrast between deliberative democracy and aggregative democracy. Deliberative democracy is organized around the idea of talk as a decision procedure. Aggregative democracy is organized around the idea of voting as a decision procedure.

Voting, notice, is a *simultaneous* process. Everyone votes at the same time. In an ideal voting system—or anyway, in the sort we would nowadays regard as ideal[7]—no one is supposed to know how anyone else has voted at the time of casting his or her own ballot. So, for example, a system where voting is spread over two days would be seriously flawed democratically if the first day's votes were counted and announced before voting began on the second day. (Indeed, it *is* a serious criticism of the US presidential elections that results of East Coast voting are often announced—or at least confidently predicted by television psephologists—before poll booths have closed on the West Coast.) In elections, people are supposed to be forming their own judgements and voting independently. That is why the secret ballot was introduced in the first place.[8]

Deliberative democrats, in contrast, are anxious for people to explain and defend their positions in the open forum. They are anxious for people to be discursively accountable to one another for the political positions they take concerning the governance of their common affairs.[9]

Talking, in contrast to voting, is a distinctly *serial* process. First one person speaks, and then the next, and then the next in turn. Furthermore, each person is supposed to listen to what others have said before and to respond appropriately. That is simply a matter of good conversational manners.

Deliberative democrats redouble the demands of sheer good conversational manners, in that respect. Listening attentively to one another is

[7] cf. Mill (1861: ch. 10).

[8] It was more often phrased in terms of preventing coercion and the selling of votes: but what is wrong with that is that votes thus influenced are not suitably 'independent'.

[9] After the fashion of Mill (1861: ch. 10). For early statements of this position within the contemporary deliberative democracy literature, see Mansbridge (1980: 33–4) and Brennan and Pettit (1990).

part and parcel of what is to deliberate together.[10] Discursive engagement requires interlocutors to pay attention to what one another is saying and to adjust their own positions and their own remarks appropriately.[11]

Translating those deliberative platitudes into the language of decision theory, that amounts to saying that deliberative democrats want '*dynamic updating* in public deliberation'.[12] In other words, deliberative democrats enjoin deliberators to revise their beliefs (broadly construed) as the conversation proceeds, speech-by-speech.

Dynamic updating is contrasted with *periodic updating*. When engaging in periodic updating, you just file away information as it comes in, and only update your beliefs on the basis of everything in the file at one particular point in time. 'Peripheral processing' discussed in Section 3.6.1 would involve merely periodic updating, whereas 'central processing' involves dynamic updating. Rousseau's suggestion that people should not talk but simply take a vote, and revise their opinions in line with the majority-that-can-never-err after the vote, would be another instance of merely periodic updating.[13] The problems I shall be discussing with talk as a decision procedure are problems that arise from dynamic updating, and my suggested solution will be to replace that with periodic updating instead.

6.1.2. Path Dependency as a Consequence

'Talk as a decision procedure'—deliberation of the form that deliberative democrats advocate—is thus a serial process with dynamic updating. Those two features combine to make that process prone to 'path dependency'.[14]

---

[10] Bickford (1996: ch. 5). This is an old thought: Sieyès said, 'It is not a question of a democratic election, but of proposing, listening, concerting, changing one's opinion in order to form in common a common will' (quoted in Elster 1998*b*: 3).

[11] In Rawls's (1997/1999: 138–9) formulation: 'The definitive idea for deliberative democracy is the idea of deliberation itself. When citizens deliberate, they exchange views and debate their supporting reasons concerning public political questions. They suppose that their political opinions may be revised by discussion with other citizens and therefore these opinions are not simply a fixed outcome of their existing private or nonpolitical interests.'

[12] In the phrase of Karpowitz and Mansbridge's (2005) subtitle. Expanding they say: 'We contend that participants in productive deliberation should continually and consciously update their understandings of common and conflicting interests as the process evolves' (2005: 238). See similarly Gutmann and Thompson's (1996: 356) discussion of the 'capacity to change'.

[13] Rousseau (1762: book 2, ch. 3).

[14] As I remarked, very much in passing, in Goodin (2003*b*: 175).

A path-dependent process displays the following features:

1. *Unpredictability*. Because early events have a large effect and are partly random, many outcomes may be possible. We cannot predict ahead of time which of these possible end-states will be reached.
2. *Inflexibility*. The farther into the process we are, the harder it becomes to shift from one path to another.
3. *Nonergodicity*. Accidental events early in a sequence do not cancel out. They cannot be treated (which is to say, ignored) as 'noise', because they feed back into future choices. Small events are remembered.
4. *Potential path inefficiency*. In the long run, the outcome that becomes locked in may generate lower pay-offs than a forgone alternative would have.

More generally, 'these are processes in which sequencing is critical. Earlier events matter much more than later ones, and hence different sequences may produce different outcomes'.[15]

One popular way of modelling such processes mathematically is through the Polya urn.[16] Here is how that works: Start with an urn containing two balls, one red and one black. Draw out one ball. Return that ball to the urn, together with another ball of the same colour. Continue the process until the urn fills up. Then tip out the balls and count how many there are of each colour.

Obviously, the outcome of this process depends crucially on what colour ball you draw first. If out of the two-ball urn you draw the red ball, and you return that ball and another red one to the urn, your chances of randomly drawing a red ball in the second round are two-to-one. If you do indeed draw a red ball in the second round, and return that and another red ball to the urn, your chances of randomly drawing a red ball in the third round are three-to-one. And so on, until the urn is almost completely full of red balls. But of course you could equally well have drawn a black ball in the first round: the chances were 50:50, after all. Had you done so, then the same process could have yielded an urn almost completely full of black balls. Or in the second round, you could (somewhat against the odds, but not wildly so) have drawn the one black ball rather than either of the two red ones. Then it would have been even money which colour ball you would randomly draw in the third round;

---

[15] Pierson (2000: 253), glossing Arthur (1994: 112–13).
[16] Once again, as described by Pierson (2000: 253), building on Arthur (1994).

and were that pattern of alternating-colour draws to persist throughout a few early rounds, you might well end up with an urn with nearly the same number of balls of each colour, pretty much regardless of what happens in later rounds.

The point of the story is simply this. First, in a Polya urn (or a path-dependent process, more generally) pretty much any outcome might eventuate. Second, which outcome eventuates depends crucially on what happens at early stages in the process.

Something very much like that the Polya urn process might occur in a conversation of the sort favoured by deliberative democrats, which is to say, in a series of conversational interjections with everyone dynamically updating their own views in light of each intervention. Here is one way in which that might happen.

Imagine a dozen-person group trying to answer a binary true–false question. Imagine that each member of the group has some private information bearing on the question, as well as the public information that is shared among everyone in the group. Suppose we are good deliberative democrats, so (*a*) we accord each other person's views the same weight as our own and (*b*) we update our own views in light of what others have said dynamically as they say it.

Now suppose we go around the table clockwise, each of us announcing his or her decision in turn.[17] The first person says 'false'. Suppose the private information available to the second person also disposed her to say 'false'—which she does all the more emphatically for having heard the first speaker's 'false'. Now comes the turn of the third man. His private information suggests that 'true' is the correct answer. But both of the first two speakers have said 'false', and he accords their views as much weight as his own. Dynamically updating his views in light of theirs, therefore, he concludes (albeit more reluctantly than the second speaker) that 'false' must be the correct answer, and reports accordingly. The weight of opinion come the fourth speaker is three-to-zero 'false'; so after dynamic updating she says 'false' even if her private information suggested 'true'. The weight of opinion come the fifth speaker is four-to-zero 'false'; so after dynamically updating he says 'false' whatever his private information. And so on around the table. In the end, the decision

---

[17] 'Announcing decisions' rather than 'reporting reasons' may sound more like an aggrega-tive process of 'sequential voting' than anything a deliberative democrat would care to countenance. I state the point in these terms first, for expository convenience. But I restate the same point in terms of 'reasons' in Section 6.2.3.

is unanimous. 'False' has emerged as the common consensus among the group.

But suppose we had gone around the table counterclockwise instead. And suppose the private information available to the first person and the second person going around in that direction suggested that the correct answer is 'true'. By exactly the same serial process of dynamic updating, the group would then have come to a unanimous decision in favour of 'true'. In short, had we gone around the table in the opposite direction, the common consensus would have been just the opposite.[18]

The general point is that conversations, seen as serial processes with dynamic updating, can easily be path dependent.[19] The outcome of the conversation depends upon the sequence of conversational moves, particularly those early in the conversation that set it off down one path rather than some other.[20]

6.2. Ways of Overcoming Discursive Path Dependency

Talk as a decision process can, therefore, be path dependent and hence fundamentally arbitrary. What might we do to overcome that problem? Here I shall consider four suggestions, the first three of which turn out not to be solutions at all. Only the last, I shall argue, offers a good solution to the problem of path dependency in political talk.

6.2.1. Simultaneous Conversations, Somehow Pooled

Some conversations are inconclusive, of course. But even where a conversation comes to some conclusion, there may be nothing special about

---

[18] Adapted from Bikhchandani, Hirshleifer, and Welch (1992, 1998).

[19] But are not necessarily so. They would not be if everyone would have said the same thing, for example: then the order in which they speak makes no difference to the outcome. Similarly, if two individuals would say the same thing, it makes no difference to the outcome which of them speaks first.

[20] It may well be that thought itself is path dependent: one idea leads to another; and if a different idea had occurred to you first, then you would have set off down a different train of thought altogether and you would have concluded something different. In the case of thoughts inside our own heads, we overcome the problem of path dependency by revisiting our own thoughts, starting from different points, from time to time. Each train of thought is still path dependent, of course. But we hold in our heads each previous train of thought (or anyway the conclusions arising from each), averaging or weighing them according to relative persuasiveness to come up with an overall assessment of a proposition.

that conclusion. Different conversations could well have come to different conclusions, depending upon the particular discursive path. Another conversation among the same people on the same topic might well have yielded a different outcome. There is no reason to privilege any particular conversation's conclusion. That is the 'arbitrariness' worry arising out of the path dependency of talk as a decision procedure.

The ordinary way we wash out the effects of arbitrariness is to pool lots of independent experiments. Assuming arbitrary effects are random, they will cancel one another out, leaving genuinely systematic effects standing out starkly. One initial thought, in trying to overcome the effects of path dependency on conversation, would therefore be to hold many conversations on the same topic and to see what (if any) larger pattern emerges across all those conversations.[21]

Here I shall offer two worries about any such strategy. First, the procedure might well be inconclusive: multiple conversations on the same topic may well not come to similar conclusions. In other words, there may be very little left after filtering out the arbitrary path-dependent effects. Second, even if the procedure does yield some determinate result, there is no reason to privilege that conclusion: it may just reflect systematic, non-random effects of path dependency.

On the first point, we mostly just have anecdotal evidence. But lawyers, for example, treat it as a platitude that 'no two juries are alike'.[22] Different groups go off in different directions. The same case presented to a different judge and jury will play out very differently.

Among deliberative democrats, the main evidence offered on the question of whether different deliberative groups come to similar conclusions derives from a series of Deliberative Polls conducted in three different locales in Texas on issues of energy policy. Fishkin proudly reports that in all three cases opinion shifted in the same direction pre- to post-deliberation, at least on three very broad questions. But although the shift of opinion was in the same direction in all three cases, the distribution of opinion within the three different groups was still very different. For example:

- After deliberating on the matter, fully half the respondents at one site thought that 'investing in conservation' was the 'option to pursue

---

[21] An alternative would be to hold many conversations on the same topic, one after another, involving the same people. But unless the conversations are separated in time sufficiently that people have forgotten the last before they begin the next, issues of path dependency arise again.

[22] Kalven and Zeisel (1966: 474).

first to provide additional electrical power to the service territory'; elsewhere under a third thought so.

- After deliberating on the matter, over a third of respondents at one site thought that 'renewable energy' should be the top option; elsewhere only a sixth thought so.

- As a result of deliberation, the percentage of people 'willing to pay at least $1 more on their monthly bill for renewable energy' increased by 23 percentage points at one site but by fully 34 percentage points at another.[23]

Thus, while it may be true to say that deliberation prompted movement in the same direction across all three deliberating groups, it cannot really be said to have led to exactly the 'same conclusions' in all three places.

Thus, we have only relatively weak evidence, at best, to suggest that different conversations on the same topic will always or even often come to the same conclusions. But even if they did, what should we make of that fact?

Nothing much, perhaps, if we are dealing with path-dependent effects of the sorts discussed above. Those effects are arbitrary, in some important sense: they are without any justification. Crucially, however, those effects are non-random. The law of large numbers will not wipe out such effects but instead will reinforce them. Pooling the results of deliberations at multiple sites will merely yield results that mirror initial biases concerning the most common conversational starting points or the most common early moves in the conversation.

To see why, return to the Polya urn example, with a slight variation. Suppose now there are three balls in the urn at the beginning of the process, one red and two black. Conduct a hundred experiments starting with such a three-ball Polya urn. Final distributions will vary from one experiment to the next. But much the most common pattern will be an almost-all-black distribution, owing to that initial 2:1 bias in favour of black.

So too in conversations: if in some cultural context there is some 'natural' starting point for conversations about any given subject, or if there are some 'natural' early moves in those conversations, that will bias the subsequent conversation towards particular outcomes associated with the conversational path determined by that starting point and those early moves.

---

[23] Fishkin (1995: 220).

If we had some independent reason for thinking that that is the right starting point for the conversation, or those are the right early moves in the conversation, then the 'bias' would be unobjectionable. The fact that conversation ended up in the conclusions it did, merely because it took the early path it did, would not constitute an objection. It would be justified by the reasons we have for thinking that that was the right path.

Ordinarily, however, we do not have reasons for thinking that whatever biases are built into ordinary discourse are justifiable. And in the absence of such explicit justifications for one conversational path rather than others, any path dependencies deriving from those biases ought to be regarded as arbitrary—however commonly they might occur.

6.2.2. Forcing Equal Conversational Representation

Suppose we had some good reason to think that the equal representation of all opinions in the conversation would be desirable. There are ways of ensuring that. Legislative assemblies typically conduct important parts of their business in just that way, with speakers from opposite sides of the floor taking turns in addressing the assembly.

If we want to overcome the indeterminacies associated with path-dependent processes of the sort described in Section 6.1.2, here is one easy way to do that. Just use a 'reverse-Polya-urn' process. When you put back the ball you have drawn, instead of adding another of the same colour, add another of the opposite colour. The effect of that will be to equalize the number of balls of each colour over time. It will do so regardless of the initial distribution of balls in the urn.

That 'reverse-Polya-urn' process would overcome the indeterminacies associated with path-dependent processes. But would it overcome the problem of arbitrariness? It would do so only if (once again) we had some good independent reason for thinking that equal representation of each position is the right outcome.

Surely in vote-counts that is not always the right outcome. Some positions are crazy. People should get to cast crazy ballots if they want. But the rules of the system should not be rigged to ensure equal representation of the sane and the stupid among all positions afoot in the community.

The right rule in a democracy is 'one person, one vote'—not 'one position, one vote'.[24] The same surely is true in terms of voice-hearing.

[24] Lest this be thought to be attacking a straw man, cf. Elster (1998b: 14).

Some positions are distinctly minority positions. It is important that they be heard. But it is not necessarily desirable that they be heard just as often or as insistently as positions that resonate. It can be a great distraction in US Presidential debates for every candidate, however lacking in credibility, to be allowed to speak for the same amount of time as the major candidates.

6.2.3. *Give Reasons, Not Merely Conclusions*

In describing the conversational analogue of the Polya urn in Section 6.1.2, I envisaged that each of the jurors simply announce a verdict, 'true' or 'false', without giving any supporting reasons for reaching that conclusion. That way of proceeding would actually be anathema to deliberative democrats, of course. It amounts to aggregating votes (albeit in a serial rather than simultaneous way) rather than giving one another reasons.

It might therefore seem that one easy way out of the path dependency we encountered there would be to follow more faithfully deliberative ideals: have jurors offer reasons rather than verdicts to one another, as they go around the table. It turns out, however, that that makes absolutely no difference to the outcome. It will be equally path dependent, equally sensitive to what early speakers have said, either way.

To show why, let me introduce some notation. Going around the table clockwise, label speakers 'Speaker 1' through 'Speaker 12'. Call the reason that Speaker 1 gives 'R_1', and so on around the table. For simplicity, assume each speaker has just one extra reason—just one piece of private information unique to himself or herself—to add to the mix.

Suppose, finally, that speakers abide by the precepts of deliberative democrats that they should listen to one another and take account of what others have said, and that they should update their own views accordingly. Indeed, let us assume once again that they take others' views as fully on a par with their own. Let us represent this in my lightly formalized schema by saying that after Speaker 2 has heard Speaker 1 give reason R_1, Speaker 2 treats that information equally to her own 'private' bit of information (R_2) and reports to the assembled group her dynamically updated view 'R_1 and R_2'.

With this apparatus in place, the path dependency that arises from the first-speaker advantage becomes immediately apparent. Speaker 1 says

'R_1'. Speaker 2, internalizing what Speaker 1 said and adding to it her own bit of private information, says 'R_1 and R_2'. Speaker 3 internalizes what the first two speakers have said—Speaker 1's report 'R_1' and Speaker 2's report 'R_1 and R_2'—and adds to that his own R_3. Speaker 4 internalizes all that has gone before—'(R_1) and (R_1 and R_2) and (R_1 and R_2 and R_3)'—and adds to it his own R_4. Notice what is happening, here: the first speaker's report is getting double- (and triple- and quadruple- and so on) counted as they go around the table.[25]

In the story in Section 6.1.2, the private information available to Speakers 1 and 2—R_1 and R_2, respectively—indicated a conclusion of 'false'. Going around the table clockwise, we end up counting those reasons multiple times; and the group ends up concluding 'false'. Had we gone around the table counterclockwise, and had the reason the first two speakers going in that direction (R_{12} and R_{11}) indicated a conclusion of 'true', the opposite verdict would have been reached by exactly the same process.

The very same thing could happen with Bayesian updating, if the updaters (wrongly) proceeded in a serial way updating their own beliefs in light of what all the previous updaters have reported. It would however be erroneous updating from a Bayesian point of view, of course, because it would amount to treating each new report as independent evidence when in fact each new report is highly intercorrelated with the immediately preceding report.

The problem thus lies with serial, dynamic updating, of the sort that deliberative democrats desire. If we listen carefully and take fully into account what the previous speakers just have said when forming our own view as to what we should say next, the conversation can be highly path dependent, and arbitrarily sensitive to what the early speakers have said. Unless there is some independent reason to think that those early interventions ought to be privileged, there is no good reason to think that the upshot of that sort of conversation should have any particular merits.

---

[25] Sometimes one reason might 'cancel' another, as Donald Wittman has pointed out to me. Speaker 1 says, 'The best way to get to ANU from the airport is to take a taxi.' Speaker 2 says, 'The best way to get to ANU from the airport is to take a taxi, but the taxis are on strike today.' Even if those two reasons keep getting repeated in all subsequent speakers' interventions, the second cancels the first in each repeated case. So the result described in the text does not necessarily always obtain. My claim is a weaker one: it may, and insofar as it does so with any frequency we should worry about 'talk as a decision process' even in the realm of reasons.

6.2.4. Wait to Update

How then can we overcome the threat of unwarranted effects of path dependency on democratic deliberations? We can only do so, I suggest, by repudiating demands that deliberators engage in dynamic updating over the course of the deliberation.

In the sorts of examples I have been discussing, that amounts to saying that deliberators should go around the table simply putting their 'private information' on the table for all to see. Instead of dynamically updating their own beliefs as others speak, they should wait to revise their beliefs until all the private information is on the table. Only at that point should they engage in 'periodic updating' of their beliefs, taking account of all the new information now in the public domain.

Talk, by all means. Accept the fact that that is inevitably a serial process, with each participant talking and listening to one another in turn. But instead of taking on board what each speaker is saying in real time, updating their own views in light of each speech as it is spoken, participants should just store up all that new information. They should update their own views in light of that new information, all at once, after all the speeches are over. In that way, they avoid the double- (triple- etc.) counting of inputs of previous speakers of the sort discussed above (in Sections 6.1.2 and 6.2.3).

If literal consensus does not emerge from that first round of updating, deliberative democrats might be tempted to suggest that we go around the room again with another round of speeches, with each speaker describing how he or she revised his or her views in light of the information garnered from the first round of speeches. There is, however, one good reason to resist that temptation, akin to the 'double-counting' objection to people dynamically updating after each speech.

The objection is simply this. There is no new information presented in second-round speeches. People have already updated their beliefs in light of all that old information. To update their beliefs again in light of the information that they have already taken into account amounts to double-counting.

You can get a consensus that way, sure enough. Here is Keith Lehrer's model of how that can happen. Imagine a two-person society (the point easily generalizes to larger societies). Suppose we each give some positive weight to the views of the other in forming our own views. Your initial estimate of the probability of some event is .30, my initial estimate of that probability is .70. We tell each other that, and explain why we think so.

We then each revise our probability estimates in light of that information. In Lehrer's model, we do not necessarily accept each other's evidence as fully on a par with our own. Your probability estimate goes up to .40, mine drops to .60. We report that to one another. Then, on Lehrer's model, we have a second round of revisions. Lo and behold, we both now hit upon a probability estimate of .50.[26]

We have reached consensus, but what is that consensus worth? Nothing, I would suggest.[27] The second round of updating is simply illicit. It takes account of something we have already taken fully into account in the first round of updating.

The reason we should ordinarily revise our beliefs in light of others' reports is that others know something we do not, something that we should take into account and revise our own beliefs in light of. The first round of updating is an appropriate response to genuinely new information in just this way. But after the first round of updating, there is no new information to take into account.

Consider an analogy from scientific laboratories. One laboratory conducts a set of experiments and estimates some value to be 5.60. Another laboratory conducts a set of experiments and estimates that value to be 5.00. They exchange notes as to their procedures and findings. On the basis of that exchange the first set of experimenters is persuaded that the true value is most probably 5.40 and the second set of experimenters is persuaded that the true value is most probably 5.20. What good would it do to exchange notes once again at that point? No new experiments have been conducted. All the relevant information has already been taken into account in each group's revised estimate.

That argument notwithstanding, there might be just some point in exchanging notes a second time, and in having a second round of speeches in the political case as well. Even if there is no new information to add, in trying to take account of what others have said in the first round it may be the case that new *interpretations* have emerged. In the scientific case, it makes perfectly good sense to discuss what theories best fit the data, even after all the data we will ever be able to collect is already in. In the political case, it makes perfectly good sense to discuss how best to understand one another, our plight and our prospects, even after all the basic facts about the situation are settled.

---

[26] Lehrer (1976, 2001*a*) and Lehrer and Wagner (1981).
[27] Goodin (2001); cf. Lehrer (2001*b*).

That is a less mechanical process than Bayesian information pooling of the first-round sort, and it is correspondingly harder to say when exactly it should stop. Still, the general shape of the argument is clear. We should stop the conversation—and simply vote—when nothing new is being added.[28] We should not keep splitting the conversational difference until we reach an artificial consensus, in the realm of interpretation any more than in the realm of information.

The best practical device for discouraging dynamic updating and replacing it with periodic updating is to institute periodic elections. That way, electors will have no pragmatic reason to update their beliefs in light of the evidence as it comes in, in between elections. Pragmatically, they need only update their beliefs in light of the accumulated evidence once the election is called.

6.3. The Benefit of Talking Before Voting

Talking together before we vote yields all sorts of benefits, in terms of understanding what we are meaning to convey to one another through our votes.[29] Many of the ways in which this might work have been canvassed in previous chapters. Here I want to add one further reason, internal to the voting process itself, for thinking it is highly important to talk before voting.

Talk can, as Section 6.1.2 has shown, be path dependent. Hence, we should not simply be counting how often any particular position comes up over the course of the conversation: that may simply be a consequence of the particular conversational path we happened to go down. Nor, for reasons given in Section 6.2.1, should we even be counting how

---

[28] Maybe the best practical solution would be this. First take a 'straw ballot' with no discussion preceding it: that is a simultaneous process with no path dependency. Then have a discussion to flush out arguments and interpretations, with no updating of beliefs until that discussion is over (to avoid conversational path dependency). Then update beliefs once the discussion is over, and take a binding vote.

[29] As Dahl and Lindblom (1953: 66) observe, 'Voting is nearly always preceded by discussion. This is a well-nigh universal association, found not merely in the theory and practice of modern polyarchies but in primitive tribes as well. Voting and discussion are commonly found together because voting is typically used where the participants want a more or less accurate indication of voters' preferences.... Conversely, when leaders do not really wish an accurate indication of voters' preferences but need the ritual of voting as an aid in propaganda or in helping to establish legitimacy, as in the plebiscites and elections of totalitarian countries, they attempt to limit or eliminate discussion.'

often any particular position comes up over the course of a large set of conversations.

What we should pay particular attention to is not the frequency with which any particular position comes up but, rather, what all different positions come up over the course of the conversation. That is to say, we should regard the conversation as elaborating the agenda for the voting as follows.[30] In vote-centric terms, the greatest value of pre-voting talk lies in expanding the menu of options from which voters will then choose.[31]

To see why this is important, we merely need go back to the Condorcet Jury Theorem discussed in Section 4.2.2. That theorem tells us that a large group of independent assessors who are on average better-than-random will be virtually certain to choose the correct option—from among those presented to them. But if the correct option is not on the menu, they cannot choose it.

To drive the point home: Suppose there is a .9999 probability that some large group will choose the correct option from among those on the agenda; but suppose there is only a .3000 chance that the correct option is actually on the agenda. What is the probability that that group will choose the correct option? It is .9999 times .3000—which is to say, just under .3000 (rather than just under 1).

Thus, among large groups of assessors, the prime determinant of whether or not they reach the correct answer (even where the assumptions of the Condorcet Jury Theorem are satisfied, and there is a correct answer to be found) is whether or not the correct answer actually appears on the menu for choice. And wide-ranging discussion is a good way to get a wide range of options on the agenda, even if groups have in the end to choose between them purely by voting.[32]

---

[30] 'Elaborating' (i.e. expanding) rather than 'setting' (i.e. restricting) the agenda for voting, notice: for if the agenda is restricted as a result of the conversations, the same discursive path dependency exposed above might introduce arbitrary constraints on what choices the electorate are offered. In practice, of course, that is precisely what typically happens. From the Athenian Boule forward, small deliberative groups have been used to set the agenda for larger deliberative assemblies and electorates (Ferejohn 2008).

[31] As noted by Fearon (1998: 49), although he missed this particular angle on that.

[32] There is a raft of evidence suggesting that the conclusions reached on the basis of group discussion are not invariably superior to those reached by individuals without any discussion (Hastie 1986; Sunstein 2006). Mostly, however, that evidence cautions against treating talk as a 'decision procedure'. We only need to be wary of treating talk as a 'discovery process' insofar as the menu of options generated by talking is inferior to that available without talking. Evidence of that is much more scarce.

6.4. Conclusion

The upshot of this chapter, and Part I of the book as a whole, is that 'talking together' is excellent as a 'discovery procedure'. In that way we can learn much that we need to know in order to make good collective decisions. But 'talking together', in and of itself, is not a particularly good 'decision procedure'. My recommendation is therefore, 'first talk, then vote'. That is to say, build discursive and deliberative elements centrally into the political process, but make the ultimate decisions through more purely aggregative procedures. Having explored the nature and functioning of micro-deliberation in Part I of the book, I shall in Part II be exploring how that fits into the sorts of macro-democratic institutions that currently characterize our political world.

Part II

Macro-Democracy

7

Who counts?

Democracy might be characterized, semi-circularly, as a matter of 'groups of people making collective decisions in a democratic way'. I employ that circularity deliberately to bracket off the part of the formula that I do not want to focus upon for present purposes.

Of course, what it is to 'make collective decisions in a democratic way' is precisely the part of the formula that traditionally preoccupies democratic theorists. Is that a matter of expressing opinions or of aggregating votes or of deliberating together? (And if 'all three', then combined how and in what proportions?) Insofar as it is a matter of aggregating votes, according to what rules? (Simple majority rule or something else?) Insofar as it is a matter of elections, what makes them free and fair? (How are campaigns to be conducted, electors apportioned to districts, and so on?) Are there any substantive constraints on what democracies may or must do? (Respect human rights, for example.) Such questions constitute the warp and the woof of democratic theory.

All that leaves to one side, however, the prior question of *who* exactly it is that is to be making those decisions in that democratic way. How do we specify the group making those decisions? That is what I shall call the problem of 'constituting the demos'.[1]

Writing in 1970, the pre-eminent democratic theorist of the previous generation complained, 'Strange as it may seem ..., how to decide who legitimately make up "the people" and hence are entitled to govern themselves ... is a problem almost totally neglected by all the great political

---

[1] I prefer that characterization to two others more common in the scant literature on this topic. Calling it 'the Boundary Problem' makes the issue seem more a matter of geography than it necessarily is; cf. Whelan (1983). Calling it 'the Problem of Inclusion' inclines us to think in terms of inclusion in some already existing decision-making group, ignoring the question (which I see as logically the crucial one) of how to constitute that group in the first place; cf. Dahl (1979: 108–29; 1989: 119–31) and Shklar (1991).

philosophers who write about democracy.'[2] Dahl himself subsequently managed only a little progress on that subject: a couple dozen pages on it in his seminal 1979 paper on 'Procedural Democracy', shrunken to half that in his consolidation text a decade later.[3] For an issue that he rightly saw as at one and the same time neglected yet central to democratic theory, that constitutes a pretty scant coverage. But Dahl is hardly alone in that respect. Virtually all democratic theorists find that they have surprisingly little to say on the topic.[4]

Neither do plausible solutions to the problem of 'constituting the demos' fall straightforwardly out of any of the larger discussions in adjacent areas of political philosophy. There might, for example, seem to be a ready solution within contractarianism: the demos, like Nozick's utopia, ought consist of all and only those persons each of whom is not rejected by any of the others as a member.[5] But that formula implausibly risks leaving large proportions of the world's population blackballed and stateless. Were we to try to avoid that outcome by stipulating 'could not be reasonably rejected', we would simply be assuming (in the standard of what is 'reasonable') precisely what this analysis is supposed to provide, which is an account of what are and are not good grounds for excluding people and hence for constituting the demos one way rather than another.[6]

Similarly, there is a large literature on political obligation which might be thought ought to bear fairly directly on questions of how to constitute the demos. The easy thought might be that all and only those persons who are (legally) obliged or (morally) obligated to obey a body of laws

[2] Dahl (1970: 60–1). He continues, 'I think this is because they take for granted that a people has already constituted itself. How a people accomplishes this mysterious transformation is therefore treated as a purely hypothetical event that has already occurred in prehistory or in a state of nature. The polis is what it is; the nation-state is what history has made it. Athenians are Athenians. Corinthians are Corinthians, and Greeks are Greeks.'

[3] Dahl (1979: 108–29; 1989: 119–31).

[4] The issue is absent altogether from Pennock's otherwise encyclopaedic *Democratic Political Theory* (1979). It gets only a brief chapter in Carl Cohen's *Democracy* (1971: 41–55) and Giovanni Sartori's *Democratic Theory* (1962: 17–30; see also 1987: 21–38). The fullest discussion remains Whelan's (1983) *Nomos* chapter on 'Democratic Theory and the Boundary Problem', from a quarter-century ago.

[5] Nozick (1974: ch. 10). cf. Whelan (1983: 24–8).

[6] This is akin to the now-standard 'Euthyphro objection' to Scanlon's *What We Owe to Each Other* (1998). Ridge's (2001) way of 'Saving Scanlon' points out that the reasons in question are (at least in important part) agent-relative, which is true and very much to that larger point. What matters for my argument here is simply that the test of what constitutes 'reasonableness' in rejecting others as co-members on grounds of those (possibly agent-relative) reasons is itself an (presumably agent-neutral) analysis of what are and are not good grounds for excluding people and hence for constituting the demos one way rather than another.

ought to be entitled to membership in the demos making those laws. But upon reflection, there turn out to be all sorts of people who are legally and morally obligated to obey our laws but who are not (and rightly not) entitled to membership in our demos: the captain of a foreign ship anchored in our harbour; any visitor to our shores; or indeed any alien illegally living among us. All are rightly bound by our laws, but none is (or ought to be) entitled to a vote in making them. How to constitute the demos is thus orthogonal to what might have initially seemed the perfectly parallel problem of justifying political obligation.

'Constituting the demos' is therefore a problem that finds no ready solution, either within democratic theory or in any of the seemingly cognate areas of political philosophy. The natural place to look for a solution is indeed in the vicinity of democratic theory itself, and I shall argue that we can indeed find one there—but not without some surprises along the way.

I shall talk in this chapter principally in terms of 'votes'—for 'constituting the demos' is traditionally cashed out in terms of 'who is entitled to a vote?' But precisely the same issues arise when the question is recast in deliberative terms as 'who is entitled to a say?' Constituting the demos is therefore a problem shared by both deliberative and aggregative democracy. Indeed, it may be even more problematic for deliberative democrats, for reasons given in Section 7.3.4.

7.1. A Silence at the Heart of Democratic Theory?

Constituting the demos is the first step in constructing a democracy. Clearly that is true temporally. Until we have an electorate we cannot have an election. But that is not just a temporal observation; it is a logical truth.[7]

It is simply incoherent to constitute the electorate through a vote among voters who would be entitled to vote only by virtue of the outcome of that very vote. That is like saying the winning lottery ticket will be pulled out of the hat by the winner of that selfsame lottery.

Logically, constituting the demos—in the very first instance, at least—cannot itself be a product of ordinary democratic decision-making.[8] At

---

[7] As noted, in different fashions, by many before me: see, e.g. Whelan (1983: 13–16, 22–4, 29–31, 41–2).

[8] 'Ordinary' here, and 'usual' in the next paragraph, in contrast to the possibility canvassed in Section 7.1.4 that there might be some 'deeper principles' (perhaps even 'deeper democratic

later stages we can *re*-constitute the demos in that way. Once we have the initial demos, its members can then vote on whom else to make members. But the initial membership of the demos, at least, must itself be constituted according to some principle independent of any decision of the demos.

That is simply to say that the decision of how the initial demos is to be constituted cannot be 'made in a democratic way'. Anyway, it cannot be made in the 'usual' democratic way, or at least not the very same ways in which the group makes its subsequent democratic decisions.

7.1.1. How Bad Would It Be?

Seen in one light, that observation might seem to suggest that democracy is inherently founded on a fraud. Democratic though the subsequent decisions may be, the initial decision of how to constitute the demos can never be democratic; and that might be thought to contaminate all subsequent democratic decisions in the same way that, for Rousseau, the initial fraud upon which property rests contaminates all subsequent transfers and titles.

Seen in another light, that observation might make us more comfortable with democracy as we know it. The need to appeal to some principle outside democracy to constitute the demos does not render democratic theory incoherent, merely incomplete. The chastening force of that observation is more akin to that of Gödel's Theorem than that of Arrow's.

Democratic theory being incomplete in this regard actually renders it powerfully permissive. It means that we do not (indeed, cannot) offend against democratic principles by organizing the demos in any manner that we choose. The upshot would be that any group of people constituted on any basis whatsoever could constitute a perfectly proper demos for democratic purposes.

7.1.2. Democratically Bootstrapping a Demos

Arbitrariness ordinarily makes moralists nervous. The proposition that we should simply take the demos as given, on any old basis it happens to have been given to us, would ordinarily be a source of unease. But there might be one way to overcome that unease.

principles') underlying both the decision as to how to constitute the demos and the decision as to what procedures the demos should use in making decisions.

Suppose it simply does not make any difference where we start, in the first instance. Once the initial demos has been constituted, among the decisions to be taken democratically is how to re-constitute the demos. Suppose there is some internal dynamic within democratic decision-making processes that naturally leads the demos to be changed over time in such a way as to include all those and only those who ought to be included.[9] Further suppose that this process is not at all path-dependent: it does not matter where you start; thanks to those internal dynamics of democratic decision-making, you always eventually end up settling on precisely the right composition of the demos.[10] Were all that true, we need not worry about how the demos is initially constituted. We could constitute that initial demos on any basis whatsoever, and set the democratic process underway to refine it; the correct composition of the demos would then automatically eventuate.[11]

On the face of it, this would seem to be an essentially empirical claim about inexorable tendencies within democratic politics. Someone arguing along these lines might, for example, point to the inexorable tendency for democratic decision procedures constantly to expand the demos, leaving ever-fewer groups disenfranchised. But that empirical observation does the normative work this argument carves out for it if and only if we have some independent reason for supposing that a maximally extensive franchise is indeed the right way to (re)constitute the demos.

More generally, unless we already knew what the right way to constitute the demos is, we have no way of knowing whether any given empirical tendencies within democratic politics would, as this argument asserts, lead them to (re)constitute the demos in precisely the right way. This argument was trying to save us from any need to stipulate appropriate principles for constituting the demos from the start. In the end, however, it requires us to be in possession of precisely such principles in

---

[9] Jürgen Habermas (2001: 774), for example, supposes that we can 'break out of the circle of a polity's groundless discursive self-constitution only if this process . . . can be understood in the long run as a self-correcting learning process'.

[10] Pause to reflect on the implausibility of that proposition. Does anyone really believe that we would end up with exactly the *same* demos, composed of exactly the same people, no matter whether we started out with two different initial pairs of demoi: in one case, England-Scotland-Wales on the one hand and Ireland on the other; in the other case, England-Scotland-Wales-Northern Ireland on the one hand and the Irish Republic on the other? Surely not, says Arrhenius (2005: 14–5), building on Whelan (1983: 23–4).

[11] Consider the analogy to Bayesian decision theory: it does not matter what prior probabilities people start with; as they update their beliefs in light of new evidence as it comes in, everyone will eventually converge on the same sets of beliefs over time, wherever they started from.

order to assess the validity of its own claim that democratic politics will (re)constitute the demos in precisely the right way.

The only alternative I can see would be for someone running this line to insist that the 'right way to constitute the demos' should be defined in purely procedural ways—and that democratic decision-making procedures invariably satisfy these procedural criteria, and furthermore that they do so regardless of the composition of the demos implementing them.[12] It is a brave democratic theorist, however, who would go the 'pure proceduralist' line, repudiating any substantive constraints on what counts as a democratic decision. And it is an even braver one who would persist in that line, confronted with any conceivable decision-making group. Does anyone really imagine that a free and fair vote among the Hitler's Cabinet would be sufficient for us to conclude that the German demos had been (re)constituted in just the right way?

7.1.3. Can It Really Not Matter?

Some commentators seem resigned simply to accepting that democratic theory is silent on the issue of how to constitute the demos.[13] Most are mildly embarrassed by the fact and tiptoe lightly around it. But a few—Schumpeter famously among them—trumpet the fact that we must 'leave every *populus* to define [it]self' on whatever basis it chooses:

[I]t is not relevant whether we, the observers, admit the validity of those reasons or the practical rules by which they are made to exclude portions of the population; all that matters is that the society in question admits it. . . . In a commonwealth of strong religious conviction it may be held . . . that dissent disqualifies or, in an anti-feminist commonwealth, sex. A race-conscious nation may associate fitness with racial considerations. And so on.[14]

Schumpeter does not approve of any of those exclusions, necessarily. He merely wants to say that we cannot 'call such societies undemocratic' by virtue of those exclusions alone.

[12] The most plausible version of that argument would perhaps be the 'consent' argument: 'people should rule and be ruled together with such people as they agree to rule and be ruled together with' (cf. Whelan 1983: 24–8).

[13] Whelan (1983: 16), e.g. writes, 'Boundaries comprise a problem . . . that is insoluble within the framework of democratic theory, and . . . democracy is practicable only when a historically given solution of this issue (justifiable or not, by some theory other than democratic theory) is acceptable. The following argument to this effect is not intended to discredit democratic theory, but only to establish one of its inherent limitations.'

[14] Schumpeter (1950: 245, 244).

For Schumpeter and those following him, 'characteristics...associated with democracy' pertain purely to how decisions are made, not to who makes them. For Schumpeter and those following him, any group that (in my bracketing formula) 'makes decisions in a democratic way' counts a democracy, however that group is itself constituted.

Most democratic theorists, however, are not as prepared as Schumpeter to bite the 'incompleteness' bullet quite so hard, and to follow it quite so far in endorsing 'anything goes' conclusions when it comes to constituting the demos. Robert Dahl protests, in uncharacteristically purple prose, 'the absurdities to which we may be led by the absence of any criterion for defining the *demos*'. He offers a litany of telling *reductios*:

> Suppose that in the [American] South, as in Rhodesia or South Africa, Blacks had been a preponderant majority of the population. Would Schumpeter still have said that the Southern states were 'democratic'?...If the rulers numbered 100 in a population of 100 million, would we call the rulers a demos and the system a democracy?...Or suppose that the Politburo were internally democratic, and ruled by the party, which ruled over the State, which ruled over the people. Then the members of the Politburo would constitute the Soviet populus, and the Soviet State would be, on Schumpeter's interpretation, a democracy.[15]

7.1.4. Tracing Shared Roots

Notice that Dahl is not simply saying that those ways of constituting the demos are evil or immoral or absurd or preposterous. He is suggesting instead that they are 'not democratic'. That, in turn, is to suggest that there are indeed principles somehow internal to the standards of democracy for preferring the demos be constituted one way or another, even in the first instance.

Recall the logical conundrum that tempted us to think otherwise. It is logically incoherent to let the composition of the initial demos be decided by a vote of the demos, because that demos cannot be constituted until after the demos votes. 'Ordinary democratic ways of making decisions'— voting and such like—cannot therefore be used to make decisions about how to constitute that initial demos. We need to constitute that initial demos on the basis of some principles other than those.

But might we find some connection, one level down, between the 'how' and the 'who' of democratic politics? Might our standards of what are 'democratic ways of making decisions' and of what are 'democratic ways

---

[15] Dahl (1979: 111–12).

of constituting the demos' both be derived somehow from one and the same underlying principle? If so, what might that principle be?

In looking for hints, we might begin by examining the bases upon which real-world demoi are most commonly constituted. Territoriality, nationality and history—'blood and soil', as the slogan goes[16]—are undoubtedly the most common. There is no principled reason for settling on any of those, in and of themselves. It is arbitrary, from a moral point of view, where we draw the lines on the map. It is arbitrary, from a moral point of view, to whom we happen to feel sentimentally attached or with whom we happen to share a common history or ancestry.

What makes those factors matter, in ways that justifies constituting our demoi around them, is the way that those factors lead to people's interests being intertwined. Geographically, people who live in close proximity to one another are typically (if not invariably) affected by what one another does. People bound by shared histories or nationalities typically (if not invariably) care about what one another does and conceive their interests as being affected by that. The reason we think that territorial or historical or national groups ought to make decisions together is that, typically if not invariably, the interests of individuals within those groups are affected by the actions and choices of others in that group. Those common reciprocal interests in one another's actions and choices is what makes those groups appropriate units for collective decision-making—at least in a rough-and-ready way.[17]

Rough-and-ready, because (as flagged by the recurring qualifier, 'typically if not invariably') the correlation between territoriality or nationality or history and shared interests is far from perfect. Not every person who lives in a given territory is affected by the actions and choices of every other person in that territory; not every person in the territory is affected by every collective decision of the demos constituted on the basis of residence in that territory. And ditto for historical or national groups.

Constituting a demos on the basis of shared territory or history or nationality is thus only an approximation to constituting it on the basis of what really matters, which is interlinked interests.[18] Sometimes the approximation is over-inclusive, including in the demos someone whose

[16] Brubaker (1992) and Soysal (1994).

[17] This is what defines a 'people' which is to be 'self-determining'. The convergence of views found among such a people is what sometimes gives credence to notions of a 'common good' or 'general will' that is sometimes taken to be required to ground the demos. See Cohen (1971: ch. 2), Sartori (1962: ch. 2; 1987: ch. 2), Mill (1861: ch. 16), Barry (1989), and Margalit and Raz (1990).

[18] Arrhenius (2005: 17–21).

interests are not affected by the decision of the demos (either in the case of this particular decision, or in general). Sometimes the approximation is under-inclusive, excluding from the demos someone whose interests are affected by the decision of the demos (either in the case of this particular decision, or in general).

The crucial thing to notice at this point, however, is the characteristic form taken by critiques of those alternative ways of constituting the demos. Counterexamples are conjured up showing that each of those ways of constituting the demos is either (or both) over- or under-inclusive, wrongly conferring membership upon people whose interests are not affected by the decisions of the demos or wrongly denying it to people whose interests are affected. Notice, however, that that is just to say that the 'all affected interests' principle is the principle that is being implicitly employed in judging all those other methods of constituting the demos, on the basis of territoriality, nationality, history, or whatever. The 'all affected interests' principle is the standard by which the adequacy of those other approximations is invariably assessed.

Such critiques can be extended even to the rule that 'all those who will be bound by a rule should have a say in making the rule'. On the face of it, that looks like an attractive principle in its own right, with a robustly democratic pedigree traceable to the notion of what it is to 'give laws to ourselves'.[19] But (unless we illicitly equate 'will be bound by' with 'will be affected by') that method of constituting the demos is invariably open to the same sorts of counterexamples as plague the others. Lots of laws have extra-territorial effects without having, literally, extra-territorial application. Imagine a German law that requires polluting factories there to build chimneys tall enough to ensure that their emissions fall to ground only beyond Germany's borders: legally, that law binds only manufacturers in Germany; but it clearly affects Scandinavians, and is indeed designed to do so. Giving only Germans (the only ones who are literally 'bound' by the law) a vote on the law, as the principle here in view envisages, would be adjudged fatally under-inclusive in consequence.[20]

---

[19] Or, as Dahl (1979: 112–3) phrases it, 'the moral axiom that no person ought to be governed without his consent....'

[20] Arrhenius (2005: 26). Examples of over-inclusiveness are harder to produce, here, precisely because anyone who is bound by (subject to) a law is *ipso facto* affected by it. But consider transients, who are indeed bound by a country's laws (at least for the duration of their stay in that country) but are not (sufficiently) affected by them over the long haul to deserve a say in making those laws. [This is to put a different gloss on Dahl (1979: 123, n. 20; 1989: 128, n. 11.)]

Protecting peoples' interests is thus the most plausible candidate principle for bringing the 'who' and the 'how' of democratic politics into alignment. That principle dictates who should constitute the decision-making group ('all affected interests should have a say'[21]). It also dictates how that group should be governed ('making decisions democratically', which well-established results tell us is the best way to protect and promote people's interests[22]).

Is that principle for constituting the demos itself a democratic principle, or do both those strands of democratic theory derive from a principle that is itself 'extra-democratic'? Well, arguably the principle is indeed 'democratic': the 'all affected interests' principle is fundamentally egalitarian, counting all interests equally; and equal political power is arguably the cornerstone of democracy.[23] But whether or not the 'all affected interests' principle is itself a democratic principle—and hence whether we can truly be said to be constituting the demos on a 'democratic' basis when adhering to it—is ultimately probably a purely terminological question of little consequence. What matters is that constituting the demos in that way is consonant with our settled views about what it is to 'make collective decisions in a democratic way' at the procedural level. Both derive from a shared root, and they are linked in that way.

7.2. Applying the 'All Affected Interests' Principle

'The Principle of Affected Interests is' thus, as Dahl says, 'very likely the best general principle of inclusion that you are likely to find.'[24] In its most generic form, the 'all affected interests' principle simply says that 'everyone who is affected by the decisions of a government should have the right to participate in that government'.[25]

---

[21] Or at least 'have a right to have a say': I leave it as an open question here whether democratic theory requires, or permits, making it obligatory for those who have such a right to exercise it.

[22] The latter formulation aims to straddle Macpherson's 'protective' and 'developmental democracy' (1977: chs. 2–3). The root intuition is traceable to James Mill's 'Essay on Government' (1823). It has been variously formalized by May (1952) and Rae (1969). The relationship between these formalizations and the Condorcet Jury Theorem are discussed in Goodin (2006).

[23] Beitz (1989).

[24] Dahl (1970: 64). Whelan (1983: 16, 19) thinks it is 'perhaps the most intuitively plausible proposal', even though he ends up rejecting it as 'fundamentally untenable'.

[25] Dahl (1970: 64). It is often added: 'and only those who are affected by a decision should have a say in it'; but in Section 7.3.1, I show that that clause can be safely omitted. Like Dahl I shall here be talking in terms of *'people's* interests', and reducing the interests of corporate

There are many possible fine-tunings of that basic 'all affected interests' principle. Perhaps, for example, not every old interest ought automatically to entitle one to a say in the matter; we may, for example, want to disenfranchise 'external preferences' (at least when they take a malevolent rather than benevolent form).[26] Perhaps other sorts of interests particularly entitle you to a say (when your basic needs or fundamental human rights are at stake, for example). Perhaps, for yet another example, people ought to be given a say not simply if their interests are affected but also in proportion to the degree to which their interests are affected.[27]

All those finer details are interesting and important in the actual application of the 'all affected interests' principle. But for present purposes I want to set all those to one side, in order to focus upon more fundamental issues that arise in choosing among various alternative forms of that principle.

7.2.1. The 'All Actually Affected Interests' Principle

According to what I shall call the 'all actually affected interests' principle, the decision-making body should include all interests that are actually affected by the actual decision. This is probably the most common form of the principle.[28] But it can be quickly shown to be simply incoherent, in the same way it is incoherent to say that the electorate should be constituted from the outset by a vote of that selfsame electorate.

The demonstration is straightforward. Notice first that whose interests are 'affected' by any actual decision depends upon what the decision actually turns out to be. Notice second that what the decision actually turns out to be depends, in turn, upon who actually takes the decision. Hence the 'all actually affected interests' principle suffers the same incoherence as discussed at the outset: it is unable to tell us who is

or collective actors to the interests of their constituent individuals (Coleman 1990: pt. IV). While that seems the obviously right way to enumerate 'all affected interests' for purposes of voting, it may well be that, because of their special information or expertise, organized groups ought to be given separate standing in deliberations (Cohen and Sabel 1997: 333).

[26] Goodin (1986: 75–101) and Dahl (1970: 66).

[27] Dahl (1970: 65) and Brighouse and Fleurbaey (2006).

[28] Dahl (1970: 64) says 'everyone who *is affected* by the decision' [emphasis added]. Whelan (1983: 19, 16) says 'all those people who *are affected*', going on to say that 'who is affected by a given law or policy depends on *which* law or policy is enacted from among the available alternatives'.

entitled to vote on a decision until after that very decision has been decided.[29]

Here is one example. Imagine we are in the process of democratizing an old feudal order, and the newly established House of Commons will henceforth be sovereign. The question now is, 'Who ought to be entitled to vote for members of the House of Commons?' Specifically: 'Ought we enfranchise nobles as well as commoners?' The 'all actually affected interests' principle instructs us to enfranchise everyone whose interests are actually affected by the decision that is actually made. If the decision is to exclude the nobles, then their interests will be affected: a House of Commons constituted in that way will (let us assume) enact legislation dispossessing nobles of their excess lands. But if the decision is to include the nobles, then their interests will not be affected: they will (let us assume) have sufficient voting power to block seizure of their lands.[30]

Here is another example. Imagine a UK referendum on the question, 'Should the UK transfer 5 percent of its GDP as restitution to its former African colonies?' Ought citizens of those former African colonies get to vote in that referendum? On the 'all actually affected interests' principle, they ought to if their interests are affected by the outcome that actually occurs in that referendum. If the decision is to give them a vote, then interests are affected: there will (let us suppose) be enough African votes in favour of the proposal to swamp the British ones against it. If the decision is to deny the Africans a vote in that referendum, their interests are not affected: the referendum will fail (let us suppose) and they will be no better or worse off than they are at present.

The general point is just this: which interests are 'actually affected' depends on who gets to vote. Hence it is incoherent to try to determine who should get to vote by asking whose interests are actually affected by the course of action actually decided upon. It is like the winning lottery ticket being pulled out of the hat by whomever has won that selfsame lottery.

[29] Whelan (1983: 17) offers a similar thought: 'In many cases...the question of who is affected by a given law or policy depends on which law or policy is enacted from among the available alternatives;...[t]hus to say that those who will be affected by a given decision are the ones who should participate in making it is to attempt to...propose what is a logical as well as procedural impossibility.'

[30] The narrow, literal understanding of what it is to 'be affected' upon which I am concentrating for the moment takes the *status quo* as the baseline, and assumes that a decision 'affects' someone or something only if it causes deviations from the *status quo*. The expansive 'possibilistic' construal to which I turn in the next section drops that assumption, which is obviously unduly restrictive.

7.2.2. The 'All Interests Possibly Affected Interests' Principle

That, clearly, is an indefensibly narrow construal of what it is to 'be affected'. Indeed, it is indefensibly narrow in two respects. First, it construes what it is to be affected as being 'actually affected by the course of action actually decided upon'. Second, the 'all affected interest' principle implicitly takes the status quo as a baseline, and supposes that your interests are affected by a decision if and only if the decision alters your position from that.

By any sensible standard, your interests are indeed affected by a decision to preserve the status quo, if the alternative to doing that would have been to leave you far worse off (or better off) than you are at present. You are surely 'affected' in the relevant sense by a decision to compensate you fully for property expropriated for some public purpose, rather than just taking the property without compensation. You would surely have been 'affected' in the relevant sense by the decision to 'open the floodgates and submerge your farm if there is another six inches of rain', even if the rain stopped and the floodgates were never actually opened.

More generally, you are rightly said to be 'affected', not merely by the 'course of action actually decided upon' but also by the consequences of not choosing any of the other alternative courses of action that could have been chosen. And you are rightly said to be 'affected', not merely by what the consequences of that decision actually turn out to be but also by what the consequences could have turned out to be.

That is simply to say that we ought to broaden our analysis of what it is to be affected by a decision to include anything that might possibly happen as a result of the decision. To decide what interests are affected in the UK referendum discussed above, we must therefore ask what interests would or could be affected by any possible outcome of that decision process. Even if the actual outcome of the referendum goes against the Africans, leaving them 'unaffected' in the sense of 'no better and no worse off than they are at present', the decision nonetheless ought to be seen as 'affecting' them in a broader sense because had it gone the other way, their interests would have been greatly advanced.

In the case of a referendum, it seems simple enough to determine what 'any possible outcome of that decision process' might be. After all, there are only two boxes on the referendum's ballot paper to choose between. The outcome of the referendum decision has to be either one or the other, either 'Yes' or 'No'.

Things might not be quite so simple even in that simple case. Although there are only two possible outcomes of the vote, it might not be straightforward determining who might possibly be affected and how much by each possible outcome of the referendum. People can disagree about that, too, giving rise to yet further hard questions. (Should 'all affected interests' include anyone who *believes* his or her interests could or would be affected by some possible outcome of the decision process, or ought we limit it to those who really would?[31]) But let us set these complications aside, once again, to focus on a more fundamental matter.

That more fundamental issue is, 'Who gets to formulate the referendum question?'—or to set the political agenda more generally? Clearly, that is a decision to which the 'all affected interests' principle must be applied, as well. But once we do that, it turns out (on the 'possibilistic' analysis I am here advocating) that we will have to give a say in *that* decision to anyone who might possibly be affected by any possible outcome of any possible question that might possibly appear on any possible ballot. That is, we will have to give a say to anyone who might possibly be affected by any possible decision arising out of any possible agenda.

By embracing all possible worlds, politically, this expansive conception of 'all possibly affected interests' causes the franchise to balloon dramatically and the scope for legitimate exclusions to shrink accordingly. Virtually (maybe literally) everyone in the world—and indeed everyone in all possible future worlds[32]—should be entitled to vote on any proposal or any proposal for proposals. A maximally extensive franchise, virtually (perhaps literally) ignoring boundaries both of space and of time, would be the only legitimate way of constituting the demos to this more defensible version of the 'all possibly affected interests' principle.

7.3. Amendments and Evasive Manoeuvres

As between those two, the 'possibilist' version is the only coherent interpretation of the 'all affected interest' principle, and that principle is the best one anyone has yet come up with for how to constitute the demos. The upshot, however, would be to extend membership in the demos to

---

[31] Dahl (1970: 66).

[32] Tännsjö (2005). And depending on one's views about the interests of the dead, past worlds as well; and depending on one's views about the interests of other sentient beings or even ecosystems, perhaps we ought on those grounds enfranchise nature as well. On the former issue, see Mulgan (1999) and Bergström (2005). On the latter, see Goodin (1996*a*) and Goodin, Pateman and Pateman (1997).

'all interests possibly affected by any possible decision under any possible agenda'.

For those who are uncomfortable with the idea of a genuinely global, timeless democracy, the challenge is to come up with some alternative— either an alternative to or an alternative formulation of the 'all affected interests' principle. Here I shall canvass four possible responses along those lines.

The first suggests an amendment to the 'all affected interests' principle that, if accepted, would block the radical expansion of the demos suggested above. Upon closer inspection, however, there prove to be no grounds for that amendment. The second response suggests an amendment to the 'all affected interests' principle that, if accepted, would reduce (but not eliminate) the expansionary tendencies of my argument above. One part of that proposal ought (usually) to be accepted, but the remaining parts must be rejected, with consequences almost as expansionary as those sketched above.

The third response suggests that the 'all affected interests' principle be deployed for a different purpose. On this proposal it would be used for specifying the decisional power of the demos, rather than for constituting the demos. The radical expansion of the demos would thus be avoided, but at the cost of reducing the decisional power of the demos just as radically.

The fourth response might be the deliberative democratic proposal, taken to extremes. One way to avoid problems that might arise from extending the franchise too widely is to avoid voting altogether, substituting talk for votes. But extending the conversation to encompass all affected interests is as problematic, if not more so, as extending the franchise that widely.

7.3.1. The 'All and Only Affected Interests' Principle

The first response suggests that the 'all affected interests' principle be construed as enfranchising all *and only* those whose interests are affected.[33] Then the expansive rendering sketched in Section 7.2.2 could be blocked on the grounds that it falls afoul of the 'and only' clause in that very principle itself.

Under the more expansive 'possibilistic' rendering of the principle in Section 7.2.2, virtually everyone would get a vote on virtually everything,

---

[33] Implicitly, 'all and only *actually* affected interests': thus raising all the objections discussed in Section 7.3.1.

virtually everywhere in the world. They would do so, on the grounds that their interests could or would be affected by some possible outcome of some possible question that might be put on some possible ballot.

For a great many of those people, however, their interests will not actually be affected by the most likely outcome of the present ballot. Their interests may not even be affected by any possible outcome of the present ballot. Their interests might be affected by some possible amendment to the present proposal, or by substituting some other proposal for the present one. But that is simply not going to happen. Their interests are simply not going to be affected by any possible outcome of the ballot presently taking place. Giving them a say in the matter, when it does not affect them, looks like a classic case of over-inclusiveness—judged according to the 'actually affected' version of that standard, anyway.

Note in passing that even on that analysis, lots of people who are not currently entitled to vote should still be entitled to a vote: Lebanese in the elections of Israelis who bombard them; Iraqis in the elections of Americans who occupy them; and so on. Without doubt, those people are actually affected by the actual outcomes of ballots that are actually taking place there. So even without the 'possibilistic' extension, merely an 'all actually affected interests' principle would lead to some pretty radical extensions of many of the more powerful demoi. That much is common ground between 'actualist' and 'possibilist' readings of the 'all affected interests' principle. The issue between them is merely how far we should go beyond that already substantial extension of those demoi.

Previous commentators have noted various inconveniences with the principle that 'all and only interests that are affected should be enfranchised'. If 'affected' is taken to mean 'actually affected by the course of action actually decided upon', then a different set of people would be affected by each different decision; and if the 'all affected principle' enfranchises all *and only* those who are affected, that 'would require a different constituency of voters or participants for every decision'. In consequence, 'the status of fellow-citizens would not be permanent,...but would shift in relation to the issue proposed'.[34] That sounds like bad news for a democratic polity. It may be a little less bad, if we recall that already 'there are 1,467 political entities in the New York Metropolitan Region'.[35] Still, were a different decision-making unit required for literally

---

[34] Whelan (1983: 19). See similarly Saward (1999: 125–6).   [35] Dahl (1970: 64).

every political decision, the proliferation would exceed that many, many times over.

This problem, notice, arises from the conjunction of the overly narrow 'actualist' construal of what it is to be 'affected', together with an 'all and only' version of the 'all affected interests' principle. I have criticized the former already. Let me now turn a critical eye to the latter. In so doing, I will be arguing not so much that it is wrong as that it is unnecessary to add the 'and only' rider to the 'all affected interests' principle.

Here is what is at stake. If we can find good grounds for dispensing with the 'and only' rider, then over-inclusiveness would cease to be a problem, while of course under-inclusiveness would remain problematic. An 'all (but not necessarily only) affected interests' principle would require us to ensure that anyone whose interests could or would be affected is included. But it would raise no objection to including, as well, various people whose interests are not affected. Notice that the most reliable way of ensuring that no one who should be included is excluded is simply to include everyone.[36] Were there no objection to including people whose interests might not be affected, that would clearly be what we should do for the sake of ensuring we do not omit someone who ought to be included. That, in turn, would yield a demos that was stable, in the sense that its composition would not change from issue to issue.

What argument might be given for thinking that over-inclusiveness is not a problem? The best one is as follows. Suppose that people vote one way or the other purely on the basis of their interests (remembering the expansive construal of 'interests' I am working with here, embracing sentiments as well as material interests). Now suppose that people are required to vote on some issue that does not affect their interests. How will they vote? Randomly, given the first hypothesis. And remember: a large number of people voting randomly distribute themselves equally across all options, leaving the overall outcome unaltered.[37]

It makes no difference to the political outcome, therefore, if we enfranchise people whose interests are not affected. All that we have to worry about is ensuring the inclusion of everyone whose interests are affected.

[36] As Arrhenius (2005: 22) observes, 'there is an obvious end to the regress: when everybody is included'.

[37] Assuming decisions do not require any 'special majority'. If only 1,000 of 1,001,000 voters are affected, and all those affected support the proposal, the statistically expected outcome of the ballot would be 501,000 for and 500,000 against. The proposal would be enacted if voting were by simple majority rules, but it would fail if e.g. a two-thirds majority were required—despite the fact that it got well over two-thirds of those who actually had a stake in the matter.

Omitting them can change the outcome, and from the viewpoint of the 'all affected interests' principle change it for the worse. Including those whose interests are not affected does not.

Restricting the 'all affected interests' principle to 'all *and only* affected interests' can thus be rejected as otiose. If the purpose of the 'all affected interests' principle is to ensure protection of affected interests, there is no need to add the 'and only' clause. On the contrary, if we want to be sure of protecting 'all affected interests', we have good reason to err on the side of over-inclusiveness—with the expansionary effects on membership in the demos noted above.

7.3.2. The 'All Probably Affected Interests' Principle

In Section 7.2.2, I argued that the 'all affected interests' principle requires us to include in the demos every interest that might possibly be affected by any possible decision arising out of any possible agenda. Those wanting to resist any such radical extension of the demos might try to do so, secondly, by substituting 'probably' for 'possibly' in that formulation.

They might begin by putting pressure on the notion of 'possibility' at work there. Consider analogous issues arising in connection with the Precautionary Principle in environmental policy-making. One strong formulation of that Principle would be: if we know that it is possible that a certain course of action might lead to a major catastrophe, but we do not know how probable that is, we ought to treat that catastrophic outcome as if it were certain until we have sufficient evidence about probabilities to justify doing otherwise.[38] But there are limits on what can count as 'possible' for purposes of triggering even so strong a Precautionary Principle as that. It is logically possible that the laws of physics might have been other than they actually are, for example; but 'possibilities' arising under laws of physics governing some possible world very different from our own actual world are surely insufficient to trigger the Precautionary Principle.[39] So

[38] For various alternative formulations, see Gardiner (2006).

[39] 'Ordinarily we think of possibility as an all-or-nothing matter', David Lewis (1973: 52) observes. 'Given the notion of comparative overall similarity of worlds, however, there is a natural comparative concept of possibility. It is more possible for a dog to talk than for a stone to talk, since some worlds with talking dogs are more like our world than is any world with talking stones. It is more possible for a stone to talk than for eighteen to be a prime number, however, since stones do talk at some worlds far from ours, but presumably eighteen is not a prime number in any world at all, no matter how remote.' Strictly speaking, therefore, in specifying what is or is not 'possible' for purposes of the Precautionary Principle or my 'all possibly affected interests' principle, we ought to think in terms of some 'threshold' defined in terms of degrees of similarity in certain relevant respects to our actual world; and the

too, most people would say, are possibilities below 'a certain threshold of scientific plausibility'.[40]

Critics of the Precautionary Principle, like those of the 'maximin' rule that it mimics, insist more generally that we ought to decide on the basis of probabilities, not sheer possibilities. Recall Harsanyi's famous riposte to Rawls:

If you took the maximin principle seriously you could not ever cross the street (after all, you might be hit by a car); you could never drive over a bridge (after all, it might collapse); you could never get married (after all, it might end in disaster), etc. If anybody really acted in this way he would soon end up in a mental institution.[41]

And sooner than Harsanyi imagines, perhaps, since 'refusing to do [each of] those... things has worst-case scenarios of its own (including death and disaster)'. In Sunstein's view, that renders the Precautionary Principle 'literally incoherent... [Because] there are risks on all sides... it forbids the very steps that it requires,... [T]he Precautionary Principle forbids action, inaction, and everything in between'.[42]

From discussions of the Precautionary Principle and the maximin rule, we have thus learned to talk in terms of 'probabilities' rather than mere 'possibilities', wherever we reasonably can.[43] Can that sort of thought help avoid the radical expansion of the demos to include every interest that might possibly be affected by any possible decision arising out of any possible agenda?

'Possibly' figures in that 'all possibly affected interests' formula at three distinct places. There is only one, I think, at which it might plausibly be substituted by 'probably'. What agendas are probable, and what outcomes under them are probable, is a function of who has voting power within the demos. But that being so, it would be incoherently circular to let who is a member with voting power in the demos depend on what is probable

dimensions in which we would demand above-threshold similarity, in order to call something 'possible' for these purposes, would include the laws of nature, logic, and metaphysics (but would conspicuously exclude political or social arrangements).

[40] 'No one thinks that it is enough if someone, somewhere, urges that a risk is worth taking seriously' Sunstein (2005: 24) continues.

[41] Harsanyi (1975: 595). Harsanyi's conclusion: 'It is extremely irrational to make your behavior wholly dependent on some highly unlikely unfavorable contingencies regardless of how little probability you are willing to assign them.'

[42] Sunstein (2005: 111, 4).

[43] 'Reasonably can' rather than 'possibly can', because even if you have absolutely no evidence bearing on probabilities it is always possible for you to assign subjective probabilities completely groundlessly. If subjective probabilities are completely (or very substantially) groundless, however, it is not at all clear that we are better off thinking in those terms than we are thinking in terms of possibilities.

in those two ways. (That is just like saying 'the person who draws the winning number out of the hat is the person who has won that very draw', once again.)

That leaves only one place in the formula where 'probably' might plausibly replace 'possibly'. That concerns the question of whether the interest in question would actually be affected (by any of the possible decisions arising out of any of the possible agendas). That is exactly the sort of issue giving rise to arguments over the Precautionary Principle and maximin; and the right answer here is whatever the right answer there turns out to be. Most of the time, we ought to indeed judge that sort of issue on the basis of probabilities rather than possibilities alone. But where (as occasionally happens) we have no reliable probability information, then we may well be forced back to reliance on possibility-based reasoning of some sort or another.[44]

How much would it help to replace 'possibly' with 'probably' at only that one of the three places it appears in the formula? Membership in the demos, on that revised account, ought extend to every interest that would probably be affected by any possible decision arising out of any possible agenda.[45] And 'any possible decision' and 'any possible agenda' still seem likely to expand the demos very substantially indeed. Restricted as it (usually) is to interests that 'would probably be affected', the revised formula might not extend membership in the demos quite as far as the version of the formula that operated in terms of 'possibly' rather than 'probably' at that point. But even the revised formula seems highly expansionary.

7.3.3. Limiting the Decisional Power of the Demos

Ordinarily, the 'all affected interests' principle is taken to be a standard for defining the scope of membership in the demos. Alternatively, or additionally, it might be used to delimit the scope of the 'decisional power' of the demos.[46]

There are of course many other things (human rights, for example) that might also legitimately limit the decisional power of the demos. Even if, as per the 'all affected interests' principle, we give a vote to everyone who

---

[44] Which could be 'maximin', or could be 'maximax', or could be a weighted average of the two as per Arrow and Hurwicz (1972).

[45] When henceforth I refer to my preferred 'possibilist' version of the 'all affected interests' principle, it is this revised version to which I shall be referring.

[46] Whelan (1983: 20) canvases a version of this.

is affected, that does not necessarily imply that the demos is empowered to decide by voting upon everything that affects its members. You may be affected by (or anyway have preferences over) what I read or the colour I paint my bathroom, but I have a right to decide those matters myself without intervention of your 'nosy' preferences.[47] Those who would want to resist the implication that the 'all affected interests' principle should give workers (and consumers and neighbours and even competitors) a right to have a say in the operations of a firm that affects them would presumably try to point to some analogous right to 'privity' within the firm.

In introducing his initial discussion of the 'all affected interest' principle, Dahl recalls the old US Revolutionary-era slogan, 'No taxation without representation'.[48] One way of meeting that demand would have been to give US colonists seats in the UK Parliament responsible for enacting the taxes in question. That is what is suggested by the 'all affected interests' principle as I have been discussing it up to this point. But a second way of meeting that demand (and what one suspects the US colonists really wanted) would have been for the UK Parliament to refrain from enacting taxes that apply to people like them who lacked representation in that Parliament.

The 'all affected interests' standard can thus be satisfied in either of two ways. One is by expanding the franchise, giving a say to all those who would be affected. Another is by restricting the power of the demos, so it is only allowed to make decisions that affect only those who do have a say.

The 'decisional power' version might, on its face, seem to be the more modest proposal: the first entails a radical expansion of the demos whereas the second requires merely restraint on the part of the demos. Such appearances are misleading, however. The second version is every bit as radical as the first, and for just the same reason. It threatens to deprive the demos of virtually all power to make any decisions whatsoever, unless the demos already includes 'all affected interests' defined in the expansive 'possibilistic' way.

On the expansive analysis of what interests might be 'possibly affected', any given decision is highly likely to affect a great many interests— at least some that are likely not to be included in any relatively restricted demos. If the 'decisional power' of the demos is restricted only to those decisions that affect only those who are members of the

[47] Barry (1986: 11–44).   [48] Dahl (1970: 64).

demos, then any such relatively restricted demos would be debarred from making those sorts of decisions—which, empirically, seems to be most decisions.

The upshot of the previous analysis was that virtually everyone, regardless of spatial or indeed temporal location, should be included in the demos. The upshot of the present analysis is that if they are not, then the 'decisional power' version of the 'all affected interests' principle would debar the demos from making virtually any decisions at all.

7.3.4. Forget the Franchise, Just Talk

Deliberative democrats suppose that their particular brand of democracy is impervious to political boundaries. As John Dryzek puts it,

[O]lder models always saw the first task in their application as specification of the boundaries of a political community. Deliberation and communication, in contrast, can cope with fluid boundaries, and the production of outcomes across boundaries. For we can now look for democracy in the character of political interaction, without worrying about whether or not it is confined to particular territorial entities. [49]

Instead of extending the franchise to include all affected interests, deliberationists would simply have us extend the conversation to include them. Conversations can be carried on across borders in a way that elections cannot. Substitute 'discursive accountability' for 'electoral accountability', and the problem of political boundaries disappears. [50]

The problem of 'constituting the demos' does not disappear, however. For deliberations to be democratic, they too must include all affected interests. They must do so, for just the same reasons as given above for including 'all affected interests' in a demos that makes decisions by voting. And if 'all affected interests' is understood in the expansionary way argued for above, that is going to be a very extensive conversational community indeed. [51]

But any much extended demos is conversationally very problematic. Listening to one another takes time, and if there are too many others

[49] Dryzek (1999: 44).

[50] Benhabib (1996: 70) and Thompson (1999: 120) offer weaker versions of the same thought.

[51] In Section 7.3.1, I argued against the 'all and only affected interests principle', on grounds that in the case of voting it was costless to include voters whose interests would not be affected: their votes would be random and hence cancel each other out. It is similarly costless to include them in the discursive case: if their interests are not going to be affected, they would have nothing to say.

involved it simply takes too much time to constitute a viable decision procedure. Remember Robert Dahl's back-of-the-envelope calculation: 'if an association were to make one decision a day, allow ten hours a day for discussion, and permit each member just ten minutes—rather extreme assumptions...—then the association could not have more than sixty members'.[52] If 600 people were involved, speaking time for each would have to drop to one minute each or the rate of decision-making would stretch out to one decision every ten working days. If there were 6,000 people, speaking time for each would drop to six seconds each or the rate of decision-making would stretch to one decision every hundred working days, or (assuming they do not work weekends) just a couple of decisions a year. If millions or billions of people were engaged in the conversation, the consequences simply do not bear thinking about.

Of course, to say that virtually everyone in the world is 'conversation-ally enfranchised' is not to say that each and every one of them will necessarily exercise that franchise. Some people will have nothing to say, either because they are not affected by the proposal that is actually on the table or because someone else has already made their point. Suppose only one in every hundred people put up their hands to speak. If there are a million people who are entitled to speak, however, that still leaves us with 10,000 names on the list wishing to speak.

Talking together is important, in all the ways discussed in previous chapters. Discursive accountability to one's peers within networks, nationally and transnationally, can be a powerful supplement to electoral accountability, as I shall go on to argue in Chapter 8. But substituting discursive accountability for electoral accountability does nothing to cure—rather, it exacerbates—the problems arising from genuinely including all affected interests among those to whom we must be accountable.

7.4. Getting Real

Dahl concludes his own initial discussion of these issues saying,

By now you may be troubled by the thought that the [all affected interests] principle has unlocked Pandora's box. Very likely it has.... [I]t forces us to ask whether there is not after all some wisdom in the half-serious comment of a friend in Latin America who said that his people should be allowed to participate in our

[52] Dahl (1970: 67–8).

[US] elections, for what happens in the politics of the United States is bound to have profound consequences for his country.[53]

Dahl cautions us not to dismiss the jest out of hand.[54] But labelling the observation 'half-serious' leaves it hovering uneasily in that infamous argumentational no-man's land between *QED* and *reductio*.

If (as I believe to be the case) the 'all affected interests' principle is the best principled basis upon which to constitute the demos, and if (as I have argued) the best interpretation of that principle is the expansive 'possibilist' form, then it does indeed provide good grounds for thinking that (at least in principle) we should give virtually everyone a vote on virtually everything virtually everywhere in the world.

If, as many would insist, that is wildly impractical then we need to begin thinking what arrangements might best approximate that ideal in some practice that is feasible. The territorially defined state is the form most commonly found in practice. For the sake of argument, let us assume that that is so for good practical reasons. Indeed, let us assume that the territorially defined state is the most practical form. Let us then proceed to ask, 'What overlays do we need to superimpose on a system of territorially defined states to approximate as closely as possible to the ideal of genuinely including "all possibly affected interests" via a universal franchise worldwide?'

Here I shall suggest two possible overlays on the existing state system for doing that. Both leave territorially defined states of the familiar sort in place. One would put a layer of 'world government' over the top of them, giving people a right to appeal over the heads of territorial states if their interests were affected by actions of territorial states in which they have no say. The other, more modestly, would put a layer of 'international law' over the top of territorial states, imposing an obligation on territorial states to honour claims for compensation from people and peoples whose interests have been affected by actions of territorial states in which they have no vote.

7.4.1. *Upward Appeal, Higher Authorities*

Even the most dewy-eyed cosmopolitans rarely envisage a centralized, unitary government issuing worldwide diktats from some Capital of the

[53] Dahl (1970: 67).

[54] 'Do not dismiss his jest as an absurdity. In a world where we all have a joint interest in survival, the real absurdity is the absence of any system where that joint interest is effectively represented' (Dahl 1970: 67).

World. The proposal is almost always for a 'world government, federal in form'.

Here, in slightly stylized form, is how federal systems in general are supposed to work: Lower-level governments do what they can do well, without undue impact on people in other jurisdictions. But things that lower-levels of government cannot do well, or that cut across jurisdictions, are kicked up to higher levels of federal authority.[55]

Wherever decision problems are 'decomposable', we can without loss assign component parts of the problem to distinct subsystems that do not interact with one another, without any higher-level system interfering.[56] Some political decisions are like that. For purposes of making those sorts of decisions, we truly can carve up the political universe into distinct self-governing units and let them rule themselves without reference to other such units and without interferences from any higher-level units. If all political decisions were like that (or back when they all were, assuming there ever was such a time), the familiar sort of territorial state would be all we would need, and there would be no need for a federal overlay on that system of territorial states.

Insofar as political decisions are not like that—insofar as the decisions made in one territorial unit affect the interests of people and peoples in other territorial units (as increasingly they do)—we need some system for 'internalizing' those externalities, making those agents who cause the effects somehow responsible for the consequences of their actions. That would be the role of the upper-tier of government, in a federal system: to entertain and adjudicate complaints from people and peoples in one jurisdiction that their interests are affected by activities in other jurisdictions in which they had no vote.

It is hard to see how exactly that would work to solve the enfranchisement problems here in view, unless the upper-tier of government was itself somehow answerable to a demos comprised in the maximally expansive way that (for the sake of the present argument) is being assumed to be impracticable. But maybe it is only impracticable to organize a demos in that maximally expansive way if the demos in question is going to be charged with making lots of decisions.

---

[55] This is the 'subsidiarity' principle, much discussed in the European Union (Delors et al. 1991; Føllesdal 1998). Once its institutional structure is fleshed out, Cohen and Sabel's proposal for a system of 'directly deliberative polyarchy' turns out to be basically just a variation on that theme (1997: 334–7).

[56] Simon (1969).

Maybe most of those impracticality worries would drop away, once we have agreed to most of the day-to-day decisions to the existing territorially based states, treating the upper-tier of government as basically a court of appeal which will adjudicate only very occasional cases. Whether or not that is plausible depends upon exactly what impracticality worries there were with directly implementing the expansive 'all possibly affected interests' ideal in the first place. Exploring that further would require a different sort of enquiry; here I merely flag that as something to explore, as part of any such enquiry.

7.4.2. *Lateral Claims to Compensation*

Interpreting the 'all affected interests' principle as delimiting the 'decisional power' of the demos—as saying that it has power to make only those decisions that affect no one except members of that demos—would in effect prohibit the demos from making any decision that has transboundary spillovers.[57]

Concern with such spillovers is common among political economists and policy-makers alike. 'Externalities', public economists say, distort public decisions. They are keen that they ought to be 'internalized'. But note well: their ordinary injunction does *not* prohibit activities altogether that have external effects. Instead their injunction is merely to 'internalize' externalities, making sure that those who produce external costs for others reimburse them, and that those who produce external benefits for others are reimbursed by them.

Likewise in international law, the rule is not 'no spillovers' but, rather, 'no *uncompensated* spillovers'. Insisting that no jurisdiction may do anything that affects any other would be unrealistically restrictive. Almost anything we do has some effects on others beside ourselves alone. International law, like public economics, is perfectly content that we should do so, just so long as we compensate others who are affected by our actions and choices.

What is adequate compensation and who gets to say what is adequate are tricky questions. Difficulties in reaching a mutually agreed resolution may constitute good pragmatic reasons for trying hard not to do anything that affects outsiders (even whilst knowing that it will never be possible to achieve that goal completely). The point remains that the basic rule in international law and public economics is something less than is proposed

---

[57] A consequence of the 'all affected interests' principle noted by Whelan (1983: 43, n. 12).

under the 'decisional power' interpretation of the 'all affected interests' principle. There is no prohibition on affecting interests that have no say. International law and public economics require, instead, simply that any interests that are affected ought to be compensated. But they insist that precisely because they have no say—precisely because these are in that sense *external* effects—these effects must be compensated.[58]

What form of compensation (if any) is appropriate for righting any particular sort of wrong is a further and deeper question. Sometimes we can provide recompense 'in-kind': monetary damages for monetary losses. Typically in tort law, however, we have to provide compensation in a form that differs in kind from the form of the losses being compensated. In such cases, there is always a question whether *any* amount of compensation can 'make the victim whole' again.[59] But that question arises with particular poignancy when the wrong involved is wrongful exclusion from the franchise.

For that reason, the compensation strategy is probably third-best, after genuinely 'enfranchising all possibly affected interests' worldwide, and after 'world government, federal in form'. Still, third-best is better than nothing.

7.5. Conclusion

The democratic ideal ought to ideally be to enfranchise 'all affected interests'. Understood in a suitably expansive 'possibilistic' way, that would mean giving virtually everyone everywhere a vote on virtually everything decided anywhere.[60]

Maybe that is not practical, for one reason or another. Maybe we will have to fall back on one of the more modest approximations just discussed. But even the more modest of those fallbacks still have important consequences.

Even if we only insist upon compensation being paid to people whose interests are affected by activities in other jurisdictions in which they do not have a vote, that would give rise to claims across borders far beyond

---

[58] Governments can, and regularly do, pass laws that help some people and harm others *within* their jurisdiction, without any requirement of compensation. It is only cross-jurisdictional effects that require compensation, under international law. For examples and further references, see Goodin (1988*b*).

[59] Goodin (1989).

[60] And it might mean that we ought take such votes on lots more than we presently do, including the activities of firms and so on.

anything we see at present. Purely as a matter of democratic third-best, the price of not enfranchising everyone we ideally should is that we would have to pay them off for any harms we inflict upon them and accede to their demands for fair recompense for any benefits we derive from the wrongfully disenfranchised.

Were we all making joint decisions together within a single demos, we would be democratically entitled to impose costs and confer benefits upon one another as part of our ongoing life together. If people whose interests we affect are kept outside our demos, we are obliged—by principles of democracy, as well as ones of justice and humanity—to settle up.

8

Modes of democratic accountability

Democratic accountability, conceived as it traditionally has been in strictly electoral terms, seems highly problematic if the franchise were extended as broadly as Chapter 7 has suggested it should be. Having everyone worldwide vote in a single polity would be visionary, to say the least.

The traditional voting-based conception of democratic accountability is not the only one available however. 'Discursive accountability' is the deliberative-democratic alternative. Democratic accountability on a global scale becomes much less problematic if we re-conceive it in broader, non-electoral terms, as encompassing accountability to disbursed networks rather than merely accountability to democratically empowered electors.[1]

In this chapter, I explore the possibilities of network-based modes of accountability. I do so by special reference to voluntary associations of civil society. As Seyla Benhabib writes,

It is through the interlocking net of these multiple forms of associations, networks, and organizations that an anonymous 'public conversation' results. It is central to the model of deliberative democracy that it privileges such a public sphere of mutually interlocking and overlapping networks and associations of deliberation, contestation and argumentation.[2]

The discursive accountability characterizing such networks is the mode of accountability that is peculiar to deliberative democracy.

This chapter develops its analysis by reference to the most formally organized tip of the civil society iceberg, non-profit corporations of the so-called 'Third Sector'. The lessons drawn from there generalize, however, to

---

[1] As Held (1995: 271) sees it, 'the case for cosmopolitan democracy arises from [the existence of] diverse networks' like this. See similarly Dryzek (1999: 44).
[2] Benhabib (1996: 73–4).

civil society as a whole. Indeed, the lessons generalize beyond the nation-state itself. These novel modes of network accountability are arguably the dominant modes of democratic accountability in the globalized world.

8.1. The Nature of Accountability

Accountability is a concept that takes a three-part predicate: the account-ability is *of* some agent *to* some other agent *for* some state of affairs. Political accountability of a democratic sort is the most familiar example, perhaps. There, the accountability is *of* elected officials *to* their electorates *for* their performance in office.

That modern, democratic version of accountability piggybacks, of course, on much earlier notions of political accountability: that *of* a servant of the Crown *to* the Sovereign *for* the performance of his or her duties. Historically, such accountability was serious stuff. It was suffi-ciently terrifying to induce Cardinal Wolsey to transfer his newly built palace at Hampton Court to his liege lord, for one famous example. Mod-ern administrative accountability pales in comparison. But we still talk of the accountability *of* public servants *to* elected officials (and through them to the electorate in general) *for* their performance in office.

Similarly, corporate accountability refers to the accountability *of* a firm's managers *to* its owners *for* their conduct of the affairs of the firm. This is where accounts and accountants come into their own.

In the case of partnerships or joint-stock companies, the owners are plural. That gives rise to political-style mechanisms of accountability at partners' or stockholders' meetings. Political those meetings may be, but they are hardly democratic: the rule is not one-person-one-vote but one-share-one-vote; and the franchise, far from being universal, is limited to those with a share in the firm.[3]

If the firm is listed on public stock exchanges, that gives rise to further layers of accountability: *of* the owners-and-managers *to* public officials (and through them to elected officials, and thence the electorate at large) *for* fair dealing as specified by relevant statutes and regulations. Thereby arise the duties of publicly listed companies to provide public accounts, compiled according to recognized and accepted accounting standards to ensure there is no fraud or deception, along with the duties not to engage in corrupt practices (insider-trading etc.).

[3] Indeed, with a 'voting share', insofar as there are non-voting shares.

Those are very familiar forms of accountability in the state and market sectors. It is often alleged that accountability is conspicuously lacking outside those sectors. Here I show that that need not be so, by focusing particularly on the most organized forms of civil society: non-government, non-profit organizations that are characteristically dubbed 'the Third Sector'. What I say about Third-Sector organizations in particular applies equally to all the more amorphous elements of civil society as a whole.

The non-state, non-market organizations of the Third Sector are often said to be sorely lacking in accountability.[4] There it is unclear *to* whom officers of the organization are to be held to account.[5] In the non-profit sector, there is simply no equivalent to 'voters' in the state sector or 'shareholders' in the market sector. And necessarily so, in the case of non-profits: the latter feature (the absence of any category of 'residual owners' akin to shareholders) is the defining feature of a non-profit organization.[6] The weak control of principals (donors, clients, constituents) over their agents (managers of non-profits) in the Third Sector is what, for example, allows the Red Cross to mount a fund-raising campaign by reference to one humanitarian crisis but then spending the monies alleviating some other.[7]

Still, there is *some* accountability. Non-profit organizations *are* typically legally incorporated. Their articles of incorporation serve to constitute the 'body corporate', provide for officers to be authorized to act on its behalf, and specify purposes of the organization. Just as with other corporations, these articles incorporating non-profits give rise to the accountability *of* officers (directors, trustees) of the body corporate *to* other officers (and through them to members of the organization entitled to vote for officers) *for* their conduct of the affairs of the organization in accordance with its stated aims and principles.[8] Depending on their aims, non-profit

---

[4] Herzlinger (1996); cf. Brody (2002); Independent Sector 2000.

[5] The 'Compact on Relations between Government and the Voluntary Sector in Wales' (United Kingdom Secretary of State for Wales 1988) offers the following laundry list:

Voluntary and community organisations and volunteering interests recognise their responsibility to be accountable to the different parties that have an interest in their work, including:

* their members;
* the people who use their services;
* the communities in which they work;
* the general public and funding bodies that support their work;
* the regulatory bodies that oversee their activities.

[6] Clark (1997). [7] Herzlinger (1996).

[8] As indicated by the fact that standing to bring a derivative suit against a 'public-benefit' (as distinct from 'mutual-benefit' or 'religious') non-profit corporation is typically limited

organizations may or may not seek tax-exempt or 'charitable' status, giving rise to another set of accountability mechanisms.

Beyond these specific accountabilities, of course, there is also the general accountability *of* all persons *to* public authorities (and through them the public at large) *for* complying with such statutes and regulations as lawfully govern their conduct. Contractual and fiduciary responsibilities, for example, give rise to the accountability *of* officers of non-profit organizations *to* their donors *for* using donations as specified by the donors.

Looking beyond legal relations, there is the even more general accountability *of* all moral agents *to* the moral community at large *for* acting in accordance with the moral law. That often takes a more concrete, conventional form in cases of role-responsibilities, which officers of private as well as public organizations sometimes powerfully internalize.[9]

Finally, there are various strategic factors that make people behave responsibly and responsively towards one another, even in the absence of any formal or informal relations of accountability. Under this heading falls the accountability *of* non-profit corporations *to* their donors *for* acting in accordance with their wishes—if they ever expect to get any more money from those donors, or from others who might take the experience of those donors to be indicative of their own prospective fates.

8.2. Dimensions of Accountability Regimes: A Basic Typology

We could, and for other purposes undoubtedly should, explore in far more detail all of those formal modes of accountability: the precise instruments giving them effect; the duties to which they give rise; the rights, powers, and remedies that they afford. For the present purposes, however, we can abstract from all those interesting and important details to identify three distinct regimes of accountability, loosely associated with each of the three different sectors (state, market, and non-profit, respectively).

What I propose doing here is analogous to what welfare-state researchers do with their notion of welfare regimes. They know fully well that any given country's welfare arrangements are a complex bundle of different policies and programmes, enacted at different times for different

to '(1) state attorneys general, (2) directors of the corporation [and] (3) members of the corporation ... [who] have "the right to vote for the election of a director or directors"'. Donors and those relying on benefits from the non-profit are typically denied standing to sue, and in that sense at least are not among the people to whom officers of the non-profit are accountable (Anon. 1992: 1594–5; see similarly ALI-ABA 1987: sec. 6.30).

[9] Day and Klein (1987).

purposes, animated by different principles and aiming at different objectives, organized in different (often fundamentally different) ways.[10] Still, it can be powerfully illuminating to abstract away from that complexity and to concentrate on certain generic forms of 'welfare regimes'. No country fits any of the models perfectly, but some come pretty close; and even for those that are an irreducible amalgam, those more abstract models help us think through the tensions and dynamics associated with such hybridization.

Here I aim to do something similar for accountability regimes. I fully acknowledge the complexity of detailed arrangements, merely hinted at by the glosses offered above. But having done so, let me step back from those complexities to allow some larger patterns of accountability to come into view.

Different accountability regimes, I shall argue, are distinguished along two dimensions: the *subject* of accountability and the *mechanism* of accountability.

There are, of course, many other dimensions along which accountability regimes might be distinguished. But those two dimensions seem to me to be the most perspicacious in illuminating the differences that are of most concern, here.

8.2.1. *The Subject of Accountability*

The 'subject of accountability' refers to what people are accountable *for*. What do people have to explain, when called to account? In what terms must an acceptable explanation be couched?

Of course, in the detailed workings of accountability regimes, people are held responsible for all sorts of different things. But abstracting away from the detail, we can say that there are generically three distinct kinds of things that people might be held accountable for:

- their actions;
- their results; or
- their intentions.

The first possible subject of accountability concerns what people *did*. Were their *performances* as prescribed (or proscribed) by the dictates of duty, or within the range of their legitimate prerogatives? If this is the subject of

---

[10] Epsing-Andersen (1990) and Goodin et al. (1999).

accountability, giving an adequate account consists in showing that you did the right (or an alright) thing.

The second possible subject of accountability concerns what happened as a *result* of what people did. Were *good consequences* produced? If this is the subject of accountability, giving an adequate account consists in showing that what you did produced good effects.

The third possible subject of accountability concerns *why* people did what they did. What were their *motives*? What outcomes were they *attempting* to produce? If this is the subject of accountability, giving an adequate account consists in showing that your aims and intentions were pure.

Perhaps these three subjects of accountability do not necessarily exhaust all logically possible ones. It is nevertheless worth observing that those do loosely correspond to the three main 'methods of ethics': deontology, consequentialism, and virtue ethics, respectively.

8.2.2. Mechanisms of Accountability

'Mechanisms of accountability' refer to the *devices* that serve to secure whatever it is (actions, results, or intentions) for which people are accountable. They are instruments for calling people to account, for judging the adequacy of the accounts rendered, and for bringing sanctions to bear for failures to produce an adequate account. Wherever these mechanisms are effectively in place, we can have some substantial confidence that accountability (of the particular sort in view, anyway) will be secured.

Any actual system of accountability usually employs a mixture of mechanisms. But generically there seem to be three distinct mechanisms by which people might be held accountable:

- through *hierarchical* systems of command and control;
- through the *competitive* discipline of the market and cognate systems of social control; or
- through *cooperative networking*, monitoring, and sanctioning with a group sharing similar norms and values.

The first mechanism of accountability operates through an authority relationship. Subordinates are accountable to their superiors, who are accountable to their own superiors in turn. Sanctions ensue if superiors deem their subordinates' performances wanting.

The second mechanism of accountability operates through the clash of interests and perspectives, orchestrated so as to ensure that good outcomes ensue. Exactly what that latter clause entails depends upon what accountabilities the competition is supposed to underwrite. If the accountability in question is to God's will, trial by ordeal might (depending on the particulars of one's theology) suffice to secure it. If the accountability in question is to the common good, as the market's purports to be, then the competition must be further hedged by the constraints (of the law of property, tort and contract) that are required to underwrite that in a reliable fashion.

The third mechanism of accountability operates through praising or shaming and shunning among a network of coequals sharing a common culture of similar norms and values, goals, and principles. That inevitably gives rise to punishments on one side, to praise and rewards and encouragements on the other. The mutual adjustments that ensue often seem to have a strategic, bargaining-like aspect to them, with people offering rewards or punishments with a view to evoking behaviour more in line with their own preferences and perspectives. But what is distinctive about accountability through shared values is that a mutual adjustment is not purely 'partisan'; the evolution of norms is not wholly instrumental.[11] Generally, participants genuinely internalize values shared by others within their network and critiques of their behaviour based on those shared values.

Again, I have no ironclad argument that these three mechanisms of accountability exhaust the realm of all possible such mechanisms. Still, they loosely correspond to the principal types of socio-political processes identified by students of social control over the past century.[12]

8.3. Three Accountability Regimes

My central theses are as follows:

- the *state sector's* accountability regime focuses relatively more heavily on the *actions* of public officials as its subject of accountability, and it

---

[11] Cf. Lindblom (1965); Axelrod (1986); March and Olsen (1995: ch. 2).

[12] Dahl and Lindblom's categories (1953) were 'hierarchical control by leaders'; systems of competition to exercise 'control over leaders' (via the 'price system' economically, the competitive political processes of 'polyarchy' electorally); and network-like 'control among leaders' (which they dub, misleadingly as I have said, 'bargaining'). Some such partitioning is inchoate in many discussions in these realms. For example, the longer laundry list of mechanisms Ross (1901) discusses in his remarkable book, *Social Control*, can be assimilated to the first and last of this trio, with his 'political' mechanisms mapping onto my 'hierarchical' and his 'ethical mechanisms' mapping onto my 'cooperative'. Williamson's *Markets and Hierarchies* (1975) obviously correspond to my categories two and one, respectively.

relies relatively more heavily upon *hierarchical* authority structures as its characteristic mechanism for achieving accountability;

- the *market sector's* accountability regime focuses relatively more heavily on *results* (mainly but not exclusively financial) as its subject of accountability, and it relies relatively more heavily upon unfettered *competition* (mainly but not exclusively between firms in the economic marketplace) as its characteristic mechanism for achieving accountability;

- the *non-profit sector's* accountability regime focuses relatively more heavily on *intentions* as its subject of accountability, and it relies relatively more heavily upon mutual monitoring and reputational sanctioning within a *cooperative network* of like-minded others as its characteristic mechanism for achieving accountability.

These propositions are encapsulated in Table 8.1.

Let me enter three caveats straightaway. First, these are 'ideal-typic' characterizations. Not all states are purely (or even predominantly) hierarchic, just as not all markets are purely (or even particularly) competitive. And, all the more so, not all non-profit accountability structures, as practiced at present, are as I shall be describing. My claim is merely that cooperative network-based accountability is something to which non-profits (and they far more than other sectors) can aspire. That is what potentially makes them importantly different in their accountability practices from the other two sectors.[13]

As a second caveat, I should also acknowledge from the start that in the real world each sector contains some elements of all these accountability regimes. No non-profit regime is sensitive *only* to intentions and wholly insensitive to results, for example—any more than any market regime can afford to be *wholly* oblivious to actions (laws restricting certain sorts of actions are constitutive of markets, after all). What my ideal regime types aspire to do is merely to describe 'dominant tendencies' or 'distinctive possibilities'. None of the three sectors, in the real world, is a pure type of any of these ideal-typic accountability regimes.

A third caveat is that the particular combinations of 'subjects of accountability' and 'mechanisms of accountability' shown in Table 8.1 do not reflect any deep necessary connections between items in the second and third columns. What they reflect, instead, are merely characteristic

---

[13] Within any given state, anyway. The accountability of states to one another in the international system could, and perhaps ideally should, also take this same form.

Table 8.1. Accountability regimes across three sectors

	Subject of accountability	Mechanism of accountability
State sector	Actions	Hierarchy
Market sector	Results	Competition
Non-profit sector	Intentions	Cooperative networks

practices of agents in the first column. It is the traditional accountability practices of the state sector, and those alone, that forge the connection shown there between 'actions' as the 'subject of accountability' and 'hierarchy' as the 'mechanism of accountability'; and so on down the list.

8.3.1. *The State Sector: Action-Based, Hierarchy-Based Accountability*

It is only a slight exaggeration to say that, within the received traditions of public administration, the two greatest sins are to perform an action either 'arbitrarily' or '*ultra vires*'.[14] What public officials are typically accountable for, within the accountability mechanisms of administrative law and administrative appeal, is acting within the scope of their authority and giving reasons for their action.

The reasons do not have to be 'good' reasons, or even the official's own 'true' reasons. They merely need to be among the legitimate grounds on which the official would be entitled to make a decision. While a court or administrative appeals tribunal might conduct a 'rationality review', it is merely to ensure that some legitimate reason was given: that the decision was not 'arbitrary' in this special, technical sense of that term. In general, courts and administrative appeals tribunals will usually not query the substantive merits of the decision.[15] The scope of officials' accountability simply does not extend that far.

The characteristic subject of accountability within the state sector is, thus, to be accountable for what one has done—the *actions* one has performed—rather than for the results that flowed from those actions

---

[14] De Smith and Brazier (1989).

[15] Behn (2001: 13). Even when they do, courts do not query the substantive merits too closely. They conduct a 'proportionality review' to ensure treatment is not wildly disproportionate across like cases. They satisfy themselves that action was 'not unreasonable', rather than asking whether it was the uniquely right thing to do. In negligence actions, they will only apply a minimal 'reasonable man' test in determining whether the 'duty of care' has been discharged. And so on.

163

or for one's intentions in so acting. For public officials, accountability requirements are characteristically satisfied when they show that the action was within the scope of their official powers, and that some reason (within the scope of legitimate reasons) was given for the action. Accountability procedures in the state sector do not enquire particularly deeply into results ('was it on balance the *right* decision?'), nor do they enquire particularly deeply into intentions ('were those the official's *real* reasons?').[16]

Traditional public-sector mechanisms of accountability operate through a set of nested hierarchies. The public sector traditionally governs through command and control, externally, and through chains of command, internally.[17] Subordinates are accountable to superiors, who are accountable to higher officials in turn, who are (after however many links in the chain) accountable to elected officials who are accountable to the electorate. The electorate thus sits at the pinnacle of a large set of nested hierarchies that constitute 'the state'.

In a democracy, the public is ultimately the sole source of sovereign authority, and it is the public to whom all public officials ought ultimately be accountable. But only elected officials are accountable to the public directly.[18] All other officials are accountable to the public indirectly, 'through' the officials (elected and appointed) to whom they are themselves directly accountable.

Unsurprisingly, this daisy chain of accountability breaks relatively quickly. Passing accounts through others is akin to a game of Chinese whispers, with all the slippage that that entails. Elected officials systematically exploit the slippage, and there seem to be strict limits in the

---

[16] Except perhaps in cases involving hypersensitivities associated with potential discrimination against 'discrete and insular minorities'. The issues of accountability with which I am principally concerned here arise predominantly in constitutional and administrative law. If we broaden our gaze to accountability under the criminal law, there intentions clearly are central to issues of *mens rea*. Note that the early history of even the criminal law, however, was characterized by a focus on actions, and distinctive wrongs which it was the task of the criminal law to label and proscribe (Horder 1997). I am grateful to Niki Lacey for these observations.

[17] 'Traditionally', because of course many have urged, with much success, that command-and-control mechanisms be replaced with looser 'management by objectives' or by 'prices' (Kneese and Schultze 1975) or that hierarchies be replaced by looser networks in systems of 'joined-up government' (Gore 1993; Considine 2002).

[18] Usually, although lower officials can, in most jurisdictions (but only recently in Britain, for example), be called to account in public hearings of the legislature, on pain of contempt; and they usually can be prosecuted in courts of law, and held to account in that way (unless they can claim immunity on grounds they were acting within the scope of their official duties).

extent to which the institutions of a free press and vibrant opposition can effectively constrain that phenomenon.[19]

A remedy of sorts used to be found in the old (now substantially defunct) traditions of ministerial responsibility, whereby the elected official formally in charge of a ministry assumed responsibility for all that happened within it, even in cases where there was no realistic way the minister could have known about or prevented the events in question.[20] But while this is a good model of 'responsible government', in the sense of always giving us someone to blame, it is hardly a model of 'accountable' government, in the sense of giving us someone from whom a first-hand account can sensibly be demanded.

Note however that this is a feature not only of the peculiar British model of 'responsible government' but is also characteristic of hierarchical models of political accountability quite generally, whereby lower officials are typically accountable 'through' higher officials ultimately to the public at large. The account is passed through many hands. Any moderately low-level official who was the efficient cause of the event is subject to the direct scrutiny of the public at large only in extraordinary cases.[21]

This is where other accountability regimes, and other sectors, come into their own, supplementing the sort of accountability regime that we typically find within the state sector. At the macro-level, politicians in a democracy are required to enter into the marketplace politically, engaging in a periodic competition for people's votes; and non-profits join in pressing their broad social concerns (in a 'non-partisan' way, if they want to retain tax-exempt status, of course) in the course of that campaign. At the micro-level, state officials subcontract public services to providers in the market or non-profit sectors, hoping that this 'purchaser–provider split' will bring better accountability (by results or by intentions) than the sort of accountability obtainable through the hierarchical action-based regime that predominates in the state sector itself.[22] All the while, the para-political portions of the Third Sector stand (sometimes ineffectual) guard against political money allowing the corporate sector to circumvent

---

[19] As the 'children overboard' affair during the 2001 Australian election shows: see Australia, Senate Select Committee on A Certain Maritime Incident 2002, esp. chs. 6–7 ('The failure to correct the record' and 'Accountability', respectively).

[20] Day and Klein (1987: ch. 2).

[21] The same is true with firms in the market sector: one does not know or care who within the firm is responsible for mistakes; one simply sues the firm as a whole, or takes one's business elsewhere, if the results are unsatisfactory.

[22] Le Grand (1991).

the democratic process and undermine accountability of elected officials to the public at large.

8.3.2. *The Market Sector: Results-Based, Competition-Based Accountability*

In the market sector, the subject of accountability is typically the financial 'bottom line'. That is basically what officers of a firm are held accountable for, when facing their shareholders.[23] Those are the terms in which officers of a firm give an account of themselves, internally.

The accountability regime of the market sector has an external face as well. The way the market sector justifies itself, both to society at large and to consumers in particular, is similarly in terms of results. The market, it is said, maximizes (economic) well-being of the community as a whole. When the market sector as a whole is held to account by the community (as opposed to particular managers being held to account by their shareholders), those are the results-based terms in which the market gives its account.

The mechanism of that sort of accountability, within the market sector, is competition. The speculations of Mandeville and Smith as formally proven by Arrow and Debreu show that (under certain ideal conditions) each attempting to maximize his or her own well-being maximizes the well-being of everyone overall.[24]

The hypothesized ideal conditions of perfect competition virtually never obtain in the real world, however. Externalities, natural monopolies, and concentrations of market power abound. Where competition is less than perfect, any guarantee of the market sector's accountability to society at large can be seriously compromised. That is where the other sectors and their distinctive accountability regimes come into play, holding the market sector accountable, politically or socially, when it is not competitively. And that is where the Third Sector has a very particular role

---

[23] Clark (1997) has shareholders saying to managers,

You are supposed to maximize our financial well-being. You meet your specific defined duties to everyone else. You pay taxes to the government, fulfill contracts to customers, obey the environmental laws, do right by your employees in accordance with the labor laws. You do all that, but what you're really supposed to maximize is the financial well-being of us, the owners, and by the way, we have the power to kick you out if you don't do it.

Significantly, the device social reformers choose for trying to make firms more socially responsible is couched in similarly results-based terms: 'the triple bottom line', accounting for social and environmental as well as financial outcomes.

[24] Mandeville (1989); Smith (1776); Arrow and Debreu (1954).

to play in pressing politicians to take action against powerful corporate interests which, in the absence of that countervailing public pressure, may well have utterly dominated political life.

8.3.3. The Non-Profit Sector: Intention-Based, Network-Based Accountability

As I said at the outset, accountability as applied to the non-profit sector is a much less well-articulated notion. The formal legal accountability that derives from non-profits' articles of incorporation is thin stuff. And the other sorts of accountabilities typically in play there—duties to obey the law and honour one's contracts, together with more diffuse duties of a moral sort—are nowise peculiar to the non-profit sector alone.

Here I shall offer an analysis of the accountability regime that is in one part very familiar and in the other part less so. The familiar part concerns the non-profit approach to what I have called the 'subject of accountability'. The novel part concerns what I have called the 'mechanism of accountability'. There, I suggest that network-based accountability could and should (and maybe even does) characterize the non-profit sector, and it predominantly (and perhaps it almost uniquely).

INTENTIONS AS A SUBJECT OF NON-PROFIT ACCOUNTABILITY

It is a familiar fact, of signal importance, that non-profits are motivationally distinct.

This motivational distinctiveness shows up, first, in how non-profits raise much of their labour and most of their funds—through voluntary donations rooted in altruistic concern with 'the cause'.[25] The fact that non-profits are pursuing charitable purposes rather than private profits is crucial in justifying the tax exemption that they enjoy.[26]

By reason of both selection and self-selection, managers of non-profits are committed to 'the cause', rather than merely to maximizing profits or managerial efficiency.[27] That fact is central to the conventional analysis of why, in a world of imperfect information and incomplete contracting, we prefer to trust non-profits rather than profit-seeking corporations: they

---

[25] Hansmann (1980: 840–1); Alexander (1987); Rose-Ackerman (1996: 702–15).

[26] The fact *that* having a 'charitable purpose' is crucial for non-profit status is clear on the face of statutes dating back to the original Elizabethan Statute of Charitable Uses of 1601 (see, latterly, Internal Revenue Code § 501(c)(3) 1988; Charity Commission for England and Wales 2002b: paras 20–3). *Why* the statutes should be written in that way is a more vexed issue (Anon. 1992: 1612–34).

[27] Brennan (1996) and Behn (2003: 52–5).

may not be as efficient, but at least they internalize the 'right' goals (which is to say, the goals we too espouse) rather than serving our goals merely as a means of making a profit for themselves.[28]

That motivational distinctiveness is a stylized fact about non-profits, the truth of which is an open empirical question. Some evidence seems to suggest that that stylized fact is indeed true.[29] But whether or not it is true does not really matter for present purposes. My point is not that non-profits *are* necessarily more deeply motivated by the charitable purposes around which they are notionally organized. My point, instead, is that that enquiry into their motives is much more central to holding them to account than such enquiries would be in either of the other two sectors.

What non-profits, their managers, and workers are responsible *for*—their 'subject of accountability'—is, to a much greater extent than in the other two sectors, manifesting good intentions appropriate to the non-profit's formal goals. When asked, 'please explain', motives figure more centrally among the terms in which those explanations may and must be cast than with agents in other sectors. That is what is distinctive about the accountability regime of the non-profit sector: the substantially greater extent to which the right intentions, in and of themselves, there count as a satisfactory account.

Certainly good intentions are not *all* that count, even in the non-profit sector. Competence in pursuing them counts, too. Maybe good intentions are not even the *main* things, when it comes to giving a good account of oneself in the Third Sector. My claim is merely that good intentions count much *more*, in the accountabilities of non-profits, than they do in any other sector. It is this substantially greater weight given to intentions, as compared to results or actions, which is distinctive about the accountability regime of the non-profit sector in terms of the 'subject of accountability'.

NETWORK-BASED MECHANISMS OF NON-PROFIT
ACCOUNTABILITY

As regards the distinctive 'mechanism' of accountability in the non-profit realm, my analysis is somewhat less mainstream.

---

[28] Newhouse (1970: 65 ff.); Hansmann (1980); Smith and Lipsky (1993: 26–31); Rose-Ackerman (1996: 716–7); Minow (2003: 6).

[29] Minow (2002: 13) and Kapur and Weisbrod (1999).

To be sure, the phenomenon I shall be describing—networking among Third-Sector actors to achieve desired results—is increasingly familiar in the real world, particularly in transnational politics.[30] The interpretation I put on it is, however, slightly different. Networking among non-governmental organizations (NGOs) is generally seen more in strategic than accountability terms. It is seen as the way the Third Sector operates. It is seen as the Third Sector's way of forcing accountability on *other* actors (ranging from firms through national governments to the World Bank). My proposal is that we should see that networking as also being a mechanism by which non-profits are *themselves* held accountable.[31]

Whether or not the Third Sector currently conceives its own accountability in network-based terms, that mode of accountability constitutes a distinctive *possibility* which is open to the Third Sector much more than to the other two sectors. For that reason if no other, I therefore feel justified in describing it as 'the' non-profit sector's distinctive accountability regime.

In developing this model, I shall be building on analyses of network-based accountabilities from various other realms: how NGOs are (or could be) held accountable, transnationally or domestically; how coordination is (or can be) achieved interdepartmentally, within the New Public Management ethos of reinvented government; how coordination has traditionally been achieved in the 'coordinated market economies' of Continental Europe. So far as I know such analyses have yet to be applied to problems of non-profit accountability as such, but I nonetheless hope they will resonate there.

Let us begin by considering briefly how goals of coordination, accountability, positive responsiveness, and mutual adjustment are accomplished in those other disparate realms.

Internationally, many commentators fear that power is being exercised by a range of organizations that themselves suffer a serious deficit of democratic accountability. Transnational NGOs are formally accountable to virtually no one; and while there are strong informal pressures for them to be accountable to publics funding and supporting them, that

[30] Sikkink (1993); Keck and Sikkink (1998); Fox and Brown (1998); Brown (2003).
[31] The Alliance for Nonprofit Management uses an open network method to promote better accountability (Light 2000: 32–4; Brody 2002: 482, 491). But the impression given is that this is not because the Alliance sees this as a distinctive form of accountability uniquely suited to the non-profit sector, but merely because networking is how non-profits do things quite generally.

often makes them accountable to the wrong people.[32] Intergovernmental organizations (IGOs) are accountable to the governments of their various member states, which are accountable in turn (after some fashion or another) to their own people.[33] But accountability based on 'one-state, one-vote' (or worse) is a far cry from a system of democratic accountability based on equal representation of all affected interests, which is conspicuously absent on the world stage.[34]

Both domestically and internationally, regulatory power is often and increasingly exercised by non-state actors. This extends from the financial discipline exercised over states by private agents like Standard and Poor's when rating sovereign risk to the regulatory power delegated to groups like the Royal Society for the Prevention of Cruelty to Animals or the General Medical Council which oversees the self-regulation of medical practitioners within the National Health Service. In the penumbra lie a range of 'private overseers of national governments', including 'international NGOs such as Amnesty International, Transparency International and Greenpeace International'.[35] Many of these

non-statutory private regulators operate complete regimes in the sense of having the capacity to set standards, to monitor and enforce without the intervention of other organizations. Where this is the case they wield more power than those public regulators which are constrained by the need to follow standards set by legislatures or government departments and to pursue litigation in order to apply legal sanctions. There is thus a remarkable concentration of private power over public organizations. This is perhaps most striking with those private regulators operating internationally whose judgements on such matters as financial or fiscal credibility, probity or greenness significantly affect decisions of notionally democratic governments.[36]

The problem, there, is how to hold such private power publicly accountable.

Another problem domestically is how to ensure coordination and accountability for activities of government that straddle conventional

---

[32] That is, 'To wealthy, relatively public-spirited people in the United States and other rich countries, who do not experience the results of their actions' (Keohane 2003: 22–3). The growth of NGOs in developing countries over recent years may ease this fear.

[33] Nye (2001). 'Mike Moore was appointed by democratically elected governments', some may say. But 'between someone who actually got elected and the director general of the WTO, there are so many miles that, in fact, he and his staff are accountable to no one' (Lori Wallach, quoted in Keohane and Nye 2001: 225, cf. 229).

[34] Nye (2001: 4).   [35] Scott (2002: 60).   [36] Scott (2002: 74).

lines of departmental responsibility, as is increasingly common under the influence of New Public Management theories ('reinvented government', 'joined-up government', etc.).[37]

The problem within Continental European economies is how to coordinate the choices of firms, and hold them accountable to their financial backers, while avoiding the cut-throat competition and short-term imperatives characterizing share markets driven by the threat of hostile takeovers.

So how are these coordination and accountability challenges met, within each of those realms? Well, slightly differently in each. But across all those realms there is a pattern of 'network-based accountability' that I want here to apply to the Third Sector.

Transnationally,

key regimes for governance [long] operated like clubs. Cabinet ministers or their equivalent working in the same issue-area, initially from a relatively small number of relatively rich countries, got together to make rules. Trade ministers dominated the General Agreement on Tariffs and Trade; finance ministers ran the IMF; defense and foreign ministers met at the headquarters of NATO; central bankers convened as the Bank for International Settlements. They negotiated in secret, then reported their agreements to national legislatures and publics. Until recently, they were largely unchallenged.[38]

In response to recent challenges, NGO representatives are sometimes co-opted onto the governing bodies of IGOs (a prime case in point being the World Commission on Dams); but since NGOs are often not themselves very accountable to anyone, incorporating them might merely exacerbate the democratic deficit.[39]

The real solution to securing accountability in such settings is through monitoring and reputational sanctioning among a group of like-minded others. The key agents, here, are networks of people sharing a common core of norms and values, mutually internalizing the views of one another. Domestically,

US institutions that are deliberately insulated from elections—in particular, the Supreme Court and the Federal Reserve Board—routinely publish their deliberations or opinions, so that not only the results, but the reasoning and disagreements involved, can be publicly known. These institutions are held accountable through criticisms by professional networks, such as legal scholars writing in law journals

---

[37] Christensen and Lægreid (2002) and Behn (2001).
[38] Keohane and Nye (2002: 220); cf. Slaughter (2000).
[39] Keohane and Nye (2002: 239, 236).

and economists writing scholarly articles and offering opinions in the public media.[40]

Internationally, likewise,

Professional associations create and maintain transnational norms to which IGOs, NGOs and government officials can be judged accountable. The practice, by non-governmental organizations and the press, of 'naming and shaming' of transnational corporations with valuable brand names also provides a sort of accountability.[41]

'An important counter to international private power generally is the formation of networks of governments and regulatory authorities, often organized around particular scientific areas..., seeking to meet the challenges of private networks of power through the development of equivalent or interdependent governmental communities'[42]—and then drawing private actors themselves into that community. Being 'strongly embedded within a wider community' of this sort may 'offer a legitimate alternative to control through democratic government channels'.[43]

Certainly it constitutes a form of accountability, anyway, and one that is potentially just as strong as the accountability that is secured through state hierarchy or market competition. How exactly it relates to democracy and wherein lies its legitimacy are issues to which I shall return below.

New Public Management likewise replaces, or supplements, 'traditional vertical accountability with new forms of horizontal recognition'. That horizontal model re-construes 'accountability as... responsiveness, obligation and willingness to communicate with others' across the various agencies (the various government departments, quasi-governmental organizations, and private contractors) constituting the relevant policy community responsible for the 'joined-up government' of, and service delivery in, that sphere.[44] The accountability that comes with these new forms of governance is, then, the mutual accountability agents and agencies linked in networks in pursuit of common projects, responsible to one another for their good-faith contributions to the shared task.[45]

Finally, consider the accountability regime within the distinctively Continental European variety of capitalism. These are 'Coordinated Market Economies', with the 'coordination' coming through 'dense networks

---

[40] Keohane and Nye (2002: 230).   [41] Keohane and Nye (2002: 239–40).
[42] Scott (2002: 76).   [43] Scott (2002: 75).
[44] Considine (2002: 21); cf. Rhodes (1997).
[45] Barker (1982) and Behn (2001: 126, 2003).

linking the managers and technical personnel inside a company to their counterparts in other firms on terms that provide for the sharing of reliable information about the progress of the firm'. This occurs through 'close relationships . . . between companies and their major suppliers and clients, . . . extensive networks of cross-shareholding and joint membership in active industry associations that gather information about companies in the course of coordinating standard-setting, technology transfer and vocational training'.

'Firms sit inside dense business networks from which potential funders can gain a considerable amount of inside information about the track record and projects of a firm'; and that in turn 'provides companies with access to finance that is not entirely dependent on publicly available financial data or current returns. Access to this kind of 'patient capital' makes it possible for firms to retain a skilled workforce through economic downturns and to invest in projects generating returns only in the long run', thereby often outperforming the more Liberal Market Economies of the North Atlantic.[46] 'Informal rules' and 'shared understandings' lie at the heart of the sort of 'network reputational monitoring' that characterizes coordination and mutual accountability within Continental European economies of this sort.[47]

After this long detour, let us now return to the issue of the accountability of non-profits. My proposal is that we model the distinctive accountability regime of the non-profit sector in broadly the same way.

Other mechanisms operate too, of course. (There is no pure case of any ideal type.) But what is or could be really distinctive about accountability in the Third Sector is this: non-profits concerned to serve some public good are enmeshed in a network of others—other non-profits, locally, nationally, and transnationally; government and quasi-governmental organizations, locally, nationally, and transnationally; donors and sponsors, both public and private, contractual or otherwise.[48]

What all the parties across that network of related non-profits, etc. share is a commitment to some particular common purpose.[49] Each no doubt

---

[46] Hall and Soskice (2001: 22–3).   [47] Hall and Soskice (2001: 13, 23).

[48] For one small example, Lyons and Chan (1999: 11–13) offer evidence that non-profit employment agencies were more inclined to work collaboratively with one another and share job vacancies, whereas for-profit agencies were less likely to do so.

[49] Just as all of the non-profits comprising the network themselves are 'self-conscious collectivities of shared sentiment that take on voluntary activities consistent with those sentiments' (Smith 1993: 85). Networks are subject-specific. But they are also multiple, porous, and overlapping. Just as there are often interlocking directorated coordinating the market sector, so too there are invariably networks of networks straddling the non-profit sector.

conceives it slightly differently: and that is good, in helping to bring not only diversity but also openness and transparency to what might otherwise be closed communities accountable to no one but themselves. Some groups inevitably have private interests operating alongside their interest in the shared cause; and in some cases the differing conceptions or conflicting interests will put a group 'outside the pale' altogether. Among the broad group of those differing groups who broadly conceive of themselves and one another as 'members of the club', each internalizes the views of the others, to some greater or lesser extent, as to how good a job they are doing.

Such networks operate essentially on the basis of trust and reputation. Trust and a reputation for trustworthiness are what lay the basis for cooperation among agents who do not *have* to cooperate.[50] A paradigm case of such agents are non-profits, which are bound to others neither by hierarchical authority nor by shared commercial interests.

Thus, while acknowledging that there are other elements of accountability sometimes at work as well, I propose that what is (or could be) really distinctive about the accountability regime of the Third Sector is that it is based on mutual monitoring of one another's performance within a network of groups, public and private, sharing common concerns.[51] That, I suggest, is the principal mechanism of accountability across the Third Sector and indeed civil society more generally; and it is something that, while also found in other sectors, is generally a distinctly subordinate element in the accountability mix characterizing those other regimes.

8.3.4. Too Neat?

As already acknowledged, there are elements of each accountability regime to be found in every sector.

The market sector clearly has elements of hierarchy. (Just think of firms, and the internal authority relations between superiors and subordinates within them.) Accountability in the market sector is sometimes for actions (officers of firms are held accountable for illegal acts, and not just because they are bad for business). And, as already discussed, in some places (famously including Continental Europe and Japan) the market sector

[50] Kreps (1990).

[51] Thus, for one small example, non-profit hospitals' concern with 'prestige' rather than 'profit' leads them to weigh 'quality' more heavily than 'quantity', as compared to for-profit hospitals (Newhouse 1970: 65 ff.).

itself is substantially coordinated and held accountable through network-based cooperative mechanisms here associated more with the non-profit sector.[52]

So too with the state sector, accountability is mixed. For a start, competition (of politicians for the votes of the electorate) is obviously absolutely central to systems of accountability in any democracy; and candidates, parties, and interest groups are all rightly drawn into this competitive accountability process. Different departments of state and different levels of government compete with one another, often fiercely. Insofar as the state contracts with private suppliers, it typically does so through a process of competitive tendering; and much of the policy dynamic within government is driven by competition between departments of state (between spending departments versus revenue-raising departments, and among competing departmental claimants for funding). So too, in the world of New Public Management, is there much network-based accountability for cooperative activities that straddle departments and hierarchical lines responsibility within them.

In the non-profit sector, likewise, accountability mechanisms have elements of hierarchy. Among them are those entailed by the employment relationship of non-profits with their own employees. There can also be elements of hierarchical public-sector style accountability as, for example, when tax-exempt non-profits in Britain are accountable to the Charity Commission, which is accountable to Parliament, which is accountable to the electorate.[53] Furthermore, non-profits are accountable not only for good intentions but also for their actions (illegalities, for example) and for their results. The consequences of medical malpractice are no less actionable in non-profit hospitals than in for-profit ones; and non-profits are increasingly accountable for meeting 'performance objectives' stipulated in contracts with public and private agents.[54] More generally, managers are blamed, even in the non-profit sector, if their organization conspicuously fails to achieve its aims, however good their intentions.

So none of these constitute pure cases. Still, the accountability regime I associate with each sector can be fairly regarded as the 'dominant motif' of accountability relations within each sector. There are other elements interspersed, to be sure. But the *principal* way in which each of these

[52] Indeed, sociologically that is perhaps the way most successful businesses operate (Macaulay 1963; Collins 1999).

[53] Charity Commission for England and Wales (2002a: 41).

[54] Smith (2002: 166–7); Young and Salamon (2002: 429); DeHoog and Salamon (2002: 335–6).

three sectors is held accountable—the *basic* mechanism at work—is the accountability regime I here associate with each.

8.4. Tri-Sectoral Democratic Accountability

Theories of democratization tend to have an unfortunate 'one size fits all' aspect to them, inter-sectorally as well as internationally.[55] Democratizing non-electoral institutions, both within the state sector and beyond it, is typically interpreted as mimicking key features of elective representative democracy.

Thus, for example, 'democratizing' the bureaucracy is often seen as a matter of making it more 'representative' of the citizenry as a whole— in just the same way as the Reform Acts democratized the legislature.[56] 'Democratizing' the economy is sometimes seen as a matter of expanding shareholding and participation in the labour market— in just the same way as expanding the franchise and participation in politics makes that more democratic. Other times 'democratizing' the economy is seen as a matter of increasing workers' control in the affairs of their firms—'shopfloor democracy', modelled on 'town meeting democracy'.[57]

The same is true of calls for 'democratizing' the Third Sector. Those often amount to pleas for giving everyone affected by organizations' activities more of a say in their decisions[58]—thus equating democratic accountability in the Third Sector to democratic accountability in the political sphere. Both the UN and the European Union, for example, form consultative or partnership relations with NGOs only on condition they have suitable internal accountability mechanisms in place.[59] Other times, 'democratizing' the Third Sector is construed in terms of making it suitably pluralistic, so that there is some non-profit representing every

---

[55] Whitehead (1996).   [56] Krislov (1974).
[57] Pateman (1970) and Greenberg (1986).   [58] Fung (2003b).
[59] Resolutions of the United Nations, Economic and Social Council (UN ECOSOC) (1996: § 12) permit it to establish 'consultative relations' with non-governmental organizations only on condition that 'The organization shall have a representative structure and possess appropriate mechanisms of accountability to its members, who shall exercise effective control over its policies and actions through the exercise of voting rights or other appropriate democratic and transparent decision-making processes' (see further Lempnien 1999; Brown and Moore 2001; cf. Keohane 2003). Likewise, the White Paper on *European Governance* of the European Union Commission (2001: 4, 16–17) endorses 'partnership arrangements' with select NGOs 'in return for more guarantees of the openness and representativity [sic] of the organizations consulted'.

interest—just as, in idealized pluralist democracy, there is some lobby group representing every interest.[60]

I do not dissent from any of those proposals. They may be good ideas, too. All I wish to add is that there is another way of democratizing society. Instead of holding each and every sector to the *same* criteria of democratic representation, we can democratize our institutions as a whole by holding each sector accountable according to some *complementary* sets of criteria.[61]

The idea is as old as notions of checks and balances and the division of labour. Those arrangements may work imperfectly, in practice, in any given instance; but it is clear enough how they might work, in theory. Different branches of government representing different interests, each with substantial (if not quite veto) power over the other, might well produce outcomes that are in the general interest.[62] Different people specializing in different tasks might well produce outcomes better for all than any could have achieved alone.

The secret to making this work lies in good institutional design. The differences must be made to actually complement one another, articulating with one another in such a way as to yield the desired outcome overall. The same is true when trying to ensure democratic accountability of our social institutions, overall, by holding each sector accountable in different but complementary ways.[63]

Devising a recipe specifying the perfect mix of the three accountability regimes is a large task, beyond the scope of the present chapter. Instead, I

[60] Douglas (1983: 155) and Minow (2002: 37, 45, 166–7).

[61] As Young and Salamon (2002: 439–40) write:

In the old order, business, government and charitable enterprise all had their particular places, and although there was much interaction among them, they remained relatively distinct in organizational terms, in motivational values, in their sources of support and in the work they carried out. That appears to be changing now ... [with] the emergence of a 'new governance'...approach to solving public problems. The heart of this approach is an emphasis not on the differences among the sectors, but on the opportunities for collaboration among them.... [T]he new clarion call is 'whatever works'—a non-formulaic, non-legalistic, non-political, non-categorical approach to getting the job done.

[62] Cf. Goodin (1996b).

[63] I thus echo Minow (2003: 36), when she writes,

Collaborations between governments and private entities—whether for-profit, secular or religious—could introduce accountability tools from the other sectors and thereby improve performance. Yet such collaborations also have the potential to divert the public trust into forms of conduct that already have faulty accountability procedures or use accountability mechanisms inadequate to the public tasks.... At minimum, the accountability framework itself must be public in the source of its norms and in its overarching authority and enforcement power.

shall confine myself to specifying the different kinds of contributions that can be made by the differing accountability regimes of the three different sectors.

8.4.1. *The Essential Core: Political Accountability*

'Democracy' means, most fundamentally, being 'systematically responsive to citizens' desires and interests'.[64] The principal political mechanism of democratic accountability is electoral, with politicians being called to account to voters at periodic elections in which the sovereign electorate has an opportunity to sanction them.[65]

That is the 'ultimate' layer of democratic accountability, so to speak. But beneath it are various complementary layers of political accountability within the state sector: the administrative accountability of appointed officials to their elected masters; the legal accountability of both appointed and elected officials to the Constitution and courts; the political accountability of all to the Fourth Estate and the court of public opinion, even between elections.[66]

Still, it is the electoral check—and the ultimate subsuming of all within the state sector, and indeed other sectors, to it—that provides the crucial guarantee of *systematic* responsiveness. Other accountability regimes respond more-or-less systematically, to some people's desires and interests more than to others'. The electoral check, in a political system with an extensive and well-exercised franchise, provides the closest thing we have to a guarantee that all citizens' desires and interests will be systematically taken into account. Other accountability regimes, insofar as they are valued as contributions to *democratic* accountability, must be seen as mere adjuncts to that—contributing where they can, but subordinate to electoral democracy where they are in conflict with that master accountability regime.[67]

8.4.2. *Useful Supplements: Market Accountability*

The market might be another way to promote systematic responsiveness of a sort to people's desires. The 'might' is a big one, depending as it does on all the familiar conditions of perfect markets and pure competition (perfect information, no market power, no externalities, and so on). Still,

---

[64] May (1978).   [65] Manin, Przeworski, and Stokes (1999).   [66] Goodin (2000*a*).
[67] Papadopoulos (2007).

under those ideal conditions markets should indeed respond to people's desires overall.

Of course, markets only respond to 'effective demand', desires backed by money. The market's rule is 'one dollar, one vote', rather than 'one person, one vote'. So if we were trusting to markets to produce democratic-like outcomes, we would need to equalize people's capacities to make their demand effective. One way to do that, without redistributing money itself, is to create separate currencies useable only for the purchase of particular goods: school vouchers, housing rebates, public health insurance, and so on.[68]

Other ways to harness the power of the market as an adjunct in the democratic project of ensuring systematic responsiveness to people's desires and interests is to introduce 'internal markets' into the operation of government itself or to contract out public services to private providers subject to market discipline.[69]

The purchasers, in these cases, are public officials, subject ultimately (if often very indirectly) to the political discipline of the ballot box. Assuming they are able to specify the goods and services they are buying relatively precisely and to monitor the quality of the goods and services received relatively effectively (big assumptions!), then imposing the discipline of the market on providers of those goods and services would (at least under ideal market conditions) contribute to making the outputs of government more systematically responsive the desires of public officials and through them (making some heroic assumptions again, this time about political responsiveness) to the interests and desires of citizens overall.

Of course, the stipulated conditions will almost never be met perfectly. Contracts are always incomplete; monitoring of contract compliance is never perfect; and for the same reasons we are tempted to contract out services (i.e. we think private actors are quicker and more creative than public ones), there are good grounds for thinking that private actors are always going to be one step ahead of government officials in finding loopholes in the contracts.[70] Still, those conditions might sometimes be sufficiently closely approximated as to make the market a useful adjunct.

---

[68] Goodin (2000a: 4); Rose-Ackerman (1983); Minow (2002, 2003).

[69] Le Grand (1991).

[70] Similarly, think about the 'hire/buy' decision. Firms hire employees, rather than buying the products that those employees produce, when it is easier to monitor the quality of their behaviour and inputs than it is to monitor the quality of their outputs (Coase 1937). Reflecting on that fact ought to lead us to prefer internalizing production of public services

8.4.3. *The Third-Sector Contribution*

Those are all familiar ways in which market-based accountabilities might enhance the systematic responsiveness of the state to citizens. Next let us consider other ways, some less familiar, in which the non-profit sector, too, might contribute to democratic accountability.

One way, which *is* familiar from the writings of everyone from Tocqueville through Habermas, is by helping to mobilize popular demand for political action.[71] Much ink is spilt extolling some often rather romanticized virtues of civil society. But to appreciate the point, one needs only recall that, legally, political parties themselves are just another instance of a non-profit corporation.[72] Mobilizing political demands is not something that every non-profit does, but many do. And that is as it should be, democratically. In a democracy, political demands should emanate from voluntary associations: certainly that rather than from the state sector, and certainly that rather than from the market sector alone.

Another way in which the non-profit sector can enhance the systematic responsiveness of the social institutions as a whole to citizens' desires and interests is by doing things that states and markets cannot do or will not do. Because Third Sector organizations are motivationally and organizationally distinct, they are capable of doing many things that neither the state nor the market sectors can do reliably or well. For one example, markets notoriously fail in the face of positive externalities, as profit-seekers prefer freeriding to contributing. But for community-oriented altruists of the Third Sector, the presence of positive externalities is merely an added inducement to contribute to such causes.[73] Or for another example, 'non-market failures' within the state sector notoriously arise from rent-seeking, as profiteers attempt to co-opt the coercive power of the state to serve their private ends. But being voluntary organizations lacking any coercive powers, non-profits are immune to that threat as

within the public sector rather than contracting it out privately to anything larger than a single-person provider. For the same reason those contractors hire employees rather than just subcontracting, so too ought the government hire people to produce those services through the public sector.

[71] Tocqueville (1835: vol. 1, pt. 2, ch. 4) and Habermas (1996). See e.g. Walzer (1991); Offe (2000); Ware (1989: ch. 8).

[72] Anon. (1992: 1656–77) and Charity Commission for England and Wales (1999).

[73] Weisbrod (1975); cf. Friedman (1962: 190–1); Goodin (1988*a*: 155–7); Andreoni (1990); Rose-Ackerman (1996: 713). Such altruism is usually limited to people in certain groups or certain situations, rather than the world at large; but while the scope of such solidarity is thus limited, there is a genuinely altruistic concern for those within its scope.

well. For those familiar reasons, there are many things that the Third Sector can do that neither of the first two sectors can do well.

Another—less familiar but potentially even more important—is that non-profit NGOs are capable of responding to *non-standard* needs that people *cannot afford* to satisfy themselves through private markets. The problem with states is that they operate according to rules. They provide standardized goods and services to people who fall within certain prescribed categories. There is always some element of discretion, but that discretion is usually pretty circumscribed. People with non-standard needs—cases that do not correspond neatly to categorical criteria—are not well catered for by the state. The market can provide tailor-made responses, for a price ('rationing by price', and ability to pay it). But people without the wherewithal to pay cannot get their non-standard needs met in the market. That is where charities have traditionally come to the fore.[74]

Yet another way in which the non-profit sector might help make social institutions systematically responsive to citizens' desires and interests is as an adjunct to the public sector in service delivery. Contracting out public services to for-profit market-based organizations promises better effectiveness and efficiency, but produces the risk that undetectable corners might be cut in quest of profits. Contracting out public services to non-profit organizations avoids that risk, at least[75]—although the absence of the profit motive also cancels any competitive guarantee of effectiveness and efficiency.[76]

Note well, however, that what enables the Third Sector to play that role in supplementing the other two sectors is that that sector *is* motivationally and organizationally distinct from the other two. Recalling that fact ought make us wary of arrangements, whether of 'partnership' or 'competition', that straddle the various sectors. The worry must be that in bringing different sectors under the same yoke, the very thing that made the Third Sector a useful adjunct to the other two sectors—its organizational and motivational distinctiveness—risks being lost.

These concerns are familiar, too. Faith-based organizations rightly worry that their sacred missions might be compromised by the conditions that the secular state imposes (and inevitably and rightly so) when

[74] Smith and Lipsky (1993: ch. 6).
[75] Unless, of course, contracts are awarded on the basis of price alone (in which case non-profits will have as much of an incentive to cut corners as for-profits in order to win the contracts); and unless, of course, any surplus garnered is appropriable for other purposes dear to the non-profit but not the contractor.
[76] Hansmann (1980: 843–5).

subcontracting public functions to outside bodies.[77] Non-profits rightly worry that in competing against for-profit organizations for public contracts, they will become not just interchangeable with but perhaps even indistinguishable from for-profit organizations, doing the same things in the same ways as for-profits would have done. And perhaps that, too, is inevitably and rightly so, given the 'level playing field' standards of fair competition that properly govern public tenders quite generally. These are risks I discuss in more detail below.

8.4.4. Networks of Mutual Accountability Across Sectors

There is yet another role, potentially an even more important one, that the voluntary sector can play in underwriting the democratic accountability of social institutions as a whole. That is linked directly to the sorts of networks of common concern that, on my account, underwrite accountability within the Third Sector itself. Those selfsame networks can constitute a 'reference group' for public policymakers: a font of information and advice and an evaluative touchstone for policy formulation and transformation.[78]

The key to the cooperative ethos of those networks is mutuality. They are bands of coequals sharing common concerns, none having any formal authority over any other. Government is crucially different in that latter respect, of course; thus government agencies probably cannot be part of those networks on exactly the same basis as non-profits themselves. Still, relevant government agencies might have an 'adjunct' standing within those networks, where they are semi-formally organized. And where they are merely informal networks of senior officers of organizations sharing the same substantive concerns, senior officials of the relevant public agencies can and ordinarily would presumably be included in that loop.[79]

This marks a distinctive sort of accountability: 'policymaking accountability', Susan Rose-Ackerman dubs it. She reports strong evidence of it in the drafting and implementation of environmental legislation in the USA

---

[77] Minow (2002).

[78] Something of this is captured in discussions of the role of 'epistemic communities' in policymaking (Haas 1989, 1992), though the contribution here envisaged for Third Sector networks extends well beyond epistemic issues, and crucially including advice based on the shared norms, values, principles, and commitments pervading the network.

[79] 'Revolving doors' also contribute: '[T]he recruitment of former managers of nonprofit agencies to high level public service positions has contributed to the homogenization of views between the two sectors...At the same time as they persuade their former colleagues in the private sector of the need for government priorities..., they seek to ameliorate government policy in directions favored by voluntary agencies' (Smith and Lipsky 1993: 145).

and Germany, and growing evidence of it in the post-communist regimes of Central and Eastern Europe, under pressure from the European Union to form area-specific Partnership Groups with non-profit organizations as a precondition of membership in the EU.[80]

This 'reference group for policymakers' function is importantly different from the first-mentioned 'lobby group' function traditionally associated with the voluntary associations of civil society. That first function refers to the mobilization of political demands, in the face of other competing demands. Mobilization is for war, in domestic politics as internationally.

Whereas the dominant ethos of 'lobbying' is essentially competitive, the dominant ethos of network-based reference groups is essentially cooperative, at least within the network. (Different networks, of course, compete with one another, in pushing their particular barrows.) Networks unite people and organizations sharing common concerns and values, on a voluntary basis. Mutuality prevails, as each internalizes the perspective of the others. Differences of opinion exist within the network, of course. But assured that they are all aiming at the same goal, participants in networks respect one another's opinions, explore the bases for their differences, and try in good faith to resolve them.[81]

This is, of course, an idealized story about what might happen within the sorts of networks that link non-profits and hold them accountable. A fuller and more realistic account would require, at the more macro-level, lots of detailed case studies exploring how disparate groups with partially overlapping (but partially diverging) interests, goals, and fundamental values come together in pursuit of the partial goals that they do share. How are shared norms socially constructed, by and within such networks? That is an important topic for further research.[82] At the more micro-level, we need lots of detailed case studies of how individuals within those networks come to internalize such norms and adjust their self-appraisals in light of them.[83] The personal phenomenology of life within such networks needs to be explored much more fully.[84]

---

[80] Rose-Ackerman (1995, 2003/2004) and European Union Commission (2001).
[81] March and Olsen (1995: ch. 2).   [82] Begun in Fox and Brown (1998).
[83] Bate (2000).
[84] An excellent start is Mansbridge's account (1995: 27–9) of what it is to feel oneself 'internally accountable' to the feminist movement:

The entity...to which they feel accountable is neither an aggregation of organizations nor an aggregation of individual members but a discourse. It is a set of changing, contested aspirations and understandings that provide conscious goals, cognitive backing and emotional support for each individual's evolving feminist identity....The discursively created movement is what the people in the movement say it is, what is taken up and held to be feminism....[T]he discursive process is always collective...The 'movement' is made up of

Those are large and important tasks, for later occasions. For now, however, it just bears emphasizing that sort of mutual accountability through networks of significant others can happen only (or anyway best) among non-profits than among organizations in the other two sectors. Mutuality of the sort that lies at the heart of this network ethos presumes a voluntary band of coequals. It assumes that none have authority over the other (as in a state's hierarchy) and that they are free from competitive pressures (as are found in markets) to cooperate in good faith with one another. This is thus a unique contribution that the Third Sector can offer towards helping public policy a more effective response to citizens' needs, interests, and aspirations.

Realistically, too, it is important not to romanticize networks. They can be conspiracies against the public, or cosy cabals covering one another's incompetence as easily as they can be collaborations in pursuit of true public good.[85] Thus, it is by no means analytic that such networks necessarily promote the public good. While fully acknowledging that fact, we can nonetheless say that there are certain sorts of public good that can only be promoted by such groups. It is a necessary, if not sufficient, condition of promoting the public good that such networks exist.

8.5. Conclusion

This chapter, then, has identified three modes of accountability. The state-based mode of accountability is, at root, a mode of electoral accountability. The market-based mode of accountability is, at root, a mode of financial accountability. The network-based mode of accountability is the one that I have been associating especially with the Third Sector, but it is found among states and throughout civil society more generally.

To give a good account of oneself in the first mode, one simply needs to say: 'I won the election and I have a right to rule in consequence; the electors will judge me come the next election.' To give a good account of

women figuring out and telling one another what they think makes sense, and what they think can explain and help crack the gender domination that they feel and are beginning to understand. I argue that this discursively created movement is the entity that inspires movement activists and is the entity to which they feel accountable.

Something like this seems true of life within 'issue networks' more generally (Mansbridge 1992: 39–40).

[85] Nicholson (1972). 'An inbred group . . . prey to lapses in judgement', as Brody (2002: 478) describes how interlocking directorates facilitated the spread of the 'Foundation for New Era Philanthropy' scam through Philadelphia's non-profit sector.

oneself in the second mode, one simply needs to say: 'I turned a profit; my shareholders will judge me, selling off their shares in my company if they disapprove.'

To give a good account of oneself in the third mode, one needs to be able to say, 'I justified my actions to the satisfaction of my peers.' That sort of network accountability is, thus, the paradigm case of discursive accountability. It is the paradigm sort of democratic accountability that deliberative democrats should wish for.[86]

---

[86] In Thompson's terms (1999: 120), it 'broaden[s] the scope of political accountability', requiring 'public officials [to] consider not only their electoral constituents but also what may be called their moral constituents, all those individuals who are bound by the decision they make, whether *de jure* or *de facto*'. Thompson goes on to observe, 'This moral constituency goes beyond the border of the nation', although he thinks (wrongly, I think) that it 'stops short of a cosmopolitan inclusion of everyone in the world who might be affected by a state's decision'. His reason for that is that 'most non-citizens are not reasonably regarded as participants in the scheme of cooperation that establishes the rights and obligations that the state enforces'. That, however, is tantamount to the 'blackball' model I reject at the beginning of Chapter 6.

9

Sequencing deliberative moments

Standard versions of deliberative democracy tend to postulate something like a unified deliberative agent of a single mind. The agent is plural, of course: it is composed of many people deliberating together in the sorts of networks just described. But that plural agent is assumed to be in pursuit of a shared purpose—the 'common good' or some such. Deliberations are assumed to be fixed on a single purpose, shared by all the component parts of that plural agent. Then and only then can we expect the full set of deliberative virtues to be fully on display in group deliberations.[1]

But politics is not like that. Real-world politics involves plural agents with partially conflicting interests, playing different roles at different stages in the process. Despite that fact, I suggest, group deliberations might still add up to something worthy of respect, if concatenated in the right way.

My aim in this chapter is to point out the possibility of 'distributed deliberation'—with different agents playing different deliberative roles—as an alternative to the 'unitary' model of deliberation that presently dominates discussion among deliberative democrats.[2] In this model of 'distributed deliberation', the component deliberative virtues are on display sequentially, over the course of this staged deliberation involving various component parts, rather than continuously and simultaneously present as they would be in the case of a unitary deliberating actor.[3]

---

[1] This is the respect in which Young (1996: 125) complains that the 'deliberative model assumes unity'. The later Habermas (1996: 304–7) critiques Cohen (1989) on precisely this point.

[2] For elaboration of the 'unitary' model, and its contrast with the 'adversary' model, see Mansbridge (1980: ch. 2). Habermas (1996: 304–7) criticizes Cohen's account (1989) of deliberative democracy for being too 'unitary' in just this way.

[3] In this, I shall be elaborating Mansbridge's (1999; cf. Hendriks 2006) notion of a 'deliberative system' in which 'the criterion for good deliberation should be not that every interaction in the system exhibit mutual respect, consistency, acknowledgment, open-mindedness and moral economy, but that the larger system reflect those goals'. Ferejohn (2008) offers a similar

9.1. Setting Discursive Standards

When it comes to setting standards for what counts as 'good' discourse and deliberation, there seems to be an impressively broad scholarly consensus.

That fact emerges most strikingly when we compare the criteria proposed by three distinct sets of scholars, working wholly independently of one another. First is the Oxford-Berkeley philosopher of language, Paul Grice. Second is a team of international relations specialists led by Knud Midgaard. Third is a team of comparative politics experts led by Jürg Steiner. Table 9.1 sets their respective criteria of 'good discourse' alongside one another.

Although organized slightly differently, these lists are remarkable for their overlaps. Those are not the product of any direct cross-fertilization: none of these teams make any explicit reference to one another's work; they apparently compiled their lists completely in ignorance of one another. Furthermore, they derive their inspiration from different sources, the Steiner team taking its orientation from Habermas, while the other two draw their inspiration explicitly or implicitly from J. L. Austin.[4]

Of course, deeper down they all share common roots. Habermas has read Austin and makes use of his insights. Both Habermas and Austin draw on many of the same sources, including most conspicuously the later Wittgenstein. Still, these constitute genuine instances of 'independent discovery', albeit within the same broad traditions.

The sheer fact of consensus does not necessarily vouchsafe the truth of a proposition, of course. Common-mode failures are common; different people can easily succumb to the same error. Nevertheless, we ought find it powerfully reassuring that independent observers as varied as these come up with such broadly similar criteria of what constitutes 'good discursive practice'.

Before we seize upon this happy news and field a large battery of operational tests of good discursive practice, we ought pause briefly to

---

analysis of the virtues of a division of deliberative labour, in his discussion of the British Columbia Citizens' Assembly on Electoral Reform. Manin (1997: ch. 6) similarly notes that 'trial by discussion' comes at different points in the political process under the three models of democracy he discusses ('Parliamentarian', 'Party Democracy', and 'Audience Democracy').

[4] Midgaard explicitly, Grice implicitly. For a measure of the extent to which Grice's account (1975) elaborates themes in the air of Austin's Oxford, consider the similarities between Grice's list and Nowell-Smith's list (1954: 81–2): the two parts of Grice's Maxim 2 correspond to Nowell-Smith's Rules 1 and 2 and Grice's Maxim 3 to Nowell-Smith's Rule 3.

Table 9.1. Standards of good discursive practice

Maxims of conversation	Rules of political interlocution	Indices of deliberative quality
1. Quantity • Make your contribution as informative as is required (for the current purposes of the exchange). • Do not make your contribution more informative than is required. 2. Quality • Do not say what you believe to be false. • Do not say that for which you lack adequate evidence. 3. Relation • Be relevant. 4. Manner • Avoid obscurity of expression. • Avoid ambiguity. • Be brief (avoid unnecessary prolixity). • Be orderly. Grice (1975)	1. Sense • Try to speak sense. 2. Sincerity • Try not to mislead by one's own use of language. 3. Relevance • Stick (in a reasonable degree) to what is relevant to the official purpose and to the addressee. 4. Attentiveness • Pay attention to what is said by the other participants. 5. Respect • Show respect towards the other participants. Midgaard, Stenstadvold, and Underdal (1973: 20) and Midgaard (1980: 87)	1. Open participation • Every competent individual should be free to take part in the discourse. 2. Justification of assertions and validity claims • Assertions should be introduced and critically assessed through 'the orderly exchange of information and reasons'. . . . • The tighter the connection between premises and conclusions, the more coherent the justification is and the more useful it will be for deliberation. 3. Consideration of the common good • [T]here should be a sense of empathy, other-directedness or solidarity that allows the participants to consider the well-being of others and of the community at large. • Someone using self-interest must demonstrate that it is compatible with or contributes to the common good. 4. Respect • [Participants should] acknowledge the needs and rights of different social groups. • [Participants should] respect the demands under discussion, as long as they can intersubjectively be seen as justified. • [Participants should show] respect towards counterarguments raised by opponents that contradict their own conclusions. . . . 5. Aim at a rationally motivated consensus • [A] discourse should at least attempt to reach mutually acceptable compromise solutions. . . . 6. Authenticity, without deception in expressing preferences. . . . • [S]tated preferences should be sincere rather than strategic. . . . Steenbergen et al. (2002: 25–6)

consider what these are tests *of*. We need to consider whether, and how, they might properly be used to study genuinely *political* interactions.

9.2. Language Games, Cooperative and Otherwise

I shall say more about the content of those lists shortly. First, however, I want to point out a deeper, structural feature underlying all these models. All represent discourse—conversation, political interlocution, or deliberation—as, fundamentally, a *cooperative* game.

That is not merely in the loose, colloquial sense that the collaboration of multiple players is required to make a conversation. More than that is involved here. Discourse is represented as a cooperative game in the technical game-theoretic sense of the term: there is no conflict of interest between any of the parties to the game; what is good for one is good for all (or anyway, good for some and not bad for any).

Grice explicitly posits a 'Cooperative Principle' as governing all conversation.[5] It is from that principle that Grice derives his other, more specific, Maxims of Conversation. But the point here is not peculiar to Grice or to his particular characterization of interpersonal communication. Instead it is rooted deeply in the nature of language as a set of conventions.

Here is the standard story. It is purely arbitrary what sign we take to signify what, whether we use the word 'blast' or 'blue' to denote the colour of the sky. What is crucial, if we are to communicate our meanings to one another, is that we share the *same* arbitrary conventions—that what I call 'blue' must also be what you understand by my saying 'blue'. Insofar as we each have an interest in communicating with one another at all, it is in the interests of each of us to share the same conventions about the usage of words (and other signs and symbols). That is the sense in which David Lewis models the conventions of language as a 'coordination game'—a subspecies of cooperative games in which, above all else, each of us wants to do the same as the other.[6]

Of course, the *uses* we make of those conventions might be anything but cooperative. We might want to use words whose meanings we share to contradict or criticize or insult one another. The point is simply that, in order to do any of that, we even more fundamentally want our messages

---

[5] To wit: 'make your conversational contribution such as is required, at the stage at which it occurs, by the accepted purpose or direction of the task exchange in which you are engaged'.
[6] Lewis (1969).

to be *meaningful* to one another. At that more fundamental level, systems of communication simply have to be, at root, a cooperative game.

One of the above standards of 'good deliberative practice' arguably follows straightforwardly from that basic analysis of the conventionality of language itself. That is the principle of veracity: saying only what you genuinely believe to be true. It is crucial that speakers generally respect that rule, in order for the rest of us even to be able to surmise what they *mean* by the propositions that they are asserting.[7] If they invariably lie, there will be no pattern for us to pick in assigning meaning to their utterances.

By and large, however, the precepts of 'good discursive practice' set out in Table 9.1 do not follow directly from the nature of language and communication itself. Instead they derive from the special requirements of special sorts of linguistic encounters: 'purposive conversations' (in Grice's case); discussions formally assigned an 'official purpose' (in Midgaard's case); deliberations aimed at joint resolution of some specific issue (in Steiner's case).

Only a philosopher could imagine that interpersonal communication is always a purely cooperative game entirely oriented towards some shared goal. Bartenders, barbers, priests, and politicians all know better. Conversation, as they know it, has many different aims. Those are different for different people, whose aims in the conversation are often cross-cutting and sometimes completely at cross-purposes. Communication in the real world is not the purely cooperative game of the philosophical imagination. Instead it is a mixed-motive game of strategy—or worse, a game of pure competition, in which one person's gains are the other's losses.

It is a massive leap of faith to suppose that all parties to a conversation-cum-deliberation share the same view of the 'purpose' of the discussion, of 'what it is about'. The topic on the table is typically one of the things up for discussion, not something taken as read from the outset. And that is as true in formal negotiations as in informal conversations. In a political discussion, particularly, a certain amount of gaming invariably surrounds the 'definition of the problem'. What is the problem under discussion and what would count as a solution are typically things to be discussed, not things fixed prior to discussion.[8]

---

[7] In Lewis's formulation (1969: 194), 'L is an actual language of [population] *P* if and only if there prevails in *P* a convention of truthfulness in L, sustained by an interest in communication'.

[8] Furthermore, discussion seems in fact help participants focus on issue dimensions structured in the same way (List et al. 2007).

Even if there is inevitably a certain amount of gaming over those issues, however, strategic actors often confront the problem of 'getting from here to there'. They are often obliged to take the 'official' topic as given, pro tem, and at least to pretend that their interventions constitute contributions towards its resolution—even if their larger agenda is ultimately to change the topic of conversation and to substitute their own definition of the problem for the one they have conversationally inherited.

Certainly the formal processes of political deliberation are organized 'as if' the group were essentially a single agent with a unified purpose. Rules of parliamentary procedure are, first and foremost, *Rules of Order*.[9] They set out procedures by which the group might systematically set about deliberating over a complex issue. Rules of parliamentary procedure prescribe for a group deliberation what the rules of logic prescribe for an individual.[10] Take one topic at a time; decompose it into its component parts; decide on each of those components in a logical sequence; stick to the point.[11]

In a way, those are familiar pieties that constitute the 'dignified' fiction upon which deliberative institutions are based. Parliamentarians pay periodic tribute to them. Their obeisance is often shallow. Rules of order and parliamentary procedures typically constitute the 'institutional rule book', the framework within which political games are played out. And in politics as in commerce, 'players' are anything but 'gentlemen'.[12] Players in parliament are invariably 'gaming the system', sailing as close to the wind of the formal rules as necessary, in order to secure their own particular objectives as best they can.[13]

Still, it is less the reality of parliamentary discourse that concerns me at this point than the fiction. The rules of parliamentary procedure invite us to see a legislature—ideally, at least—as a unified deliberative agent, which ought operate according to the same standards of logic, order, coherence, etc. as ought a single natural individual deliberating on the same matter. The rules of parliamentary procedure invite us to suppose that legislatures, and collective deliberations more generally, ought to be governed according to the ideals of good deliberative practice set out in the final column of Table 9.1.

---

[9] Robert (1876/1951).
[10] Oakeshott (1975: 43–6, 173–80) would fiercely resist the particular analogy, as applied to individual deliberation or that of a civil association either. But he would, I think, take the larger point.
[11] Jefferson (1801/1988: §17, p. 274) and Robert (1876/1951: §43, pp. 180–2).
[12] Coleman (1973).   [13] Goodin (2000d).

9.3. Another Model of Group Deliberation: Distributed Deliberation

'The fundamental right of a deliberative assembly', General Robert writes in the introduction to his *Rules of Order*, is 'to have questions thoroughly discussed before it is called upon to take action upon them'.[14] But 'having a question thoroughly discussed' does not necessarily imply that the discussion necessarily occurred, exclusively (or perhaps even principally) *in that place.*

As General Robert goes on to point out, 'the work of Congress is enormous and is mostly done by standing committees....' Indeed, 'it is usual in deliberative assemblies' quite generally 'to have all preliminary work in the preparation of matter for their action done by means of committees'.[15]

Those committees are creatures of the parent assembly. They deliberate on issues assigned to them by the parent assembly. They report back to the parent assembly, and their reports then partly form the basis for subsequent deliberations of the parent assembly. In short, the parent assembly delegates certain elements of its deliberative task to these other subgroups.[16]

Furthermore, those delegated deliberations proceed in slightly different ways than do delegations in the parent assembly. General Robert tells us that the rules of procedure governing committees are broadly the same as those governing the parent assembly.[17] But having said that, General Robert immediately proceeds to itemize a litany of important differences that belie that general rule. For example:

- Members can speak as often as they like on a motion in committee, but only once (or with special dispensation twice) on the floor.
- Any member can move to reconsider past action in committee, whereas only a member who voted on the winning side can bring a motion to reconsider on the floor.

[14] Robert (1876/1951: 16).

[15] Robert (1876/1951: 19; §52, pp. 210–11). Cox (2006) shows why that is a good idea, in terms of limiting demands on 'plenary time' and avoiding giving virtually every representative a veto. James Madison tried to persuade the first Congress 'to determine the outlines of all business in the Committee of the Whole', but even then other members thought it better for motions be referred first 'to a subcommittee to digest'; otherwise it was as if 'they were building the house before the plan was drawn' (quoted in Mansbridge 1988: 66).

[16] As Robert (1876/1951: §52, p. 220) remarks, 'When a committee is properly selected, in nine cases out of ten its action decides that of the assembly'.

[17] Robert (1876/1951: §52, p. 211).

- In committee, the chairperson takes an active part in the deliberations, whereas in the legislative chamber itself the chair's role is more
  purely procedural.

To some extent those differences can be explained by the sheer fact of size
of the respective groups. Being smaller, committees can afford to dispense
with some of the formality that is required to manage business in an
orderly fashion in larger assemblies.[18] But to some extent the differences
in procedure reflect the fact that different tasks are being performed by
the committee and the parent assembly.

The committee is engaged in drafting (and redrafting) proposals; in
giving detailed consideration to proposals line-by-line; in fact finding and
in framing appropriate responses to the facts found.[19] This is creative,
cooperative work. The parent assembly, in contrast, is more in the business of disposing of proposals, affirmatively or negatively.[20] Discourse in
the former venue is aimed more at refining proposals. In the latter venue
it is aimed more at rationalizing acceptance or rejection.

These are all familiar facts about legislative assemblies. My proposal here
is that they be generalized to deliberation *tout court*. My suggestion is that
it is always possible, and with large groups almost always desirable, to
divide up the deliberative task in such ways.

Different parts of the deliberative task can then be assigned to different
subsets of the larger group. The deliberations of these sub-units serve as
background and inputs into the deliberations of the larger group with
overall deliberative responsibility.

Furthermore, just as with legislative committees, the terms on which
those sub-units conduct their delegated deliberative business can (and
probably ordinarily should) differ somewhat from the terms on which
the larger group conducts its own deliberations.[21]

---

[18] Robert (1876/1951: §50, p. 208; §52, p. 213).

[19] Robert (1876/1951: §§52–4; §69, pp. 279–83).

[20] Notably, when it cannot do that, the larger assembly takes on the committee form:
'When an assembly has to consider a subject which . . . is not well digested and put into proper
form for its definite action' the assembly will typically 'resolve itself into a committee of the
whole', which 'allows the freest discussion of the subject' (Robert 1876/1951: §55, pp. 229,
233).

[21] Or, more precisely, should have conducted its deliberations had it decided the matter
itself directly, without any such delegation. It may be the case that the larger groups should
conduct its deliberations differently, for having delegated part of the deliberative task to sub-
units, than it would have done had it not done so. (The legislative analogue is presumably
going into 'committee of the whole' to consider matters that have not first been sifted by a
standing committee.)

In short, the procedures—and deliberative standards—to which we should hold deliberative agents in such a system of 'distributed' or 'delegated' deliberation are not necessarily the same as those to which we would rightly hold a single, unified deliberative agent. In a world of delegated deliberation, where different parts of the deliberative task are divided up and shared among various different agents, appropriate behaviour within each component part of that distributed deliberation is not necessarily the same as appropriate behaviour where one body is performing the whole deliberative task on its own.

9.4. Different Steps, Different Deliberative Expectations

In light of all that, let us now consider four different steps in the operation of ordinary representative democracy and what might be considered as constituting 'good deliberative practice' within each of them.

The exercise is intended to be illustrative rather than exhaustive. There is much more that goes on within representative democracy that ought also be held up to ethical scrutiny. There are various other ethical standards to be brought to bear besides merely the deliberative one. Representative democracy both embodies and is embedded in broader networks of accountability as sketched in Chapter 8.

Still, focusing on these four stages of ordinary representative democracy will suffice to illustrate my basic point, here. And for these purposes, it also suffices to simply take the 'indices of deliberative quality' developed by the Steiner team as our evaluative concerns.[22] Having gotten the point onto the table by reference to stages and standards of those familiar sorts, we can then begin to ponder how to broaden it to other stages (deliberation in civil society or the administrative process, for example) or other standards (of rhetoric, for example).

Minimally contentiously, representative democracy might be envisaged as proceeding in the following four stages.[23] First, let us suppose, there is the 'caucus room' deliberation, where all the Members of Parliament (MPs) of a single party get together to formulate their own programme. Second, let us suppose, there is the 'parliamentary debate', when MPs from all parties publicly present arguments for their preferred position

[22] Steenbergen et al. (2002).
[23] Modelled loosely on the British case (Birch 1964). For underappreciated early treatments of 'government by discussion' along similar lines, see Lindsay (1935: Lecture 3) and Barker (1958; resurrected by Majone 2006: 233–4).

and against other positions. Third, let us suppose, there is an 'election campaign', in which parliamentary candidates compete for office based on the policy positions their parties have taken. Fourth, let us suppose, there is 'post-election bargaining', in which party leaders negotiate policy deals with one another based on the number of representatives they elect. As I say, this is a highly stylized characterization of a much messier political reality; it is in no way exhaustive of all alternative possibilities. Still, it will do for the purposes.

What we ought naturally to expect is that each of those 'stages of the deliberative process' will display different virtues, judged by the Indicators of Deliberative Quality. Table 9.2 reproduces those Indicators and foreshadows the conclusions of the following remarks as to where in the deliberative process each of those deliberative virtues is most likely to be found.

The caucus room is first and foremost a place for candour. Members can speak freely, knowing that what is said in the caucus room stays in the caucus room. There, deliberations can achieve 'authenticity, without deception' (Indicator 6) in ways that elsewhere in the process they cannot.

Of course, that desideratum is not necessarily met perfectly even in the caucus room. Even within a single party, there are differences of opinion, factional fights, and hence motives for dissembling and deceiving one another. Still, it seems reasonable to expect less of that there than elsewhere in the overall deliberative process. And, of course, 'authenticity' is not the only deliberative virtue on display in the caucus room. Insofar as the party trying to come up with a position that can be defended in open debate to the public at large, it must be a position capable of being backed by argument (Indicator 2), ideally in terms of the common good (Indicator 3).[24] And of course internally, all the other deliberative desiderata are met: participation is open, at least to everyone who is a member of the caucus (Indicator 1); if their votes are to be won, respect must be shown (Indicator 4), albeit again only to members of the caucus; and the aim of the discussion is to produce a rationally motivated consensus (Indicator 5), at least among members of the caucus.[25]

[24] The fact that the caucus must sell its proposals through the parliament to the electorate in general is what prevents the insularity that Lindsay (1935: 40–1) fears with small closed sects, generally. As Bolingbroke wrote in *The Idea of a Patriot King*, 'A man who has not seen the inside of parties, nor had opportunities to examine their secret motives, can hardly conceive how little a share principle of any sort, tho principle of some sort or other be always pretended, has in the determination of their conduct' (quoted in Hofstadter 1969: 21).

[25] In Manin's account (1997: 217) of 'Party Democracy', it is 'in the intra-party exchanges that precede parliamentary debates, participants truly deliberate. The party leadership and Members in Parliament debate among themselves what collective position should be adopted.

Table 9.2. Deliberative expectations of representative democracy

	Caucus room	Parliamentary debate	Election campaign	Post-election bargaining
1. Open participation				
Every competent individual should be free to take part in the discourse.	−	−	+	−
2. Justification of assertions and validity claims				
(a) Assertions should be introduced and critically assessed through 'the orderly exchange of information and reasons'....	−	+	−	−
(b) The tighter the connection between premises and conclusions, the more coherent the justification is and the more useful it will be for deliberation.	−	+	−	−
3. Consideration of the common good				
(a) [T]here should be a sense of empathy, other-directedness or solidarity that allows the participants to consider the well-being of others and of the community at large.	−	−	+	−
(b) Someone using self-interest must demonstrate that it is compatible with or contributes to the common good.	−	−	+	−
4. Respect				
(a) [Participants should] acknowledge the needs and rights of different social groups.	−	−	−	+
(b) [Participants should] respect the demands under discussion, as long as they can intersubjectively be seen as justified.	−	−	−	+
(c) [Participants should show] respect towards counterarguments raised by opponents that contradict their own conclusions.....	−	+	−	−
5. Aim at a rationally motivated consensus				
[A] discourse should at least attempt to reach mutually acceptable compromise solutions....	−	−	−	+
6. Authenticity, without deception in expressing preferences				
[S]tated preferences should be sincere rather than strategic....	+	−	−	−

Hence, in saying that 'authenticity' is the *principal* deliberative virtue on display in the caucus room, I do not mean to imply that either it is completely on display there or none of the other deliberative virtues are on display there to any extent. Authenticity is simply the principal virtue of the caucus deliberation, and the caucus is the principal place in the deliberative process where it is found.

The parliamentary chamber is first and foremost a place to 'put one's case'. Each party sets out the most coherent and persuasive justification it can, for its preferred position. Like barristers arguing a brief, MPs do their best to set out their arguments in an orderly, logical fashion (Indicator 2). Insofar as counterarguments of their opponents threaten to undermine their own case, they respectfully register those arguments and attempt to refute them (Indicator 4c). But in parliamentary debate, no one seriously expects to change any other MP's mind.[26] 'It is the business of an opposition to oppose.'[27] The various parties are merely 'making their pitch' to the media (lobby correspondents in the old days, television cameras nowadays), and through them to the electorate at large.[28]

Once again, parliamentary debates do not always completely realize this ideal. They are not always completely logical and argument driven. But they display those deliberative more than most other aspects of the overall deliberative process, that is, the primary deliberative virtue of this stage of the process. Once again, too, parliamentary debates display to some other of the other deliberative virtues, such as (ostensible) concern for the common good and rationally motivated consensus and authenticity (Indicators 3, 4a,b, 5, 6) in anticipation of the need to sell one's case to the electorate. And participation in parliamentary debates is open, at least to all MPs (Indicator 1).

And in that debate, the participants are able to change their minds as a result of the exchange of arguments'.

[26] '[R]epresentatives do not vote in light of the arguments exchanged in Parliament, but as a result of decisions formed elsewhere' (Manin 1997: 216–7; see similarly Young 1996: 121). That explains the findings in Steenbergen et al. (2002: 40) that, in House of Commons debates, 'respect for others' demands' (Indicator 4b) is conspicuously missing. As Hobbes (1651: ch. 6) says, you deliberate before you have decided; the 'end' of 'deliberation' is to settle on some particular course of action, to put an end to 'liberty' you previously had to choose any of them. Couched in those terms, we might say MPs having conducted their 'deliberation' in the caucus room are no longer at liberty to change positions on the floor.

[27] Lindsay (1935: 47). See similarly Hobbes's critique (1647/1998: ch. 10, §12) of the factionalism inevitable in large deliberative assemblies.

[28] 'Much of what is said on the floor is designed primarily for the record or for home consumption' (Mansbridge 1988: 64). But as Lindsay (1935: 42) puts it, parliamentary 'discussion is to take place, if possible, with the invisible public listening; and the function of a general election is not simply to choose representatives but to express the approval or disapproval of the general public on the doings of the representative assembly'.

So once again in saying that conjuring up 'rational justifications' is the *principal* deliberative virtue on display in parliamentary debates, I do not mean to imply that either it is completely on display there or all other deliberative virtues are totally absent. 'Rational justification' is simply the principal deliberative virtue of the parliamentary debate, and that is the principal place in the deliberative process where it is found.

The election campaign is the point in the deliberative process where 'participation' is most 'open' to everyone (Indicator 1). Partly in consequence of that, it is also the place where considerations of the 'common good' are most likely to come to the fore (Indicator 3).[29]

Of course, the participation in question here is discursive, not just electoral. Just as many qualified electors fail to vote, so too (all the more so) do many affected parties fail to speak. The criterion is couched in terms of possibility rather than actuality ('every competent individual' being '*free* to take part in the discourse', rather than necessarily actually doing so). Still, there are strict limits on even the sheer possibility of every member of a large electorate having his or her voice heard by all others who are supposed to be party to that same discourse.[30] The most we can realistically expect is that citizens talk to one another, who talk to still others in turn, and that some 'six degrees of separation' sort hypothesis holds sufficiently to ensure that everyone in the community is connected directly or indirectly to everyone else in this discourse.[31]

---

[29] The causal conjecture is based on evidence about how communication increases cooperative play in Prisoner Dilemma games (Orbell et al. 1988; Dawes, Kragt, and Orbell 1990; Frey and Bohnet 1996). Note Bagehot's parallel comments (1867/1966: 152) on expanding one's horizons through petitions of grievances:

In old times one office of the House of Commons was to inform the sovereign what was wrong. It laid before the Crown the grievances and complaints of particular interests. Since the publication of the Parliamentary debates a corresponding office of Parliament is to lay these same grievances, these same complaints, before the nation, which is the present sovereign. The nation needs it quite as much as the king ever needed it. A free people is indeed mostly fair, liberty practices men in give-and-take, which is the rough essence of justice.... But a free nation can rarely be ... quick of apprehension. It only comprehends what is familiar to it—what comes into its own experience, what squares with its own thoughts. "I never heard of such a thing in my life," the middle-class Englishman says, and he thinks he so refutes an argument. The common disputant cannot say in reply that his experience is but limited, and that the assertion may be true, though he had never met with anything at all like it. But a great debate in Parliament does bring home something of this feeling. Any notion, any creed, any feeling, any grievance that can get a decent number of English members to stand up for it, is felt by almost all Englishmen to be perhaps a false and pernicious opinion, but at any rate possible—an opinion within the intellectual sphere, an opinion to be reckoned with. And it is an immense achievement.

[30] Goodin (2003*b*: ch. 7).   [31] Lindsay (1935: 38–9).

Similarly, there is no guarantee that discussions spread across a broad public will necessarily focus attention on what is in the common good of that whole public. Still, when parties are trying to appeal to the public as a whole, they will be strategically tempted at least to pretend that what their plan is good for the public at large, as well as for their own supporters (Indicator 3b). As Manin puts it,

Competition among the different . . . candidates . . . encourages each protagonist to make use of those principles and arguments likely to win the largest possible agreement . . . In order to increase its support, each party has an interest in showing that its point of view is *more general* than the others'. . . . [T]he structure of the deliberative system [in an election] usually makes the protagnoists strive to enlarge their points of view and propose more and more general positions. There is a sort of competition for generality.[32]

On the part of voters themselves, there is evidence that people vote 'sociotropically', on the basis of what they perceive to be good for the country as a whole rather than on the basis of what is good for them personally.[33] Insofar as they do (or, rather, insofar as parties perceive that they do) it makes good strategic sense for parties to orient their appeals in that way. And insofar as voters are oriented towards the common good in this way, they will orient their own conversations surrounding the election in this way.

While those two deliberative desiderata—openness and a common-good focus—are likely to be most strongly present in election campaigns than other stages of the deliberative process, other deliberative desiderata may well be less markedly present. Public debate during an election campaign will be a pale shadow of parliamentary debates in the run-up to the election. Coherent, rational arguments involving careful deduction of conclusions from well-grounded premises (Indicator 2) are far less likely.[34] In parliamentary debates, rules require MPs to behave as if 'it is not the man, but the measure, that is subject of debate'[35]; election campaigns are bound by no such rule and are characterized, if anything, by the

---

[32] Manin (1987: 358–9).

[33] Kinder and Kiewiet (1981); Kiewiet (1983); Rohrschneider (1988).

[34] What Hobbes (1647/1998: ch. 10, §11) says contra deliberation in large assemblies is all the more apt apropos large electorates: 'votes are cast not on the basis of correct reasoning but on emotional impulse. This is not the fault of the *man* but of *Eloquence* itself, whose end (as all the masters of Rhetoric point out) is not truth (except by accident) but victory; and its task is not to teach but to persuade'. The media, even in Bagehot's day (1867/1966: 153), 'only repeat the side their purchasers like: the favourable arguments are set out, elaborated, illustrated, the adverse arguments maimed, misstated, confused'.

[35] Robert (1876/1951: §43, p. 180).

opposite tendency. In divisive election campaigns, respect for opposing groups, their interests, and their arguments (Indicator 4) are also likely to suffer. In an election, the aim is to secure the numbers, not to build a unanimous consensus (Indicator 5).[36] And in an election, strategic manoeuvring (contra Indicator 6) is a fact of life, for parties and voters alike. So while election campaigns might display two key deliberative virtues (openness and concern for the common good), they often fall far short on other deliberative dimensions.

Finally, once the election is over, parties come to the bargaining table. Sometimes bargaining is required to form government itself, if no single party commands a workable majority in the legislature. Sometimes bargaining is required between the different chambers of a bicameral legislature, where different chambers are controlled by different parties. Sometimes bargaining is required between chambers or between factions within the governing party, insofar as they differ over their preferred form legislation should take.

At the bargaining table, the deliberative virtue most on display is 'respect for demands' (Indicator 4b). Bargainers come to the table with settled preferences and firm conclusions. They are not trying to change one another's minds through the force of better arguments. They are not driven by any empathetic desire to help others further their ends. Bargainers acknowledge the 'rights and needs of other groups' (Indicator 4a), if only because they respect the bargaining power of those groups. Bargainers seek 'a mutually acceptable compromise' (Indicator 5)—not so much a 'rationally motivated consensus' as simply a solution. Bargainers merely want to 'do a deal'. Insofar as bargainers are making at least partly conflicting demands (and bargaining would not be required unless they were), each bargainer is attempting to maximize satisfaction of her demands with minimal sacrifice of other things she also demands. All this bargaining is purely in terms of demands, with minimal reference to reasons.

Of course, no bargaining game is purely a matter of utterly conflicting demands. If it were, there would be nothing on the 'contract curve', no solution that makes both parties better off than leaving the matter unresolved. In consequence of that fact, there will always be a certain amount

---

[36] This is conspicuously true in first-past-the-post electoral systems like Britain's. But even in countries with systems of proportional representation, where power-sharing post-election is the norm, the parties' aim of the election campaign itself is primarily to maximize their vote and hence the number of seats in parliament that they take into the bargaining that then follows over government formation.

of reasoned argument and attempted consensus-building, as bargainers try to persuade one another that this or that solution really is good for both of them and not just for the speaker alone.

9.5. Sequenced Deliberation

Perhaps what is most to be desired from a deliberative perspective is represented by the ideal described in Section 9.1. Perhaps the best form of deliberation would indeed be akin to a cooperative game among all the participants, with all the deliberative virtues being simultaneously and continuously on display.

My point is simply that politics is not like that, at least not in the sorts of representative democracies that (and we are by and large glad that) now predominate. But while we cannot seriously expect all the deliberative virtues to be constantly on display at every step of the decision process in a representative democracy, we can realistically expect that different deliberative virtues might be on display at different steps of the process.

The question then is whether that can ever be 'good enough', from the point of view of the deliberative ideal. I presume the answer must surely be, 'It depends'. First, it presumably depends on having all of the deliberative virtues on display at *some* point or another in the decision process. We know from the 'general theory of second best' that if the ideal is unobtainable, the next best thing might be something very different from the ideal in all dimensions.[37] In the ideal speech situation, for example, (i) no one would lie and (ii) no one would question the sincerity of others. The second best would clearly not be one in which the condition (ii) is met even if condition (i) is not.[38]

Second, it presumably depends on the deliberative virtues coming in the right combinations and the right order. There are presumably interactions between different deliberative virtues, and across stages of the deliberative process, which must be taken into account in sequencing the deliberative virtues.

Third, it presumably depends on interactions among parts of the sequence. Having different deliberative virtues on display might lead different stages of the process to work at cross-purposes, from a democratic point of view. The caucus stage may generate proposals that are

---

[37] Lipsey and Lancaster (1956) and Goodin (1995).   [38] Markovits (2006).

more extreme than the general population would favour. Or anticipating having to face an election campaign mediated through the mass media might induce political leaders to produce proposals that would appeal to populist sentiments, but that would not withstand the scrutiny of calm reason.

Different ways of arranging our political affairs have different implications for the sequencing of deliberative virtues. The particular way of sequencing deliberation within representative democracy that I have been discussing is just one among many, albeit presumably a common one.

What I have been describing is a model of political deliberation where parties propose and electors dispose. Different parties work out their positions behind closed doors, making the deliberative virtue of 'authenticity' possible there. They set out 'reasoned arguments' for their positions in parliamentary debates, governed by rules promoting deliberative virtues of that sort. Those arguments are then put to the 'maximally expansive' deliberative body, the public at large, at an election where the premium is on deliberatively virtuous 'common-good' talk. Once voters have electorally determined the distribution of power in parliament, party leaders convene a probably only semi-public session to cut deals—'mutually acceptable compromises', based on deliberatively virtuous respect for the 'demands' ('rights and needs'—and power) of each respective group.

This model might be semi-provocatively dubbed 'deliberative Schumpeterianism'. In the classical Schumpeterian model of 'minimalist democracy' sketched in Chapter 1, the role of parties is to develop coherent policy packages which they then offer to the electorate. In the 'deliberative Schumpeterian' alternative, the role of parties is to develop coherent policy *arguments*, which they then offer to the electorate. Those arguments then become the subject of subsequent debate among the public.[39] Deliberatively endorsing one or other set of policy proposals—and, crucially,

---

[39] In roughly the ways Lindsay (1935: 42) described:

In a healthy and educated democracy, discussion ... will not be confined to the discussions of the representative assembly. [Instead] the discussion of the assembly will define issues. Profitable discussion in even the smallest group ... needs a chairman to define issues and focus attention on the points where discussion will be profitable. In a healthy democracy the discussions of the representative assembly will as it were act as chairman for the multifarious informal discussions of the nation as a whole, and the measure of the successful working of democracy is the extent to which the voting of the ordinary man and woman has been informed by this widely diffused public discussion'.

See similarly Bagehot's discussion (1867/1966: ch. 4, pp. 152–3) of the 'informing' and 'educative' functions of the House of Commons.

the ratio offered for it—is the essence of democratically 'giving law to ourselves', Chapter 10 will argue.[40]

There may well be other ways to sequence the deliberative process.[41] The British Columbia Citizens' Assembly on Electoral Reform offers another model: a deliberative mini-public is empowered to propose a referendum proposition and a ratio for it, and the electorate then votes on that. The stages and sequences of a 'referendum democracy' organized along those lines would distribute 'deliberative expectations' differently than that set out in Table 9.2, obviously. But that too would be a deliberative process characterized by different stages, with different deliberative virtues on display at each stage.

The larger point is that distributing deliberative virtues across different stages of a deliberative process might be 'good enough', if not perhaps ideal, from a deliberative point of view. It is, in any case, probably the most to which we can realistically aspire.

---

[40] Parties may not be the only groups that can serve a policy-development function. Voluntary associations (Lindsay 1935: 39–40) and interest groups (Mansbridge 1992) do that, as well. But alone among them parties are in a position to enact their policies and their associated ratios into law.

[41] Parkinson (2006: 166–73) sketches another way of conceptualizing the stages of the 'deliberative system'.

10

The place of parties

The great American legal philosopher Joel Feinberg opened his justly famous essay on 'The Nature and Value of Rights' with a quintessentially philosophical thought experiment:

Try to imagine Nowheresville—a world very much like our own except that no one...has *rights*.... We can make [Nowheresville] as pretty as we wish in other moral respects.... [M]ake the human beings in it as attractive and virtuous as possible.... Fill this imagined world with as much benevolence, compassion, sympathy and pity as it will conveniently hold... [1]

Still, Nowheresville would be lacking something that Feinberg finds of fundamental moral importance—rights.

In lacking rights, Nowheresville lacks any way in which people can make *claims* against one another, demanding what is due them. 'The activity of claiming', to Feinberg's way of thinking, is what 'makes for self-respect and respect for others, [and] gives...sense to the notion of personal dignity'. That, he concludes, is what 'distinguishes [our] otherwise morally flawed world from the even worse world of Nowheresville'. [2]

I do not particularly want to defend Feinberg's conclusion here, nor do I even want to talk further of his particular topic of 'rights'. I do, however, want to borrow his philosophical methodology. Trying to imagine what exactly our world would be like if just one crucial piece of our actual world were missing proves to be a very good way of trying to determine what, exactly, that missing piece is doing for us in our actual world. The philosophical foundations of social forms and practices, rendered familiar from long acquaintance, can thus be effectively excavated.

My particular concern is with political parties. Chapter 9 has described what sort of role they *could* play in a system of distributed democratic

---

[1] Feinberg (1970: 143).   [2] Feinberg (1970: 155).

deliberation. But *should* they? This chapter asks whether political parties, playing that sort of role, serve a democratically important purpose. To foreshadow, I shall derive the justification for having political parties, of a very particular sort, from the very notion of what it is democratically to 'give law to ourselves'.

Once we have philosophically explored what justifies political parties normatively, we can and should of course turn to other more empirical modes of enquiry to determine whether or not parties actually are discharging the role that democratic theory thus carves out for them, and whether or how their performance in that regard can be improved. But first things first. Until we are clear on the justificatory question, we cannot assess what empirical facts morally matter to democratic theory.

10.1. No-Party Democracy

The thought experiment I propose is this: let us try to imagine what it would be like to have a No-Party Democracy. We know (some of us better than others) what it is like to live in a 'multi-party democracy' or in 'two-party democracy' or indeed in a 'One-Party Democracy'. But what would it be like to have a *No-Party Democracy*?[3]

In engaging in this thought experiment, let us—following Feinberg's model—hold all other features of our actual world absolutely constant. In particular, let us imagine a world whose political arrangements are every bit as *democratic* as our own (or maybe even a little more so). Let us suppose that everyone who lives in the jurisdiction is entitled to vote, and let us suppose that a great majority of people do vote (maybe everyone is even compelled to vote, as in Australia.) Let us suppose that the votes are counted absolutely fairly. Let us suppose that the candidate with the most votes is faithfully installed in office, and reliably vacates office upon losing a subsequent election. Let us suppose that elections are held at periodic intervals, and are well publicized in advance. Neither candidates for office nor elected officials, let us suppose, ever lie, cheat, steal, take bribes, or in any other way pervert the electoral process. There are, let us suppose, always multiple candidates standing for every office; and those candidates are, let us suppose, different from one another in as many respects as we can imagine. In short, let us conjure up in our mind's eye the most perfectly democratic system that we can imagine.

---

[3] My model of 'No-Party Democracy' sketched below is broadly similar to the model of 'Parliamentarianism' that Manin (1997: ch. 6) contrasts to 'Party Democracy'.

Let us suppose that political system is missing just one element that is present in contemporary democracies as we now know them. In this wonderful democracy we are imagining, there are simply no political parties. Each candidate for office, let us imagine, stands entirely in his or her 'own right', rather than as in any way part of an organized 'list', 'slate', 'party', 'faction', or 'group'.

Some candidates may, of course, be more alike than others, in some dimensions (maybe, or maybe not, in all dimensions). Electors who prefer one may also prefer others who are similar, for the same reason. So there may thus be some pattern in the electoral returns, systematically favouring candidates who are similar in certain ways over others.

The key feature of this No-Party Democracy, however, is that there is no *intentional* action on the part of politicians—before, during, or after the election—to coordinate their own political actions with those of any other politician. Certainly, they do not constitute themselves a 'collective agent', with an internal decision-making structure all its own. Neither do they even 'act in unison' in any more loosely coupled sort of way. In this No-Party world, each person acts wholly independently of every other. Any commonalities that might exist across their political behaviours are, let us suppose, wholly unintended by them.[4] That is the sort of world I am asking you to imagine, for purposes of this thought experiment.

Things would still get done, policies made. But each act of the legislature would be a one-off—the product of a coalition assembled around a particular piece of legislation that carries over to no other. Representatives would have to be persuaded, one-by-one, on each new piece of legislation, one-by-one.

10.1.1. *An Older Ideal*

This may seem a fanciful scenario from today's perspective. True, at least one distinguished democratic theorist recommended something close to it, though the proposal is nowadays not much discussed.[5] And while occasional African regimes—Museveni's in Uganda, Rawlings' in Ghana[6]—style themselves 'No-Party Democracies', those seem actually to have been more like One-Party Democracies rather than No-Party ones. Local government, in certain places, might be the closest contemporary approximation we can find to No-Party Democracy.

---

[4] cf. Bratman (1992, 1993), French (1979), and Gilbert (1989).
[5] Ostrogorski (1902).   [6] Kasfir (1998) and Crook (1999).

From a broader historical perspective, however, No-Party Democracy seems far less eccentric. Schisms among governing elites have occurred since time immemorial, of course. But political parties as an organizational form are a relatively modern innovation, arising in their modern form only in the nineteenth century.[7]

Before that, all we find are constant complaints about the disharmony introduced by 'factions', 'cabals', and the 'spirit of party'. Those complaints are found in all the familiar English sources on the subject: Francis Bacon, Thomas Hobbes, and Viscount Bolingbroke and, in more resigned tones, in David Hume and Edmund Burke.[8] More surprising (in light of parties' subsequent flourishing there[9]) is the animus against parties and factions found among the Founders in the early American Republic.

The *Federalist Papers* are replete with worries about the 'spirit of faction'. Nowhere is that more evident than in the famous 'Federalist No. 10', which many say serves as the 'basic rationale for the American political system'.[10] 'Federalist No. 10' is no celebration of party politics: just the opposite. Madison's explicit aim is to find what he called some 'method of curing the mischiefs of faction'. Those he defined in the following, distinctly unflattering terms:

By a faction I understand a number of citizens, whether amounting to a majority or minority of the whole, who are united and actuated by some common impulse of passion, or of interest, adverse to the rights of other citizens, or to the permanent and aggregate interests of the community.[11]

Accepting that there is no way to 'remove the causes' of factionalism without sacrificing liberty itself, Madison contents himself with 'controlling its effects' by (among other things) pitting factions against one

---

[7] Hofstadter (1969: ch. 6) and Duverger (1959: xxiii–xxxvii).

[8] Bacon (1597), Hobbes (1651: ch. 22), Bolingbroke (1733-4, 1749), Hume (1760), and Burke (1770).

[9] Behold Lord Bryce's description of *The American Commonwealth* circa 1897: 'The whole machinery, both of national and state governments, is worked by the political parties. The spirit and force of party has in America been as essential to the action of the machinery of government as steam is to a locomotive engine; or, to vary the simile, party association and organization are to the organs of government almost what the motor nerves are to the muscles, sinews and bones of the human body. They transmit the motive power, they determine the direction by which the organs act.... The actual working of party government is ... so unlike what a student of the Federal Constitution could have expected or foreseen, that it is the thing of all others which anyone writing about America ought to try to portray' (quoted in Hofstadter 1969: 71).

[10] Dahl (1956: 5).

[11] Madison (1787/1961: 57). See similarly Rousseau (1762: book 2, ch. 3).

another.[12] Even though he thus found a way to use parties against parties, Madison was clearly a foe rather than a friend of party politics.[13]

So too, of course, was George Washington. In his last political testament, the 'Farewell Address' (drafted for him first by Madison and then by Hamilton) the 'Father of his Country' proclaimed unequivocally:

...the common and continual mischiefs of the spirit of party are sufficient to make it the interest and duty of a wise people to discourage and restrain it.[14]

A dozen years later one senator went so far as to propose amending the Constitution to make the president be chosen purely by lot from among retiring senators, precisely on the grounds that ending the popular election of the president was the only way to 'cut-off the head of the demon...of party spirit...which is engendered by factions...'[15]

Let us leave history there. These texts were all written with aims more political than philosophical. The political world that they addressed was only a very partially democratized one. There are limits to what such history can teach us.

Still, I find it an agreeable irony that, were we trying to imagine what a No-Party Democracy might be like, we can do no better than to try to imagine ourselves into the ideal political world of the American Founders themselves.

10.1.2. *What Political Life Might Be Like*

Let us take instead a more theoretical, a priori tack in addressing the question of what political life would be like in a No-Party Democracy.

By stipulation, the politics would be democratic. Various people would compete with one another for office. On the basis of the outcome of the election, a government would be formed, with someone or another at its head and various others occupying subsidiary offices of state as required. In all those ways, life under a No-Party Democracy would be just the same as at present.

The main differences would lie in the bases upon which, in the absence of any formal or informal party organizations, politicians would compete with one another for office and cooperate with one another in the exercise of office. What grounds would voters have for choosing one

---

[12] Madison (1787/1961: 58).   [13] Hofstadter (1969: chs. 1–3).
[14] Washington (1796/1966: 201).
[15] Hillhouse (1808/1967: 233). Tellingly, Hillhouse was himself retiring from the Senate.

candidate rather than any other? What grounds would elected representatives have for joining one another in support of legislative proposals, much less joining together in government? I can think of several, which could, of course, be combined in varying proportions in any actual instance.

First and foremost, No-Party Democracy would be a world of 'personalistic politics'. People stand for office as individuals, completely in their own right. They therefore commend themselves to voters, first and foremost, on the basis of their own personal characteristics. Those are of course many and varied: amiability, eloquence, charm, beauty, compassion, competence, integrity, intelligence. Some of those might seem better bases for political office-holding than others. The point is simply that, when choosing among candidates purely on the basis of their personal merits, such characteristics as these inevitably loom large. So too would personality form the basis for partnerships on the floor of parliaments thus elected.[16] In both respects, then, it is only natural to expect that a No-Party Democracy would be relatively more prone to 'personality cults'.[17]

(So they seem to be. For the limiting case, consider the deification of George Washington in the No-Party Democracy of the early American republic. But a personalistic focus seems to have been characteristic even of more mundane political figures in more ordinary elections of that era.[18])

---

[16] 'How men can proceed without any connection at all is to me utterly incomprehensible. Of what sort of materials must that man be made, how must he be tempered and put together, who can sit whole years in Parliament, with five hundred and fifty of his fellow-citizens, amidst the storm of such tempestuous passions, in the sharp conflict of so many wits, and tempers and characters, in the agitation of such mighty questions, in the discussion of such vast and ponderous interests, without seeing any one sort of men, whose character, conduct, or disposition would lead him to associate himself with them, to aid and be aided ...?' (Burke 1770: 123).

[17] Such 'personal friendships and animosities' and 'attachments to particular families and persons' can of course go on to form the basis of 'factions' (Hume 1760). Here we are contemplating the case in which they do not.

[18] Hofstadter (1969: 47–8) writes, 'In eighteenth-century Virginia men were elected not because of the group they were associated with or what they proposed to do about this or that issue but because of what they were. An election promise might be made here or there—though political promises were rather frowned on and might even be made the object of investigation or cause an elected candidate to be refused his seat—but in the main men put themselves forward on their social position and character and manners, and on their willingness to treat their constituencies in the right and liberal fashion, not least on their willingness to ply them with rum punch. It was rare for a man to run on issues or policies; and no one could run on factional identifications, since these were thin, ephemeral and spare of meaning.'

Second, No-Party Democracy would be a world of 'clientelist politics', of patrons and clients.[19] People are linked to particular other people through personal ties of allegiance. In the legislative assembly of a No-Party Democracy, coalition-building is personal, ad hoc and *ad hominem*. Likewise the bond between electors and the elected is a personal one, of clients to patrons.

Third, following from that, No-Party Democracy would be a world of 'patronage politics'. The premium would be on constituency service, 'ward-heeling', 'bringing home the bacon'. In a No-Party Democracy, the primary function of the elected member is to serve as an ombudsperson vis-à-vis central government authorities and to secure public services and private benefits for the district. Those are the things with which incumbents bribe their constituents. It is those favours for which incumbents are rewarded with re-election.[20]

(Again, the experience of the No-Party Democracy of the early American republic bears out those predictions. Recall that the most famous case in the early history of the US Supreme Court arose over a case of patronage, Marbury being one of the many 'midnight judges' appointed to the federal courts on the eve of President Adams handing office over to his rivals.[21])

Fourth, following from all that, No-Party Democracy would be a world less of 'politics' than of 'administration'. Where politicians' appeals to the voters are largely personalistic, and where their links to one another are likewise personalistic, there is little basis for any concerted action to institute any systematic, coherent set of policies. What representatives do have is a consistent and ongoing interest in the administration of the affairs of state, and how that impacts on their constituents. That is the key to their re-election. That is where the focus of a representative's attention would naturally fall in a No-Party Democracy.

Fifth, No-Party Democracy would be characterized by identity-group politics. Insofar as it has any systematic substantive content at all, No-Party Democracy would presumably be addressed primarily to

---

[19] Lemarchand and Legg (1972).

[20] For a fairly fully elaborated model of how this would work, see Weingast and Marshall's model of 'the industrial organization of Congress', which explicitly assumes away 'parties' (1988: 137).

[21] Furthermore, the decision itself was arguably directed at curtailing the 'mischiefs of faction', once again. 'Significantly', Tribe (1988: 25) remarks, 'Marshall decided *Marbury v. Madison* at a time when the idea that legislatures would ignore principle in order to please controlling "factions" was widely shared but the idea that courts were similarly political was not yet current (although it would be within a few decades).'

'demographically shared interests'. People might vote for someone who is 'like themselves'—who lives where they live, who is of the same class or race or ethnicity or gender. The thought is that if the representative is sufficiently like them, then in serving her own interest the representative will incidentally serve theirs as well.[22]

Again, identities and shared interests can give rise to organized factions, and hence parties, as Hume saw clearly.[23] But even without any formal or informal organization of a party in the electorate, the sheer fact of these shared features can lead many voters independently to vote for the same candidate who also shares those features. And even without any formal or informal organization of a party in the parliament, the sheer fact of these shared features can lead many representatives independently to vote for the same enactment that well serves people with those shared features.

(Something like this happened in the era before anything remotely resembling organized political parties in England. People enjoying royal favour stood to benefit from expanding government and military adventures, and hence supported such schemes; large landowners, who had to pay for it all, had interests and hence opinions that were diametrically opposed. As each elected people like themselves, and as people with like interests voted in like manner in parliament, voting blocks formed without anyone directly intending them: they were called 'Court party' and the 'Country party', but they were more 'parts' than 'parties' in the modern sense; they were defined by a convergence of interests, not formal, intentional organization.)

10.1.3. What Would Be Missing

What must necessarily be missing in a No-Party Democracy is any systematic pursuit of 'principles' in politics. What is lacking is the 'politics of ideas', practiced in any systematic way.[24]

Of course, even in a No-Party Democracy individual candidates for office offer their own particular ideas in the course of trying to recommend themselves to electors. And even in a No-Party Democracy individual representatives offer their own ideas on proposed legislation, as

---

[22] Miller and Stokes (1963).   [23] Hume (1760).

[24] Phillips (1995). And a good thing too, Hume (1760) would say: 'Parties from principle, especially abstract speculative principle, are known only to modern times and are, perhaps, the most extraordinary and unaccountable phenomenon that has yet appeared in human affairs.... Each naturally wishes that right may take place, according to his notions of it. But where the difference of principle is attended with no contrariety of action, but every one may follow his own way, without interfering with his neighbour, as happens in all religious controversies; what madness, what fury can beget such unhappy and such fatal divisions?'

211

it comes up for a vote on the floor of the legislative assembly. But in a No-Party Democracy, all of them would, by definition, be doing so independently of one another. There is no common thread (or anyway, no mechanism for guaranteeing there is any common thread) uniting their thinking.

In the case of the politics of interests—which is very much the standard story about parties, in pluralist terms—I have indicated how 'coincidences of interests' might be able to substitute for any intentionally 'concerted action'.[25] But whereas distinct interests are few and coincidences among them common, distinct ideas are many and coincidences among them rare. So too, in consequence, would be non-intentional coalitions among people who just coincidentally happen to hit upon the same ideas of a policy-specific sort. The sorts of general ideas upon which people might converge without intentionally trying to do so—overarching ideologies and the like—are simply indeterminate at the level of fine-grained policy detail.

In the absence of some mechanism of intentional coordination, like a party unified around a common platform, different people would get elected from different constituencies on the basis of the different ideas that they espoused from their respective stumps. And different legislators, in their turn, would vote for any given enactment on the basis of those different ideas.

To be sure, a vote is eventually taken, and something eventually gets decided. But in the absence of any thread unifying the intentions of the various independent actors, what is decided is merely 'what we shall do?'—not 'why?' Our collective purpose, in deciding this way rather than that, has been 'left undecided'.[26]

Now, I take it that the *essence* of democracy lies in a community's being 'self-legislating', understood as 'giving laws to itself'. One familiar face of that is the principle of 'self-determination'. To be democratic, a community must give its laws to itself, rather than laws being given to it from the outside. A second aspect of the community's 'giving laws to itself' is the principle of the 'rule of law'. That is to say, to be democratic, a community must rule itself through law—rules that citizens can understand and internalize—rather than arbitrary edicts that cannot be anticipated or comprehended.

'Giving laws to ourselves', collectively, necessarily involves some collective determination not just of 'what to do' (a bare command: 'do

---

[25] Crick (1962) and Aldrich (1995: ch. 2).   [26] Sunstein (1996a, 1996b).

this', 'do not do that') but also of 'why' (the *ratio*, rationale, or grounds behind the law). That is true, if for no other reason, merely because we—citizens, as much as judges—need to know the underlying *ratio* in order to interpret and apply the law as we attempt to 'follow' it. On other analyses, the law's *ratio* might be thought to provide a rationale to legitimize the law substantively. On the present analysis, the need for the law to have a single, coherent *ratio* derives simply from what is involved in rule-following at all.[27]

Law is not just a system of 'orders backed by threats'. If it were, law's commands would be indistinguishable from the highwayman's. Law differs because, and insofar as, people in general 'internalize' it, taking a 'critical reflective attitude' towards law and shaping their own conduct accordingly. That is a familiar argument, made famous by H.L.A. Hart almost a half century ago.[28] My point is just this: in order for people to do any of that, there needs to be some *ratio* that people can internalize, rather than just some bare command for them to comply with.

But that, as I have said, is precisely what is missing in the absence of any intentional agent (like a political party) to coordinate the intentions of the disparate legislators or voters. Their isolated acts of assent might issue in 'legislation' of some sort or another. But in a No-Party Democracy without any mechanism for aligning their intentions, one person votes for the enactment for one reason, another for another. There is no single, coherent *ratio* underlying the enactment, which anyone can internalize and act upon. In that important sense, the community in this No-Party world is not 'giving *law* to itself'. It is, at most, giving orders or commands or edicts to itself. That is something substantially less—and, importantly, less democratic.

In summary, let us now put all those pieces together to see exactly what is wrong with No-Party Democracy.

1. Democracy requires that a community is collectively self-legislating.
2. A *ratio* is required to have truly 'given a law to yourself', and to be 'self-legislating' in that sense.

---

[27] Our 'aim in making law is to lay down rules by which people may guide their [own] conduct', as Fuller (1971: 88) says. For Hart (1961: 202), certain formal features that law must display derive from 'what is ... involved in any method of social control—rules of games as well as law—which consists primarily of general standards of conduct communicated to classes of persons, who are then expected to understand and conform to the rules without further direction'.

[28] Hart (1961: 55–7).

3. A collective *ratio* is necessarily absent from the uncoordinated votes of independent actors in a No-Party Democracy.

From the combination of these three propositions, it follows that

4. No-Party Democracy is not democracy at all.

People there cannot be self-legislating, precisely because there cannot be a collective *ratio* for decisions taken by uncoordinated agents in a No-Party world.

10.1.4. *Parties as Ideational Facts*

Empirical studies of political parties see them, first and foremost, as organizations. Their function is to coordinate the actions of their members, to make them 'toe the party line'. Parties 'discipline' their members. And it is the discipline of party membership that makes members act in a unified way. In one dimension, these studies tell us, parties provide the glue that connects voters with elected officials. Parties organize and mobilize voters, nominate and elect candidates. In another dimension, parties provide the glue that connects politicians to one another. Parties form the basis for organizing the legislature.[29] Party loyalty binds disparate actors, first and foremost not only within a single assembly but also across different branches of government and across separate jurisdictions.[30] In yet another dimension, therefore, parties also provide the glue that connects political activity in separate venues. In election campaigns, the party is what connects different candidates standing in separate constituencies. In the operation of government, shared party loyalties can unify (and differing party loyalties divide) the actions of different branches and levels of government.[31]

In all those ways, empirical analyses of political parties treat political parties first and foremost 'organizational facts'. Political parties are 'organizations' not just in some loose sociological sense but in a rigorously legal one. They are typically incorporated under Company Law, as 'non-profit' (albeit, precisely because political, definitely not 'charitable') corporations. They have articles of incorporation, stipulating goals and

[29] Cox (2006: 147–9).

[30] In an archaic usage which the *Oxford English Dictionary* dates to Jacobean England, a 'party-man' is 'a soldier belonging to, or officer commanding, a party'—a 'partisan', in more contemporary usage.

[31] Sorauf (1968) and Mayhew (1991).

internal procedures. They have officers, with defined responsibilities. And so forth.

Obviously, I do not want to deny that organizational side to political parties, nor do I want to deny the importance of their organizational life to the practice of democratic politics. But as a supplement to that analysis, we ought to remind ourselves that party discipline is an 'ideational fact' as well as an 'organizational' one.

Empirically, those two might well be in tension in the actual practice of party politics. Insofar as they do, the organizational may well triumph over the ideational (it is, after all, presumably the more useful of the two, seen purely as instruments in the quest for political power). There is evidence aplenty of this, too, in empirical studies of politics in many places, not least the United States again.[32] But there is also evidence aplenty of programmatic differentiation of parties.[33]

As I emphasized at the outset of this chapter, however, this is an exercise in political philosophy, not political empirics. My question here is what can justify having political parties at all, in a democratic system of government. If the best justification that can be found turns out to be one that involves something that it is impossible to implement in practice, then of course that will be an empirical fact of great normative consequence. But again, first things first: we must establish what is the philosophical justification of parties in a democracy, before proceeding to enquiries in another mode as to the feasibility of procuring parties of that sort.

From a philosophical point of view, the justification that I have arrived at here for parties is indeed an ideational one. Burke's definition captures the point precisely: 'Party is a body of men united for promoting by their joint endeavours the national interest, upon some particular principle in which they are all agreed.'[34]

---

[32] Lord Bryce (1897: vol. 2, p. 5) remarked of political parties in America's Guilded Age, 'the fewer have become their principles and the fainter their interest in those principles, the more perfect has become their organization.' At the middle of the last century, the same complaint came from the American Political Science Association's famous report, 'Toward a more responsible two-party system': 'Historical and other factors have caused the American two-party system to operate as two loose associations of state and local organizations, with very little national machinery and very little national cohesion. As a result, either major party, when in power, is ill-equipped to organize its members in the legislative and the executive branches held together and guided by the party program. Party responsibility at the polls thus tends to vanish. This is a very serious matter, for it affects the very heartbeat of American democracy. It also poses grave problems of domestic and foreign policy in an era when it is no longer safe for the nation to deal piecemeal with issues that can be disposed of only on the basis of coherent programs' (Schattschneider 1950: v).

[33] Klingemann, Hofferbert, and Budge (1994). Page (1978).   [34] Burke (1770: 119).

10.2. How Many Parties Does Democracy Require?

On the preceding discussion, what would be missing from a No-Party Democracy is anything like a coherent *ratio* for government enactments, which is required in 'giving laws to ourselves'. That lack is what prevents a No-Party Democracy from being truly democratic. That is what parties supply, coordinating the disparate intentions of members of the party through the collective agency of the party and its programme. How well or badly parties do that in practice, that is what they are most fundamentally supposed to do, in terms of democratic theory.

Given that analysis of the justificatory function of political parties in a democratically self-governing community, what might we further infer about the number of such parties required to discharge that function?

10.2.1. *At Least Two*

All that is required to provide a *ratio* for the law's pronouncements is a unified agent with a coherent rationale for the legislation that it promulgates. That requirement can of course be satisfied in various ways, some distinctly non-democratic. If the law's having a *ratio* is all we want, that demand can be satisfied by rule by edicts backed by rationales supplied by Bolingbroke's Patriot King.[35] It is a necessary condition of democratic rule that the law has a *ratio*, but that is far from being a sufficient condition for the system's being democratic.

Just as the law can acquire a *ratio* by being handed down by an unelected Patriot King, so too can the law acquire a *ratio* by being handed down by duly elected representatives in a One-Party Democracy. Focusing just on the need for the law to have a *ratio*, there is no need for more than a single party to provide that. Indeed, in a Two-Party Democracy, it will typically be a single party—the governing party—whose unified programme provides the *ratio* for legislation that is enacted.

If there is something to be said in favour of competition among two or more parties, it is not to be found in the argument about the need for the law to have a *ratio* in order for us to 'give laws to ourselves' in a democratic way.

---

[35] Bolingbroke (1749). Or by 'parliamentary parties' that are unconnected to any 'electoral parties', as in Britain in the eighteenth century: the Parliamentary parties provided a *ratio*, but in the absence of parties campaigning for office on that basis the *ratio* thus provided was undemocratic, without electoral endorsement.

The need for a *ratio*, and the capacity of unified party programmes to provide one, speaks to the issue of what it is to 'give *laws* to ourselves'. A *ratio* is needed in order for it to be a *law*, at all: in order for subjects to be able to internalize it themselves.

Democracy requires that that the *ratio* be provided by a programme that has been endorsed by the citizens. That speaks to the issue of what it is to 'give laws to *ourselves*'. A Patriot King can provide decrees with a *ratio*. Only a party that has been duly elected can provide a *ratio* that satisfies that further requirement of *democratic* rule.

The case for multiple parties offering competing programmes and alternative *ratios* for legislation, as opposed to single-party rule, derives from yet another aspect of that same basic principle. We can be said to have *'given* laws to ourselves' only if we had the alternative of doing otherwise. Where there is only a single party, with a single programme and a single *ratio*, the electorate does not have the alternative of doing otherwise. Any given elector might of course deface her ballot or refuse to vote. But where there is only one possible outcome of the election, there is only one option available to the electorate as a whole.

The outcome of an election involving only one party cannot be democratic. The reason is simple. 'Democracy' requires that the outcome of the election is 'the people's choice'; and a 'choice' by definition can only be made among two or more options.[36] In a one-party system, there is only one option.[37] The only party there is always the winner.[38]

A great many rulers have from time to time found it desirable to secure electoral endorsement of their rule, but to do so in ways that avoided the divisiveness of party competition. Post-colonial rulers in Africa often echoed calls by leaders in post-Revolutionary America for One-Party Democracy, organized around a single 'party of national unification'.[39] Even Bolingbroke, opposed though he generally was

---

[36] Lindsay (1935: 35).

[37] Assuming 'none of the above' is not an option from which any meaningful consequences follow. In some systems (particularly in Eastern Europe), if no candidate wins at least 50% of votes then the returning officer declares that no candidate is elected. But either that leads to new elections, or else (or in addition) it leads to decisions being made by those who won more than 50% of votes in their constituencies, the other seats being left unfilled (Dryzek and Holmes 2002: 117).

[38] There may be factions within the One Party, much though they may aspire for there to be 'no opposition party and no opposition within the party' (Lindsay 1935: 35). But in a One-Party system it is rarely the electorate as a whole that gets to determine which faction will rule.

[39] Zolberg (1966) and Hofstadter (1969: 16–7).

to parties, could countenance a single overarching party 'authorized by the voice of the country' and 'formed on principles of common interest'.[40]

Insofar there is a programme that the One Party is putting to the people, and a party unified behind it, such a One-Party Democracy is importantly different from No-Party Democracy. No-Party Democracy is not really democracy at all, because legislation enacted by it lacks the sort of *ratio* that 'giving *laws* to ourselves' requires. If there is a party and programme, even if there is just one, that problem can be solved—provided the One Party chooses to rule by law rather than edict.[41]

Another problem necessarily arises, however. Insofar as the citizens' choice is limited to a single party and a single programme, the citizens cannot really make a choice—or hence *'give* themselves laws', either. So One-Party Democracy is undemocratic, too. It is undemocratic in an interestingly different, but connected, way to that in which No-Party Democracy is undemocratic.

People wanting to advocate One-Party Democracy need to justify why *any* political party should exist and why *only one* should exist. That is to say, they need to argue why there should be *at least* one party, and they need to argue why there should be *at most* one party. The best argument I have found for there being at least one party—couched in terms of what is involved in democratically 'giving law to ourselves'— implies that there should be more than one party. That argument for organizing democratic politics around a party seems to me to imply that democracy requires multiple competing parties. Those who would advocate One-Party Democracy need either to find some other argument for having any political party at all, or else they need to find some flaw in my derivation of the implications of what it is to 'give law to ourselves'.

---

[40] Bolingbroke (1733–4: Letter IV, p. 37) hastens to add, however, that 'A party, thus constituted, is improperly called party. It is the nation, speaking and acting in the discourse and conduct of particular men'.

[41] It may well not. Empirically, one might well conjecture that in the absence of competitive politics to keep One-Party politics focused on ideas and principles, it may well degenerate in effect into No-Party politics. In that connection, note the many similarities between No-Party rule as described in Section 10.1.2 and the actual experience of One-Party rule wherever it has lasted for protracted periods. Personalistic politics of the sort that led to the deification of Washington in the early American Republic is not importantly different from the sort that led to the deification of Mao in the One-Party Democracy of China (Apter 1987). And the clientelistic, patronage politics that dominated the early American Republic is replicated, perhaps, in what is seen as pervasive corruption of in the One-Party Democracy of China.

10.2.2. *Perhaps No More*

No-Party Democracy fails the test of democratic self-government because, in the absence of a single, coherent ratio underlying enactments, we cannot be 'giving law to ourselves'. Multi-party politics, notice, might pose similar problems.

The clearest case concerns governments composed of a coalition of many parties. Sometimes those parties will have gotten together, either ahead of the election or in its immediate aftermath, to hammer out a common programme backed by a single coherent rationale. More often, coalitions will have been formed after the election on the basis of horse-trading and portfolio-swapping. One party gets the Health portfolio, to be run according to that party's goals and precepts; another party gets the Finance portfolio, to be run according to that party's differing goals and precepts. The edicts emanating from any one Ministry might be backed by a coherent *ratio*, traceable to the party with power over that portfolio. But the policy and legislation of the Government overall—composed as it is of multiple parties with differing goals, precepts, and resulting ratios—does not manifest any single coherent *ratio*.

There are various ways around that, of course. The most robust way would be for the coalition partners to negotiate a common programme backed by a clear *ratio*. In its strongest form, this would involve hammering out a joint programme ahead of the election, and meeting together in a 'joint party room' while in government to monitor and update it. (The 'Bourgeois parties' in Norway used to do that, for example, as does 'the Coalition' of the Liberal and National Parties in Australia.) Weaker forms of coordination, and correspondingly less unified *ratios* for policies being pursued, might be achieved through various devices within the executive (Cabinet committees, interdepartmental committees, formal or informal 'shadowing' practices[42]) or the legislature (committees and other forms of parliamentary scrutiny[43]).

How well such mechanisms might work is, of course, an empirical question demanding investigation of a different sort. But where those mechanisms do not achieve coordination on a single *ratio* to any great extent—where compromises are ungrounded in any coherent principle, and purely the product of vote-trading—my argument would seem to suggest that coalition government can be undemocratic for the same reason as is No-Party politics.

[42] Thies (2001).   [43] Martin and Vanberg (2005).

10.2.3. *The Need for Ideationally Unified Parties*

Notice that similar worries as I have been expressing with multi-party government can also arise in Two-Party Democracy. Such problems might arise in three distinct ways.

First, the governing party in a Two-Party Democracy might lack strong internal discipline, being itself composed of multiple vying factions each with its own distinct goals and precepts. Then the rules and legislation emanating from that government would once again lack a single coherent *ratio*. That is of course famously true of Washington most of the time, and even of Westminster on some famous occasions (as during the long power struggle between Tony Blair and Gordon Brown for control of the Labour Government's agenda).

Second, in Two-Party Democracy, there can be 'divided government', with different parties in control of different branches of government or different chambers of the legislature.[44] Then even if each party is tightly unified and its proposals all have a single coherent *ratio*, the rules and legislation that emerge from negotiations among different parties in control of different parts of the government will be the product of a horse-trade or log-roll, with no coherent *ratio*.

Again, there are ways around problems of both those problems. Factionalism within each party can be addressed, to some extent, by party conventions charged with working out a coherent manifesto, with proposals backed by a single coherent *ratio*. Of course, manifestos of faction-ridden parties are often themselves the product of factional horse-trades, and lack a *ratio* of the right sort; still, some such mechanism might conceivably work to overcome these problems within parties. Problems introduced by 'divided government' can be similarly addressed by 'conference committees' between different chambers controlled by different parties, with the 'conference committee' being charged with the task of coming up with not just a compromise piece of legislation but also a proper *ratio* for it. In practice, again, what emerges out of conference committees is often little more than a horse-trade, with no suitable *ratio* underlying the terms of the trade; still, there is hope that some such mechanisms might work to unify the products of divided governments in the right way. How well or badly such remedies work in practice is, once again, an empirical question demanding investigation of a different sort. But what those empirical investigations ought to be looking for, if they are to address

[44] Mayhew (1991).

what is the central question from the viewpoint of normative democratic theory, is the capacity of such mechanisms to evoke a single coherent ratio in enactments emanating from factionalized parties or divided governments.

There is a third worry that seems even harder to assuage. Even if parties in Two-Party Democracies are themselves highly unified actors, and even if the same party controls all branches of government, it is in the nature of democracy that parties ought to be expected to alternate in power. Hence the laws enacted by one party, for one set of purposes, will be amended from time to time by another party, for a rather different set of purposes. With the accretion of amendments with rather different underlying rationales, the law once again ceases to have a single, coherent *ratio* of its own. Courts might assuage such worries by adopting the doctrine of *stare decisis*, but that solution is unavailable to sovereign democratic legislatures: part and parcel of their sovereignty is being bound by the decisions of no other body, including past assemblages of the same body.

10.3. Beyond Party Democracy?

So far I have been talking about party democracy. But democracies have other institutions, beyond political parties. Those other institutions might complement party democracy, in ways that further aid us in 'giving laws to ourselves'.

Institutionally, of course, when the *ratio* of legislation is unclear, it is the courts to which we then turn. They are charged with imposing a *ratio* on the legislation, when interpreting and applying it. On the face of it, that looks pretty undemocratic: judges are not electorally accountable, after all; so if it is judges who get to choose the *ratio* for our laws, we are not exactly 'giving laws to *ourselves*'. We might as well revert to Bollingbroke's Patriot King.

That dismissal might be a little too quick, however. It is the task of judges to choose which of the competing rationales for legislation that can be found in the legislative record ought to be treated as 'the' rationale, for purposes of interpreting and applying that legislation. But they are not democratically permitted to impose just any old rationale that they please: they are limited in their search to rationales that are arguably available in the legislative record. The democratic process may be slightly indeterminate, in leaving various options as equally democratically eligible; and judges are charged with choosing among them. Still, the options are constrained to those that have some democratic warrant in the legislative record.

Juridical democracy thus construed might seem too minimally democratic to qualify for that status at all. There is one other way of giving rules a *ratio* that, while optimistic, might not be completely utopian. This involves 'deliberative democracy' of the distinctive sort I have been advocating in Chapters 8–9: distributed governance across a network with no central authority.

The thought is just this: maybe we do not need political parties to tell us what the options are and how we ought to think about them, when construing their rationale and purpose. Maybe we can think through that for ourselves, as a democratic public reasoning together.

Of course, if the aspiration is for our rules to have a single, coherent rationale, then that deliberation in civil society must not just move towards consensus as to which option ought to be chosen. It is also necessary that the deliberation move towards a consensus as to why that option ought to be chosen, a consensus as to the *ratio* for that law. Then and only then will people be democratically 'giving laws to themselves'.[45]

We can have agreement of the second sort without that of the first. People can agree what is some rule's *ratio*, while disagreeing over whether the rule with that *ratio* ought to be adopted as law. And there is some evidence to suggest that deliberation can indeed contribute bringing people's views into better alignment in that more modest way.[46]

Still, what parties do relatively effortlessly discursive engagement across any very large community accomplishes only laboriously, and even then only very partially.[47] Maybe Pericles' Athens was different. But as Manin remarks,

In highly complex systems, the cost of exploring all possibilities, even if that were theoretically possible, would be enormous. Chess players, for example, cannot examine all possible moves with all their consequences; they examine only certain types of moves, and explore only those moves that seem most promising. This situation characterizes deliberation. It is not possible to deliberate all possible

[45] A court deciding 'what to do' can leave 'why' undecided (Sunstein 1996a, 1996b). Democratic communities 'giving laws to themselves' cannot.

[46] List et al. (2007).

[47] Furthermore, insofar as that discursive engagement is intended by those involved to coordinate with others as to what law should be enacted with what *ratio*, that intentional coordination itself the assumptions of a No-Party Democracy. Those intentionally coordinating their acts with others in this way are, in effect, *forming* parties.

outcomes; the range of proposed solutions must by necessity be limited. In the political arena, the limited pluralism of parties is required for effective deliberation.[48]

It is a philosophical fact that 'giving laws to themselves' requires people to be able to collectively choose between different potential laws, each with a well-defined *ratio*. As a practical matter, much the best way to do that seems to be for there to be competing parties offering alternative policy packages and *ratios* for them.

[48] Manin (1987: 357).

11

Democratic mandates

with Michael Saward

The democratic aspiration of rule by the people implies some minimal idea that the people know—are told—what they are really voting on. The clarity and consistency of messages from candidates to voters therefore matters deeply to the quality of democracy. What sort of a mandate a government can claim—what a government is entitled to do in office—depends heavily upon how the campaign messages are conveyed. If campaign messages are mixed, strong mandates do not follow.

This point will be illustrated and elaborated in this chapter by particular reference to a new and particularly pernicious campaign technique, 'dog-whistle politics'. That is a way of sending a message to certain potential supporters in such a way as to make it inaudible to others whom it might alienate. The classic case, perhaps, is the 'Are you thinking what we're thinking?' campaign mounted by the Tories in the 2005 British general election by Lynton Crosby, who had perfected the technique in highly successful campaigns to re-elect John Howard in Australia.

Just how powerful dog-whistle politics is as a mechanism of manipulatory politics is, perhaps, an open question. The fact that the practice is noticed, that it has acquired a name and a bad press, suggests that the message is not literally inaudible to others beyond its intended target. They have noticed it. And by identifying the trick and giving it its name, they have (after a fashion) worked out a way around it. When politicians engaged in dog-whistle politics deny that they ever said anything racist, their opponents' ready rejoinder is 'Of course not; you were practising dog-whistle politics'.

The effectiveness of that rejoinder depends upon the willingness of people to punish politicians for a message that they have not themselves heard. Presumably, a party's own supporters will ordinarily be disposed to think well of it. When told that a message was sent that they could not themselves hear but of which they would disapprove, supporters will most likely be disposed to trust their own ears and deny that any such message was sent. Or where they heard a message that could be interpreted in multiple ways, they opt for some more innocuous version. So dog-whistle politics is mostly a way of attracting certain other voters without losing existing support from people who would disapprove of what the party has to say to attract those new groups.

Dog-whistle politics is just the latest instantiation of a larger and more familiar class of campaign techniques. It merely resurrects a practice common in the days of 'whistle-stop campaigns' and segmented news markets, when candidates could say different things to different audiences in complete confidence that no one would ever notice the discrepancies. Clever marketing techniques do for today's politicians what moving trains and localized newspapers did for those of a previous generation.

Sending divergent messages to different audiences is typically a better way of getting elected than it is of getting re-elected. Or at least that is so insofar as the messages entailed promises to undertake some relatively specific actions once in office. Come re-election, electors can judge candidates not so much on the basis of what they say as on the basis of what they have done (although the interpretation of that is subject to a certain amount of dog-whistling too). If the candidates had engendered incompatible expectations in different segments of their constituency, they will inevitably have disappointed some of them. Retrospective electoral accountability thus provides a partial check to the persisting abuse of dog-whistle politics.

11.1. Distinguishing Two Kinds of Mandates

The concerns of this chapter are prospective rather than retrospective, however. The question that concerns us is to what extent might dog-whistle politics undermine the possibility of any genuine democratic mandate?

Mandates come in two forms. One—the first-mentioned in the *Oxford English Dictionary*—is simply 'the commission to rule ... conferred by electors on their elected representatives'. This is a purely procedural right, with the substance of rules left to be subsequently specified. A 'mandate' in this sense is the right to govern, to occupy offices of state, and to discharge the duties and exercise the prerogatives appertaining thereto. Call this a 'mandate to rule'.

The question to be asked of any given government is whether it has another sort of mandate as well. That second sort of mandate is 'the commission to...pursue stated policies conferred by electors on their elected representatives'. This is a right with substantive referents, a right to implement a specific set of policies explicitly stipulated during the election and explicitly endorsed by the electorate at that election. Call this a 'policy mandate'.

This second sort of mandate would be something over and above the first. Any government that is duly elected has the first sort of mandate, a mandate to rule. That is just what it means to have been 'duly elected': to have the right to rule. And part and parcel of what it is 'to rule' is to enact and enforce rules of one's choosing (within limits of course: set by constitutions, conventions, moral codes, international treaties, and so on).

If a government has the second sort of mandate as well as the first—a policy mandate as well as a mere mandate to rule—then it has not only the general right that all duly elected governments have to enact and enforce rules of their choosing but also a special right to enact and enforce the specific policies for which they have that second sort of mandate.

It is immediately apparent what the political cash value of a mandate of the first sort is: the keys to office. What might be the political cash value of a mandate of the second sort is less immediately apparent. After all, one already has the keys to office, the right to rule. The second sort of mandate, however, provides one with an 'especially strong right to rule' on the particular points of substantive policy covered by that mandate.

That is a right against others—other people and parties who lost the election, other chambers of the legislature, other branches of government—not to obstruct a government with a mandate of the second sort in pursuing the policies it has been mandated to pursue. Losers always have an obligation to vacate office and let winners rule. But where winners have a policy mandate as well as a mere mandate to rule, losers have a particular obligation not to obstruct winners' rulings on the policies covered by the mandate.

In general, 'the duty of the opposition is to oppose'. 'Loyally' perhaps, 'constructively' perhaps—but 'to oppose' nonetheless. A government's having a mere mandate to rule obviously does nothing to undermine that. But where a government has a policy mandate, the opposition's duty to oppose is replaced by a 'duty to defer'. And whatever general reason that unelected or malapportioned upper chambers might have to defer to the people's house, or unelected courts to popularly elected legislatures and executives, that duty is redoubled when they have a policy mandate as well as a mere mandate to rule.

What winners of a policy mandate get is a 'right to rule unobstructed', at least on the policy covered by the mandate. A right is not a duty, though. While it would be odd for a party to seek and secure a policy mandate from voters that it then opts not to exercise, one can imagine circumstances in which that might make sense. Circumstances might have changed: indeed, they might have changed simply in consequence of winning the mandate (had Heath secured a mandate on the question of 'Who rules Britain?' and the miners meekly succumbed to the industrial relations legislation already on the books, nothing more would have been required).

Of course, neither sort of mandate—a mandate to rule nor a policy mandate to rule unobstructed in some policy area—is absolute. Nothing the lower house does ought ever to be entirely free from scrutiny by the house of review; nothing the legislature or executive does ought ever to be entirely free from scrutiny by the courts. Still, a policy mandate—where it exists—gives political actors a particularly strong hand.

11.2. Knowing What We Are Voting On

The concern of this chapter is with the ways in which certain campaign techniques, like dog-whistle politics, weaken that hand. Elections are elections, and winners are winners. So long as the election was free and fair, its winner always enjoys a mandate of the first sort, a right to rule. But insofar as the winner's victory was tainted by dog-whistle politics, the second sort of mandate proves more elusive.

In order to secure a mandate to implement any policy in particular, candidates must first tell people what specific policy or policies they propose to implement if elected.[1] Only then can they claim to have some special mandate to implement that policy in particular (as opposed to 'rule' more generally), should they win the election in the particularly convincing way that is ordinarily thought to confer a mandate.

---

[1] Parties in search of a policy mandate must, however, avoid bundling together too many disparate policies, lest they undermine any mandate they hope to claim for any one of them in particular. Seeking a mandate for a bundle of policies at the same time works best when the bundle constitutes a logically or ideologically linked set which voters all perceive as such.

Politicians engaging in dog-whistle politics are doing almost the opposite of that. They are not telling everyone what specific policies they propose to implement if elected. Instead, they tell one group of voters one thing, while allowing (and indeed, encouraging) another group to believe another. If they win the election on the basis of such mixed messages, what does their victory add up to in substantive policy terms? Nothing, we suggest.

Consider an analogy. In California, voters often have to vote on several different referendum or initiative proposals in any given election. Imagine in this year's elections they are asked to vote yea or nay on two propositions: Proposition 1 would outlaw gay marriage, and Proposition 2 would outlaw abortion. But suppose the numbering of the propositions somehow gets garbled. Imagine a mischievous hacker, for example, has programmed electronic voting machines so they periodically reverse the numbers of the two propositions. So what some voters see on the voting screen as Proposition 1 is the 'outlaw abortion' text that is officially supposed to constitute Proposition 2, and what some voters see on the screen as Proposition 2 is the 'outlaw gay marriage' text that is officially supposed to constitute Proposition 1. Further, suppose that the trick is discovered only after voting is over, and that there is no way to retrieve information about which mode the voting machine was in ('true' or 'trick') when any given voter cast his or her ballot. The machines only tally how many people voted for Propositions 1 and 2 respectively (under whichever descriptions the voters happened to see on the screen).

Imagine, now, the State Electoral Commissioner declaring the results of the poll: 'Proposition 1 secured 52% of votes and is carried; Proposition 2 secured only 41% of votes and has failed.' What on earth are we supposed to make of that? Is gay marriage outlawed? Well, the returning officer has told us that Proposition 1 was carried; and outlawing gay marriage is what the proposition that was supposed to be Proposition 1 would have done. But thanks to the hacker's mischief, some (indeterminate number of) people instead saw Proposition 1 as the proposal to outlaw abortion. Did the ban on abortion fail? Well, Proposition 2 failed, and that was supposed to be the one banning abortion. But again, some indeterminate number of people instead saw Proposition 2 as the gay marriage ban.

When voters are voting on literally different propositions, adding up their votes amounts to a nonsense. In the Californian fantasy just described, the only reasonable course of action would be to declare the election null and void, and re-run the poll.

11.3. Mixed Messages Undermine Policy Mandates

The key difference between that Californian fantasy and actual dog-whistle politics is a difference between 'why' people vote and 'on what' people vote. In the Californian fantasy, people were voting on different propositions; and adding up the numbers of votes for Proposition 1, when Proposition 1 contained a different text for some voters than for others, is nonsense. In the case of dog-whistle politics, and other forms of 'mixed-message politics' more generally, people are voting 'on' the same propositions (understood as 'Should candidate X be elected?'); people merely vote the way they do for different reasons.

Dog-whistle politics (like whistle-stop politics in an earlier era) is the limiting case of mixed-message politics. In that limiting case, one subset of the audience is not even cognisant of the message that is crucial in leading others to vote as they do. A more moderate case of 'mixed-message politics' might involve differing emphases among differing audiences, either in the way the message was sent or in the way the message was received.

The latter point is of signal importance. Political candidates typically take stands across a wide range of issues. Party manifestos typically are omnibus affairs, making promises on many fronts. Different constituencies attach differential importance to different parts of the overall package. So even if the politicians and parties are putting out an utterly univocal message, the uptake of the message will inevitably differ among electors with different interests. The upshot is that different voters always end up voting for the same candidate or party for at least partly different reasons.

Clearly, that is not quite as bad as voting on literally different referendum propositions, as in the Californian fantasy case. Still, when different people perform the 'same' action with different intentions, it is inevitably tricky trying to adduce any 'collective intention' behind their joint action. Philosophies of law that enjoin courts to interpret legislation according to the 'original intent' of the legislators have come to grief over this conundrum: if different legislators voted for the same legislation intending it to have different effects and for it to be applied and interpreted differently, there simply is no collective intent across the legislature as a whole upon which judges can base their interpretations.[2]

[2] MacCallum (1966).

The same problems arise in interpreting the outcomes of elections involving mixed-message politics, more generally. Whichever candidate or party collects the requisite number of votes wins the election, thereby acquiring a mandate to rule. But insofar as their victory is built out of a classic 'coalition of minorities', with different people voting for them for different reasons, there is no single, coherent policy mandate that the winner can credibly claim. Or to put the point in scalar rather than absolute terms: the winner can credibly claim a mandate only to the extent that all voters are voting predominantly on the basis of the specific issue or set of connected issues for which the mandate is being sought.

This difficulty of inferring a mandate from mixed-message politics is redoubled in cases of dog-whistle politics. Imagine a particularly extreme example. A conservative party dog-whistles an encouraging message to racists that its own traditional supporters would instantly repudiate. It wins the ensuing election. Half its voters voted for it purely because of its (coded) support for racist policies; half voted for it purely because of its traditionally decent policies on race. Clearly, the party won a majority; clearly, it has a mandate to rule. But under those circumstances, it equally clearly could not claim a policy mandate to pursue either of the two contradictory policies that won it its votes.

11.4. How to Secure a Policy Mandate

What then is a party to do, if it wants to claim any particularly strong policy mandate, over and above a mere mandate to rule?

One minimum condition would be not to send mixed campaign messages, by engaging in dog-whistle politics and such like. Parties might win office that way. But no matter how large an electoral majority they might amass in that way, it never gives rise to a policy mandate. The cost of parties sending mixed messages in that way is to deprive themselves of the special sort of claim that can come from decisive electoral support for any particular piece of legislation. There are no good democratic grounds for other parties, chambers, or branches of government necessarily deferring to the legislative programme of a party whose electoral majority has been amassed via dog-whistle politics.

But as I have said, even politics-as-usual involves mixed messages. Ordinary campaign manifestos are a grab bag combining a variety of diverse and disjointed programmes. Different aspects of the manifesto appeal to different parts of a party's constituency. Any electoral majority it amasses might well represent a coalition of minorities, with each subgroup voting for the party overall because they approve of its policies on issues dearest to it, but with no single proposition in the manifesto commanding the support of a majority of voters overall.

The traditional solution was for a party that was seeking a strong policy mandate to enact one particular piece of controversial legislation to explicitly fight the issue on one issue and one issue alone. Ted Heath turned the February 1974 general election into a referendum on the question 'Who rules Britain?'—himself or the miners. Had he won the election, and done so convincingly, he could credibly have claimed a policy mandate for his industrial relations policies.

It is rare for a party to be quite so monomaniacal. But perhaps that is simply to say, it is rare for a party to want, or need, the special powers that come from possessing a policy mandate: a mere mandate to rule, subject to the ordinary obstructions that come from other legitimate actors in the political process, is good enough for most purposes and for most parties.

11.5. Referenda

If there is some particular proposal that needs a special warrant, then it might be far better to seek the mandate for the policy directly, in referendum, rather than to seek a policy mandate for some party to carry it out.[3]

Note that the same mixed-message phenomena can be found with referendums as well. Different people can vote in favour of a referendum proposition for different reasons. Indeed, organizers of referendum campaigns can engage in dog-whistle politics just as surely as can parties standing for office. In such cases, purely advisory referendums would confer no more of a policy mandate upon elected politicians charged with implementing them than would an overwhelming parliamentary majority won through the same techniques.

Binding rather than purely advisory referendums would not solve all those problems. Where messages about voters' collective intentions are mixed in such ways, for example, judges would have as much trouble trying to adduce the 'original intent' of a group of voters who enacted the proposal in referendum as they would in trying to adduce the original

[3] Budge (1996).

intent of a group of legislators who had very different intentions in voting for the same enactment.

But making referendums binding rather than purely advisory would solve the key problem in view here. Notice that where direct democratic devices make law directly, it does not matter whether or not the referendum vote constitutes a policy mandate: it constitutes law. The function of a policy mandate, recall, is to make others back off in their opposition to proposed legislation. When we are talking about a referendum that directly enacts a proposition into law, rather than about candidates and parties elected to make laws, there is simply no space between a mandate to rule and a policy mandate. Winning at referendum mandates the policy to rule as law.

Now, undermining the policy mandate that parties can claim is perhaps not the worst thing that dog-whistle politics does, democratically. Deception and self-deception, through rhetorical trickery and various other means, is perhaps a far deeper sin against the ideals of self-rule.[4] And dog-whistle politics in the course of binding referendum campaigns can commit that deeper sin, even if it avoids the lesser one.

11.6. Conclusions

It is worth firmly reminding political parties that when they engage in dog-whistle politics in ordinary general elections, the same phenomenon that they are counting on to increase their share of votes also undercuts the authority that they might secure by winning the vote. Parties practising dog-whistle politics might thereby win a mandate to rule, but doing so in that way deprives them of the possibility of winning a policy mandate. In terms of democratic self-rule, mixed-message campaign techniques like dog-whistle politics are not merely morally tainted but also fundamentally counterproductive.

---

[4] Goodin (1980*b*).

12

Representing diversity

Enfranchising all affected interests, as Chapter 7 has shown, involves extending the franchise way beyond the bounds of what most people would regard as realistically practicable. Certainly it would be impracticable for such a large group to constitute a directly deliberative democracy, with each and every person having a say before decisions are made. If the group thus enfranchised is very diverse (as such a group is very likely to be), then it might be impracticable for it even to be *indirectly* deliberative, with each distinct subgroup being represented by its own party or spokesperson in the decision-making forum. The argument of this chapter is that democratic ideals can nonetheless be furthered, even if not perfectly realized, by a politics of 'partial presence', chastening decision-makers by reminding them of the sheer fact of diversity among those for whom they are legislating.

This is a very old discussion, in a way. At America's founding, John Adams insisted that a legislature 'should be an exact portrait, in miniature, of the people at large, as it should feel, reason and act like them'.[1] Others demurred. Most famous were federalist patricians such as Alexander Hamilton; blessed with a touching faith in the capacity and willingness of the 'better classes' faithfully to represent the rest, they thought it unnecessary (as well as unwise) for the legislature to mirror the population at large.[2] Anti-federalists in contrast thought it highly desirable—but also, in so large a union, wildly impractical—for the legislature to mirror the

---

[1] Adams (1776: 205), quoted in Pitkin (1972: 60).

[2] 'It is said to be necessary that all classes of citizens should have some of their own number in the representative body, in order that their feelings and interests may be better understood and attended to. But . . . under any arrangement that leaves the votes of the people free . . . the representative body . . . will be composed of land-holders, merchants, and men of the learned professions. . . . [W]here is the danger that the interests and feelings of the different classes of citizens will not be understood or attended to by these three descriptions of men?'; quoted in Hamilton (1788).

population as a whole. The pseudonymous pamphleteer 'Brutus' put the point most forcefully:

Is it practicable for a country so large and so numerous . . . to elect a representation that will speak their sentiments, without their becoming so numerous as to be incapable of transacting public business? . . . The United States includes a variety of climates. The production of the different parts of the union are very variant, and their interests, of consequence, diverse. Their manners and habits differ as much as their climates and productions; and their sentiments are by no means coincident. The laws and customs of the several states are, in many respects, very diverse, and in some opposite . . . [O]f consequence, a legislature, formed of representatives from the respective parts, would not only be too numerous to act with any care or decision, but would be composed of such heterogeneous and discordant principles, as would constantly be contending with each other.[3]

By The Federalist's (which is to say, Hamilton's) own account, this was the most serious, or anyway the most common, objection to the proposed US Constitution: 'the house of representatives is not sufficiently numerous for the reception of all the different classes of citizens, in order to combine the interests and feelings of every part of the community, and to produce a due sympathy between the representative body and its constituents.'[4]

That in my view remains one of the most serious worries to be faced by modern mirror-style models of representation, most notably Anne Phillips's *Politics of Presence*.[5] Such proposals are a response to the fact of diversity.[6] But with too much diversity, those proposals prove impossible to implement. Too little diversity, and a 'politics of presence' is unnecessary. Too much, and it is impossible.

---

[3] Brutus (1787).   [4] Hamilton (1788: 218).

[5] Phillips (1995). There is more to the 'politics of presence' than simple mirror representation, in ways I acknowledge and incorporate in my critique at footnotes 24, 29, and 44. I focus here purely on legislative representation, although similar issues would presumably arise in trying to make all relevant differences physically present in executive or judicial settings as well.

[6] To quote Phillips (1995: 5): 'Many of the current arguments over democracy revolve around what we might call demands for political presence: demands for the equal representation of women with men; demands for a more even-handed balance between the different ethnic groups that make up each society; demands for the political inclusion of groups that have come to see themselves as marginalized or silenced or excluded. In this major reframing of the problems of democratic equality, the separation between "who" and "what" is to be represented, and the subordination of the first to the second, is very much up for question. The politics of ideas is being challenged by an alternative politics of presence.' Iris Marion Young (1990: 184) similarly insists that democracy 'should provide mechanisms for the effective recognition and representation of the distinct voices and perspectives of those of its constituent groups that are oppressed and disadvantaged'; this passage is quoted by Phillips (1995: 21).

Of course, the Goldilocks possibility remains: the amount of diversity might be 'just right' for the politics of presence to prove both necessary and feasible. Phillips offers good reasons for thinking that that will prove true in some genuinely important cases.[7] But in other important cases—and perhaps, upon closer inspection, even in some of Phillips's own—that will not be true.

For cases when diversity is too great for the politics of presence to work in the ordinary way, I shall propose a variant on that strategy. There, the chief function of the physical presence of others who differ from you is, in that connection, merely to remind you of the 'sheer fact of diversity' within your community.

In that variant, there is no pretence that the particular others who happen to be present alongside you in the deliberative assembly are a fully representative sample of that diversity. The diversity is too great for a really representative sample to assemble together to deliberate anything. Still, merely being reminded of the sheer fact of diversity can have salutary effects on the behaviour of such representatives as are assembled. Being reminded that we are diverse, in ways the present assembly has no hope of fully capturing, might even make representatives more solicitous of those not present than they would have been had there been a reliable sample of all distinct groups present in the chamber.

12.1. Representation with Mirrors

The 'mirror' model of representation recurs throughout modern political history. It figured in feminist pleas in revolutionary France.[8] It figured in Sidney and Beatrice Webb's complaints against the unreformed House of

---

[7] Phillips (1995: 7) insists that her proposals operate 'not [in] the world of mind-stretching political utopias, but one of realistic—often realized—reforms'. She offers as examples 'the quota systems that have been adopted by a number of European political parties to deliver gender parity in elected assemblies, or the redrawing of boundaries around black-majority constituencies to raise the number of black politicians elected in the USA'. Those, I shall be arguing, are exceptional cases rather than typical ones.

[8] 'Just as a nobleman cannot represent a plebeian and the latter cannot represent a nobleman, so a man, no matter how honest he may be, cannot represent a woman', asserted a group of Frenchwomen petitioning for a place in the Estates General in 1789; quoted in Phillips (1995: 52).

Lords.[9] It figured in the McGovern reforms to the Democratic National Convention in 1972.[10]

Throughout this long history, the exact nature and grounds for mirror representation have tended to vacillate between two logically quite distinct propositions. Sometimes the claim seems to be that demographically unrepresentative assemblies cannot (or anyway usually do not, in practice) represent well the *ideas and interests* of excluded groups.[11] Other times the claim seems to be a more symbolic one, that demographically unrepresentative assemblies cannot represent the *identities and images* of the excluded.[12]

There is generally no need to choose between those two grounds for a politics of presence, however. In the typical case, both of those propositions are true. Making the assembly mirror the identities and images of people in the larger society is typically one good way to help ensure representation of their ideas, interests, and opinions, as well.[13]

Occasionally of course there may be no systematic difference in the policy preferences of different groups in society. Survey research showed none between men and women in the period of the McGovern reforms to the US Democratic National Convention, for example. That was taken to undercut arguments for demographically balanced representation, insofar

[9] 'It was', they said, 'the worst representative assembly ever created, in that it contains absolutely no members of the manual working class; one of the great class of shopkeepers, clerks, and teachers; none of the half of all the citizens who are of the female sex'; quoted in Pitkin (1972: 61).

[10] And disastrously so, according to Kirkpatrick (1975). For a more even-handed account see Ranney (1975).

[11] The 1789 petition from the women of revolutionary France goes on to assert that 'between the representatives and the represented there must be an absolute identity of interests', which is lacking where one social group is representing another. As one of the first political scientists to make a systematic study of legislative behaviour testily remarks, 'Facts about the men who enact statutes are, presumably, significant only if they bear some relation to legislative behaviour—significant only if they affect the content or form of laws, or influence the procedure by which laws are enacted'; Hyneman (1940), quoted in Pitkin (1972: 89).

[12] Thus, for example, Lani Guinier (1989: 421) says, 'Blacks cannot enjoy equal dignity and political status until black representatives join the council of government'. See similarly Mansbridge (1999: 648–52).

[13] Giving rise to the model of 'introspective representation' discussed in Mansbridge (2003). The existence of a rough-and-ready correlation between these two represents common ground in the debate between Griffiths (1960) and Wollheim (1960) over 'How Can One Person Represent Another?' Wollheim (1960: 210) writes, 'If our concern is that a country's assembly should be the forum for every opinion that the country contains, then it is natural and reasonable to suggest that the assembly should be composed of descriptive representatives drawn from every opinion-holding group', where he takes every descriptively different group to hold a distinctive opinion as well. This is also one way of construing what John Adams meant when saying that the legislature 'should be an exact portrait ... of the people at large, as it should feel, reason and act like them'.

as those arguments were couched in terms of ideas and interests.[14] But it leaves untouched (if anything, gives freer rein to[15]) justifications couched in terms of symbolism, identities, and images.

I assume that 'no systematic difference of opinion' constitutes a rare and special case, however. Certainly as between men and women, that is now a thing of the past. An appreciable 'gender gap' has now opened up in political opinions on a wide range of topics, across a wide range of countries. And the same is true in trumps of opinions of different racial, ethnic, religious, etc. groups on many important political issues. Here, therefore, I am going to concentrate on cases, which I take to be both more common and also more pressing, where there are systematic differences in ideas and interests among different groups in society.

'Ideas' may be too cognitive a way of putting it, and 'interests' may be too crass. It might be better to talk in terms of 'perspectives' or 'standpoints' or 'experiences' or whatever.[16] Phrase it as you will, the point is just that in the cases upon which I focus: (a) each different group brings something distinctive to the deliberation and (b) that can be articulated or otherwise evoked more effectively by members of the group than by anyone else.

12.2. Circumstances of Moderate Diversity, and Beyond

The argument of this chapter turns on a distinction between representing the *fact* of diversity and representing the *particulars* of diversity in a democratic polity.

The politics of presence focuses primarily on the latter. The reason it is important to have individuals from different groups in society personally

[14] That is Kirkpatrick's claim (1975).

[15] If demographic balance makes no material (i.e. idea- or interest-based) difference to the deliberations, then there is no reason (in those terms, anyway) *not* to allow full symbolic representation of everyone's images and identities in the representative assembly; see Goodin (1977).

[16] Phillips (1995: 52, 176) and Young (2000: ch. 4). Both are rightly wary of essentialism here, though. People who 'share' experiences do not have the 'same' experiences. The 'shared experience' of slavery was nonetheless very different for field slaves and house slaves (and, judging from various 'slave narratives' that mushroomed on the eve of the Civil War, very different yet again within each of those groups). Even where experiences are more literally and less metaphorically 'shared', they are still not the same. Two inmates who share the same cell, nonetheless, have different experiences of prison; two partners who share the same bed have different experiences of marriage.

present in a representative assembly so that they can 'speak for themselves'. Only in that way can their distinctive perspective be adequately represented in the assembly's deliberations.[17]

That strategy could only possibly work, however, under certain very special conditions.[18] With due apologies to Hume and Rawls, I dub these, collectively, 'circumstances of moderate diversity'. Diversity must be no more than moderate in three particular respects:

- First, there must be relatively *few distinct groups* requiring representation in this way. Otherwise—in a really diverse society—there may be too many different groups for them all to be represented by a physical presence in the assembly chamber.

- Second, each of those groups must be *internally relatively homogenous*. Otherwise—if there is great diversity within groups—too many members of each group would be required to sit in the assembly in order to represent that within-group variation.

- Third, the dimensions of difference must be *relatively uncomplicated*, in the sense of not cutting across each other in too many diverse ways. If they do, then the number of distinct constituencies needed to mirror all the various combinations mushrooms exponentially, as I shall show.

In what follows, I take up each of those issues in turn.

In circumstances where diversity is more than merely moderate, the ideals of democratic representation and of deliberation come into tension with one another. Insofar as the claims of the politics of presence are right, certain sorts of people can only truly be represented by people 'like them' in the relevant respects. But in circumstances of immoderate diversity, that requires the physical presence of too many people for the representative assembly to remain a genuinely deliberative one.

---

[17] For 'politics of presence' theorists, the representation of the viewpoints in the actual deliberation is crucial. Other sorts of 'mirror theorists' might focus instead on improving democratic representation purely through ensuring that all groups have been assured a demographically appropriate share of the votes in aggregative, vote-counting mechanisms. But for a 'politics of presence' theorist, 'It is primarily when we ask how to improve deliberation ... that we discover the virtue of shared experience, which lies at the core of descriptive [mirror] representation'; Jane Mansbridge (1999*b*: 629).

[18] Another, which I shall not elaborate further here, is that our policies affect ourselves alone. Often we are doing things that affect others far away in time or space: it is logically impossible for future people to be made physically present here and now; and it is often practically difficult for a representative sample of all the different foreign peoples affected by our policies to be made physically present in our representative assemblies.

The problem is not just one of physical space in the legislative chamber in which all this diversity is to be made physically present. We can always build a bigger House. The point is instead that, beyond some point, it ceases to be a *deliberative* assembly in any meaningful sense at all.

Crass though they may seem, problems of 'size' have long been recognized as crucial in other ways in debates about democracy. Problems of 'size' are what drive us from direct to representative democracy in the first place. So said the American Founders.[19] So said the French revolutionaries.[20] And so say most contemporary advocates of representative democracy.[21]

Just as problems of size make representation necessary, so too might problems of size make it impossible for the deliberative assembly to contain a physical presence of all groups deserving of representation in that way. That is a challenge that existing theories of a politics of presence are often at risk of failing. That is the challenge to which my alternative approach hopes to help them meet.

I desist from trying to specify too precisely what the upper limit might be on the size of a workable legislative assembly. But clearly there are limits, if the legislature is to serve as the sort of deliberative assembly that advocates of the politics of presence envisage. Their aim is not merely to increase the number of votes of oppressed groups within the legislature. Advocates of the politics of presence would not be content turning the legislative assembly into a mini-referendum, where everyone had the right number of votes but none interacted with any other beyond simply the casting of votes. Instead, they want representatives of each distinct group to explain or somehow manifest their own distinct perspective to one another.

If that is the aim, however, then there are strict limits as to how many members the assembly may have: a few hundred, rather than many thousands. Dahl's calculation discussed is relevant here, once again: 'if an association were to make one decision a day, allow ten hours a day for

---

[19] 'Representation is made necessary only because it is impossible for people to act collectively', says one; 'In a community consisting of large numbers, inhabiting an extensive country, it is not possible that the whole should assemble', said another. Both are quoted in Pitkin (1972: 87). And the argument between The Federalists and Anti-Federalists was over the appropriate size and scale of government.

[20] '[W]hen Mirabeau compared a legislature to a map of the nation he added that representation is necessary wherever "a nation is too numerous to meet in a single assembly"' (Pitkin 1972: 87).

[21] Although that is not the only thing to be said in favour of representative democracy: cf. Kateb (1981) and Riker (1983).

discussion, and permit each member just ten minutes—rather extreme assumptions...—then the association could not have more than sixty members.'[22] Even if we think in terms of representatives 'manifesting' their distinct perspectives to one another in non-verbal ways (through their distinctive dress, for example[23]), the assembly needs to be small enough for everyone to be able to see one another.

12.2.1. Too Many Groups

The first problem—the problem of too many groups—might in principle seem easily resolvable within the terms of Phillips's proposal. Whether it is resolvable in practice remains an open empirical question.

The representation that a politics of presence requires, Phillips sensibly says, is not of every conceivable group: 'pensioners, beekeepers, and people with blue eyes and red hair'.[24] Plainly, not every conceivable group needs to be represented by physical presence in the legislative chamber. That is a pressing need only for those groups with a continuing history of being oppressed, excluded, and discriminated against.[25]

It is an open empirical question as to which, and how many, groups are (or conceive themselves as being) oppressed, excluded, and discriminated against in these ways. 'New social movements' quite generally tend to organize themselves around some such premise. 'This', Phillips says, 'has generated a more identity-based politics which stress[es] the self-organization of those most directly oppressed.' Among the dimensions of difference, Phillips herself mentions as relevant in this way, at one point or another in her book, are race, gender, ethnicity, sexual orientation, disability, language, Aboriginality, immigrant status, national origin.[26] Thus, there might in principle be quite a few different groups which

[22] Dahl (1970: 67–8). The Internet does not help, either: just change 'ten minutes listening to each person's speech' to 'ten minutes reading each person's posting', and Dahl's result remains. See generally Goodin (2003: ch. 9).

[23] As is done by the Sami in Scandinavian political meetings: I am grateful to Michele Micheletti for this example.

[24] Phillips (1995: 46).

[25] Phillips (1995: 46, 171), building explicitly on Young (1990). As Phillips (1995: 47) explains, 'The underlying preoccupation is not with pictorial adequacy—does the legislature match up to the people?—but with those particularly urgent instances of political exclusion which a "fairer" system of representation seeks to resolve'. Of course, it is important for majority groups (and indeed the oppressors) to be represented in the assembly as well; but we can safely assume they will be anyway, and focus our efforts on ensuring inclusion for oppressed and discriminated groups that might otherwise be excluded.

[26] Phillips (1995: 8–9, 46, ch. 5).

need to be accommodated through a physical presence in the legislative chamber.

Much depends on whose standard of 'discrimination' is applied. One way of defining 'discrimination' is in terms of the self-conscious intentions of the discriminators. In that case, perhaps the number of categories ('descriptions') under which people are explicitly discriminated against is strictly limited. Fine-grained though the discrimination of caste or status societies may be, even the most bigoted societies rarely manage to keep more than a half-dozen basic categories constantly in play at any one time.[27] And if it is the intentions of the discriminators—the 'descriptions under which they discriminate against others'—that determine the rights of discriminated-against groups to a physical presence in the legislature, then the entitlement of those groups to separate seats in the legislative assembly is correspondingly limited.

That is not the only plausible way to cash out the key term 'discrimination' in the theory, however. Arguably what we should privilege here are not the descriptions in terms of which discriminators discriminate, but rather the self-descriptions which are internalized by the discriminated-against themselves.[28] The contrast might best be illustrated by reference to the Indian Constitution's special protections for 'Scheduled Castes'. What those castes generically have in common is their 'untouchability'. That, presumably, is the description under which oppressors discriminate against, oppress, and exclude members of those classes. But from the point of view of the self-conceptions of members of the Scheduled Classes themselves, presumably, there is a world of difference among the vast multitude of castes, all of which are categorized generically as 'untouchable' and are Scheduled in consequence. And that is presumably all true among the various Scheduled Tribes (as distinct from Castes) that the Indian Constitution entitles to the same special protections.[29]

Anne Phillips is duly attentive to the risk that people might not think themselves well represented by some member of a group which the majority community, but not they themselves, see as being in the 'same' generic

---

[27] As suggested by the discussion of 'the rank order of discrimination' in the American South (Myrdal 1944: ch. 3, §4, pp. 60–7). Similarly, despite all the fine distinctions among castes and tribes in India, discrimination and the Constitutional remedies for it are couched in relatively simple terms of 'untouchability' of certain sets of castes and 'backwardness' of certain sets of tribes; see Galanter (1984: chs. 5, 9).

[28] Saward (2006) correctly describes the processes of representative democracy in terms of would-be representatives lodging 'claims' to represent certain people, and the crucial issue is then whether those they claim to represent accept that claim.

[29] Galanter (1984).

category. She sees clearly that having a reserved an 'ethnic minority' seat at the table, when the minority in view is supposed to embrace Indians as well as Pakistanis as well as West Indians, is wholly unsatisfactory from the point of view of the represented.[30] She seems to regard that as wholly unsatisfactory not only from their point of view but also her own. The relevant groups she wants to see physically present are, in that case, absent.

The trouble with this move on her part is that we no longer have the reassurance of any strict limit on the number of groups who are supposed to be entitled to a physical presence in the legislative chamber. Moving away from oppressors' intentions and towards oppressed's self-conceptions, we multiply the credible claimants—perhaps well beyond the bounds of feasible accommodation within any realistically delibera-tive assembly.

12.2.2. Too Much Heterogeneity within Groups

The second problem—heterogeneity within groups—exacerbates those problems.

Contemporary advocates of the politics of presence carefully eschew 'essentialism'. In so doing, they disassociate themselves from any thought that there is an essence of, for example, 'woman', such that any *one* woman can represent *all* women. And likewise (one sometimes gets the feeling that they would like to say 'all the more so') for all other groups that they discuss. Thus, for example, Phillips writes,

[I]nterests may be gendered without any implication that all women share the same set of interests; racial and ethnic minorities may have a strong sense of themselves as a distinct social group, but this can coincide with an equally strong sense of division over policy goals; territorial minorities may see their own interests and concerns as ignored by the wider community, but still have to grapple with their internal diversity.... [T]he dominant discourse in contemporary feminism stresses differences *between* women almost as strenuously as differences between women and men.[31]

Lani Guinier is likewise anxious to emphasize that 'racial groups are not monolithic, nor are they necessarily cohesive': they are rent

---

[30] Phillips (1995: 169).

[31] Phillips (1995: 145, 55–6); this is a theme to which she returns time and again (e.g. pp. 53–4, 68–9, 83, 104–06, 146, 168, 188). See similarly Mansbridge (1999: 637–9) and Young (2000: 122, 142–3).

by divisions of gender, age, class, and so on.[32] Likewise gays and lesbians.[33]

The internal heterogeneity of those groups makes it impossible for *one single* woman to represent the diverse perspectives of many different women.[34] But that does not mean that it is impossible *tout court* to represent those perspectives through a politics of presence.[35] What that means is that, if we want to have each woman represented by women with an identity and self-conception similar to her own, we will need a larger number of representative women to mirror statistically the diverse identities found among women. One woman cannot represent the heterogeneity of all women. But, statistically, a thousand women can constitute a good representative sample of all women (as good as a Gallup poll is of the electorate at large, anyway).[36] And so on for all the other groups in question.

[32] Guinier (1993: 1622), quoted in Phillips (1995: 104). Appiah (1996: 76) concurs, adding, 'Earlier in American history, the label "African" was applied to many of those who would later be thought of as Negroes, by people who may have been under the impression that Africans had more in common culturally, socially, intellectually, and religiously than they actually did.'

[33] Halley (1998).

[34] Young (2000:143–4, 148) uses 'perspective' in a technical which sense she wants to distinguish from 'interests' on the one hand and 'opinions' on the other. 'To the extent that what distinguishes social groups is structural relations, particularly structural relations of privilege and disadvantage, and to the extent that persons are positioned similarly in those structures, then they have similar perspectives both on their own situation and on other positions in the society.' Young thinks that there are far fewer distinct structural locations (and hence far fewer distinct 'perspectives') in society that require representation than there are distinct interests and opinions. But she concedes that 'there are good grounds for questioning an assumption that a social perspective is unified to the extent that all those positioned by structures in a similar way will express issues conditioned by this situated perspective in the same way'. For that reason, she recommends 'pluralizing' representation of perspectives, so a decision-making body 'can contain some of the perspectival differences that cross the group'. Depending on exactly how many distinct perspectives there are, how internally heterogeneous they are, and (to anticipate Section 12.2.3) how seriously they cut across one another, the same problems of scale discussed here in relation to representation of ideas and identities might re-emerge in relation to representation of Young's 'perspectives'.

[35] Nor does it therefore automatically imply, as Phillips seems to suppose, that we have to bolt some mechanisms of 'accountability to the group' onto mirror theories of representation. In her closing pages, Phillips ponders the question of on what basis 'representatives can claim to represent "their" people or group', and offers this conclusion: 'Once we give up on the guarantees that would come with notions of an essential identity, the only sure basis for such claims would lie in alternative mechanisms of accountability that depend on the self-organization of the relevant group. . . . Changing the composition of elected assemblies only improves the representation of excluded groups in what we might call a statistical sense; failing the development of more sustained conditions for consultation and discussion, it is an enabling condition, and still rather a shot in the dark. It is a better guarantee than we enjoy at present, which is enough to make it a political priority. But the real force of political presence lies in this further development' (Phillips 1995: 188).

[36] Young (2000: 147–8) likewise recommends women be represented by a 'committee' of women.

The problem, once again, lies merely in the maximum feasible size of a genuinely deliberative legislative chamber. Suppose there are several groups that ought to be represented by a physical presence in the chamber. Suppose that each of those groups is moderately diverse, and that multiple spokespersons are thus required from each of them to represent that intra-group diversity. Even if (contrary to my concerns above) the number of different groups to be represented is tolerably small, the number of representatives required from each group for them to constitute a representative sample of a diverse group can swell well beyond the numbers that can be present in a single deliberative chamber.

One solution might be to let each group deliberate in a chamber all its own—just as the First, Second, and Third Estates met separately under the *ancien régime* in pre-revolutionary France—and for the decisions of each separately deliberating group to be carried forward by a delegate to the overarching decision-making body. Associational democrats from G. D. H. Cole forward have long urged us to reconceptualize democracy in mass society along some such lines, with many different groups organized along different lines making representational claims of many different sorts.[37]

That solution, however, is unavailable to advocates of a politics of presence. The whole point of the politics of presence is for representatives of all the distinct oppressed groups to be present in the *same* place, speaking and being spoken to in turn by one another. For the same reason that multiple representatives of each internally heterogeneous group are required to be physically present somewhere in the representative machinery, those multiple representatives of each group need to be physically present in the same chamber as representatives of all other groups. Only through multiple physical presences in the same deliberative assembly can those heterogeneous groups represent themselves fully to one another.[38] The ghettoization of deliberation of each group in its own chamber, with only a handful of representatives carrying that chamber's views forward to the general assembly of all, would be clearly contrary to this requirement of the politics of presence.

---

[37] Cole (1950: chs. 6–7). See most recently Saward (2003).

[38] While it is essential that all those multiple members of heterogeneous groups be physically present in the same deliberative assembly, advocates of the politics of presence are not necessarily committed to the principle [attributed to them by Wollheim (1960: 215–8)] that each of those multiple members have one vote in the assembly. The demands of physical presence are perfectly consistent with schemes of weighted voting to ensure that each group gets only its due share of power within the assembly.

12.2.3. *Too Many Cross-Cutting Groups*

The third problem—cross-cutting memberships—is more problematic yet again.

The starting point, once again, is the question of 'who can speak for or on behalf of another'. As Phillips says,

> [O]nce men were dislodged from their role of speaking for women, it seemed obvious enough that white women must also be dislodged form their role of speaking for black women, heterosexual women for lesbians, and middle-class women for those in the working class. The search for authenticity . . . then makes it difficult for anyone to represent an experience not identical to her own and, taken to this extreme, renders dialogue virtually impossible.

Phillips reports that 'most feminists have resisted this deadening conclusion'; and she goes on to add that 'recent contributions have reframed the question of authenticity very much in terms of achieving equality of presence'.[39] My question is simply what 'equal presence' might mean, and how it might be achieved, in a situation of multiple cross-cutting identities and memberships.

The basic premise of the politics of presence is that no one can speak for members of another group. Members of each distinct group must be physically present to speak for themselves. Distinct groups are defined, for these purposes, in terms of identities and self-conceptions which are rooted in an ongoing practice of discrimination and oppression.

My point is just this. Any given person might be a member of, and construct his or her identity in terms of, multiple groups of precisely that sort.[40] Furthermore, he or she might have suffered discrimination by virtue of that conjunction of identities—as a lesbian Latina, for example, rather than (or in addition to) the discrimination she suffered as a lesbian on the one hand and as a Latina on the other.[41] Under those circumstances, the politics of presence test would be met; and we should require physical presence in the assembly not just of lesbians and of Latinas but also of lesbians who are also Latinas. And so on for all other conjunctions of group memberships which give rise to identities and discriminations in the conjunct, over and above the identities and discriminations involved in their component parts.

---

[39] Phillips (1995: 9).

[40] The point is actually Simmel's, who analyzed individuality in terms of a person's unique location in a network of overlapping group affiliations of this sort (1955).

[41] Halley (1998) and Barvosa-Carter (2007).

The problem to which this gives rise is, once again, a problem of the size of the assembly potentially required to represent all conjunct groups of this sort.

Here is one way of coming to appreciate the problem. The most natural mechanism for ensuring that the representative assembly is a mirror image of the larger society is by creating distinct electoral registers for each distinct group, as with the Maori in present-day New Zealand or with Oxford and Cambridge graduates in the British House of Commons up to 1948. And that is easy enough, where there is just one dimension of difference (Maori/Pakeha, graduate/non-graduate) to represent.

Things get more complicated, however, where there are multiple cross-cutting dimensions that have to be represented by a physical presence in the assembly. Where there are two cross-cutting dimensions (ethnicity and gender, say), we will need four separate electoral registers to represent all the categories (male Maori, female Maori, male Pakeha, female Pakeha). Where there are three cross-cutting dimensions (ethnicity, gender, and class), we need eight (male Maori, rich and poor; female Maori, rich and poor; male Pakeha, rich and poor; female Pakeha, rich and poor). In general, where there are x different binary dimensions along which people differ, we will need 2^x different electoral registers to accommodate them.

Of course, if the differences cannot be represented as simple binary contrasts, the number increases even more rapidly. But stick to that simplest binary case for the moment. Even in that simplest case, it would take only 9 cross-cutting dimensions of difference to generate 512 distinct electoral registers—which is about the size of most national representative assemblies. If one or more dimensions are more than binary (as ethnicity, religion, national origin, or even race is likely to be[42]), or if some groups are larger than others and deserve more than a single representative in the chamber, or if some of those groups are internally heterogeneous in ways that require multiple representatives, the requirements of physical presence then burst the bounds of any workable deliberative chamber.

[42] Suppose that each of these four dimensions point to four basic categories of people requiring physical presence in the assembly, each of which cuts across each other and across the basic binary distinctions of gender and sexual orientation. Then we would need $4 \times 4 \times 4 \times 4 \times 2 \times 2 = 1024$ separate electoral registers, with at least one seat each in the chamber.

12.3. Representing Instead the Sheer Fact of Diversity

The upshot of exceeding the bounds of 'moderate diversity' in any (still more, all) of those dimensions is simply this: it will be physically impossible for each group deserving a physical presence in the deliberative assembly to have one, and for that assembly to remain remotely 'deliberative'.[43]

One natural response at this point might be to abandon mirror representation and the politics of presence altogether, or to confine it to a narrow range of cases where the 'circumstances of moderate diversity' obtain. Another might be to abandon hopes for a politics of full presence and accept instead that the most you can aspire to is *partial* presence, mirroring only some of the 'most important' differences within the community.

The latter approach certainly describes the politics of representation as we know it. Every political coalition, party, or movement is internally disparate in ever so many ways. Part and parcel of ordinary politics is overlooking many things that divide us in order to more effectively pursue certain other things on which we are as one. Some differences get ignored in order that other 'more important' dimensions of difference can be represented.

Normatively, however, there is a world of difference between what is appropriate political practice in a world of full presence and in a world of partial presence. Political horse-trading of a sort that might be a satisfactory way of settling competing claims if every distinct group were properly represented in the chamber will be unsatisfactory precisely to the extent that some are left out of the chamber. Those with no votes to trade have no power in this bargaining game.

Nonetheless, some presence is better than none, even if 'full presence' for all relevantly different groups is impossible. To argue why, we need to conceptualize differently the exact role that 'presence' is supposed to play in circumstances where more-than-moderate diversity means that only 'partial presence' will ever be possible.

When it proves to be impossible to represent the *particulars* of diversity within the assembly, it nonetheless remains possible—and in that case, particularly desirable—to represent within the representative assembly

---

[43] Note that 'serial deliberation', rotating different groups in the legislative assembly, would fail in the same way as the Estates model discussed above to satisfy the 'politics of presence' desideratum of having representatives of all distinct groups deliberating together with one another: that requires that they be in the same place (the same assembly) at the same time (rather than some serving in the assembly earlier and others later).

the *sheer fact* of diversity.[44] By 'the sheer fact of diversity', I mean the fact that our society is diverse in a great many respects that genuinely matter in framing public policy.

For that sheer fact of diversity to be represented, some substantial diversity has to be made manifest in the assembly. But if the aim is to represent the sheer fact of diversity, rather than the exact parameters of that diversity, a fully representative sample is not strictly necessary. A suitably diverse representative body can instantiate the fact of diversity, reminding us what a diverse society we are, without instantiating all the particulars of that diversity.

The point of reminding legislators of the sheer fact of diversity, in turn, is merely to remind them that whatever laws they make will apply to a wide range of people who differ in a multitude of ways, the details of which are partially opaque to them when legislating. With that thought firmly in mind, the representatives assembled ought to incline more towards 'minimally presumptuous' policy-making.[45] This, as I shall show, is importantly different from what would follow if legislators could presume that the particularities of diversity were fully physically present in the chamber.

12.3.1. *The Difference that Presence Might Make*

In purely power-political terms, getting representatives of minority communities into the legislative chamber might not make much difference. Minorities who have historically been marginalized outside of parliament can easily enough be marginalized inside parliament, in much the same way, for much the same reasons, with much the same effect.

In discussing what material effect she envisages the physical presence of previously excluded groups making to the deliberations of a political assembly, Phillips points to its consciousness-raising function, both for members of the group themselves and especially for other members of the assembly.

The real importance of political presence lies in the way it is thought to transform the political agenda, and it is this that underlies the greater priority now accorded to gender and ethnicity and race.... We ... need to be represented in ways that will get new issues on to the political agenda, and will challenge the false consensus

---

[44] In Phillips's dichotomy (1995), this amounts to representing 'ideas and interests'—but in a very different way than before.

[45] 'Basic income' is preferable to categorical social assistance on those grounds, for example; Goodin (1992*b*, 2000*b*).

that keeps so many out. If all the options were already in play, or all needs and preferences already clearly defined, then the priority would more properly lie with getting more vigorous advocates. This certainly plays its part in the argument for more women in politics, and it plays an even greater part in the argument for minority representation in the USA; but all those pressing the inclusion of the previously excluded also stress the hegemonic power of dominant perspectives and the way these have blocked thinking on what else could be done. [46]

Literally expanding the legislative agenda—literally getting more motions onto the table for a vote—is, I take it, much the smaller of these contributions. [47] Far the greater contribution, presumably, lies in expanding perceptions of legislators (and of previously excluded groups themselves) as to what 'personal troubles' ought properly be considered 'public problems', appropriate for concerted social action through authoritative channels with powers of social sanctions. [48] This, in turn, is mostly a matter of 'expanding the perspectives' of representatives of the historically dominant community, so they can 'see things' from the point of view of those who had previously been excluded.

This much is common ground among political philosophers from Mill to Rawls. The latter remarks, in *A Theory of Justice*, upon how 'in everyday life the exchange of opinion with others checks our partiality and widens our perspective; we are made to see things from the standpoint of others and the limits of our vision are brought home to us ... ' Those lessons, Rawls supposes, carry over to legislative deliberations as well. [49]

J. S. Mill is even firmer on this point. In his *Considerations on Representative Government*, Mill emphasizes how, 'in the absence of its natural defenders, the interest of the excluded is always in danger of being overlooked'—or, 'when looked at, ... seen with very different eyes from those of the persons whom it directly concerns'. The prime example in his own day was that of the working classes, then effectively 'excluded from all direct participation in the government':

I do not believe that the classes who do participate in [government] have in general any intention of sacrificing the working classes to themselves... [I]n the

[46] Phillips (1995: 176, 158). In this, she is explicitly borrowing and elaborating arguments of Sunstein (1991: 33–4), quoted in Phillips (1995: 152–3). In 'Beyond the Republican Revival', Sunstein (1988: 1588, n. 262) himself traces the observation, in turn, to Rawls's *Theory of Justice* (1971: 358–9).

[47] Just as there are limits to the number of people who can genuinely deliberate together, so too might there be limits on the number of things they can genuinely deliberate together about, however.

[48] The phrase is that of Mills (1959). The point is emphasized by Mansbridge (1999: 643–8).

[49] Rawls (1971: 358–9).

present day their ordinary disposition is the very opposite.... Yet does Parliament, or almost any of the members composing it, ever for an instant look at a question with the eyes of a working man? I do not say that the working men's view of these matters is in general nearer to the truth than the other: but it is sometimes quite as near; and in any case it ought to be respectfully listened to, instead of being, as it is [now], not merely turned away from but ignored. On the question of strikes, for instance, it is doubtful if there is so much as one among the leading members of either House, who is not firmly convinced that the reason of the matter is unqualifiedly on the side of the masters, and that the men's view of it is simply absurd.... [H]ow different, and how infinitely less superficial a manner the point would have to be argued, if the classes who strike were able to make themselves heard in Parliament.[50]

12.3.2. Partial Presence and Legislative Reticence

Physical presence of excluded others is for Phillips, like Mill before her, absolutely crucial in forcing that expansion of perspectives.

With the best will in the world (and all too often we cannot rely on this), people are not good at imagining themselves in somebody else's shoes. We may get better at such acts of imaginative transcendence when our prejudices have been more forcefully exposed, but this happens only when the 'other' has been well represented.[51]

Where direct discursive engagement with others is possible, that is surely superior to mere imaginative engagement with mental reconstructions of them.[52] Where that is not possible (for reasons of time, distance, or, here, sheer limits to the size of genuinely deliberative groups), imaginatively projecting oneself into the place of others—however imperfect it inevitably is—is nonetheless better than not. 'Democratic deliberation

---

[50] Mill (1861: ch. 3, p. 188).

[51] Phillips (1995: 53); see further Young (1996/1997a, 1997b). John Stuart Mill (1861: ch. 7, p. 277) makes a similar point, in arguing for expansion of the franchise: '[E]ven in a much more improved state than the human mind has ever yet reached, it is not in nature that those ... [without a voice] should meet with as fair play as those who have a voice. Rulers and ruling classes are under a necessity of considering the interests and wishes of those who have the suffrage; but of those who are excluded, it is in their option whether they will do so or not; and however honestly disposed, they are in general too fully occupied with things which they *must* attend to, to have much room in their thoughts for anything which they can with impunity disregard.'

[52] As Montaigne (1580: 1045) says, 'Studying books has a languid feeble motion, whereas conversation provides teaching and exercise all at once. If I am sparring with a strong and solid opponent, he will attack me on the flanks, stick his lance in me right and left; his ideas send mine soaring. Rivalry, competitiveness and glory will drive me and raise me above my own level'.

within' can be a valuable adjunct when direct deliberative engagement is simply infeasible.[53]

Maybe Phillips is right, however, that we are not particularly good at imagining fully what it is like to be in radically different people's positions.[54] If so, that means that we will not be able to make very well-informed choices as to what would be good from their point of view.

Still and all, simply reflecting upon the fact and extent of difference across the community might make legislators more cautious and circumspect in their policy-making. That might help legislators avoid imposing 'one-size-fits-all' policies, oblivious to the extent of differences afoot in their community.

Even if they cannot anticipate exactly what variations in the application of the policy might be required, legislators sensitive to the sheer fact of diversity within their society will appreciate that variations of some sort will be necessary.[55] That will lead them to provide mechanisms within their legislation for making such variations; to write 'loose laws', setting out goals and principles without picking out any narrow set of ways of meeting or satisfying them; to leave room for flexibility in interpretation and application of the rules, and considerable latitude for different groups to meet the basic requirements of the law each in their own ways.[56]

Legislators can do all of this without knowing anything much about the particular facts of diversity among the people for whom they are legislating. All that is required is for them to know the sheer fact of diversity: that the people subject to their legislation are diverse, *and* that they are diverse in ways not fully knowable from within the legislature.

12.3.3. *Contrast with the Pretence of Full Presence*

This is very different from the way the role of representatives is conceived, and the way legislators behave in consequence, in a chamber purporting to represent the full particularities of societal diversity.

Where representatives are persuaded that the assembly fully captures the particulars of that diversity, representatives could—and should—feel

[53] Goodin (2000c, 2003b).

[54] Legislative dynamics, driven by closed mindsets instilled by party-based organization of the chamber, might make that particularly hard for legislators to do: mainstreaming the oppressed and making their just treatment more the responsibility of responsive administrators, instead, may therefore be particularly to be commended. I am grateful to Judith Squires for this thought.

[55] In much the same way that Rorty (1989) supposes observing cruelty of one form sensitizes to cruelty in general.

[56] Goodin (1982: ch. 4).

morally at liberty simply to cut deals among themselves.[57] They could do so, morally confident in the knowledge that all interested parties were adequately represented by an appropriately sized physical presence at the bargaining table. If every interested party truly were represented at the table, with power proportional to their legitimate stake in the issue, there would be no reason *not* to proceed with political horse-trading in that ordinary way.[58]

Lacking that confidence, representatives should (and hopefully would) instead be more genuinely solicitous of the views of others—those who are absent as well as those who are physically present. Representatives should (and hopefully would) be genuinely more sensitive to the demands of diversity, rather than merely mechanically sensitive to the demands of particular others in the legislative horse-trading.

The presence of diverse groups within the assembly is a powerful aid to this way of thinking. It helps 'ensure that processes of deliberation are not distorted by the mistaken appearance of a common set of interests on the part of all concerned'. In that way, diversity among the groups assembled helps to 'increase the likelihood that political outcomes will incorporate some understanding of the perspective of all those affected'. But on this alternative understanding of how a 'politics of partial presence' might work, that is accomplished 'not primarily [by] . . . allow[ing] each group to have its "piece of the action"', after the standard pluralist horse-trading fashion.[59] Instead, it is accomplished by letting such diversity as is present serve as a reminder of the even-wider-diversity that is absent.

12.4. Getting a Grip, Motivationally

A politics of presence designed to represent the 'sheer fact of diversity' would be designed to remind such representatives as are present in the assembly of the yet greater diversity that remains unrepresented, absent,

---

[57] Sunstein (1988: 1587) raises this issue clearly: 'the most significant problems with proportional representation are that it threatens to ratify, perpetuate, and encourage an understanding of the political process as a self-interested struggle among "interests" for scarce social resources, that it may discourage political actors from assuming and understanding the perspectives of others. . . . [I]n some incarnations, proportional representation tends to accept the basic premises of pluralist politics; it simply reallocates the distribution of power that underlies interest-group (even racial) struggle. The reallocation of power is in some settings highly desirable, but the improvement in politics is only partial.'

[58] Which is to say, horse-trading would in those circumstances be extensionally equivalent—would have the same outcome—as every representative internalizing fully the interests of all in the way Sunstein (1988), among many others, would wish.

[59] Sunstein (1988: 1588).

and opaque. That, in turn, should hopefully have two effects on representatives who internalize that lesson. First, it should make them more
reluctant merely to cut a deal among those who happen to be present,
cutting out of those who happen not to be. Second, it should make
representatives reticent, writing their laws in ways that are open to diversity along dimensions they have no serious expectation of being able to
anticipate in advance.

In brute terms of power politics, of course, there is little reason for
representatives to do either. Those present can simply carve up the spoils
for themselves, leaving nothing for those who lack any presence or hence
power in the assembly. All that might restrain *realpolitik* actors from doing
so is the thought that they might be setting a precedent that could be used
against them at some time when they happen to be the ones absent from
the assembly.

Even just minimally conscientious legislators, however, will see much
stronger reasons than that for being motivated to internalize the 'sheer
fact of diversity' and to act upon its implications. Making laws that
are suitable to the community is part and parcel of the legislator's job
description; it is tied to that role by a 'logic of appropriateness'.[60]

Motivationally, it is a tolerably small leap from accepting a role to
internalizing the norms that come with that role. 'Why should I be
moral?' may be a hard question to answer to a wholly *realpolitik* egoist.
'Why should I do the job I have agreed to do?' is a much easier question
to answer in terms that might get a grip on the agent concerned.[61]

12.5. Conclusion

Advocates of 'the politics of presence' rightly point to the ways in which
direct engagement with others who are importantly different from ourselves can broaden our own perspectives and lead to a fairer and more
just social outcome. They rightly want to broaden the range of social
groups (particularly oppressed groups) represented in social decision-
making bodies, accordingly.

But Brutus was right. In any large and interestingly diverse community,
mirror representation will probably prove impossible. The number of representatives required to represent that diversity would burst the bounds

[60] March and Olsen (1995: ch. 2). For a discussion of the ways in which American legislators
conceptualize their roles in these respects, see Maas (1983).
[61] Goodin (2000a: 233–50).

of any properly deliberative assembly.[62] The politics of presence would require the presence of too many people for them all genuinely to be 'present' to one another at all.

The Federalist then would say that we just have to trust those who are present to represent faithfully those who are absent. 'They cannot', advocates of the politics of presence would retort. But in a large and diverse community, The Federalist would reply, 'we cannot do any better'. The politics of full presence is rendered impossible by problems of sheer size and immoderate diversity.

The Federalist is right. In those circumstances, we have to trust some to legislate on behalf of others very unlike themselves. If advocates of the politics of presence are right, however, that amounts to legislating partially in ignorance. The realization of that fact ought to prompt a certain degree of legislative reticence and modesty, and a search for forms of rules appropriate for governing a people who are diverse in ways not fully known or knowable to the makers of the rules.

A politics of presence, partial though it may be, has a role to play in inducing that attitude towards the legislative task. Even if the full particulars of the diversity cannot be represented in a genuinely deliberative assembly, the presence of some substantial diversity within the legislature can serve as an important reminder to legislators of the 'sheer fact of diversity'. That there are appropriate and inappropriate ways to rule a diverse society is a principle that legislators can know and act on, without knowing the full details of the diversity. Reminding deliberators of that fact is further function, more modest but no less useful, that the politics of presence can perform, even in circumstances of more-than-moderate diversity.

---

[62] Constraints derived from the size of a genuinely deliberative legislative assembly might of course be overcome by shifting some of the representational burden onto the executive. Administrators can invite submissions from all interested parties before making rules. Ideas and interests can be represented in these ways, but the ideal of a politics of presence cannot.

13

Conclusion

This book has approached the problem of democratic renewal from two ends. One is the 'micro-deliberative', the other the 'macro-political'.

I explored in Part I the innovative use of 'deliberative mini-publics'—Citizens' Juries, Consensus Conferences, Deliberative Polls, and the like. There I was asking how those mechanisms worked, and what might reasonably be expected of the sorts of micro-deliberative processes embodied in them. I found that they have much to contribute. They allow us both to pool our information and to probe each other's premises. Hearing one another's reasons rather than merely their conclusions, talking together rather than just mutely counting ballots, allows us to understand better the deeper meaning of one another's attitudes, actions, and behaviour.

Deliberative talk of that sort, admirable though it is as a 'discovery procedure', ought not in and of itself constitute our 'decision procedure', however. One reason emerged at the end of Part I: talk is a serial process that can be arbitrarily path dependent if people are responsive to one another in ways deliberative theorists desire. That is why Chapter 6 concluded that we should adopt the rule, 'first talk, then vote'. That conclusion is reinforced once we saw, at the beginning of Part II, just how radical an expansion of the demos really is morally required. It is hard enough to implement genuinely deliberative processes among more than a few hundred citizens, with each talking and being talked to in turn. It is quite impossible if we expanded the demos, as Chapter 7 showed we should, to 'all affected interests' worldwide.

So in Part II of the book, I turned to approach the problem from the other, more 'macro-political' end. Start from where we presently are—at best, in a world of independent representative democracies—and ask how deliberative ideals can be better incorporated into that. Electoral accountability is obviously democratically invaluable, so far as it goes. But many people other than elected officials do things that affect the interests of others, both inside and outside their own polity, in ways for which they ought to be held accountable. What alternative forms of accountability might be employed in those contexts? Chapter 8 has shown how the notion 'network accountability' can help make public officials and private actors more accountable to civil society, domestically and transnationally.

13.1. A Deliberative System

In any large and complex community, deliberation cannot realistically take place in the agora (or its electronic equivalent), with everyone potentially affected by the decision taking an active part in all the deliberations. Deliberative democracy, in such a world, simply has to work on and through our inherited institutions of representative democracy.[1]

Revisioning those institutions through a deliberative lens, we can think of them as constituting a 'deliberative system', with different parts of the deliberative task being allocated to each in the ways sketched in Chapter 9. Even if we cannot fit representatives of every distinct affected interest into the legislative chamber, the diversity found there can serve to remind those who are present of the still-greater diversity among those who are absent, as Chapter 12 has suggested.

For critics of 'minimalist democracy', the most contentious part of my proposal will no doubt lie in its according so important a role to political parties. 'Responsible two-party government' has long been seen as the cornerstone of democracy in the reviled 'minimalist' mode.[2] In that model, parties propose and voters dispose; voters choose but then let parties get on with the job of ruling. For minimalists, periodic moments of electoral accountability are sufficient to vouchsafe the democratic credentials of the system overall. Not so, for critics of minimal democracy[3]— deliberative democrats conspicuously among them.

But to refuse parties such a near-exclusive role in democratic politics is not necessarily to say that they should not have a nonetheless crucial

---

[1] As Squires (2002: 134) rightly remarks, 'while the current institutions of representative democracy are explicitly critiqued within the deliberative democracy literature, they are also—I suggest—implicitly assumed'. In Bohman's (1998) terms, recognition of this fact constitutes the 'coming of age of deliberative democracy'.

[2] Schattschneider (1950) and Schumpeter (1950).

[3] Famously including Rousseau: 'The people of England regards itself as free; but it is grossly mistaken; it is free only during the election of members of parliament. As soon as they are elected, slavery overtakes it, and it is nothing' (Rousseau 1762: book 3, ch. 15).

(albeit less exclusive) role to play in it. Tellingly, some of the most prominent deliberative democrats conspicuously agree. Recall Bernard Manin's remark, quoted at the end of Chapter 10: 'In the political arena, the limited pluralism of parties is required for effective deliberation.'[4] Similarly, Joshua Cohen's seminal discussion of deliberative democracy ends with the conclusion that 'political parties supported by public funds play an important role in making deliberative democracy possible'.[5]

Notice, most especially, that political parties also figure centrally in the 'two-track model' of deliberative democracy proposed by Jürgen Habermas himself. In that model, one track is 'democratic opinion-formation' occurring in the public sphere outside the formal apparatus of the state. The other track is 'democratic will-formation' occurring through authoritative acts of the legislature, executive, and judiciary. Political parties and elections are, for Habermas, one crucial (though hardly the only) mechanism by which opinions formed in the public sphere are brought to bear on 'democratic will-formation'.[6]

Other deliberative democrats are of course more implacably opposed to parties and indeed organized politics in any form. Movement politics is, for them, the be all and end all. Clearly, social movements have a very important role to play in democratic politics, and how they articulate with the state apparatus matters hugely.[7] But, realistically, they cannot wholly take the place of parties—or anyway they cannot do so without themselves in effect becoming parties.

What we should be doing is, I suggest, to find a proper place for political parties—along with all the other institutions of real-existing

[4] Manin (1987: 357). His reason for saying so, recall, is that 'it is not possible to deliberate all possible outcomes; the range of proposed solutions must by necessity be limited', and this is what parties do for deliberation.

[5] Cohen (1987: 31). Elaborating, he continues, 'They can provide the more open-ended arenas needed to form and articulate the conceptions of the common good that provide the focus of political debate in a deliberative democracy'; 'parties', he adds in a footnote, 'are required to organize political choice and to provide a focus for public deliberation'.

[6] As Habermas (1996: 368) writes, 'The political system, which must remain sensitive to the influence of public opinion, is intertwined with the public sphere and civil society through the activity of political parties and general elections.' Elsewhere, he cites approvingly Fröbel's characterization of parties as 'bringing influence to bear, primarily through arguments, on the process of public opinion- and will-formation. They represent the organizational core of an enfranchised public citizenry that, engaged in a multivocal discussion and deciding by majority, occupies the seat of the sovereign' (p. 476). Elsewhere, yet again, Habermas notes another crucial contribution of parties to deliberative democracy of the sort he advocates: 'why should voters base their ballot choices on, as we here assume, a more or less discursively formed public opinion, instead of ignoring the legitimating reasons? It is because normally they can choose only between the highly generalized policies and vague profiles of popular parties...' (p. 487).

[7] Dryzek (1990: 48 ff.) and Dryzek et al. (2003).

representative democracy—within a larger deliberative system. The crucial role Chapter 10 has identified for political parties is to serve an 'ideational coordination function' for voters. Parties can enable voters truly to 'give laws to themselves' by elaborating proposals and associated *ratios* for those proposals which mass electorates could either endorse or not through the ballot box.[8]

Political parties are merely acting as 'consolidators' in this matter, however. There is no reason to suppose that those proposals and *ratios* should necessarily emanate only from the party room or party headquarters. They can and should be shaped by input from all those who will be affected by the laws, through various deliberative fora. Broad public discussion, through the mass media and otherwise, is one mechanism.[9] Broad discussion within the party, at branch meetings and national conventions, is another.[10] Public hearings of the old-fashioned sort are yet another. Formally organized micro-deliberations, employing mini-publics of the sort discussed in Chapter 2, are yet others.

13.2. Connecting the Public Sphere

The notion of 'civil society' or 'the public sphere' looms large in virtually all theories of deliberative democracy. As Habermas defines it,

[T]he public sphere consists of an intermediary structure between the political system, on the one hand, and the private sectors of the lifeworld and functional systems, on the other. It represents a highly complex network that branches out into a multitude of overlapping international, national, regional, local, and subcultural areas....[11]

It follows, as Seyla Benhabib says, that

a deliberative...model of democracy...privilege[s] a plurality of modes of association in which all affected can have the right to articulate their point of view. These can range from political parties, to citizens' initiatives, to social movements, to voluntary associations, to consciousness-raising groups and the like....[O]ur

---

[8] As Young (2000: 135) says, 'Political parties are the most common vehicle for the representation of opinions. Parties often put forward programmes that less express the interests of a particular constituency, and more organize the political issues of the day according to principles, values and priorities the party claims generally to stand for.' She goes on to observe that 'smaller or more specialized associations...can and often do form to represent opinions in public life and influence policy'. But unless they manage to get their proposal and associated *ratio* onto the ballot paper (in a referendum, e.g.), people cannot democratically vote to give that law to themselves.

[9] Page (1996).   [10] Ranney (1975).   [11] Habermas (1996: 373–4).

guiding model has to be that of a medium of loosely associated, multiple foci of opinion formation and dissemination which affect one another in free and spontaneous process of communication.

In short, 'a normative theory of deliberative democracy requires a strong concept of the public sphere as its institutional correlate. The public sphere replaces the model of the general deliberative assembly found in early democratic theory'.[12]

Still, the 'public sphere' does not itself issue any authoritative enactments. In order for all the deliberative energies manifested there to impact on the law and official policies of the land, the public sphere must somehow connect to the legitimate organs of 'democratic will-formation'—the legislature, the executive, the judiciary.

'Loose connections' is the summary judgement John Dryzek passes on Habermas' analysis of how, exactly, the 'public sphere' has any 'influence on government'.[13] That the public sphere does influence government decision-making, and that it is important, is absolutely undeniable. But how exactly that happens is hard to say. Certainly it is hard to say anything much about it in any interestingly general terms.[14]

Habermas rightly remarks upon how 'the civil-social periphery, in contrast to the political center, [has] the advantage of greater sensitivity in detecting and identifying new problem situations'. We see evidence of that in all 'the great issues of the last decades':

Consider, for example, the spiraling nuclear-arms race; consider the risks involved in the peaceful use of atomic energy or in other large-scale technological projects and scientific experimentation, such as genetic engineering; consider the ecological threats involved in an overstrained natural environment (acid rain, water pollution, species extinction, etc.); consider the dramatically progressing impoverishment of the Third World and problems of the world economic order; or consider such issues as feminism, increasing immigration, and the associated

[12] Benhabib (1996: 73–4) and Dryzek (2000: 171 and ch. 4 *passim*). '[D]eliberation in a strong democracy should occur in many fora', as Young (2000: 167) paraphrases Gutmann and Thompson (1996), before going on to take them to task for the fact that 'most of their examples of deliberation involve public officials within state institutions'. See similarly Fraser's (1997: 81) call for multiple 'subaltern counterpublics' and Cohen and Rogers' (1995) call for 'associative democracy' working through a plethora of 'secondary associations' outside the state; Cohen and Sabel (1997) give the latter proposal more institutional structure.

[13] Dryzek (2006: 61).

[14] Habermas' (1996: 28) formulation is: 'Informal public opinion-formation generates "influence"; influence is transformed into "communicative power" through the channels of political elections; and communicative power is again transformed into "administrative power" through legislation.' That, I submit, is simply *too* general to be interestingly informative.

problems of multiculturalism. Hardly any of these topics were *initially* brought up by exponents of the state apparatus, large organizations or functional systems. Instead, they were broached by intellectuals, concerned citizens, radical professionals, self-proclaimed 'advocates', and the like.

Clearly civil society gets worried about all those sorts of things, long before the state does. But how exactly do those civil-society concerns make their way into the formal political process? Habermas canvasses a range of disparate informal mechanisms:

Moving in from this outermost periphery, such issues force their way into newspapers and interested associations, clubs, professional organizations, academies and universities. They find forums, citizen initiatives, and other platforms before they catalyze the growth of social movements and new subcultures. The latter can in turn dramatize contributions, presenting them so effectively that the mass media take up the matter. Only through their controversial presentation in the media do such topics reach the larger pubic and subsequently gain a place on the 'public agenda'. Sometimes the support of sensational actions, mass protests and the incessant campaigning is required before an issue can make its way via the surprising election of marginal candidates or radical parties, expanded platforms of 'established' parties, important court decisions and so on, into the core of the political system and there receive formal consideration.[15]

That is about as far as Habermas' analysis goes, however. And in a way, excusably so. By definition, the public sphere is not formally organized; and it is inherently chaotic and unruly in consequence.[16] There is simply no telling what creative and opportunistic norms entrepreneurs might get up to in the public sphere, or what exactly might occur in consequence. Generalizations in these realms are hard to come by. So too are institutional prescriptions for governing or guiding such a lightly institutionalized sphere of life.

Thus, it often seems inevitable that theorists must be left just offering up examples. They do so, basically in the spirit of 'proof of concept'. The actual is *ipso facto* possible. 'We know such and such a thing can happen— that ideas about abolishing the slave trade for example can develop in civil society and force their way into the political process and onto the statute books. We know such a thing can happen, because we know

---

[15] Habermas (1996: 381). This, I take it, is Habermas' answer to Dryzek's (2000: 26) challenge, 'What are we to make of the multiple channels of influence that for better or worse do not involve elections—such as protests, demonstrations, boycotts, information campaigns, media events, lobbying, financial inducements, economic threats, and so forth?'

[16] It is 'a "wild" complex that resists organization as a whole', according to Habermas (1996: 307). Young (2000: 168) too makes great play of this fact.

that once it did happen, and here is how.'[17] There are many fascinating case studies showing how movement politics can penetrate (or be co-opted by) the state, and how non-governmental organizations network with one another, with state agencies and with intergovernmental and transnational organizations to effect policy change.[18]

Those are often compelling examples. But subsuming them into a genuinely informative general analysis proves difficult. Pressed to go beyond a laundry list of the sort quoted above, deliberative theorists often tend to 'go meta' and start talking in pretty ungrounded ways. Habermas constitutes a conspicuous case in point when he starts waxing lyrical about 'subjectless forms of communication':

Subjectless and anonymous, an intersubjectively dissolved popular sovereignty withdraws into democratic procedures and the demanding communication presuppositions of their implementation. It is sublimated into the elusive interactions between culturally mobilized public spheres and a will-formation institutionalized according to the rule of law. Set communicatively aflow, sovereignty makes itself felt in the power of public discourses.[19]

Analysis has given way to pure poetics at this point.

The analysis of 'network accountability' offered in Chapter 8 is an attempt at occupying the middle ground between metaphysical flights of fancy and micro case studies. It attempts some modest middle-level generalizations about some of the mechanisms whereby civil society shapes public policy. It attempts to do so in an all-the-more grounded way by focusing particularly on the more 'organized' end of the public sphere, non-profit organizations of the Third Sector.[20]

Why such networks form, and how they work, might best be analysed through the notion of a 'veil of vagueness'.[21] Why do people cooperate, even in circumstances in which they would do better for themselves if they did not? The standard social science explanation has to do with the way in which 'the shadow of the future' influences repeat-players: I cooperate now, even though it would be to my advantage to defect, in

---

[17] Thomas (1997: books 5–6).

[18] See, e.g.: Finnemore and Sikkink (1998), Keck and Sikkink (1998), Risse, Ropp and Sikkink (1999), and Dryzek et al. (2003).

[19] Habermas (1996: 486). Dryzek (2006: 61–2) derides Habermas' notion of 'subjectless communication' although his concept of 'discourses among discourses' sometimes comes perilously close to that (Dryzek and Niemeyer 2006).

[20] For a case study on the less organized end of movement politics, see Schlosberg's (1999) account of the environmental justice movement growing out of Love Canal.

[21] For a fuller discussion see Gibson and Goodin (1999).

order to induce you to cooperate on some future occasion when it would be in your interest to defect.[22]

The real world is rarely as well-structured as a game theory payoff matrix, however. The future is uncertain in all sorts of ways. We do not know who we will need, or what we will need them for. We do not know what problems we will collectively face, or what strategies might be available to us for confronting them. All we know is that, given our respective roles and interests, we seem to keep bumping into one another from time to time.

Such uncertainties constitute a 'veil of vagueness' that serves sociologically as the functional equivalent of Rawls's 'veil of ignorance'. We agree to 'work together', in ways that remain to be specified. We 'agree to agree', details of the agreement left to be hammered out. We agree to pursue certain ends jointly, with means left to be determined[23]; or we agree to procedures, with where they will end up being left open. Or we agree to some relatively specific course of action, but one to be undertaken fairly far in the future, and hence in circumstances the details of which are hard to foresee with any precision.[24]

Regular interactions among people and groups networked in that way lead to trust-building and a sense of shared commitment. Recurring interactions within such networks provide regular occasions for people to demand and give accounts of themselves to one another. Knowing that, they are reluctant to let one another down. Among the networks responsible for negotiating environmental policy within the European Union, for example,

it is rare . . . for negotiations to fail. . . . An important factor seems to be the dynamics of long-lasting negotiations: i.e., the 'entanglement' of the negotiations which ultimately exerts such pressure on the representatives of dissenters (especially where there is only one dissenting state) that a compromise can be reached . . . [O]n the whole, no member state is willing to assume the responsibility for causing the failure of negotiations that have lasted for years and in which mutual trust in the willingness of all negotiators to contribute to an agreement has been built up.[25]

This is how the 'veil of vagueness' mechanism works. Starting with agreements on the terms of interaction that are deliberately vague and general, the network progressively refines, clarifies, and specifies in ever more detail what is to be done under the terms of those earlier agreements.

---

[22] Axelrod (1984) and Goodin (1992a: ch. 2).   [23] Scharpf (1988) and Peters (1997).
[24] Goodin (1992a: ch. 3).   [25] Rehbinder and Stewart (1985: 265).

Having agreed the generalities, agents within the network feel committed to and bound by the elaborations that emerge subsequently.

If an organization acquires a certain stability and settles down to a tradition of work, one implication is usually that on the whole the same state officials come together at regular intervals. If in addition it becomes repeatedly utilized for reaching inter-governmental agreements in a given field, it may acquire a certain institutional weight and a momentum. Certain substitutes for real political sanctions can then gradually be built up. They are all informal and frail. They assume a commonly shared appreciation of the general usefulness of earlier results reached, the similarly shared pride of, and solidarity towards, the 'club' of participants at the meetings, and a considerable influence of the civil servants on the home governments in the particular kind of questions dealt with in the organizations.... Not upholding an agreement is something like a breach of etiquette in a club.

That is Gunnar Myrdal's description of how things worked in the early days of the United Nations' Economic Commission for Europe, when he served as its original Executive Secretary.[26] Through such network dynamics, that relatively weak intergovernmental organization grew, first into the European Economic Community and eventually into the European Union.

So too it is likely to be, with discursive accountability networks more generally. An initially vague sense of shared concerns and interests brings individuals and groups into repeated interaction. That in turn gives rise to shared commitments, initially vague but increasingly refined over time. Through their repeated interactions, members of the network increasingly come to regard one another as constituting a reference group of significant others, to whom explanations and apologies are owed when defaulting on those commitments. That seems to be the way things work within policy networks, both internationally and domestically. It also offers a good way of thinking about how civil-society networks might hold public officials to account.

13.3. Embedding Deliberation Institutionally

We know what the institutional architecture of 'minimalist democracy' amounts to. It is just those things sketched at the beginning of Chapter 1: people vote; votes are counted and winners declared; those elected rule for a time, facing the electorate once again at the end of that time.

[26] Myrdal (1955: 8, 20).

The question I want now to address is: 'What is the best institutional architecture for a realistically feasible deliberative democracy?'[27] A robust public sphere is of course a *sine qua non*.[28] But what is the most hospitable structure of state institutions for accommodating and incorporating its input?

Let us begin by mapping the space, through a typology categorizing democratic institutions on two cross-cutting dimensions.

- On the first dimension, democratic institutions can be either *aggregative* or *deliberative*. In aggregative democratic institutions, political decisions are made by counting votes; in deliberative democratic institutions, political decisions are made by talking together.[29]

- On the second dimension, institutions can be either *directly* or *indirectly* democratic. In directly democratic institutions, public policy is determined directly by a vote or deliberation among everyone potentially affected by the decision; in indirectly democratic institutions, public policy is determined by a vote or deliberation among people who are in turn electorally or discursively accountable to those who are potentially affected by the decision.

---

[27] Thus, I wholeheartedly endorse the view of Fearon (1998: 64) when he writes, 'the main problem is to explain how it is even possible to have a "discussion" among thousands or millions of people. Any call for broader "deliberation" in . . . politics is simply meaningless without specific recommendations about how the broader discussion would be institutionally structured and an analysis of how those institutions would condition the discussion that resulted'.

[28] In its many forms, surveyed in Chambers and Kopstein (2006).

[29] Some of those who are advocating making political life more 'deliberative' have deliberation among public officials primarily in mind. The phrase 'deliberative democracy' was coined by Bessette (1981, 1994), whose primary concern is with deliberation in Congress rather than deliberation across the whole community; John Rawls (1993: 23) famously pronounced that 'the Supreme Court is the branch of government that serves as the exemplar of public reason'. In 'The idea of public reason revisited', Rawls (1997/1999: 133–4) expanded: 'It is imperative to realize that the idea of public reason does not apply to all political discussions of fundamental questions, but only to discussions of those questions in what I refer to as the public political forum . . . : the discourse of judges in their decisions, and especially of the judges of a supreme court; the discourse of government officials, especially chief executives and legislators; and finally, the discourse of candidates for public office and their campaign managers, especially in their public oratory, party platforms, and political statements. . . . The idea of public reason does not apply to the background culture with its many forms of non-public reason nor to media of any kind.' In characterizing 'deliberative *democracy*', however, it is deliberation among the citizenry at large rather than merely among public officials that is of central concern. Rawls (1997/1999: 135) squares this circle in his own terms by saying 'that ideally citizens are to think of themselves as if they were legislators and ask themselves what statutes, supported by what reasons satisfying the criterion of reciprocity, they would think it most reasonable to enact'.

Table 13.1. A typology of democratic institutions

	Aggregative	Deliberative
Direct	Referendum	New England town meeting
Indirect	Representative democracy—Schumpeterian 'minimalism'	Representative democracy—with micro-deliberative input

These two dimensions cut across one another, yielding Table 13.1. In the cells of that table are what I take to be paradigm cases of each model. None are pure cases, perhaps. Voters always engage in conversations with one another before they vote.[30] The point in calling a referendum or an election an 'aggregative' democratic institution is just that it is people's votes, rather than their conversations, that directly determine public policy. Or again, even in the most direct democracy, people's votes never directly determine public policy unmediated by absolutely *anything* else: there is always a voting machine, or a public servant charged with implementing the decision, standing in between.

As Table 13.1 makes plain, the form of direct democracy with which we have most experience—the referendum—is just as aggregative as any election. Its outcome is decided purely by adding up votes for and against the proposition on the ballot. Of course voters talk with one another before voting; but of course that is true when they are electing representatives as well. In both cases, it is how voters vote, not how they talk, that decides the outcome.

Deliberative democracy in its purest form would be 'directly deliberative', on the model of the New England town meeting.[31] That is fine for a small-scale society. But for pragmatic reasons, it simply cannot work in any large-scale society: with large numbers of people involved, it would

[30] As Cohen (1996: 99–100) says, 'a deliberative view [of democracy] cannot be distinguished simply by its emphasis on discussion' because 'any view of democracy—indeed any view of intelligent political decision-making—will see discussion as important, if only because of its essential role in pooling information against a background of asymmetries in its distribution'.

[31] Mansbridge (1980). Notice, however, that Cohen (1989: 30) cautions against jumping to the conclusion that 'a direct democracy with citizens gathering in legislative assemblies is the only way to institutionalize a deliberative procedure... In fact, in the absence of a theory about the operations of democratic assemblies—a theory which cannot simply stipulate that ideal conditions obtain—there is no reason to be confident that a direct democracy would subject political questions to deliberative resolution.... [F]ar from being the only deliberative scheme, direct democracy may not even be a particularly good arrangement for deliberation'.

simply take too long for everyone to have his or her say, however briefly, before we reached a decision.[32] The path dependency of conversations discussed in Chapter 6 provides a further, more principled reason why we should not use talk as our decision procedure, even if pragmatically we could.

Deliberative democrats tend to be participatory democrats, too. So if their preferred model of 'directly deliberative democracy' is ruled out, for reasons either of pragmatism or of principle, it is unclear whether their second choice would be 'aggregative direct democracy' or 'indirect deliberative democracy'. Doubtless different deliberative democrats would jump different ways when faced with that choice; and doubtless some would opt for one model for some sorts of decisions and the other for others.

Table 13.1 shows 'representative democracy' straddling both 'indirect deliberative' and 'indirect aggregative' models. It is indirectly aggregative, insofar as representatives' determinations of policy are based on formal electoral inputs of their constituents. It is indirectly deliberative, insofar as representatives' policy determinations of policy are based on formal deliberative inputs of their constituents. Representatives in a purely trustee role would be an example of the former, representatives who are delegates bound by a mandate deliberatively determined would be an instance of the latter.

In real-world representative democracies, most constituent input—both aggregative and deliberative—is far less formal than that. The aggregation that counts, the one that empowers representatives to represent, is of course the aggregation of votes on election day. But in between elections representatives weigh opinion more informally, studying public opinion surveys and monitoring their mailbags, as well as occasionally receiving petitions and delegations.

The public's deliberative inputs, too, come in varying degrees of formality. Occasionally they are part of the formal political process, as in the case of Participatory Budgeting in Porto Alegre discussed in Chapter 2. There, recall, popular Regional Assemblies that are open to everyone determine budget priorities and elect members' higher councils to carry them out. Somewhat more often, mini-publics are organized by public authorities

---

[32] Recall Dahl's (1970: 67–8; Goodin 2000c, 2003b: ch. 9) back-of-the-envelope calculation referred to in Section 7.3.4. Benhabib (1996: 73) agrees that it is 'undoubtedly true' that 'any... deliberative model of democracy is prima facie open to the argument that no modern society can organize its affairs along the fiction of a mass assembly carrying out its deliberations in public and collectively'—although in her view 'more than an issue of size is at stake'.

to provide deliberative input of a non-binding but often very influential sort. Citizens' Juries in Britain and Canada, Planning Cells in Germany, Consensus Conferences in Denmark, and Deliberative Polls in Texas and now China have all played that role, as Chapter 2 has also shown. More often still, deliberative mini-publics are organized by outside groups, but the results of their deliberations are monitored carefully by and can be highly influential on policymakers. A prime example of that from Chapter 2 is the America*Speaks* 'Listening to the City' Town Meetings.

13.4. Mini-Publics in Macro-Democracy

Not all micro-deliberative events will be a success, either in terms of meeting high deliberative standards or in terms of their further influence on policy. Sometimes those events will be co-opted or subverted by interested parties, be they politicians or stakeholders. But while there is no guarantee that deliberative mini-publics will always succeed, the evidence of Chapters 2 and 3 suggests that they can work well in their own terms and that they can have important input into the larger political process.

There are various *modes of influence* by which these micro-deliberative events might affect public policy. They can themselves be formally part of the policymaking process (as with Participatory Budgeting in Porto Alegre) or feed directly into it (as with the Zeguo Deliberative Poll). They can inform public debates more generally (as do well-publicized Deliberative Polls, America*Speaks* Town Meetings, and Kettering Foundation National Issues Forums). They can serve as opportunities for politicians to market-test policy proposals (as with the UK's 'GM Nation?' exercise). They can help to legitimate policy (as with the Leicester Citizens' Jury deliberations on hospital closures). They can even serve a community-building function (as in the South Carolina project Reconstructing Communities and Schools).

There are also various different *sites* at which deliberative mini-publics might usefully be drafted into the service of democratic decision-making. Within government itself, there is a role for deliberative mini-publics in all three branches. Within the legislative branch, they can assist in framing legislation, as do Danish Consensus Conferences. Within the executive branch, they can assist in discharging the 'public consultation' obligations associated with administrative rule-making, as in the case of the Texas Deliberative Polls. Within the judicial branch, too, deliberative mini-publics even have an important role to play: remember, juries are deliberative mini-publics par excellence.[33]

Outside the formal political system, deliberative mini-publics can play an equally or perhaps even more important role in guiding policy development. After all, it behoves governments and parties facing the prospect of an election to pay careful attention to what people say about some policy proposal, once they have had a chance to inform themselves and talk about it.

Dahl thinks of it in high-minded way, as a matter of democratic legitimacy.[34] But no need to moralize, here. We can think of it in lowly terms of democratic prudence. If governments and parties cannot sell a policy proposal to a deliberative mini-public, even after it has been given full information and plenty of time to discuss the proposal, then they are unlikely to be able to sell the proposal to the larger public. Conversely, if they can sell the proposal to a deliberative mini-public then there is at least some hope of selling it to the larger public.

Thus, the New York Port Authority found that they could not sell its initial plan for redeveloping the World Trade Centre site to the 'Listening to the City' Town Meetings, and it withdrew the plan. The Texas utility commissioners found, to their surprise, that they could sell renewables to participants in Deliberative Polls, and they began investing heavily in them. Recent US legislation has mandated 'that ethical, legal, environmental and other appropriate social concerns... are considered during the development of nanotechnology', through 'mechanisms such as citizens' panels, consensus conferences and educational events, as appropriate'.[35] Expect to see much more of that sort of thing appearing on the statute books.

Beyond informing policymakers, deliberative mini-publics can play an important role in informing fellow citizens about what they might themselves think about the matter, had they the same opportunity to study and discuss the matter intensively with one another.

---

[33] Abramson (1993).

[34] Remember his words, quoted in Chapter 2: 'The judgment of a minipopulous would "represent" the judgment of the demos. Its verdict would be the verdict of the demos itself, if the demos were able to take advantage of the best available knowledge to decide what policies were most likely to achieve the ends it sought. The judgments of the minipopulous would thus derive their authority from the legitimacy of democracy' (Dahl 1989: 342). Mansbridge (2003a: 193) similarly says, 'I suggest thinking of the individuals who do attend deliberative assemblies as informal representatives of those who do not attend'—although the extent to which the 'informality' of that relationship vitiates the 'representative claim' (Saward 2006) is an open question.

[35] US Congress (2003).

The British Columbia Citizens' Assembly on Electoral Reform is perhaps the best example to date of a deliberative mini-public serving this sort of function. The proposal it put forward won an impressive 57.7 per cent of votes in the ensuing referendum, and it did so apparently precisely because voters trusted in the representativeness and competence of the Citizens' Assembly itself.[36]

The British Columbia Citizens' Assembly is just the sort of deliberative innovation that this book has been advocating. It respects the principle, 'first talk, then vote'. It takes full advantage of the virtues of a deliberative mini-public to probe the strengths and weaknesses of a wide range of options from many perspectives. But at the end of the day, the matter was decided by a vote: in the first instance within the Citizens' Assembly itself[37]; and in the second instance by a vote of the people as a whole, which is crucial for democratic legitimacy. Indeed, the deliberations of the Citizens' Assembly provided the electorate with not just a proposal but also a ratio for that proposal, thereby serving the function that I see as ordinarily being reserved for political parties.

There probably are strict limits on the number of issues that can be handled in quite that way, with a deliberative mini-public being authorized to put a proposition directly to a vote of the people. There may also be limits to the number of deliberative mini-publics that can be convened, if they are to seize the public imagination and inform public debates.[38] Thus, there is no realistic prospect of deliberative mini-publics systematically supplanting the institutions of representative democracy. There is, however, every hope that deliberative mini-publics can serve as truly invaluable adjuncts to those other familiar features of the democratic process.

[36] That was short of the 60% required to trigger the government's promise to legislate the referendum result into law, but informed observers say it is far higher than the same proposal would have secured if coming from the legislature itself (Cutler and Johnston 2008).

[37] Although the final vote within the Assembly was near-unanimous: 146 to 7.

[38] The sheer logistics also militate against having too many Citizens' Assembly-style events: 160 people spending at least 13 weekends together over the course of 11 months, supported by a strong secretariat, is not a model than can be replicated too often (Warren and Pearce 2008).

References

Abramson, Jeffrey (1993). 'The Jury and Democratic Theory', *Journal of Political Philosophy*, 1: 45–68.

Ackerman, Bruce A. (1989). 'Why Dialogue?', *Journal of Philosophy*, 86: 5–22.

——and James S. Fishkin (2002). 'Deliberation Day', *Journal of Political Philosophy*, 10: 129–52. Reprinted in Fishkin and Laslett (2003: 7–30).

——— (2004). *Deliberation Day*. New Haven, CT: Yale University Press.

Adams, John (1776). Letter to John Penn. vol. 4, p. 205 in *Works of John Adams*. Boston, MA: Little, Brown, 1951.

Aldrich, John H. (1995). *Why Parties?* Chicago, IL: University of Chicago Press.

Alexander, Jeffrey C. (1987). 'The Social Requisites for Altruism and Voluntarism: Some Notes on What Makes a Sector Independent', *Sociological Theory*, 5 (2): 165–71.

ALI-ABA (American Law Institute American Bar Foundation) (1987). *Model Nonprofit Corporation Act (Revised)*. Available at: http://www.muridae.com/ nporegulation/documents/model_npo_corp_act.html (accessed 5 Jan. 2003).

Andreoni, James (1990). 'Impure Altruism and Donations to Public Goods: A Theory of Warm-Glow Giving', *Economic Journal*, 100: 464–77.

Anon (1992). 'Developments in the Law: Nonprofit Corporations', *Harvard Law Review*, 105: 1578–699.

Appiah, K. Anthony (1996). 'Race, Culture, Identity: Misunderstood Connections', in K. Anthony Appiah and Amy Gutmann (eds.), *Color Conscious: The Political Morality of Race*. Princeton, NJ: Princeton University Press, pp. 30–105.

Apter, David E. (1987). 'Mao's Republic', *Social Research*, 54: 691–729.

Aristotle (1984a). *Nicomachean Ethics*, trans. W. D. Ross and J. O. Urmson, vol. 2, pp. 1729–867 in J. Barnes (ed.), *The Complete Works of Aristotle*. Princeton, NJ: Princeton University Press.

——(1984b). *The Politics*, trans. B. Jowett, vol. 2, 1986–2150 in J. Barnes (ed.), *The Complete Works of Aristotle*. Princeton, NJ: Princeton University Press.

——(1984c). 'Rhetoric', trans. W. R. Roberts, vol. 2, pp. 2152–269 in J. Barnes (ed.), *The Complete Works of Aristotle*. Princeton, NJ: Princeton University Press, pp. 2152–269.

Arrhenius, Gustaf (2005). 'The Boundary Problem in Democratic Theory', in Folke Tersman (ed.), *Democracy Unbound: Basic Explorations I*. Stockholm: Filosofiska Institutionen, Stockholms Universitet, pp. 14–29.

Arrow, Kenneth J. and Gerard Debreu (1954). 'The Existence of an Equilibrium for a Competitive Economy', *Econometrica*, 22: 265–90.

—— and Leonid Hurwicz (1972). 'An Optimality Criterion for Decisions-Making Under Ignorance', in C. F. Carter and J. L. Ford (eds.), *Uncertainty and Expectations in Economics*. Oxford: Blackwell, pp. 1–11.

Arthur, W. Brian (1994). *Increasing Returns and Path Dependence in the Economy*. Ann Arbor: University of Michigan Press.

Asch, Solomon E. (1956). 'Studies of Independence and Conformity: A Minority of One Against a Unanimous Majority', *Psychological Monographs*, 70 (416).

Aumann, Robert J. (1976). 'Agreeing to Disagree', *Annals of Statistics*, 4: 1236–9.

Austen-Smith, David (1990). 'Information Transmission in Debate', *American Journal of Political Science*, 34: 124–52.

—— and Jeffrey S. Banks (1996). 'Information Aggregation, Rationality and the Condorcet Jury Theorem', *American Political Science Review*, 90: 34–45.

—— and Timothy J. Feddersen (2006). 'Deliberation, Preference Uncertainty and Voting Rules', *American Political Science Review*, 100: 209–17.

Austin, J. L. (1962). *How to Do Things with Words*. Oxford: Clarendon Press.

Australia, Senate Select Committee on a Certain Maritime Incident (2002). A *Certain Maritime Incident*. Available at: http://www.aph.gov.au/Senate/committee/ maritime_incident_ctte/maritime/report/contents.htm (accessed 5 Jan. 2003).

Australia, Senate, Finance and Public Administration References Committee (2003). *Commonwealth Contracts: A New Framework for Accountability*. Final Report on the Inquiry into the Mechanism for Providing Accountability to the Senate in Relation to Government Contracts. Available at: http://www.parliament.qld.gov. au/Comdocs/Public_Accounts/CICInfoPaper.pdf (accessed 13 Jan. 2003).

Axelrod, Robert (1984). *The Evolution of Cooperation*. New York: Basic Books.

—— (1986). 'An Evolutionary Approach to Norms', *American Political Science Review*, 80: 1095–1112.

Bacon, Francis (1597). 'Of faction', Essay 51 in Bacon (ed.), *Essays*. New York: William J. Black, Inc., 1942.

Bagehot, Walter (1966). *The English Constitution*. Ithaca, NY: Cornell University Press; originally published 1867.

Baiocchi, Gianpaolo (2001). 'Participation, Activism and Politics: The Porto Alegre Experiment and Deliberative Democratic Theory', *Politics & Society*, 29: 43–72. Reprinted in Fung and Wright (2003: 45–76).

Barber, Benjamin (1984). *Strong Democracy: Participatory Politics for a New Age*. Berkeley: University of California Press.

References

Barker, Ernest (1958). *Reflections on Government*. Oxford: Oxford University Press.

Barker, Anthony (1982). 'Governmental Bodies and Networks of Mutual Accountability', in A. Barker (ed.), *Quangos in Britain*. London: Macmillan.

Baron, Robert S. et al. (1996). 'Social Corroboration and Opinion Extremity', *Journal of Experimental Social Psychology*, 32: 537–60.

Barry, Brian (1964). 'The Public Interest', *Proceedings of the Aristotelian Society*, (Supplement) 38: 1–18.

—— (1986). 'Lady Chatterley's Lover and Doctor Fischer's Bomb Party: Liberalism, Pareto Optimality and the Problem of Objectionable Preferences', in Jon Elster and Aanund Hylland (eds.), *Foundations of Social Choice Theory*. Cambridge: Cambridge University Press, pp. 11–44.

—— (1989). 'Self-Government Revisited', in Barry (ed.), *Democracy, Power & Justice*. Oxford: Oxford University Press, pp. 156–86.

Barvosa-Carter, Edwina (2007). 'Mestiza Autonomy as Relational Autonomy: Ambivalence, Integrity and the Social Character of Free Will', *Journal of Political Philosophy*, 15: 1–21.

Bate, Paul (2000). 'Changing the Culture of a Hospital: From Hierarchy to Networked Community', *Public Administration*, 78: 485–512.

Behn, Robert D. (2001). *Rethinking Democratic Accountability*. Washington, DC: Brookings Institution.

—— (2003). 'Rethinking Accountability in Education: How Should Who Hold Whom Accountable for What?', *International Public Management Journal*, 6 (1): 43–73.

Beitz, Charles (1989). *Political Equality*. Princeton, NJ: Princeton University Press.

Benhabib, Seyla (1996). 'Toward a Deliberative Model of Democratic Legitimacy', in Benhabib (ed.), *Democracy & Difference*. Princeton, NJ: Princeton University Press, pp. 67–94.

Bentham, Jeremy (1827). *Rationale of Judicial Evidence*, vols. 6–7 in J. Bowring (ed.), *Works*. Edinburgh: W. Tait, 1843.

Bergström, Lars (2005). 'Democracy and Future Generations', in Folke Tersman (ed.), *Democracy Unbound: Basic Explorations I*. Stockholm: Filosofiska Institutionen, Stockholms Universitet, pp. 190–2.

Bessette, Joseph M. (1981). 'Deliberative Democracy: The Majority Principle in Republican Government', in Robert Goldwin and William Shambra (eds.), *How Democratic Is the Constitution?* Washington, DC: American Enterprise Institute, pp. 102–16.

—— (1994). *The Mild Voice of Reason: Deliberative Democracy and American National Government*. Chicago, IL: University of Chicago Press.

Bickel, Alexander (1962). *The Least Dangerous Branch: The Supreme Court at the Bar of Politics*. New Haven, CT: Yale University Press.

Bickford, Susan (1996). *The Dissonance of Democracy: Listening, Conflict and Citizenship.* Ithaca, NY: Cornell University Press.

Bikhchandani, Sushil, David Hirshleifer, and Ivo Welch (1992). 'A Theory of Fads, Fashion, Custom and Cultural Change as Informational Cascades', *Journal of Political Economy*, 100 (5): 992–1026.

————— (1998). 'Learning from the Behavior of Others: Conformity, Fads and Informational Cascades', *Journal of Economic Perspectives*, 12 (3): 151–70.

Birch, A. H. (1964). *Representative and Responsible Government: An Essay on the British Constitution.* London: Allen and Unwin.

Blinder, Alan S. and John Morgan (2000). 'Are Two Heads Better Than One?', an Experimental Analysis of Group vs. Individual Decisionmaking. Working Paper No. 7909. Cambridge, MA: National Bureau of Economic Research. Available at: www.nber.org/papers/w7909 (accessed 8 Sep. 2007).

Bohman, James (1995). 'Public Reason and Cultural Pluralism: Political Liberalism and the Problem of Moral Conflict', *Political Theory*, 23: 253–79.

—— (1996). *Public Deliberation.* Cambridge, MA: MIT Press.

—— (1998). 'The Coming of Age of Deliberative Democracy', *Journal of Political Philosophy*, 6: 400–25.

—— and William Rehg, eds. (1997). *Deliberative Democracy: Essays on Reason and Politics.* Cambridge, MA: MIT Press.

Bolingbroke, Henry St. John, Viscount (1733–4). 'A Dissertation upon Parties', in David Armitage (ed.), *Bolingbroke: Political Writings.* Cambridge: Cambridge University Press, 1997, pp. 1–192.

—— (1749). 'The Idea of a Patriot King', in David Armitage (ed.), *Bolingbroke: Political Writings.* Cambridge: Cambridge University Press, 1997, pp. 217–94.

Bond, R. and P. Smith (1996). 'Culture and Conformity: A Meta-Analysis of Studies Using Asch's Line Judgment Task', *Psychological Bulletin*, 119: 111–37.

Bovens, Mark (2002). 'Information Rights', *Journal of Political Philosophy*, 10: 317–41.

Brandt, Richard B. (1979). *A Theory of the Good and the Right.* Oxford: Clarendon Press.

Bratman, Michael (1992). 'Shared Cooperative Activity', *Philosophical Review*, 101: 327–41.

—— (1993). 'Shared Intentions', *Ethics*, 104: 97–113.

Brennan, Geoffrey (1996). 'Selection and the Currency of Reward', in R. E. Goodin (ed.), *The Theory of Institutional Design.* Cambridge: Cambridge University Press, pp. 256–75.

—— and Philip Pettit (1990). 'Unveiling the Vote', *British Journal of Political Science*, 20: 311–34.

Brighouse, Harry and Marc Fleurbaey (2006). On the fair allocation of power. Available at: http://cerses.shs.univ-paris5.fr/marc-fleurbaey_eng.htm (accessed 29 June 2006).

British Columbia Citizens' Assembly on Electoral Reform (2004). *Making Every Vote Count: The Case for Electoral Reform in British Columbia.* The British Columbia Citizens' Assembly on Electoral Reform Technical Report. Available at: www.citizensassembly.bc.ca/resources/TechReport(full).pdf (accessed 13 July 2005).

Brody, Evelyn (2002). 'Accountability and the Public Trust', in Salamon (2002: 471–98).

Brown, L. David (2003). 'Multiparty Social Action and Mutual Accountability', Mimeo, Hauser Center for Nonprofit Organizations, Kennedy School of Government, Harvard University.

——and Mark H. Moore (2001). 'Accountability, Strategy and International Non-Governmental Organizations', Hauser Center for Nonprofit Organizations, Kennedy School of Government, Working Paper No. 7. Harvard University. Available at: http://www/ksg.harvard.edu/hauser/useableknowledge/working_papers/7.pdf (accessed 28 Dec. 2002).

Brown, Mark B. (2006). 'Citizen Panels and the Concept of Representation', *Journal of Political Philosophy*, 14: 203–25.

Brubaker, Rogers (1992). *Citizenship and Nationhood in France and Germany.* Cambridge, MA: Harvard University Press.

Brutus (1787). Letter to the *New York Journal*, 18 Oct. 1787. Reprinted in Herbert J. Storing (ed.), *The Anti-Federalist.* Chicago, IL: University of Chicago Press, pp. 114–5.

Bryce, James (1897). *The American Commonwealth.* London: Macmillan.

Budge, Ian (1996). *The New Challenge of Direct Democracy.* Oxford: Polity.

Burke, Edmund (1770). *Thoughts on the Present Discontents.* London: Cassell, 1886.

Burnheim, John (1985). *Is Democracy Possible?* Berkeley: University of California Press.

Carson, Lyn and Brian Martin (1999). *Random Selection in Politics.* Westport, CT: Praeger.

Chaiken, S., W. Wood, and A. H. Eagley (1996). 'Principles of Persuasion', in E. T. Higgins and A. W. Kruglanski (eds.), *Social Psychology: Handbook of Basic Principles.* New York: Guilford Press, pp. 702–42.

Chambers, Simone (1996). *Reasonable Democracy: Jürgen Habermas and the Politics of Discourse.* Ithaca, NY: Cornell University Press.

——and Jeffrey Kopstein (2006). 'Civil Society and the State', in John S. Dryzek, Bonnie Honig, and Anne Phillips (eds.), *Oxford Handbook of Political Theory.* Oxford: Oxford University Press, pp. 363–81.

Charity Commission for England and Wales (1999). *CC9—Political Activities and Campaigning by Charities.* Available at: http://charity-commission.gov.uk/publications/cc9.asp (accessed 28 Dec. 2002).

——(2002*a*). *Giving Confidence in Charities.* Annual Report 2001–2002. London: Stationery Office. Available at: http://www.charity-commission.gov.uk/tcc/pdfs/annrep2002pt1.pdf (accessed 28 Dec. 2002).

——(2002b). *CC21—Registering as a Charity*. Available at: http://charity-commission.gov.uk/publications/cc21.asp (accessed 28 Dec. 2002).

Christensen, Tom and Per Lægreid (2002). 'New Public Management: Puzzles of Democracy and Influence of Citizens', *Journal of Political Philosophy*, 10: 267–95.

Civic Alliance to Rebuild Downtown New York (2002). *Listening to the City: Report of the Proceedings*. New York: Civic Alliance. Available at: www.listeningtothecity.org (accessed 12 July 2005).

Clark, Robert (1997). *Structuring the Accountability of Nonprofit Organizations*. Proceedings of the April 1997 Inaugural Conference, Hauser Center for Nonprofit Organizations, Harvard University. Available at: http://www.ksg.harvard.edu/hauser/useableknowledge/arcives/Innaugural%2Conference%20Proceedings.pdf (accessed 28 Dec. 2002).

Coase, R. H. (1937). 'The Nature of the Firm', *Economica*, 4: 386–405.

Cohen, Carl (1971). *Democracy*. New York: Free Press.

Cohen, Joshua (1989). 'Deliberation and Democratic Legitimacy', in A. Hamlin and P. Pettit (eds.), *The Good Polity*. Oxford: Blackwell, pp. 17–34.

——(1996). 'Procedure and Substance in Deliberative Democracy', in S. Benhabib (ed.), *Democracy and Difference*. Princeton, NJ: Princeton University Press, pp. 95–119.

——(1998). 'Democracy and Liberty', in Elster (1998a: 185–231).

——and Joel Rogers (1995). *Associations and Democracy*, ed. Erik Olin Wright. London: Verso.

——and Charles Sabel (1997). 'Directly-Deliberative Polyarchy', *European Law Journal*, 3: 313–42.

Cole, G. D. H. (1950). *Essays in Social Theory*. London: Macmillan.

Coleman, D. C. (1973). 'Gentlemen and Players', *Economic History Review*, 26 (Feb.): 92–116.

Coleman, James S. (1990). *Foundations of Social Theory*. Cambridge, MA: Harvard University Press.

Collins, Hugh (1999). *Regulating Contracts*. Oxford: Oxford University Press.

Condorcet, Marie Jean Antoine Nicolas de Caritat, Marquis de (1785). *Essai sur l'application de l'analyse à la probabilité des décisions rendues à la pluralité des voix*. Paris: l'Imprimerie Royale.

Considine, Mark (2002). 'The End of the Line? Accountable Government in the Age of Networks, Partnerships and Joined-Up Services', *Governance*, 15: 21–40.

Coote, Anna and Jo Lenaghan (1997). *Citizens' Juries: Theory into Practice*. London: Institute for Public Policy Research.

Corfman, Kim P. and Barbara E. Kahn (2005). 'The Influence of Member Heterogeneity on Dyad Judgment: Are Two Heads Better than One?', *Marketing Letters*, 6: 23–32.

Cox, Gary W. (2006). 'The Organization of Democratic Legislatures', in Barry R. Weingast and Donald A. Wittman (eds.), *The Oxford Handbook of Political Economy*. Oxford: Oxford University Press, pp. 141–62.

References

Crick, Bernard (1962). *In Defence of Politics*. London: Weidenfeld & Nicholson.

Crook, Richard C. (1999). ' "No-party" Politics and Local Democracy in Africa: Rawlings' Ghana in the 1990s and the "Ugandan model" ', *Democratization*, 6: 114–38.

Crosby, Ned and Doug Nethercut (2005). 'Citizens Juries: Creating a Trustworthy Voice of the People', in Gastil and Levine (2005: 111–9).

Curtis, Polly (2007). 'Researchers See Bias in Industry Funded Studies', *Guardian Weekly*, 19–25 (Jan.), p. 21.

Cutler, Fred and Richard Johnston (2008). 'The BC Citizens' Assembly as Agenda Setter: Shaking up the Referendum Process', in Warren and Pearse (2008*a*).

Dahl, Robert A. (1956). *A Preface to Democratic Theory*. Chicago, IL: University of Chicago Press.

—— (1970). *After the Revolution*. New Haven, CT: Yale University Press.

—— (1979). 'Procedural Democracy', in P. Laslett and J. S. Fishkin (eds.), *Philosophy, Politics and Society*. Oxford: Blackwell, pp. 97–133.

—— (1989). *Democracy & Its Critics*. New Haven, CT: Yale University Press.

—— and Charles E. Lindblom (1953). *Politics, Economics and Welfare*. New York: Harper & Row.

Dawes, Robyn M., Alphons J. C. van de Kragt, and John M. Orbell (1990). 'Cooperation for the Benefit of Us—Not Me, or My Conscience', in Jane J. Mansbridge (ed.), *Beyond Self-Interest*. Chicago, IL: University of Chicago Press, pp. 97–110.

Day, Patricia and Rudolph Klein (1987). *Accountabilities: Five Public Services*. London: Tavistock.

De Smith, Stanley and Rodney Brazier (1989). *Constitutional and Administrative Law*, 6th edn. Harmondsworth, Mddx.: Penguin.

—— and Lester M. Salamon (2002). 'Purchase-of-Service Contracting', in Salamon and Elliott (2002: 319–39).

Delors, Jacques et al. (1991). *Subsidiarity: The Challenge of Change*. Maastricht: European Institute of Public Administration.

Dienel, Peter C. (1999). 'Planning Cells and Citizens' Juries—Foundations of Political Engineering of the Future', available at: http://www.planet-thanet. fsnet.co.uk/groups/wdd/99_planning_cells.htm (accessed 11 July 2005).

Dillehay, R. C., C. A. Insko, et al. (1966). 'Logical Consistency and Attitude Change', *Journal of Personality & Social Psychology*, 3: 646–54.

Douglas, James (1983). *Why Charity? The Case for a Third Sector*. Beverley Hills, CA: Sage.

Druckman, James N. and Arthur Lupia (2000). 'Preference Formation', *Annual Review of Political Science*, 3: 1–24.

Dryzek, John S. (1990). *Discursive Democracy*. Cambridge: Cambridge University Press.

—— (1999). 'Transnational Democracy', *Journal of Political Philosophy*, 7: 30–51.

—— (2000). *Deliberative Democracy and Beyond*. Oxford: Oxford University Press.

——(2001). 'Legitimacy and Economy in Deliberative Democracy', *Political Theory*, 29: 651–69.

——(2006). *Deliberative Global Politics*. Cambridge: Polity Press.

——and Leslie Holmes (2002). *Postcommunist Democratization*. Cambridge: Cambridge University Press.

——and Simon Niemeyer (2006). 'Discursive Representation', paper presented at Rethinking Democratic Representation Conference, University of British Columbia, 18–19 May 2006. Available at: http://deliberativedemocracy. anu.edu.au/references/DiscursiveRepresentation.pdf (accessed 15 Sep. 2007).

——David Downes, Christian Hunold, David Schlosberg, with Hans-Kristian Hernes (2003). *Green States and Social Movements*. Oxford: Oxford University Press.

Duverger, Maurice (1959). *Political Parties*, trans. Barbara and Robert North, 2nd edn. London: Methuen.

Edelman, Murray (1988). *Constructing the Political Spectacle*. Chicago, IL: University of Chicago Press.

Elster, Jon (1986). 'The Market and the Forum: Three Varieties of Political Theory', in Elster and A. Hylland (eds.), *Foundations of Social Choice Theory*. Cambridge: Cambridge University Press, pp. 103–32.

——ed. (1998*a*). *Deliberative Democracy*. Cambridge: Cambridge University Press.

Elster, Jon (1998*b*). 'Introduction', in Elster (1998*a*: 1–18).

Esping-Andersen, Gøsta (1990). *The Three Worlds of Welfare Capitalism*. Oxford: Polity.

Estlund, David (1993). 'Making Truth Safe for Democracy', in David Copp, Jean Hampton, and John E. Roemer (eds.), *The Idea of Democracy*. New York: Cambridge University Press, pp. 71–100.

European Union, Commission (2001). *European Governance: A White Paper*. COM(2001)428 final. Available at: http://europa.eu.int/comm/governance/ white_paper/index_en.htm (accessed 27 Feb. 2003).

Fearon, James (1998). 'Deliberation as Discussion', in Elster (1998*a*: 44–68).

Feddersen, Timothy J. and Wolfgang Pesendorfer (1998). 'Convicting the Innocent: The Inferiority of Unanimous Jury Verdicts Under Strategic Voting', *American Political Science Review*, 92: 23–36.

Feinberg, Joel (1970). 'The Nature and Value of Rights', *Journal of Value Inquiry*, 4: 243–57. Reprinted in Feinberg, *Rights, Justice & the Bounds of Liberty*. Princeton, NJ: Princeton University Press, 1980, pp. 143–58.

——(1985). *Offense to Others*. New York: Oxford University Press.

Ferejohn, John (2008). 'The Citizens' Assembly Model', in Warren and Pearse (2008*a*).

Finnemore, Martha and Kathryn Sikkink (1998). 'International Norm Dynamics and Political Change', *International Organization*, 52: 887–917.

Firth, Roderick (1952). 'Ethical Absolutism and the Ideal Observer', *Philosophy & Phenomenological Research*, 12: 317–45.

Fisher, R. and W. Ury (1983). *Getting to Yes: Negotiating Agreement Without Giving In.* Harmondsworth, Mddx.: Penguin.

Fishkin, James S. (1991). *Democracy and Deliberation: New Directions for Democratic Reform.* New Haven, CT: Yale University Press.

—— (1995). *The Voice of the People.* New Haven, CT: Yale University Press.

—— (1997). *The Voice of the People,* rev. edn. New Haven, CT: Yale University Press.

—— (2003). 'Consulting the Public Through Deliberative Polling', *Journal of Policy Analysis and Management,* 22 (1, Winter): 128–33.

—— and Peter Laslett, eds. (2003*a*). *Debating Deliberative Democracy.* Philosophy, Politics and Society, series 7. Oxford: Blackwell.

—— —— (2003*b*). 'Introduction', in Fishkin and Laslett (2003*a*: 1–6).

—— and Cynthia Farrar (2005). 'Deliberative Polling: From Experiment to Community Resource', in Gastil and Levine (2005: 68–79).

—— Robert C. Luskin, and Henry E. Brady (2003). 'Inform Public Opinion About Foreign Policy: The Uses of Deliberative Polling', *Brookings Review,* 21 (3, Summer): 16–19.

—— Baogang He, Robert C. Luskin, and Alice Siu (2006). 'Democracy in an Unlikely Place: Deliberative Polling in China', available at: http://cdd.stanford.edu/research/papers/2006/china-unlikely.pdf (accessed 20 Sep. 2007).

Føllesdal, Andreas (1998). 'Subsidiarity', *Journal of Political Philosophy,* 6: 231–59.

Fox, Jonathan A. and L. David Brown, eds. (1998). *The Struggle for Accountability: The World Bank, NGOs and Grassroots Movements.* Cambridge, MA: MIT Press.

Fraser, Nancy (1997). 'Rethinking the Public Sphere: A Contribution to the Critique of Actually Existing Democracy', in Fraser (ed.), *Justice Interruptus.* New York: Routledge, pp. 69–98.

French, Peter A. (1979). 'The Corporation as a Moral Person', *American Philosophical Quarterly,* 16: 207–15.

Frey, Bruno S. and Iris Bohnet (1996). 'Cooperation, Communication and Communitarianism: An Experimental Approach', *Journal of Political Philosophy,* 4: 323–36.

Friedman, Milton (1962). *Capitalism and Freedom.* Chicago, IL: University of Chicago Press.

Fuller, Lon (1971). *Anatomy of the Law.* Harmondsworth, Mddx.: Penguin.

Fung, Archon (2001). 'Deliberative Democracy, Chicago Style: Grass-Roots Governance in Policing and Public Education', *Politics & Society,* 29: 73–104. Reprinted in Fung and Wright (2003: 111–43).

—— (2003*a*). 'Recipes for Public Spheres: Eight Institutional Choices and Their Consequences', *Journal of Political Philosophy,* 11: 338–67.

—— (2003*b*). 'Servants of the Poor: An Account of Democratic Accountability in Non-Profit Organizations', paper presented to Crisis of Governance Conference, Hauser Center for Nonprofit Organizations, Kennedy School of Government, Harvard University, April 2003.

—— (2004). *Empowered Participation: Reinventing Urban Democracy*. Princeton, NJ: Princeton University Press.

—— (2005). 'Deliberation Before the Revolution: Toward an Ethics of Deliberative Democracy in an Unjust World', *Political Theory*, 33: 397–419.

—— (2006). 'Democratizing the Policy Process', in Michael Moran, Martin Rein, and Robert E. Goodin (eds.), *Oxford Handbook of Public Policy*. Oxford: Oxford University Press, pp. 669–87.

—— and Erik Olin Wright (2003a). 'Thinking About Empowered Participatory Governance', in Fung and Wright (2003b: 3–44).

—— —— eds. (2003b). *Deepening Democracy: Institutional Innovations in Empowered Participatory Governance*. London: Verso.

Galanter, Marc (1984). *Competing Equalities: Law and the Backward Classes in India*. Delhi: Oxford University Press.

Galloway, Gloria (2004). Ontario Asks Citizen Juries for Advice on Budget. Globe & Mail, 8 Jan. Available at: www.oacas.org/Whatsnew/newsstories/04/jan/8advice.pdf (accessed 2 Aug. 2005).

Gamson, William A. (1992). *Talking Politics*. Cambridge: Cambridge University Press.

Gardiner, Stephen M. (2006). 'A Core Precautionary Principle', *Journal of Political Philosophy*, 14: 33–60.

Gastil, John and Peter Levine, eds. (2005). *The Deliberative Democracy Handbook*. San Francisco, CA: Jossey-Bass.

Gaus, Gerald F. (1997). 'Does Democracy Reveal the Voice of the People? Four Takes on Rousseau', *Australasian Journal of Philosophy*, 75: 141–62.

—— (2003). *Contemporary Theories of Liberalism*. London: Sage.

Gibson, Diane and Robert E. Goodin (1999). 'The Veil of Vagueness', in Morten Egeberg and Per Lægreid (eds.), *Organizing Political Institutions: Essays for Johan P. Olsen*. Oslo: Scandinavian University Press, pp. 357–85.

Gibson, Gordon (2002). *Report on the Constitution of the Citizens' Assembly on Electoral Reform*. Available at: www.citizensassembly.bc.ca/resourcesgibson_report.pdf (accessed 13 July 2005).

Gilbert, Margaret (1989). *On Social Facts*. London: Routledge.

Goodin, Robert E. (1977). 'Convention Quotas and Communal Representation', *British Journal of Political Science*, 7: 255–72.

—— (1980a). 'Making Moral Incentives Pay', *Policy Sciences*, 12: 131–45.

—— (1980b). *Manipulatory Politics*. New Haven, CT: Yale University Press.

—— (1982). *Political Theory and Public Policy*. Chicago, IL: University of Chicago Press.

—— (1986). 'Laundering Preferences', in J. Elster and A. Hylland (eds.), *Foundations of Social Choice Theory*. Cambridge: Cambridge University Press, pp. 75–101.

—— (1988a). *Reasons for Welfare*. Princeton, NJ: Princeton University Press.

—— (1988b). 'What is so Special About Our Fellow Countrymen?', *Ethics*, 98: 663–86.

Goodin, Robert E. (1989). 'Theories of Compensation', *Oxford Journal of Legal Studies*, 9: 56–75.

—— (1992*a*). *Motivating Political Morality*. Oxford: Blackwell.

—— (1992*b*). 'Toward a Minimally Presumptuous Social Welfare Policy', in Philippe Van Parijs (ed.), *Arguing for Basic Income*. London: Verso, pp. 195–214.

—— (1995). 'Political Ideals and Political Practice', *British Journal of Political Science*, 25: 37–56.

—— (1996*a*). 'Enfranchising the Earth, and Its Alternatives', *Political Studies*, 44: 835–49.

—— (1996*b*). 'Institutionalizing the Public Interest: The Defense of Deadlock and Beyond', *American Political Science Review*, 90: 331–43.

—— (2000*a*). 'Accountability—Elections as One Form', in Richard Rose (ed.), *The International Encyclopedia of Elections*. Washington, DC: Congressional Quarterly Press, pp. 2–4.

—— (2000*b*). 'Crumbling Pillars: Social Security Futures', *Political Quarterly*, 71: 144–50.

—— (2000*c*). 'Democratic Deliberation Within', *Philosophy & Public Affairs*, 29: 79–107. Reprinted in Fishkin and Laslett (2003: 54–79) and revised in Goodin (2003*b*: 169–93).

—— (2000*d*). 'Institutional Gaming', *Governance*, 13: 523–33.

—— (2001). 'Consensus Interruptus', *The Journal of Ethics*, 5: 121–31.

—— (2002). 'The Paradox of Persisting Opposition', *Politics, Philosophy and Economics*, 1: 109–46.

—— (2003*a*). 'Heuristics of *Public* Administration', in Mie Augier and James G. March (eds.), *Models of a Man: Essays in Honor of Herbert A. Simon*. Cambridge, MA: MIT Press, pp. 233–50.

—— (2003*b*). *Reflective Democracy*. Oxford: Oxford University Press.

—— (2006). 'Truth, Justice and Democracy', in Giuseppe Eusepi and Alan Hamlin (eds.), *Beyond Conventional Economics: The Limits of Rational Behaviour in Political Decision-Making*. Cheltenham: Elgar, pp. 81–107.

—— (2007*a*). 'The Epistemic Benefits of Multiple Biased Observers', *Episteme*, 3: 166–74.

—— (2007*b*). 'Rationalizing Discursive Anomalies', *Theoria*, Forthcoming.

—— Bruce Headey, Rudd Muffels and Henk-Jan Dirven (1999). *The Real Worlds of Welfare Capitalism*. Cambridge: Cambridge University Press.

—— and Frank Jackson (2007). 'Freedom from Fear', *Philosophy & Public Affairs*, 35: 249–65.

—— Carole Pateman, and Roy Pateman (1997). 'Simian Sovereignty', *Political Theory*, 25: 821–49.

Gore, Al (1993). *From Red Tape to Results: Creating a Government that Works Better and Costs Less*. Report of the National Performance Review. Washington, DC: Government Printing Office.

Gould, Carol (1988). *Rethinking Democracy*. Cambridge: Cambridge University Press.

Greenberg, Edward S. (1986). *Workplace Democracy: The Political Effects of Participation*. Ithaca, NY: Cornell University Press.

Grice, H. Paul (1975). 'Logic and Conversation', in Donald Davidson and Gilbert Harman (eds.), *The Logic of Grammar*. Encino, CA: Dickenson Publishing Co, pp. 64–75.

——(1989). *Studies in the Way of Words*. Cambridge, MA: Harvard University Press.

Griffiths, A. Phillips (1960). 'How Can One Person Represent Another?' Proceedings of the Aristotelian Society, Supplementary Volume, 34: 187–208.

Grofman, Bernard and Scott L. Feld (1988). 'Rosseau's General Will: A Condorcetian Perspective', *American Political Science Review*, 82: 567–76.

——Guillermo Owen, and Scott L. Feld (1983). 'Thirteen Theorems in Search of the Truth', *Theory & Decision*, 15: 261–78.

Grønbjerg, Kirsten A. and Lester M. Salamon (2002). 'Devolution, Marketization and the Changing Shape of Government-Nonprofit Relations', in Lester M. Salamon (ed.), *The State of Nonprofit America*. Washington, DC: Brookings Institution, for the Aspen Institute, pp. 447–70.

Guinier, Lani (1989). 'Keeping the Faith: Black Voters in the Post-Reagan Era', *Harvard Civil Rights-Civil Liberties Law Review*, 24: 393–435.

——(1993). 'Groups, Representation and Race-Conscious Districting: A Case of the Emperor's Clothes', *Texas Law Review*, 71: 1589–642.

Gutmann, Amy and Dennis Thompson (1996). *Democracy and Disagreement*. Cambridge, MA: Harvard University Press.

Gutmann, Amy and Dennis Thompson (2002). 'Deliberative Democracy Beyond Process', *Journal of Political Philosophy*, 10: 153–74.

——— (2004). *Why Deliberative Democracy?* Princeton, NJ: Princeton University Press.

Haas, Peter M. (1989). 'Do Regimes Matter? Epistemic Communities and Mediterranean Pollution Control', *International Organization*, 43: 377–403.

——(1992). 'Epistemic Communities and International Policy Coordination', *International Organization*, 46: 1–35.

Habermas, Jürgen (1979). *Communication and the Evolution of Society*. Boston, MA: Beacon Press.

——(1982). 'A Reply to My Critics', in John Thompson and David Held (eds.), *Habermas: Critical Debates*. Cambridge, MA: MIT Press, pp. 219–83.

——(1984). *The Theory of Communicative Action: Volume 1*, trans. T. McCarthy. Boston, MA: Beacon Press.

——(1987). *The Theory of Communicative Action: Volume 2*, trans. T. McCarthy. Boston, MA: Beacon Press.

——(1995). 'Reconciliation Through the Public Use of Reason: Remarks on John Rawls's *Political Liberalism*', *Journal of Philosophy*, 92: 109–31.

Habermas, Jürgen (1996). *Between Facts and Norms*, trans. W. Rehg. Cambridge: Polity Press; originally published 1992.

—— (2001). 'Constitutional Democracy: A Paradoxical Union of Contradictory Principles?', *Political Theory*, 29: 766–81.

Hajer, Marten (2003). 'Policy Without a Polity? Policy Analysis and the Institutional Void', *Policy Sciences*, 36: 175–95.

Hall, Peter A. and David Soskice, eds. (2001). *Varieties of Capitalism*. Oxford: Oxford University Press.

Halley, Janet E. (1998). 'Gay Rights and Identity Imitation: Issues in the Ethics of Representation', in David Kairys (ed.), *The Politics of Law: A Progressive Critique*. New York: Basic Book.

Hamilton, Alexander (1788). 'Federalist No. 35', in Jacob E. Cooke (ed.), *The Federalist*. Middletown, CT: Wesleyan University Press, 1961, pp. 220–1.

Hansmann, Henry B. (1980). 'The Role of Nonprofit Enterprises', *Yale Law Journal*, 89: 835–901.

Hanson, Robin (2003). *Shall We Vote on Values, But Bet on Beliefs?* Available at: hanson.gmu.edu/futarchy.pdf (accessed 26 Sep. 2007).

Harsanyi, John C. (1975). 'Can the Maximin Principle Serve as a Basis for Morality? A Critique of John Rawls' Theory', *American Political Science Review*, 69: 594–606.

Hart, H. L. A. (1961). *The Concept of Law*. Oxford: Clarendon Press.

Hastie, Reid (1986). 'Experimental Evidence on Group Accuracy', in B. Grofman and G. Owen (eds.), *Information Pooling and Group Decision Making*. Greenwich, CT: JAI Press, pp. 129–57.

Held, David (1995). *Democracy and the Global Order*. Oxford: Polity.

Heller, Richard (2004). *GM Nation? The Findings of the Public Debate*. Report of the GM Public Debate Steering Board. Available at: www.gmnation.org.uk/ut_09/ut_9_6.htm (accessed 11 July 2005).

Hendriks, Carolyn M. (2005*a*). 'Consensus Conferences and Planning Cells: Lay Citizen Deliberations', in Gastil and Levine (2005: 80–110).

—— (2005*b*). 'Public Deliberation and Interest Organisations', Ph.D. thesis, Australian National University.

—— (2006). 'Integrated Deliberation: Reconciling Civil Society's Dual Role in Deliberative Democracy', *Political Studies*, 54: 486–508.

—— John S. Dryzek, and Christian Hunold (2007). 'Turning up the Heat: Partisanship in Deliberative Innovation', *Political Studies*, 55: 362–83.

Herzlinger, Regina (1996). 'Can Public Trust in Nonprofit and Governments Be Restored?', *Harvard Business Review*, 9 (2): 98–108.

Hillhouse, James (1808). Speech by the Senator from Connecticut, April 12, 1808. *Annals*, 10th Congress, 1st Session, pp. 332–58. Reprinted in part at pp. 231–35 in *A Second Federalist: Congress Creates a Government*, eds. Charles S. Hyneman and George W. Carey. New York: Appleton-Century-Crofts, 1967.

Hobbes, Thomas (1647). *De Cive*. Translated as *On the Citizen*, eds. and trans. Richard Tuck and Michael Silverthorne. Cambridge: Cambridge University Press, 1998.

—— (1651). *Leviathan*, ed. M. Oakeshott. Oxford: Blackwell, 1946.

Hofstadter, Richard (1969). *The Idea of a Party System*. Berkeley: University of California Press.

Holmes, Stephen (1988). 'Gag rules, or the Politics of Omission', in J. Elster and R. Slagstad (eds.), *Constitutionalism and Democracy*. Cambridge: Cambridge University Press, pp. 19–58.

Hooker, Richard (1989). *Of the Laws of Ecclesiastical Polity*, ed. A. S. McGrade. Cambridge: Cambridge University Press; originally published 1554–1600.

Horder, Jeremy (1997). 'Two Histories and Four Hidden Principles of *Mens Rea*', *Law Quarterly Review*, 113: 95–119.

Horlick-Jones, Tom, John Walls, Gene Rowe, Nick Pidgeon, Woulter Poortinga, and Tim O'Riordan (2004). *A Deliberative Future? An Independent Evaluation of the GM Nation?* Public debate about the possible commercialisation of transgenic crops in Britain, 2003. Norwich: Understanding Risk Programme, University of East Anglia. Available at: www.uea.ac.uk/env/pur/gm_future_top_copy_12_feb_04.pdf-8 Jul 2005 (accessed 10 July 2005).

Hume, David (1760). 'Of Parties in General', in Part I, chap. 8 of *Essays: Literary, Moral and Political*. London: A. Millar.

Hyneman, Charles S. (1940). 'Who Makes Our Laws?', *Political Science Quarterly*, 55: 556–81.

Jacobs, Lawrence, Theodore Marmor, and Jonathan Oberlander (1999). 'The Oregon Plan and the Political Paradox of Rationing', *Journal of Health Policy, Politics & Law*, 24: 161–80.

Janis, Irving L. (1982). *Groupthink*, 2nd edn. Boston, MA: Houghton Mifflin.

Jefferson, Thomas (1801). 'Manual of Parliamentary Practice', in W. S. Howell (ed.), *Jefferson's Parliamentary Writings*, papers of Thomas Jefferson, 2nd series. Princeton, NJ: Princeton University Press, 1988, pp. 353–426.

Johnson, B. (1989). 'Effects of Involvement on Persuasion: A Meta-Analysis', *Psychological Bulletin*, 106: 290–314.

Johnson, Genevieve Fuji (2007). 'The Discourse of Democracy in Canadian Nuclear Waste Management', *Policy Sciences*, 40: 79–99.

Joss, Simon and John Durand, eds. (1995). *Public Participation in Science: The Role of Consensus Conferences in Europe*. London: Science Museum.

Kahneman, Daniel, Paul Slovic, and Amos Tversky, eds. (1982). *Judgment Under Uncertainty: Heuristics and Biases*. Cambridge: Cambridge University Press.

—— and Amos Tversky, eds. (2000). *Choices, Values and Frames*. Cambridge: Cambridge University Press.

Kalven, Harry Jr. and Hans Zeisel (1966). *The American Jury*. Chicago, IL: University of Chicago Press.

Kapur, Kanika and Burton A. Weisbrod (1999). 'The Roles of Government and Nonprofit Suppliers in Mixed Industries', WP-99-9, Institute for Policy Research, Northwestern University. Available at: http://econpapers.hhs.se/paper/wopnwuipr/99-9.htm (accessed 12 Feb. 2003).

Karpowitz, Christopher F. and Jane Mansbridge (2005). 'Disagreement and Consensus: The Importance of Dynamic Updating in Public Deliberation', in Gastil and Levine (2005: 237–53).

Kasfir, Nelson (1998). ' "No-Party Democracy" in Uganda', *Journal of Democracy*, 9: 49–63.

Kateb, George (1981). 'The Moral Distinctiveness of Representative Democracy', *Ethics*, 91: 357–74.

Keck, Margaret and Kathleen Sikkink (1998). *Activists Beyond Borders: Advocacy Networks in International Politics*. Ithaca, NY: Cornell University Press.

Keohane, Robert O. (2002). *Power and Governance in a Partially Globalized World*. London: Routledge.

——(2003). 'Global Governance and Democratic Accountability', in D. Held and M. Koenig-Archibugi (eds.), *Taming Globalization: Frontiers of Governance*. Oxford: Polity Press, pp. 130–59.

——and Joseph S. Nye, Jr. (2001). 'The Club Model of Multilateral Cooperation and Problems of Democratic Legitimacy', in R. B. Porter (ed.), *Efficiency, Equity and Legitimacy: The Multilateral Trading System at the Millennium*. Washington, DC: Brookings Institution. Reprinted in pp. 219–44 in R. O. Keohane, *Power and Governance in a Partially Globalized World*. London: Routledge, 2002.

Kiewiet, D. Roderick (1983). *Micropolitics and Macroeconomics*. Chicago, IL: University of Chicago Press.

Kinder, Donald R. R. and Donald Herzog (1993). 'Democratic Discussion', in G. E. Marcus and R. L. Hanson (eds.), *Reconsidering the Democratic Public*. University Park: Pennsylvania State University Press, pp. 347–77.

——and Lynne M. Sanders (1996). *Divided by Color: Racial Politics and Democratic Ideals*. Chicago, IL: University of Chicago Press.

——and D. Roderick Kiewiet (1981). 'Sociotropic Politics: The American Case', *British Journal of Political Science*, 11: 129–61.

Kirkpatrick, Jeanne (1975). 'Representation in the American National Conventions: The Case of 1972', *British Journal of Political Science*, 5: 265–322.

Klingemann, Hans-Dieter, Richard I. Hofferbert, and Ian Budge (1994). *Parties, Policies & Democracy*. Boulder, CO: Westview.

Kneese, Allen V. and Charles L. Schultze (1975). *Pollution, Prices and Public Policy*. Washington, DC: Brookings Institution.

Knight, Jack and James Johnson (1994). 'Aggregation and Deliberation: On the Possibility of Democratic Legitimacy', *Political Theory*, 22: 277–96.

Kocher, Martin G. and Matthias Sutter (2005). 'The Decision Maker Matters: Individual Versus Group Behaviour in Experimental Beauty-Contest Games', *Economic Journal*, 115: 200–23.

Kreps, David M. (1990). 'Corporate Culture and Economic Theory', in J. Alt and K. Shepsle (eds.), *Perspectives on Positive Political Economy*. Cambridge: Cambridge University Press, pp. 90–143.

Krislov, Samuel (1974). *Representative Bureaucracy*. Englewood Cliffs, NJ: Prentice-Hall.

Kuran, Timur (1995). *Private Truths, Public Lies*. Cambridge, MA: Harvard University Press.

Laslett, Peter (1956). 'The Face to Face Society', in P. Laslett (ed.), *Philosophy, Politics and Society*, 1st series. Oxford: Blackwell, pp. 157–84.

Le Grand, Julian (1991). 'Quasi-Markets and Social Policy', *Economic Journal*, 101 (408): 1256–67.

——Dan Corry, and Rosemary Radcliffe (1997). *Public Private Partnerships*. London: Institute for Public Policy Research.

Lehr, R. L., W. Guild, D. L. Thomas, and B. G. Swezey (2003). 'Listening to Customers: How Deliberative Polling Helped build 1000 mw of new renewable energy projects in Texas', Technical Report NREL/TP-620-33177. Golden, CO: National Renewable Energy Laboratory.

Lehrer, Keith (1976). 'When Rational Disagreement Is Impossible', *Noûs*, 10: 327–32.

——(2001*a*). 'Individualism Versus Communitarianism: A Consensual Compromise', *Journal of Ethics*, 5: 105–20.

——(2001*b*). 'The Rationality of Dissensus: A Reply to Goodin', *Journal of Ethics*, 5: 132–6.

——and Carl Wagner (1981). *Rational Consensus in Science and Society: A Philosophical and Mathematical Study*. Dordrecht: Reidel.

Lemarchand, René and Keith Legg (1972). 'Political Clientelism and Development: A Preliminary Analysis', *Comparative Politics*, 4: 149–78.

Lempinen, Miko (1999). 'Consultative Relationship Between the United Nations and Non-Governmental Organizations', Mimeo, Institute for Human Rights, Åbo Akademi University, Åbo/Turku, Finland. Available at: http://www.abo.fi/instut/imr/norfa/miko_ngo.pdf (accessed 28 Dec. 2002).

Lenaghan, Jo, Bill New, and Elizabeth Mitchell (1996). 'Setting Priorities: Is There a Role for Citizens' Juries?', *British Medical Journal*, 312 (7046): 1591–4.

Lesser, Leard I., Cara B. Ebbeling, Merrill Goozner, David Wypij, and David S. Ludwig (2007). 'Relationship Between Funding Source and Conclusion Among Nutrition-Related Scientific Articles', *PLOS Medicine* 4(1): e5. Available at: <doi:10.1371/journal.pmed.0040005> or <medicine.plosjournals.org/perlserv/?request=get-document&doi=10.1371%2Fjournal.pmed.0040005>.

Levine, Peter, Archon Fung, and John Gastil (2005). In Gasti and Levine (2005: 271–88).

Lewis, David (1969). *Convention*. Oxford: Blackwell.

——(1973). *Counterfactuals*. Cambridge, MA: Harvard University Press.

Light, Paul C. (2000). *Making Nonprofits Work*. Washington, DC: Aspen Institute, Brookings Institution Press.

Lindblom, Charles E. (1965). *The Intelligence of Democracy*. New York: Free Press.

——(1977). *Politics and Markets*. New York: Basic Books.

Lindsay, A. D. (1935). *The Essentials of Democracy*, 2nd edn. London: Oxford University Press; originally published 1929.

Lipsey, Richard G. and Kelvin J. Lancaster (1956). 'The General Theory of Second Best', *Review of Economic Studies*, 24: 11–33.

List, Christian and Robert E. Goodin (2001). 'Epistemic Democracy: Generalizing the Condorcet Jury Theorem', *Journal of Political Philosophy*, 9: 276–306.

——Robert C. Luskin, James S. Fishkin, and Iain McLean (2007). 'Deliberation, Single-Peakedness, and the Possibility of Meaningful Deliberation: Evidence from Deliberative Polls', Available at: http://cdd.stanford.edu/research/papers/2007/meaningful-democracy.pdf (accessed 28 July 2007).

Locke, John (1975). *An Essay Concerning Human Understanding*, ed. Peter H. Nidditch. Oxford: Clarendon Press.

Luker, Kristen (1984). *Abortion and the Politics of Motherhood*. Berkeley, CA: University of California Press.

Lukensmeyer, Carolyn J., Joe Goldman, and Steven Brigham (2005). 'A Town Meeting for the Twenty-First Century', in Gastil and Levine (2005: 154–63).

Lupia, Arthur (1994). 'Shortcuts Versus Encyclopedias: Information and Voting Behavior in California Insurance Reform Elections', *American Political Science Review*, 88: 63–76.

——(2002). 'Deliberation Disconnected: What it Takes to Improve Civic Competence', *Law & Contemporary Problems*, 65 (2): 133–50.

Lupia, Arthur (2003). *Necessary Conditions for Improving Civic Competence*. Available at: http://www-personal.umich.edu/~lupia/necessary.pdf (accessed 17 Apr. 2003).

——and John G. Matsuaka (2004). 'Direct Democracy: New Approaches to Old Questions', *Annual Review of Political Science*, 7: 463–82.

Luskin, Robert C., James S. Fishkin, and Roger Jowell (2002). 'Considered Opinions: Deliberative Polling in Britain', *British Journal of Political Science*, 32: 455–87.

Lyons, Mark and Vanessa Chan (1999). 'The Effect of Competitive Markets on Nonprofit Organisations—The Case of Employment Services', paper presented to the National Social Policy Conference, University of New South Wales, Sydney, 22 July.

Maas, Arthur (1983). *Congress and the Common Good*. New York: Basic Books.

Macaulay, Stewart (1963). 'Non-Contractual Relations in Business: A Preliminary Study', *American Sociological Review*, 28: 55–67.

MacCallum, Gerald C. Jr. (1966). 'Legislative Intent', *Yale Law Journal*, 75: 754–87.

Macedo, Stephen, ed. (1999). *Deliberative Politics*. New York: Oxford University Press.

Mackie, Gerry (1996). 'Ending Footbinding and Infibulation: A Convention Account', *American Sociological Review*, 61: 999–1017.

——(1998). 'All Men Are Liars: Is Democracy Meaningless?', in Elster (1998*a*: 69–96).

——(2003). *Democracy Defended*. Cambridge: Cambridge University Press.

Mackinnon, Catharine A. (1993). *Only Words*. Cambridge, MA: Harvard University Press.

Macpherson, C. B. (1973). *Democratic Theory*. Oxford: Clarendon Press.

——(1977). *The Life and Times of Liberal Democracy*. Oxford: Oxford University Press.

Madison, James (1787). 'Federalist No. 10', in Jacob E. Cooke (ed.), *The Federalist*. Middletown, CT: Wesleyan University Press, 1961, pp. 56–65.

Majone, Giandomenico (2006). 'Agenda Setting', in Michael Moran, Martin Rein, and Robert E. Goodin (eds.), *Oxford Handbook of Public Policy*. Oxford: Oxford University Press, pp. 228–50.

Mandeville, Bernard (1989). *The Fable of the Bees*, ed. Philip Harth. Harmondsworth, Mddx.: Penguin.

Manin, Bernard (1987). 'On Legitimacy and Political Deliberation', *Political Theory*, 15: 338–68.

——(1997). *The Principles of Representative Government*. Cambridge: Cambridge University Press.

——Adam Przeworski, and Susan C. Stokes (1999). 'Elections and Representation', in Przeworski, Stokes and Manin (eds.), *Democracy, Accountability and Representation*. Cambridge: Cambridge University Press, pp. 29–54.

Mansbridge, Jane J. (1980). *Beyond Adversary Democracy*. New York: Basic Books.

Mansbridge, Jane J. (1988). 'Motivating Deliberation in Congress', vol. 2, in Sarah Baumgartner Thurow (ed.), *Constitutionalism in America*. New York: University Press of America, pp. 59–86.

——(1992). 'A Deliberative Theory of Interest Representation', in Mark P. Petracca (ed.), *The Politics of Interests*. Boulder, CO: Westview, pp. 32–57.

——(1995). 'What Is the Feminist Movement?', in Myra Marx Ferree and Patricia Yancey Martin (eds.), *Feminist Organizations: Harvest of the New Women's Movement*. Philadelphia, PA: Temple University Press, pp. 27–34.

——(1999*a*). 'Everyday Talk in the Deliberative System', in Macedo (1999: 211–42).

——(1999*b*). 'Should Blacks Represent Blacks and Women Represent Women? A Contingent "Yes" ', *Journal of Politics*, 61: 628–57.

——(2003*a*). 'Practice-Thought-Practice', in Fung and Wright (2003*b*: 175–99).

——(2003*b*). 'Rethinking Representation', *American Political Science Review*, 97: 515–28.

March, James G. and Johan P. Olsen (1995). *Democratic Governance*. New York: Free Press.

Margalit, Avishai and Joseph Raz (1990). 'National Self-Determination', *Journal of Philosophy*, 87: 439–61.

Markovits, Elizabeth (2006). 'The Trouble with Being Earnest: Deliberative Democracy and the Sincerity Norm', *Journal of Political Philosophy*, 14: 249–69.

Martin, Lanny W. and Georg Vanberg (2005). 'Coalition Policymaking and Legislative Review', *American Political Science Review*, 99: 93–106.

May, John D. (1978). 'Defining Democracy: A Bid for Coherence and Consensus', *Political Studies*, 26: 1–14.

May, Kenneth O. (1952). 'A Set of Independent, Necessary and Sufficient Conditions for Simple Majority Decision', *Econometrica*, 20: 680–4.

Mayhew, David (1991). *Divided We Govern*. New Haven, CT: Yale University Press.

McKinney, R. J. and E. A. Sweet (2002). *Federal Legislative History Research: A Practitioner's Guide to Compiling the Documents and Sifting for Legislative Intent*. Washington, DC: Law Librarian's Society of Washington, DC. Available at: http://www.llsdc.org/sourcebook/fed-leg-hist.htm (accessed 16 May 2002).

Melville, Keith, Taylor L. Willingham, and John R. Dedrick (2005). 'National Issues Forums: A Network of Communities Promoting Public Deliberation', in Gastil and Levine (2005: 37–58).

Mendelberg, Tali (2001). *The Race Card: Campaign Strategy, Implicit Messages and the Norm of Equality*. Princeton, NJ: Princeton University Press.

Midgaard, Knut (1980). 'On the Significance of Language and a Richer Concept of Rationality', in Leif Lewin and Evert Vedung (eds.), *Politics as Rational Action*. Dordrecht: Reidel, pp. 83–97.

——Halvor Stenstadvold, and Arild Underdal (1973). 'An Approach to Political Interlocutions', *Scandinavian Political Studies*, 8: 9–36.

Mill, James (1823). 'Essay on Government', in T. Ball (ed.), *James Mill: Political Writings*. Cambridge: Cambridge University Press, 1992.

Mill, John Stuart (1859). *On Liberty*. Harmondsworth: Penguin, 1974.

——(1861). 'Considerations on Representative Government', in Richard Wollheim (ed.), *John Stuart Mill, Three Essays*. Oxford: Clarendon Press, 1975.

Miller, David (1992). 'Deliberative Democracy and Social Choice', *Political Studies*, 40 (5): 54–67.

Miller, Warren E. and Donald E. Stokes (1963). 'Constituency Influence in Congress', *American Political Science Review*, 57: 45–56.

Mills, C. Wright (1959). *The Sociological Imagination*. New York: Oxford University Press.

Minow, Martha (2002). *Partners, Not Rivals: Privatization and the Public Good*. Boston, MA: Beacon Press.

——(2003). 'Public and Private Partnerships: Accounting for the New Religion', *Harvard Law Review*, 116: 1–41.

Montaigne, Michel de (1580). *On the Art of Conversation*. Book 3, essay 8, in M. A. Screech (ed. and trans.), *The Essays of Michel de Montaigne*. Harmondsworth, Mddx.: Allen Lane/Penguin, 1991, pp. 1044–69.

Mulgan, Richard (1997). 'Contracting Out and Accountability', *Australian Journal of Public Administration*, 56: 106–16.

——(2001). 'The Accountability of Community Sector Agencies: A Comparative Framework', *Third Sector*, 7 (1): 89–105.

Mulgan, Tim (1999). 'The Place of the Dead in Liberal Political Philosophy', *Journal of Political Philosophy*, 7: 52–70.

Murphy, F. (1942). Opinion of the US Supreme Court. *Chaplinsky v. New Hampshire*, 315 U.S. 568.

Myrdal, Gunnar (1944). *American Dilemma: The Negro Problem and Modern Democracy*. New York: Harper & Row.

——(1955). 'Realities and Illusions in Regard to Inter-governmental Organizations', L. T. Hobhouse Memorial Trust Lecture, No. 24; delivered at Bedford College, London, 25 February 1954. London: Oxford University Press.

Nagel, E. and Newman, J. R. (1964). *Gödel's Proofs*. New York: New York University Press.

Newhouse, Joseph P. (1970). 'Toward a Theory of Nonprofit Institutions: An Economic Model of a Hospital', *American Economic Review*, 60: 64–74.

Nicholson, Michael (1972). *Oligopoly and Conflict*. Liverpool: Liverpool University Press.

Niemeyer, Simon J. (2002). 'Deliberation in the Wilderness: Institutional Influences on Preferences and their Discursive Transformation', Ph.D. dissertation, Australian National University.

——and Russell K. Blamey (2003). *Report of the Far North Queensland Citizens' Jury*. Canberra: Land and Water Australia and Research School of Social Sciences, Australian National University.

Norman, Wayne (1998). 'Inevitable and Unacceptable? Methodological Rawlsianism in Anglo-American Political Philosophy', *Political Studies*, 46: 276–94.

Norris, Pippa (2001). *Digital Divide*. Cambridge: Cambridge University Press.

Nowell-Smith, P. H. (1954). *Ethics*. Harmondsworth, Mddx.: Penguin.

Nozick, Robert (1974). *Anarchy, State and Utopia*. Oxford: Blackwell.

Nye, Joseph S. Jr. (2001). 'Globalization's Democratic Deficit: How to Make International Institutions More Accountable', *Foreign Affairs*, 80 (4): 2–6.

Oakeshott, Michael (1975). *Of Human Conduct*. Oxford: Clarendon Press.

Offe, Claus (2000). 'Civil Society and Social Order: Demarcating and Combining Market, State and Community', *Archives Européenes de Sociologie*, 41: 71–94.

Orbell, John M., Alphons J. C. von de Kragt, and Robyn M. Dawes (1988). 'Explaining Discussion-Induced Cooperation', *Journal of Personality and Social Psychology*, 54: 811–19.

Ostrogorski, Moisei (1902). *Democracy and the Organization of Political Parties*, trans. F. Clarke. London: Macmillan.

Page, Benjamin I. (1978). *Choices and Echoes in Presidential Elections*. Chicago, IL: University of Chicago Press.

——(1996). *Who Deliberates? Mass Media in Modern Democracy*. Chicago, IL: University of Chicago Press.

Palmer, Elizabeth (2002). 'Should Public Health Be a Private Concern? Developing a Public Service Paradigm in English Law', *Oxford Journal of Legal Studies*, 22: 663–86.

Papadopoulos, Yannis (2007). 'Problems of Democratic Accountability in Network and Multilevel Governance', *European Law Journal*, 13: 469–86.

Parkinson, John (2003). 'Legitimacy Problems in Deliberative Democracy', *Political Studies*, 51: 180–96.

——(2004a). 'Hearing Voices: Negotiating Representation Claims in Public Deliberation', *British Journal of Politics & International Relations*, 6: 370–88.

——(2004b). 'Why Deliberate? The Encounter Between Deliberation and New Public Managers', *Public Administration*, 82: 377–95.

——(2006). *Deliberating in the Real World: Problems of Legitimacy in Deliberative Democracy*. Oxford: Oxford University Press.

Pateman, Carole (1970). *Participation and Democratic Theory*. Cambridge: Cambridge University Press.

Pennock, J. R. (1979). *Democratic Political Theory*. Princeton, NJ: Princeton University Press.

Peters, B. Guy (1997). 'Escaping the Joint Decision Trap: Repetition and Sectoral Politics in the European Union', *West European Politics*, 20 (2): 22–36.

Petty, R. E. and J. Cacioppo (1986). *Communication and Persuasion: Central and Peripheral Routes to Attitude Change*. New York: Springer-Verlag.

Phillips, Anne (1995). *The Politics of Presence: Democracy and Group Representation*. Oxford: Clarendon Press.

Pierson, Paul (2000). 'Increasing Returns, Path Dependence and the Study of Politics', *American Political Science Review*, 94: 251–68.

Pitkin, Hanna F. (1972). *The Concept of Representation*. Berkeley: University of California Press.

Posner, Paul L. (2002). 'Accountability Challenges of Third-Party Government', in Salamon and Elliott (2002: 523–51).

Przeworski, Adam (1998). 'Deliberation and Ideological Domination', in Elster (1998a: 140–60).

——(1999). 'Minimalist Conceptions of Democracy: A Defense', in I. Shapiro and C. Hacker-Cordón (eds.), *Democracy's Value*. Cambridge: Cambridge University Press, pp. 23–55.

Rae, Douglas W. (1969). 'Decision-Rules and Individual Values in Constitutional Choice', *American Political Science Review*, 63: 40–56.

Ranney, Austin (1975). *Curing the Mischiefs of Faction*. Berkeley: University of California Press.

Rawls, John (1971). *A Theory of Justice*. Cambridge, MA: Harvard University Press.

—— (1993). *Political Liberalism*. New York: Columbia University Press.

—— (1997). 'The Idea of Public Reason Revisited', *University of Chicago Law Review*, 94: 765–807. Reprinted in pp. 129–80 in Rawls, *The Law of Peoples*. Cambridge, MA: Harvard University Press, 1999.

—— (2001). *Justice as Fairness: A Restatement*, ed. E. Kelly. Cambridge, MA: Harvard University Press.

Raz, Joseph (1975). *Practical Reason and Norms*. London: Hutchinson.

Rehbinder, Eckard and Richard Stewart (1985). *Environmental Protection Policy*. Berlin: Walter de Gruyter.

Rhodes, R. A. W. (1997). *Understanding Governance: Policy Networks, Governance and Accountability*. Buckingham: Open University Press.

Ridge, Michael (2001). Saving Scanlon. *Journal of Political Philosophy* 9: 471–80.

Riker, William H. (1983). *Liberalism Against Populism*. San Francisco: W. Freeman.

Risse, Thomas, Stephen C. Ropp, and Kathryn Sikkink, eds. (1999). *The Power of Human Rights: International Norms and Domestic Change*. Cambridge: Cambridge University Press.

Robert, Henry M. (1876/1951). *Robert's Rules of Order*, rev. edn. Chicago, IL: Scott, Foresman.

Rohrschneider, R. (1988). 'Citizens' Attitudes Toward Environmental Issues: Selfish or Selfless?', *Comparative Political Studies*, 21: 347–67.

Rorty, Richard (1989). *Contingency, Irony and Solidarity*. Cambridge: Cambridge University Press.

Rose-Ackerman, Susan (1983). 'Social Services and the Market', *Columbia Law Review*, 83: 1405–39.

Rose-Ackerman, Susan (1995). *Controlling Environmental Policy: The Limits of Public Law in Germany and the US*. New Haven, CT: Yale University Press.

—— (1996). 'Altruism, Nonprofits and Economic Theory', *Journal of Economic Literature*, 34: 701–28.

—— (2003/2004). 'Public Participation in Consolidating Democracies: Hungary and Poland', in J. Kornai and S. Rose-Ackerman (eds.), *Building a Trustworthy State in Post-Socialist Transition*. New York: Palgrave.

—— (2003). *'Listening to the City': Rebuilding at New York's World Trade Center Site*. Kennedy School of Government Case Program, Case Reference No. 1687-0. Cambridge, MA: Kennedy School of Government, Harvard University.

Ross, Edward Alsworth (1901). *Social Control: A Survey of the Foundations of Order*. New York: Macmillan. Reprint of a series of articles in *American Journal of Sociology*, 1896–1898.

Rousseau, Jean-Jacques (1762). 'The Social Contract', trans. G. D. H. Cole, in G. D. H. Cole (ed.), *The Social Contract and Discourses*. New edn. London: Everyman/Dent, 1973, pp. 164–278.

Ryfe, David M. (2005). 'Does Deliberative Democracy Work?', *Annual Review of Political Science*, 8: 49–71.

Salamon, Lester M., ed. (2002). *The State of Nonprofit America*. Washington, DC: Brookings Institution, for the Aspen Institute.

—— with Odus V. Elliott, eds. (2002). *The Tools of Government: A Guide to the New Governance*. New York: Oxford University Press.

Sanders, Lynn (1997). 'Against Deliberation', *Political Theory*, 25: 347–76.

Sartori, Giovanni (1962). *Democratic Theory*. Detroit: Wayne State University Press.

—— (1987). *The Theory of Democracy Revisited*. Chatham, NJ: Chatham House.

Saward, Michael (1992). *Co-Optive Politics and State Legitimacy*. Aldershot, Hants: Dartmouth.

—— (1998). *The Terms of Democracy*. Cambridge: Polity Press.

—— (2003). 'Enacting Democracy', *Political Studies*, 51: 1–19.

—— (2006). 'The Representative Claim', *Contemporary Political Theory*, 5: 297–318.

Scanlon, T. M. (1998). *What We Owe to Each Other*. Cambridge, MA: Harvard University Press.

Scharpf, F. W. (1988). 'The Joint Decision Trap: Lessons from German Federalism and European Integration', *Public Administration*, 66: 239–78.

Schattschneider, E. E., chair. (1950). 'Toward a More Responsible Two-Party System', Report of the Committee on Political Parties of the American Political Science Association, *American Political Science Review*, 44 (3, pt 2, Supplement).

Schauer, Frederick (1999). 'Talking as a Decision Procedure', in Macedo (1999: 17–27).

Schlessinger, Arthur M., Jr. (1973). *The Imperial Presidency*. Boston, MA: Houghton Mifflin.

Schlosberg, David (1999). *Environmental Justice and the New Pluralism*. Oxford: Oxford University Press.

Schumpeter, Joseph (1950). *Capitalism, Socialism & Democracy*, 3rd edn. New York: Harper&Row.

Sclove, Richard E. (2005). 'Town Meetings on Technology: Consensus Conferences', Available at: www.loka.org/pubs/techrev.htm (accessed 10 July 2005).

Scott, Colin (2002). 'Private Regulation of the Public Sector: A Neglected Facet of Contemporary Governance', *Journal of Law & Society*, 29: 56–76.

Sears, David O. (1993). 'Symbolic Politics: A Socio-Psychological Theory', in S. Iyengar and W. J. McGuire (eds.), *Explorations in Political Psychology*. Durham, NC: Duke University Press, pp. 113–49.

Selznick, Philip (1949). *TVA and the Grassroots: A Study of Politics & Organization*. Berkeley: University of California Press.

Shapin, Steven (1994). *A Social History of Truth: Civility and Science in Seventeenth-Century England*. Chicago, IL: University of Chicago Press.

Shapiro, Ian (1999). 'Enough of Deliberation: Politics is About Interests and Power', in S. Macedo (ed.), *Deliberative Politics*. New York: Oxford University Press, pp. 28–38.

——(2002). 'Optimal Deliberation?', *Journal of Political Philosophy*, 10: 196–211.

Shklar, Judith N. (1991). *American Citizenship: The Quest for Inclusion*. Cambridge, MA: Harvard University Press.

Sikkink, Kathryn (1993). 'Human Rights, Principled Issue-Networks and Sovereignty in Latin America', *International Organization*, 47: 411–41.

Simmel, Georg (1955). 'The Web of Group Affiliations', in *Simmel, Conflict and the Web of Group Affiliations*, trans. Kurt H. Wolff and Reinhard Bendix. Glencoe, IL: Free Press, pp. 125–95.

Simon, Herbert A. (1969). *The Science of the Artificial*. Cambridge, MA: MIT Press.

Slaughter, Anne-Marie (2000). 'Governing the Global Economy Through Government Networks', in M. Byer (ed.), *The Role of Law in International Politics*s. Oxford: Oxford University Press.

Smith, Adam (1776). *The Wealth of Nations*, ed. R. H. Campbell and A. S. Skinner. Oxford: Clarendon Press, 1976.

Smith, Steven Rathgeb (1993). 'Managing the Community: Privatization, Government and the Nonprofit Sector', *Journal of Political Philosophy*, 1: 82–104.

——(2002). 'Social Services', in Salamon (2002: 149–86).

Smith, Graham (2005). *Beyond the Ballot: 57 Democratic Innovations from Around the World*. A report for the POWER Inquiry. London: The POWER Inquiry. Available at: www.powerinquiry.org/publications/index.php (accessed 1 July 2005).

——and Corinne Wales (2000). 'Citizens' Juries and Deliberative Democracy', *Political Studies*, 48: 51–65.

Smith, Steven Rathgeb and Michael Lipsky (1993). *Non-Profits for Hire: The Welfare State in an Age of Contracting*. Cambridge, MA: Harvard University Press.

Sniderman, Paul M. (1993). 'The New Look in Public Opinion Research', in A. W. Finifter (ed.), *The State of the Discipline II*. Washington, DC: American Political Science Association, pp. 219–46.

Sorauf, Frank J. (1968). *Party Politics in America*. Boston: Little, Brown.

Soysal, Yasemin (1994). *Limits of Citizenship: Migrants and Postnational Membership in Europe*. Chicago, IL: University of Chicago Press.

Squires, Judith (2002). 'Deliberation and Decision Making: Discontinuity in the Two-Track Model', in Maurizio Passerin d'Entrèves (ed.), *Democracy as Public Deliberation: New Perspectives*. Manchester: Manchester University Press, pp. 133–56.

Steenbergen, Marco R., André Bächtiger, Markus Spörndli, and Jürg Steiner (2002). 'Measuring Deliberation: A Discourse Quality Index', *Comparative European Politics*, 1: 21–48.

Steiner, Jürg, André Bächtiger, Markus Spörndli, and Marco R. Steenbergen (2004). *Deliberative Politics in Action: Cross-National Study of Parliamentary Debates.* Cambridge: Cambridge University Press.

Stevens, I. E., Royal Commissioner (1996). The Hindmarsh Island Bridge Royal Commission: transcript of proceedings. Available at: http://library. adelaide.edu.au/gen/H_Islnd/ (accessed 19 Dec. 2002).

Stokes, Susan C. (1998). 'Pathologies of Deliberation', in Elster (1998*a*: 123–39).

Storing, Herbert J., ed. (1981). *The Anti-Federalist.* Chicago, IL: University of Chicago Press.

Sunstein, Cass R. (1988). 'Beyond the Republican Revival', *Yale Law Journal*, 97: 1539–90.

——(1991). 'Preferences and Politics', *Philosophy & Public Affairs*, 20: 3–34.

——(1996*a*). 'Leaving Things Undecided', *Harvard Law Review*, 110: 4–101.

——(1996*b*). *Legal Reasoning and Political Conflict.* New York: Oxford University Press.

——(2000). 'Deliberative Trouble? Why Groups Go to Extremes', *Yale Law Journal*, 110: 71–119.

——(2002). 'The Law of Group Polarization', *Journal of Political Philosophy*, 10: 175–95. Reprinted in Fishkin and Laslett 2003, pp. 80–101.

——(2005). *The Laws of Fear.* Cambridge: Cambridge University Press.

——(2006). *Infotopia.* New York: Oxford University Press.

Tännsjö, Torbjörn (2005). 'Future People and the All Affected Principle', in Folke Tersman (ed.), *Democracy Unbound: Basic Explorations I.* Stockholm: Filosofiska Institutionen, Stockholms Universitet, pp. 186–9.

Taylor, S. (1981). 'The Interface of Cognitive and Social Psychology', in J. Harvey (ed.), *Cognition, Social Behavior, and the Environment.* Hillsdale, NJ: Lawrence Erlbaum Associates.

Tetlock, Philip (1983*a*). 'Accountability and the Perseverance of First Impressions', *Social Psychological Quarterly*, 46: 285–92.

——(1983*b*). 'Accountability and Complexity of Thought', *Journal of Personality and Social Psychology*, 45: 74–83.

——(1985). 'Accountability: A Social Check on the Fundamental Attribution Error', *Social Psychological Quarterly*, 48: 227–36.

Thies, Michael F. (2001). 'Keeping Tabs on Partners: The Logic of Delegation in Coalition Governments', *American Journal of Political Science*, 45: 580–98.

Thomas, Hugh (1997). *The Slave Trade: The Story of the Atlantic Slave Trade, 1440–1870.* New York: Simon and Schuster.

Thompson, Dennis F. (1999). 'Democratic Theory and Global Society', *Journal of Political Philosophy*, 7: 111–25.

——(2008). 'Who Should Govern Who Governs? The Role of Citizens in Reforming the Electoral System', in Warren and Pearse (2008*a*).

Thucydides (1972). *History of the Peloponnesian War*. Harmondsworth, Mddx.: Penguin.

Tocqueville, Alexis de. (1835). *Democracy in America*, trans. George Lawrence, ed. J. P. Mayer and Max Lerner. New York: Harper & Row, 1966.

Torgerson, Douglas. (2003). 'Democracy Through Policy Discourse', in Maarten Hajer and Hendrik Wagenaar (eds.), *Deliberative Policy Analysis*. Cambridge: Cambridge University Press, pp. 113–38.

Tribe, Laurence H. (1988). *American Constitutional Law*, 2nd edn. Mineola, NY: Foundation Press.

Uhr, John. (1998). *Deliberative Democracy in Australia*. Cambridge: Cambridge University Press.

UK Department for Environment, Food and Rural Affairs (UK DEFRA) (2004). *The GM Dialogue: Government Response*. Available at: www.defra.gov.uk/environment/gm/debate/pdf/gmdialogue-response.pdf (accessed 11 July 2005).

Ullmann-Margalit, Edna and Sidney Morgenbesser (1977). 'Picking and Choosing', *Social Research*, 44: 757–85.

United Nations, Economic and Social Council (UN ECOSOC) (1996). Resolution 1996/31: Consultative Relationship Between the United Nations and Non-Governmental Organizations (adopted at 49th plenary meeting, 25 July 1996). Available at: http://www.un.org/documents/ecosoc/res/1996/eres1996–31.html (accessed 28 Dec. 2002).

United Kingdom, Secretary of State for Wales (1988). *Compact Between the Government and the Voluntary Sector in Wales*. Cm 4107. London: Stationery Office. Available at: www.archive.official-documents.co.uk/document/cm41/4107/4107.htm (accessed 6 June 2003).

US Congress (2003). 21st Century Nanotechnology Research and Development Act. 15 USC 7501. Available at: /frwebgate.access.gpo.gov/cgi-bin/getdoc.cgi?dbname=108_cong_public_laws&docid=f:publ153.108 (accessed 5 Aug. 2005).

US Court of Appeals, Ninth Circuit, Office of the Circuit Executive (2002). *Manual of Model Criminal Jury Instructions*. Available at: http://www.ce9.uscourts.gov/web/sdocuments.nsf/crim (accessed 13 May 2002).

Vanstone, Amanda (1996). 'Reforming Employment Assistance—Helping Australians into Real Jobs', Budget Statement, Minister of Employment, Education, Training and Youth Affairs, Commonwealth of Australia, 20 August 1006. Available at: http://www.dest.gov.au/archive/publications/budget/budget96/budget_statement/minstindex.htm (accessed 12 May 2003).

Waldron, Jeremy (1989). 'Democratic Theory and the Public Interest: Condorcet and Rousseau Revisited', *American Political Science Review*, 38: 1322–8.

—— (1999). *Law and Disagreement*. Oxford: Clarendon Press.

—— (2003). 'Security and Liberty: The Image of Balance', *Journal of Political Philosophy*, 11: 191–210.

Walzer, Michael (1991). 'The Idea of Civil Society: A Path to Social Reconstruction', *Dissent*, 38: 293–304.

Ware, Alan (1989). *Between Profit and State*. Cambridge: Polity Press.

Warren, Mark and Hilary Pearse, eds. (2008*a*). *Designing Deliberative Democracy: The British Columbia Citizens' Assembly*. Cambridge: Cambridge University Press.

——— eds. (2008*b*). 'Introduction', in Warren and Pearse (2008*a*).

Washington, George (1746). *Rules of Civility and Decent Behaviour in Company and Conversation*. Bedford, MA: Applewood Books, 1988.

——(1796). 'Farewell Address', in Daniel J. Boorstein (ed.), *An American Primer*. Chicago, IL: University of Chicago Press, 1966, pp. 192–210.

Weatherford, M. Stephen and Lorraine M. McDonnell (2007). 'Deliberation with a Purpose: Reconnecting Schools and Communities', in Shawn W. Rosenberg (ed.), *Deliberation, Participation and Democracy: Can the People Decide?*. London: Palgrave, 184–218.

Webb, L. J. (1984). 'Scientific values of the rainforests of the Douglas Shire', School of Australian Environmental Studies, Working Paper No. 15. Brisbane: Griffith University.

Weingast, Barry R. and William Marshall (1988). 'The Industrial Organization of Congress; or, Why Legislatures, Like Firms, Are Not Organized as Markets', *Journal of Political Economy*, 96: 132–63.

Weisbrod, Burton A. (1975). 'Towards a Theory of the Voluntary Nonprofit Sector in a Three Sector Economy', in E. S. Phelps (ed.), *Altruism, Morality and Economic Theory*. New York: Russell Sage Foundation, pp. 171–95.

Whelan, Frederick G. (1983). 'Democratic Theory and the Boundary Problem', in J. R. Pennock and J. W. Chapman (eds.), *Nomos XXV: Liberal Democracy*. New York: New York University Press, pp. 13–47.

White, Stephen K. (1980). 'Reason and Authority in Habermas: A Critique of the Critics', *American Political Science Review*, 74: 1007–17.

Whitehead, Laurence (1996). 'Comparative Politics: Democratization Studies', in R. E. Goodin and H.-D. Klingemann (eds.), *A New Handbook of Political Science*. Oxford: Oxford University Press, pp. 353–71.

Wildavsky, Aaron (1979). *Speaking the Truth to Power*. Boston, MA: Little, Brown.

Williamson, Oliver E. (1975). *Markets and Hierarchies*. New York: Free Press.

Wollheim, Richard (1960). 'How Can One Person Represent Another?', *Proceedings of the Aristotelian Society, Supplementary Volume*, 34: 209–24.

Young, H. Peyton (1988). 'Condorcet's Theory of Voting', *American Political Science Review*, 82: 1231–44.

Young, Iris Marion (1990). *Justice and the Politics of Difference*. Princeton, NJ: Princeton University Press.

——(1996/1997*a*). 'Communication and the Other: Beyond Deliberative Democracy', in Seyla Benhabib (ed.), *Democracy and Difference*. Princeton, NJ: Princeton

University Press, 1996, pp. 120–36. Reprinted in pp. 60–74 in Young, *Intersecting Voices*. Princeton, NJ: Princeton University Press, 1997.

——(1997*b*). 'Asymmetrical Reciprocity: On Moral Respect, Wonder and Enlarged Thought', in Young (ed.), *Intersecting Voices*. Princeton, NJ: Princeton University Press. pp. 38–60.

——(2000). *Inclusion and Democracy*. Oxford: Oxford University Press.

——(2001). 'Activist Challenges to Deliberative Democracy', *Political Theory*, 29: 670–90.

Young, Dennis R. and Lester M. Salamon (2002). 'Commercialization, Social Ventures and For-Profit Competition', in Salamon (2002: 423–46).

Zaller, J. R. (1992). *The Nature and Origins of Mass Opinion*. Cambridge: Cambridge University Press.

Zolberg, Aristide R. (1966). *Creating Political Order: The Party States of West Africa*. Chicago, IL: Rand McNally.

Index

Note: Rhet as 'democratic' failure
practice' in Nietzche's future
— possible to promote acceptance
to achieve by cultivating uncertainty
d technique of rhet
— but not guaranteed — rhet can be
used badly/anti-democratically